History

First Published 1949

MADE AND PRINTED IN GT. BRITAIN
BY CRAMPTON AND SONS, LIMITED
SAWSTON, CAMBRIDGE
FOR
CLONMORE AND REYNOLDS, DUBLIN,
EYRE AND SPOTTISWOODE, LONDON.

THE IRISH MILITIA
1793—1816

A Social and Military Study

BY

SIR HENRY MCANALLY

CLONMORE AND REYNOLDS, DUBLIN
EYRE AND SPOTTISWOODE, LONDON

Preface

If Crofton Croker is right when he says that " the history of all political events is best written after the lapse of one or more centuries, while the anecdotes which form important historical illustrations are best related as soon as possible after the occurrence ", then the time may be considered to have about come for writing the history of the Irish militia of the period of the Napoleonic wars. It seems to be considered by many that the absence of such an account constitutes a gap in Irish history requiring to be filled. If I have attempted to do this, that has not been because I do not recognise that others could have accomplished the task better than myself who am not a historian by training.

If I have, as I hope, been able to bring to it a live interest that has been due to personal circumstances. Without such interest the difficulties might have deterred. The absence of consecutive records has been the chief obstacle. Herbert Wood's *Guide to the Records in the Public Record office of Ireland* (1919) specifies many papers which I should have dearly liked to consult. The history of the Longford regiment (H. A. Richey, 1894) is about the sole piece of consecutive narrative written from those records stated (p. vi) then to have been " both voluminous and in excellent preservation ".

Nevertheless it has been possible, I think, to piece together almost the ' entire ' of the story and I do not feel that, as I now present it, substantial facts are absent. The Wonder is that it has been possible to carry investigation so far. Certainly the passage of one and more centuries, as desiderated by Croker, does not leave it easier to write about past events if contemporary records of basic facts are no longer available.

I have contemplated this task as a historical revision. It has seemed to me that though the Irish militia of 1793-1816 was not perhaps an important military force—and this is probably the reason for its neglect by military historians, and others,—it is entitled to be judged fairly as much as any other institution of the past. This I have endeavoured to do. The respects in which I feel that many, if not all, of the casual judgments which have been passed are erroneous are sufficiently, but I hope reasonably, stated in the book and I need not, otherwise than to confess to a certain hereditary prepossession, refer to them further here.

I began the foundation work of this book in about 1934-5 and arrangements for its publication had been made just before the last war began, but effect could not be given to these. Access to the greater part of the records and documents on which it has been based then became interrupted and has to a large extent remained so. Nevertheless I have carried through a revision. The title page will indicate the double scope, both parts of which are in my opinion of importance. It has been said that " even now, more than a century after, the structure of the Napoleonic epoch has not been perfectly articulated ". Well, this book is an articulation of a very limited portion of that field of survey. It would have been easier if someone had carried out the larger articulation —of the social and military import of the militia, and the other non-regular forces of Great Britain, during the Revolutionary period.

My thanks are due, and most cordially paid, to many persons who have helped me. Dr. Chart (who read many chapters in ms), Dr. Dudley Edwards and Dr. Moody have given me much help, guidance and encouragement. Mr. Tennison Groves, Mr, Philip Crosslé, Professor Waddell and various correspondents have allowed me access to their accumulated knowledge. Lord Camden permitted me to consult the Camden papers at Bayham Abbey and the late Mr. Clements of Cellbridge was good enough to lend me a very useful series of contemporary records of the Donegal militia left by Lord Leitrim. For permission to quote from the Blacker papers (see *History of Trinity College, Dublin* 1591-1892 by Dr. Constantia Maxwell, Dublin 1946, pp. 257-258) I am indebted to the living representative of the writer. I consulted the letters of Lord Castlereagh to his wife in a transcript in possession of the late Lord Londonderry and received permission to quote from them from the late Lord Lothian.

The National Library of Ireland have helped me much over consultation of the Kilmainham papers and of the Irish newspapers of the period. At an early stage the importance of these latter as a contemporary authority was impressed on me in Dublin. To Mr. Charles J. Coghlan, now assistant librarian of the Public Library at Bray, I am indebted for a most comprehensive examination of these. He has provided me with a great deal of information which was unobtainable otherwise and my narrative is constantly in his debt positively and, negatively, facts he has supplied have often prevented me from making statements and deductions which I might otherwise have made. I must also thank Mr. T. G. F. Paterson for continuous help; Professor Bruce Dickins, of Cambridge University, for advice on a special part of the narrative;

and finally my wife for unending assistance in getting the book through the press and my great grandfather (and Mr. Tempest of the Dundalgan Press) for having made it possible to present in colour the frontispiece illustration of a militia subaltern of 1793 (who was also a militia surgeon).

H. M.

Cambridge,
July 1949.

Contents

I

Antecedents

The story of the principle and practice of ' militia ' in Ireland begins early in the seventeenth century. But the militia created in 1793, which was in active service down to 1816, is not organizationally or otherwise related to the earlier militia, the existence of which anyhow tended to be intermittent. It is not necessary therefore, as a preliminary to giving the picture of the militia of the period of the revolutionary wars, to present in any detail, even if this were possible[1], the early history prior to 1778 from which year the story has closer relevance. Several indeed of those who in that year were actively interested in the militia question were still active in 1793 and possibly were able to contribute something to the building of the militia then created.

No militia *eo nomine* existed before 1660. In the years before 1700 the principal names connected with it are, from differing points of view, those of Ormond (three times lord lieutenant), the earl of Orrery, Arthur Capel, earl of Essex, Tyrconnel and Sir Richard Cox. ' Militia ' was of course in England ' familiar .. as a household word ' at the time of the Civil war ; and, on the restoration, the position, in the English sphere, of militia was regulated by statute. In Ireland the first militia regulating statute was in 1715. But whatever militias were then and later instituted were *created* under the prerogative powers ; and, at the end of the seventeenth century, the militia of James ii and that of William differed in complexion. Militarily, the wars in Ireland of those two monarchs were the time, so far as there was one, of the testing of the institution as an active force. But, these wars ended, there was no[2] active service for militia in Ireland for the hundred years ending in 1793. In this period however a political militia question always existed in the background and had intermittently some importance ; the militia acts of the first three quarters of the eighteenth century are numerous. The demise of militia in relation to the rise of Volunteers has as yet not been elucidated. With the militia act of 1778 (17-18 Geo. iii. chap. 13) the horizon in this matter clears somewhat and it is at this point that the history of the Irish Militia, for the purposes of this book, begins.

There is a contemporary (February 1780) account[3] of the circumstances which led to this act 'The prevailing and popular opinion in Ireland had long been that without a considerable standing army there was no security to the protestant interest in that country. That army it had always been the policy of England to recruit in England'. In 1775 the parliament of Ireland gave 4,000 men for the war in America but refused to receive an equal number of foreign troops 'and an opinion of the country.. to its own defence began to spread'. In 1767[4] a fairly detailed militia scheme had been elaborated in a pamphlet entitled *An essay on the use and necessity of establishing a militia in Ireland and some hints towards a plan for that purpose, by a country gentleman.* Still earlier Henry Flood was interested in the militia question. He speaks (March 1766) of 'the fate of my militia bill' and says further 'the whole power of government was set against it, merely because I was the proposer of it'.[5] In 1768 he delivered printed heads of a bill to the house of commons and this bill (or these heads of a bill) was, it appears, revived by Mr. Ogle, at least as early as 1776.[6]

The account quoted continues: 'In the beginning of 1778 the prospect of an approaching war with France, the defenceless situation of the country and the decline of trade manufacture and revenue occasioned much uneasiness and, though the contest with America was very unpopular in Ireland, yet, when the French declaration [i.e. recognizing independence] appeared, unanimity for a time seemed to take place. A militia act was passed and opposition not only joined in but moved for the vote of £300,000 granted expressly for the defence of the country. In the beginning of the summer the apprehension of an invasion increased; the greatest part of the troops (by now 15,000) were drawn together and encamped in the South where the danger was most to be apprehended'.

This act of 1778 might be called Ogle's act. George Ogle (a privy councillor of Ireland in 1783) was at the time one of the two members for Wexford County. Between 1778 and 1793 he was very prominent as a volunteer; he was a general in the force and has been described as a pillar of Irish protestantism; he opposed the catholic relief bills of 1792 and of 1793. By 1785 he had become less enthusiastic about the Volunteers: in the debates of that year he supported the Gardner amendment to the Brownlow resolution (see page 6). He is one of the links between the Volunteers and the militia as finally constituted. He did not accept a commission in the new force which was in fact the ultimate realization of his earlier efforts. The *Freeman's Journal* wrote as follows in commenting on the militia bill (19 March 1793): 'some former administrations by crafty arts defeated the effects of a militia bill which the spirit and perseverance of Mr. George Ogle had procured for this country '. In the debates of 1785 Sir Hercules Langrishe said he remembered for a course of years the repeated but disappointed efforts of patriotism to obtain a national militia ; that when it was gained from government eight or nine years ago it was considered a great acquisition ; and the right honourable gentleman whose efforts obtained it, received the acknowledgment of his country for it[7].

The preamble of the act of 1788 recites that ' a well-regulated militia would conduce to strengthen the civil power and to protect the land '. The double duty, the two sides of which proved ultimately to be fundamentally incompatible to a very large extent, is thus already envisaged. The local quasi-police and the national contra-invasion duties are sharply contrasted by the provision (clause 31) that when the militia of any county were employed ' in suppressing insurrections and outrageous tumults and in pursuing, apprehending and attending the execution of notorious offenders ' the pay of the privates was to be charged to the county but that when 'they shall be called out by order of the government for the purpose of repelling an invasion or for the public service ' they were to be paid out of public funds.

The scheme as it emerged from discussion, of which little is known, did not contemplate the formation of militia all over Ireland, in every county. It was left to the government to decide ' the number of companies to be raised in any county '. In those counties in which they decided there should be militia various steps had to be taken by commissioners of array which eventuated in the convening of ' the several Protestant inhabitants of the districts '. Attendance at this meeting was compulsory but there were enlisted only ' such and so many of the inhabitants of the district as shall voluntarily offer themselves to be enlisted '. The scheme was apparently a compromise ; the *Belfast News Letter* (23-26 June 1778) says : ' the militia bill..was read a third time....The compulsory clauses are all struck out, so ' that every person, who enters into the militia must be a volunteer in the Service....' it is also remarked that it was ' to consist of independent companies '.*

This militia scheme in the initial form of ' heads of bill ' was, after full discussion in the house of commons, presented, under order of the house, to the lord lieutenant by Mr. Ogle that it might be ' transmitted into Great Britain in due form '[8] and the ' heads ' would have received formal approval in London before being introduced as the bill ; it was then, rapidly, passed through

*The ' company ' is the only unit contemplated in the act.

the two houses. From what was afterwards said, during the debates of 1785, it was not very acceptable to the government. In those debates the attorney general dealt with[9] the question why ministry which formerly opposed a militia law then (1785) granted it.

Perhaps, therefore, it is not surprising that, as appears to have been the case, little use was made of the Act. Equally with the money grant (£300,000), it seems to have been forced upon the government which possibly never had the intention of taking any action. It had been passed in June but in August lord Hillsborough writes[10] (the 22nd of that month) : ' if however the militia is to be embodied, I apprehend that I must contrive to slip over for a few weeks, for as I am lieutenant of Down I would not wish the militia of that great protestant county should be regulated without me '; and he asks the lord lieutenant to send him instructions. It is not clear to what he refers in speaking of embodiment.

Lord Carlisle arrived in Ireland as lord lieutenant in 1780, and was immediately confronted with the problem of the volunteer corps. He considered he had no option but ' to accept their eventual services in case of necessity '. There was a vote of thanks to them in the two houses of parliament early in October 1781. ' No possible exertion ', he writes about this, ' could have ' turned the tide which gave the thanks to the volunteer corps, ' and I am far from being convinced that if we had succeeded in ' opposing that measure, any real advantages would have resulted ' in the end to government '.[11]

' Nothing ', writes[12] lord Westmoreland in 1790, ' that I can learn was done in consequence of it [the act of 1778] : it seems very defective '. Absence of administrative action on the act, which, however, in its terms was not mandatory, is confirmed by what was said in the 1785 debates.* As there appeared to be no intention to take advantage of the militia act and array it ' in spite of the liberal grant '[13] and as troops were declared to be unavailable to help, the people began to form military associations. This was the beginning of the Irish Volunteers, the rapid growth of which has been called by a recent writer ' one of the most striking phenomena of Irish history '.[14]

The non-realization of a militia seems to have been acquiesced in even by those who had been prominent in securing the act of 1778. George Ogle himself, as stated, became a Volunteer

*Some independent companies seem to have been formed but newspaper references usually do not distinguish militia and volunteers. The most specific statement I have found is (*Belfast News Letter*, 26 Sept. 1778) that the general ' has ordered the several independent companies of militia, both of foot and horse, throughout this kingdom, who have voluntarily associated and trained themselves to arms, to be prepared......'.

general; and there seems no record of any reversion to the idea of creating a militia for Ireland until after the duke of Rutland had succeeded lord Northington as lord lieutenant in February 1784. In November he talks of the establishment of a national protestant militia as his[15] 'favourite project' and states that he has consulted 'various persons who have expressed approbation in warmest terms'. The idea received support from English ministers. Pitt was ready and anxious to break the power of the Volunteers and lord Sydney wrote that 'there can be no doubt of the expediency and necessity of putting the armed force of Ireland into a legal form', and he directed Rutland to take advice and to transmit a scheme for the previous consideration of his majesty. 'In the present situation of Ireland the militia should consist of protestants only'. It soon appeared, however, that the British ministers wanted a consideration in exchange for any concessions they made to Irish insistency; this was that the Irish government should procure the assent of the Irish parliament to a contribution to the British revenue in aid of the general defence expenditure.

On 15 February, 1785, Rutland is going to send a 'sketch of the plan and a general idea of the bill to be brought into parliament'. He had already the previous day carried the matter somewhat further. In the house of commons that day the right hon. Luke Gardner (afterwards lord Mountjoy and under the 1793 act colonel of the Dublin county militia) moved to grant £20,000 'for raising and cloathing a militia in such manner as parliament shall direct'. That he was put up to make this motion (on which Grattan spoke) there seems little doubt: his action was referred to in the debate as 'the little artifice of a government measure proceeding from the mouth of a country gentleman';[16] and Curran who spoke in opposition said that he had not at first perceived that 'the question was undoubtedly ministerial'. The attorney general's speech left no room for question on this point: he acknowledged the intention of government to establish a militia and said the reason for making the motion at that time was that the militia act (i.e. that of 17-18 George iii) was expired* and another act cannot be framed unless this resolution shall pass, for on this resolution the new act must be founded. Intervening again in the debate, which was very animated and did not end until 4 a.m., he argued that the grant of the sum proposed, to enable government to array a militia, did not 'of necessity

*By 21 and 22 Geo. iii. Chap. 40 cf. 5 (a general act for revising, continuing and amending temporary statutes) the Act of 17-18 Geo. iii was continued in force until 24 June 1787 and to the end of the then next session of parliament. It is not, therefore, clear why, in 1785, the act was stated to be expired—unless the act 21 and 22 Geo. iii had been overlooked.

oblige government to adopt the measure, it only empowered them to adopt it if the exigency of the times should ever render it necessary ',

The debate abounded in highly pitched and rather extravagant eulogy of the Volunteers : the motion ' aspersed them '; ' it traduced them by a side wind '; ' it gave a vital stab to the volunteer institution '. They were referred to as ' the glorious saviours of their country '. It was also said that the creation of a militia would ' enrage the volunteers '; ' that to institute them was a very unnecessary and profligate profusion '; and that ' militia would increase the enormous power of ministry '. Some of these arguments were to do duty again. But what is more important than this rather frothy praise are the substantial grounds urged for the militia, as against the volunteer, system. For use either on the quasi-police internal duty or for contra-invasion service a force was needed which would infallibly be there when the moment came for action, and for action the nature and scope of which should be determined, not by those who had constituted themselves into authorities and leaders, but by the established authorities of the state. ' How ', argued the attorney general, ' could they be sure that if the enemy was upon our coasts and the volunteers had retired to their ploughs they could be immediately assembled so as to protect the kingdom ?' Fine protestations would not ensure this protection being available when wanted ; the volunteers had, in fact, been backward in quelling disturbances ; it was impossible to bring them under subordination. In Rutland's phrase, the ' restoration of the sword to the executive[17] ' was supremely necessary.

The result of the long debate which ended in a vote of 139 in support and 63 against was described by the lord lieutenant as ' our triumph on the militia question '. A day or two later ' leave was given to bring in a bill for establishing a militia ' and George Ogle was one of the five who were to bring it in. But all was not over. On 18 February, William Brownlow, one of the members for Armagh county, considering that the resolution carried in Supply aspersed the volunteers, moved a motion[18] that ' the volunteers of Ireland have been eminently useful to their country, by the protection they afforded against a foreign enemy and by their frequent exertions in support of its police '. To this Luke Gardner moved to add ' and that this House highly approves of the conduct of those who, since the conclusion of the war, have retired to cultivate the blessing of peace '. After a very long debate (which covers more than thirty pages in the *Parliamentary Register*) the amendment was carried by 179 to 57 and then the amended motion without a division. This debate, in which the Gardner amendment was described by one member as a 'dirty sarcasm', roamed over the same ground as that which had preceded it. The attorney general again spoke strongly against the volunteers. It is interesting to observe that several members anticipated that many of the 'real' or 'original' volunteers would be 'officers and soldiers of a militia'; it was also stated that 'the original volunteers were the real militia of the country'; and that 'the original volunteers cannot finish their glorious race with more consistent splendour than by merging in a national militia'.

This might well have happened if a militia had been set up at that time. It is not clear whether the matter ever got so far as a draft bill. On 1 April, 1785, lord Mornington writes[19] to London: 'our militia bill has not yet been discussed in the House of Lords; indeed the bill is not yet brought into the house of Commons'. Lord Charlemont writes on 29 March:

> What the cursed militia bill will be I cannot discover, though I have left no means untried to come at its contents.... It ought certainly to be impossible that it should contain anything of the nature to which you allude. Yet such is the madness of the time that nothing can be wild enough to be absolutely impossible. Still, however, I hope the best and am rather inclined to believe that nothing more unpalatable than a mere militia will ensue.[20]

On 3 April Hillsborough writes to Rutland that he hopes 'still to be in time to lay before you my thoughts upon the militia bill'.

Though, as stated, it is not clear whether the matter eventuated in a bill, Mr. Samuel Hayes of Avondale, one of the two members for the borough of Wicklow—he had formally seconded the Gardner motion and had been one of the five to whom leave to bring in the bill was granted—studied the question and afterwards, when consulted by Hobart in December 1792, made his results available. 'I was desirous', he writes[21] 'of procuring some ground to go on in apportioning the numbers which each county should furnish. I therefore got a return of the computed number of inhabitants, the computed number of protestants, and the actual number of freeholders who had voted at the preceding election. From these returns I sketched out what I thought each county might very well furnish, which amounted in the whole to about 12,000 men'. With his letter to Hobart he sends a rather elaborate table. The following are his figures for county Armagh:—

> Computed number of inhabitants 84,000; freeholders who polled at the last election 2,400; computed number of protestants 28,000. In respect of these numbers he allowed a regiment of 10 cos or 400 men.

It will be seen later how Hillsborough arrived at the figures which were embodied in the 1793 bill.

Rutland's ardour for his 'favourite project' gradually cooled off; by July 1785 he was 'in doubt whether we shall be able to contend with the volunteers this year and establish a militia'. Pitt and Sydney were still more reluctant to commit themselves in the matter; if it were to be pursued they thought that the country gentlemen and men of property 'should be so worked that they demand vigorous measures in their support and keeping under of disorder by something more than volunteers chiefly catholics'. By January 1786 Rutland was 'persuaded of the wisdom of leaving this evil [i.e. the Volunteers] *for the present* to remedy itself'. Already in the previous year there had been, in the words of another observer, 'a total stagnation to their spirit', and in July, 1787, Rutland was able to report to ministers in London that 'tranquillity prevails at present throughout Ireland'. In October of that year he was under no great apprehensions about the revival of the volunteers; he also thought that 'a militia bill has its objections and its difficulties here....that measure may, however, be the consideration of a future day, if we should ultimately be obliged to have recourse to any such expedients'.

That month he died. There is no evidence of any revival of the militia project under his successor the marquis of Buckingham. Tranquillity continued for a time but, by the middle of 1789 at least, there was ample need in the north for the restraints of military force. But the object of the Irish government—so it is alleged[22]—was to connive at dissensions which would keep catholics and dissenters from arriving at any political rapprochement. Lord Westmoreland who succeeded Buckingham arrived in Ireland early in 1790, and in May of that year W. W. Grenville revives the project: 'perhaps the most desirable of all objects, in the present state of things, would be the establishment of a militia in Ireland. This idea has sometimes been not unpopular there, as I believe'; and he asked to be furnished with Westmoreland's sentiments on the matter. Westmoreland would have none of it: 'the establishment of a militia in Ireland seems attended with unsurmountable difficulties; if it could be raised it would be burthensome and oppressive to a great degree, especially considering the disproportion of protestants and catholics'. In any dispute between England and Ireland it [i.e. a militia] would be actuated by popular opinion—which would be embarrassing. It would form an argument against the necessity of so large a military force; it would "transfer the power of the sword, *lex ultima regum*, from the English army to the gentlemen of the country';[23] this was, in effect, much the view of the militia which Cornwallis seems subsequently to have held.

He had much more to urge against the idea, which, he said, had in Rutland's day been found so unpopular and difficult that it was given up. 'I am told', he added, 'that the duke afterwards was very happy that the plan had failed'. There was only one contingency in which he would entertain the project: the renewal of the volunteering spirit. But he caustically commented on this that he 'was not quite decided whether he should not think the militia the more dangerous force' from its greater permanence—in which quality, however, the volunteers had not been so very wanting, as we have seen. He had consulted the most able and confidential persons who 'fairly stated the impropriety and danger of arming the country and thought the plan would be unpopular and inefficacious'.

One step however was taken in 1790 which had definite importance when the month of December, 1792, was reached. In the 1785 debates slighting things had been said of the act of 17 and 18 Geo. iii: it was stated, for instance to have been 'felt so useless as not to be called into action'. But, in spite of this, as we have seen, it had been continued in force. By 1789 it had really expired but, under the general statute of that year for amending reviving and continuing temporary statutes, it was revived and continued in force to 24 June, 1796 (and the end of the then next session of parliament), so that it was in force right up to the coming into operation of the 1793 act, by which 'all former acts of parliament relating to the militia' were repealed. Whether this step was taken with Westmoreland's assent or in fact prior to his arrival as viceroy depends on the date of the omnibus act of 1789 and on the date of his taking up the reins in Dublin. At all events, however much or little the matter of a militia had been agitated in the period down to June, 1792, in that month Westmoreland expressed[24] to Hillsborough (letter of 25 June) the conviction that 'some other mode *besides soldiers* must be devised to check *defenderism*'.

In November, 1792, the progress of events compelled him to give close attention to the matter; his official correspondence is full of it. To a letter of his on the subject Pitt replied[25] that he had 'not local knowledge enough to judge what difficulties may be in the way of a militia but if it can be put on a good footing it seems the most likely way to check the spirit of volunteering and to maintain the peace of the country'. A fully considered statement of the views held by the confidential servants of the king in Ireland urged the formation of a protestant militia. Westmoreland, forwarding this, comments[26] as follows:

The laws at present in force might be sufficient perhaps for raising a volunteer militia but it is thought advisable not to move on this subject till at the meeting of parliament the gentlemen of the country have an opportunity of consulting together. It seems to me possible to form a militia that may tend very much to strengthen the hands of government and enable his majesty whenever occasion requires to employ elsewhere his British forces. I am aware however that it is a question of great nicety and difficulty and I should hesitate somewhat more on the subject if I were not apprehensive that a general arming of volunteers....was about to be renewed.

He thinks that the proposal might prepare the way for abolishing volunteers and afford an ample protection to protestants and possibly be a useful instrument to government for enforcing the law. On 24 November he believes his cabinet ' will lean to a militia ' and on the 28th he does not know ' how far a militia will be practicable '; the great difficulty with him was to find the men ; ' the gentlemen to whom militia has been mentioned very generally approve '. Next day, writing to London, he has ' some hopes of being able to set on foot a militia that may render individual arming unnecessary '. On the 13th Hobart[27] the chief secretary had referred to the attorney general, the question : had the lord lieutenant the power under the act of 17 and 18 Geo. iii of arraying companies of militia, the protestants being volunteers (sic), in any county that he might decide ? The answer was probably affirmative.

On 1st December Westmoreland writes to Pitt that, after ' a whole day of conference ' the Irish Cabinet had decided that the volunteering spirit must be put down and, on the 4th, in a further long letter he writes that ' uniforms and hats are making in a most public manner ' and adds : ' I think it essential to strengthen ourselves without loss of time with a militia if we can get one ; I expect the city will make movements towards it in a day or two '.

It has seemed important to give in some detail Westmoreland's views on the policy of instituting a militia. In his early days in office, he had been adverse and the quotations given suffice to show that he had never warmly supported the policy, though, just as much as Rutland, he regarded the volunteers as an incubus. There had been indecision on this point over the whole period from 1778-93 and it is probable that, but for the manifestations of December, 1792, which seriously alarmed the Irish government, Westmoreland would have continued, up to the end of his period of office, to waver. Hobart had become convinced earlier than Westmoreland and the various steps taken in December 1792 look rather like efforts on his part to screw his chief's courage to the sticking point. From any aspect it was a misfortune for the force which was to come into existence that it should be, as it apparently was, so unwelcome to the lord lieutenant ; there is no record of him showing any marked or substantial solicitude. Having launched the militia policy, he does not seem to have acted on the view that the proper course in the public interest was to pursue it with the maximum vigour. His successor in office, lord Camden, frequently reviewed the militia units. There is another reason why Westmoreland might have been expected to show this formal interest; from the beginning the Irish public —at all events that portion which a lord lieutenant rested upon and might have wished therefore to conciliate—seems to have taken the force into its favour. It is not, therefore, surprising that Camden and Pelham when they succeeded should have found the force, as they apparently did, unprovided as regards various essentials; on the other hand it is to be noted that the idea of a long continuing war was not finally accepted before 1795.

To return now to December 1792. Early in that month several parades of the volunteers were held in various parts of the country. 'Every volunteer', says the *Hibernian Journal* on 7 December, 'who was enrolled at the time of the threatened invasion of their country when its protection was left by the then government to our armed citizens—these men everywhere now come forward and are again arraying to maintain peace. In Dublin our volunteers are mustering....having but one view, that of the protection of the persons and property of the citizens, the maintenance of the peace and of the laws and the prevention of riot and disorder'. In administration circles December was undoubtedly a month of feverish activity and in the country of interested conjectures. On 17 November the *Dublin Evening Post* had had the announcement: 'the measure of raising and embodying an efficient militia in this kingdom is said to be determined on by the administration and that it will be submitted to the consideration of parliament in the ensuing session. Their number will be 20,000'.

The volunteer demonstrations were a challenge to the government which they were not going to pass over: if it was necessary to provide a force in Dublin, then they were going to see to it that the sword should be restored to the executive. When volunteer bodies were formed under the style of National Guards it was time to be acting. The outcome of the consultations on the 4th was that a proclamation was settled against 'this particular new corps'. But the government was still timid about the possibility of offence to 'the old volunteers' and Hobart, in a letter[28] written to Hillsborough on 9 December, seems to regard 'the manner in which the old volunteers are adverted to' (in the proclamation which was issued on the 8th with an imposing list of signatures attached) as open to objection. The volunteers are not directly named but persons are referred to who 'by colour of laudable associations heretofore formed in this kingdom by his majesty's loyal subjects for repelling foreign invasion' are appearing in arms. The government's policy was not, however, merely prohibitive. The proclamation had not been very successful and Westmoreland laments, in his despatches of this month, the unarrested increase of the volunteering spirit. By the 9th the government had decided to have some sort of militia demonstration, though on the 11th Westmoreland is still impressed with the act being 'full of difficulties '[29], but he is going to do the utmost he can for a militia. Apparently the idea then was to make use of the existing act. In Hobart's letter of 9 December to Hillsborough (then in England) he had said : 'the nature of a militia you must know is attended with very great difficulties, but necessity impels us to resort to it, and we propose forthwith, *even under the present act*, to endeavour to carry it into effect', and then he adds, 'for that purpose [i.e. presumably in order to help in the militia business] and more especially because affairs here are so extremely critical, I cannot help earnestly pressing upon you for your own sake as well as that of the government to come *immediately* '; he also says that they 'hope to mould some of them [i.e. of the old volunteers] into a militia '.

On 14 December Hobart sent out a circular[30] to various gentlemen enquiring 'their sentiments on the subject of establishing a militia in their counties '. Persons to whom it is known that this letter was sent are Mr William Brownlow of co. Armagh ; Mr R. Dawson of co. Monaghan ; Mr Samuel Hayes (see p. 7) ; the mayors of Waterford and of Cork ; and Mr Richard Longford of Cork. One of the replies recites that the writer has 'laid before the principal gentlemen the offer of a militia *in the form and manner directed by the act of parliament for that purpose* '. This seems to indicate that an entirely new act was not as yet in contemplation.

The prospect of a militia challenged the volunteers to spurts of demonstrative energy. On the other hand these signs of revival of volunteering stimulated the government, though neither in Dublin nor in Belfast was the movement on any considerable scale. Westmoreland himself admits[31] that he does not believe 'more than 400 or 500 in Dublin are concerned in this. As to Belfast not above 200 or 300 volunteers have ever appeared in the town '. Nevertheless the government decided on positive action, though possibly the steps taken were no more than a piece of bluff. In the middle of December the lord mayor of Dublin received an official letter from the chief secretary informing him that a commission was being issued to array a militia in the city of Dublin and that the plan would be put into effect with the utmost expedition that legal forms would admit—to which announcement the *Hibernian Journal* adds : 'it is now upwards of 40 years since there was a militia in the city, though it must be admitted there is an existing act of parliament for that express purpose '. On the 18th Hobart again writes[32] to Hillsborough:

' I cannot help indulging a hope that you are on your way to this country. You cannot conceive how much your exertions are wanted '. On the 19th letters patent[33] passed the great seal of the kingdom for commissions for arraying the militia for the county of the city of Dublin and *for the county and town of Drogheda.* It seems possible that the latter move was by way of warning to Belfast, indicating what was in store for them if volunteering did not stop. Though the *Dublin Evening Post* on 22 December carried the matter a stage further and mentioned certain probable appointments and salaries to be paid (in particular to the recorder as commissioner of array) there seems no evidence that any actual arraying ever took place and the conclusion is that the government were, in fact, bluffing and spinning out time until with the opening of the session they could hold consultations with the country gentlemen. On 8 November, as already stated, Westmoreland had[34] taken the view that it was not advisable to move on this subject till at the meeting of parliament the gentlemen of the country have an opportunity of consulting together ', and on 7 December[35] he told Pitt : ' Our conduct for the next month is " most critical ".'

The letters patent under the great seal referred to in the last paragraph no longer exist. Presumably they were issued under powers contained in the act 17-18 Geo. iii. chap. 13. The reference to the appointment of a commissioner (i.e. commissioner of array) supports this view, in reference to which it is further to be noted that on 22 December the *Freeman's Journal* printed, for the information of its readers, ' particulars of the militia bill existing in this kingdom '. So far there is still nothing to show that a new bill was contemplated. The lord lieutenant's speech on 10 January opening parliament did not carry the matter much further : he spoke of ' measures for the maintenance of tranquillity, and for this purpose to render more effectual the law for establishing a militia in this kingdom '. Possibly even yet the government had not settled their policy* as regards legislation. The address in reply to the speech from the throne only repeated the lord lieutenant's phrase. In a debate on 5 February, in which Hillsborough took part, a militia force of 16,000 was mentioned—the number ultimately proposed. On 10 February, in reply to a question, the chancellor of the exchequer said that the ' plan of the militia was not ready '. Not till 4 March was the bill presented and then it was ' a bill for amending and reducing into one act of parliament the laws relating to the militia in Ireland.' It was on that day read a first time and ordered to be printed. After the long period of hesitation the die was now at length cast.

*When at length the militia bill came, its preamble stated forthrightly : " the militia laws now in force in this kingdom have been found incapable of effecting the purposes of their institution '.

II

The Bill of 1793

If the act of 17 and 18 Geo. iii had been Ogle's, then that of 1793 is at least as much Hillsborough's. General Robert Cunninghame, the commander in chief in 1793, tells Hillsborough, in a letter written at the end of that year, that he considers him 'as the father of all the militia in this country '.[1] When he made this remark he was writing on some point connected with the Down militia only. It may, of course, have been simply flattery, but the general impression remained that Hillsborough had really done much to get the militia for Ireland. There were, however, dissenting voices. When on 13 January, 1794, in the Dublin Guild of Merchants, an address to the marquis of Downshire—he had succeeded to the title in the previous October—was moved, thanking him 'for the acquisition of the militia law in this country '[2] there was opposition ; one member thought 'a compliment to an individual would be contributive of offence to the whole legislative body '; and the address was withdrawn and the meeting adjourned. The matter came forward again at the end of April, with greater success ; the address was then ordered to be presented in a gold box. Reference was made to Hillsborough's exertions in 'digesting, preparing and bringing forward the militia bill' and another member of the guild said that 'for a period of four months the digestion of the militia bill had occupied the indefatigable attention of the noble lord by day and night, sometimes for fourteen hours at a sitting[3] '.? But another member said 'he was taught to understand the measure had proceeded from administration and that the noble marquis was only manager to bring it forward '.

The references given in the last chapter show that the Westmoreland administration attached importance to obtaining Hillsborough's active co-operation. But he does not appear to have responded very promptly to urgent requests for his presence sent on 9 and 18 December 1793. He was at a meeting held at Downpatrick on 21 January (at which the formation of a militia was pronounced 'unnecessary and inexpedient ') and it is stated that he had then just returned from England.[4] He may of course, if, as is probable, he was in London when Hobart's summonses reached him, have spent time there in procuring information about the English militia. Speaking on the militia question on 5 February, he said 'he would wish to form the bill he was moving for leave to bring in, as nearly as circumstances would permit, on the same plan as that of England'.[5] The militia law of England had been codified in 26 Geo. iii chap. 107, and this act had no doubt been closely studied in the office of the law officers in Dublin as soon as it was probable that a bill would be wanted. No doubt there were conferences between the attorney general, Hobart and Hillsborough. The last-named was not of course a member of the administration; against this, there was the great territorial position of his father, lord Downshire, and the fact that he himself had, or had had, a commission in an English militia regiment: these were reasons why he was chosen for the task. Hobart appears to have remained studiously in the background during most of the debates, but he did intervene to make the point that 'the measure was not a measure of government but of the country and that which (Grattan) called clamour was, in truth, the honest effusions and cordial concurrence of country gentlemen'.[6] Hillsborough also made the point that it was not his intention to increase government influence. The complaints which were made of the delay in bringing forward the measure, were answered not by government but by Hillsborough: 'The reason why he had not brought it forward sooner was that some difficulties he had not foreseen had occurred which were now removed'.

It is legitimate to suspect that one of these was: how was the religious question to be handled? We have seen that up to at least 17 November Westmoreland's advisers were thinking exclusively of a wholly protestant militia; but the bill when it was introduced did not exclude catholics but seems to have required the oaths of supremacy and abjuration. It is clear from a letter written from India in February 1795 by Hobart, that Hillsborough and Hobart had not seen entirely eye to eye on this point. 'I am happy', says Hobart, 'to find by your letter that the militia have proved themselves such good soldiers; and I trust you will now forgive me for having urged the propriety of not excluding Roman catholics from the militia, as the particular service to which you allude has manifested that they will fight without enquiry into the religion of the persons they are ordered to contend with'.[7]

The principal debate on this question was in the house of lords. 'The lords in and about town' had been specially whipped for the second reading, but, though the house was extremely full, nothing was said against the committal of the bill; it was committed and reported without any amendments. On 25 March the commons sat waiting to receive it. But at 6.30 p.m. they found themselves obliged to adjourn, having been in session for some time 'without doing any business or having received the militia bill from the lords'.[8] Irish parliamentary procedure admitted of amendments being moved on the third reading; and what had happened in the lords was a last hour appeal from lord Farnham that the 'oath of supremacy should be required as an indispensable preliminary to the receiving any command in the militia'.

Though the journal of the house of lords does not record any amendment as having been moved on this matter at any stage, a newspaper report[9]—no other authority is available— speaks of a definite amendment on 25 March; and there seems to have been a division. In the debate it was stated that the bill was first introduced (i.e. in the commons) without the clause lord Farnham now proposed to amend. But an amendment was adopted which left the relevant clause (ii) as follows* : 'Every deputy governor and commissioned officer shall....take such oath or oaths and make and sign such declaration or declarations as is, are, or shall be required to be taken, made and signed by the officers of his majesty's other forces in this kingdom.'[10] No account of the debates on this point in the commons exists. But it was pointed out in the lords debate that the 'amendment now proposed (i.e. by lord Farnham) went to do away that which in the other house seemed of so much necessity and importance'. The result of carrying the amendment would have been, as the bishop of Cork pointed out that the other house must meet again to reconsider the subject.

The arguments used on either side will be obvious. The lord chancellor's attitude was to make concessions in the smallest possible instalments; the catholics had been admitted to civil and political power; satisfaction of their aspirations to military power should stand over—to see how things went. He raised some bogies: the catholics had been levying taxes 'for some secret purpose'; they 'assumed a sort of democracy in the country'. Several speakers pointed out the inconsistency of admitting catholics to the army and rejecting their admission to the militia; amongst these was Lord Dunsany, who also energetically attacked the lord chancellor, though subsequently, on the lord chancellor protesting, he apologized 'for anything which might have fallen from him in the warmth of misinformation'. The bishop of Cork strongly opposed the illiberal course suggested in the amendment. 'Was this', he asked, 'a time for procrasti-

*The oaths to be taken respectively by the balloted man (cl. 24); the substitute (cl. 25); the sergeants and corporals (cl. 65) and by the men 'voluntarily offering (33 Geo. iii. Chap. 33, cl. 13) and 35. Geo. iii. Chap. 8, cl. 16) alike contain the undertaking to 'be faithful and bear true allegiance' and that is all.

nation when a French fleet of twelve sail of the line hovered in the chops of our channel; when a British ship of war which was sent to Cork for the convoy of our outward bound trade fleet to the West Indies was ordered back to England with all expedition, in order to act for the more pressing emergency of home defence?' He was not afraid of the fidelity or the gallantry of the Roman catholics which had been proved in every quarter of the globe. Finally he was persuaded that in many counties it would be difficult to officer the militia regiments with protestants. The archbishop of Cashel thought that a discretionary power might be given to the king of dispensing with the oath of supremacy on the appointment of militia officers and of substituting another in its place. Lord Clonmel wound up the debate by saying that he should oppose the amendment as being 'probably unjust' and 'clearly impossible'. On the division being taken the Farnham amendment was rejected, the 'contents' being 10 and the 'non-contents' 23.[11] It is interesting to observe that lord Charlemont[12] voted for the amendment. So the enactment was left as the commons had decided.

The course of the discussion on this matter, at a vital stage of a great and prolonged fundamental controversy, has been worth describing at some length. It was the most controversial that arose. The bill was a long one; it ran to sixty eight pages and Grattan complained, in the second reading debate on 7 March, that it had been rather hurled at the heads of members; in the lords the duke of Leinster protested 'because his motion for printing so long a bill, that it might have due deliberation had been refused'.[13] It was in committee in the commons on 8 and 9 March and then reported with amendments. As stated, it was recommitted and again reported, when, as already stated, the clause about the oath was amended. Some other amendments also were then made the most important of which enabled surgeons and mates to hold combatant commissions without having a property qualification.[14] Generally speaking, the number of amendments made seems small in proportion to the length and detailed character of the bill.

The *Belfast Newsletter* reports an interesting committee debate on the 8 March. The property qualification for a colonel in the English militia (which had been followed) was 'but £1,000 a year'. Mr Conolly (one of the richest men in Ireland and afterwards colonel of the Londonderry militia) insisted that this would not ensure getting the first gentlemen in the country. 'This is a job', he said,[15] 'engrafted on a militia to give the minister a power of setting up, at the head of the different counties, inferior men, their own creatures and their followers who are to propagate the influence over the head of the first gentlemen of property and distinction in the kingdom '. He urged that the qualification of the colonel should be raised to ' some thousands a year '. Such alteration was necessary, he urged, to make the bill a militia bill; ' it is now a police bill '. As a result the qualification of the lieutenant colonel was raised from £1,000 to £1,600 and that of the colonel to £2,000 a year. This claim of a position of considerable independence for the militia magnates is an early exhibition of what was going to be a permanent embarrassment for the lords lieutenant: Dublin Castle always had to reckon with the susceptibilities of the ' colonels '; a quasi-diplomatic preparation of any substantial contemplated changes was usually to be found necessary. Illustrations of this will appear from time to time.

It has been seen that Mr Conolly had a definite idea of what constituted a militia bill. In later parliamentary discussions it emerged that, just as a militia was not a militia if the big county magnates had not a dominant position, so a militia raised without the ballot was not the real thing. Discussion of the idea of a militia had been going on in Ireland for a long time. The Dublin pamphlet of 1767[16] had contemplated the private men being chosen by ballot; it had also contemplated the officers being similarly chosen. In the discussions on the bill of 1793 the principle of the ballot does not appear to have been a matter for controversy. It is safe to say that in the debates there was no discussion either of the principle or of the details of the ballot proposal which was not entirely a new departure*. There were anyhow, in the Irish parliament, no tribunes of the people to harangue about it. The very lengthy debates of 1785 (see p. 5) may be regarded as in some sense a second reading debate of the bill of 1793. But, even in those wide-ranging discussions, no exception was taken to the principle of raising men by ballot. What was emphasized rather in the second reading on 7 March was that the bill was ' a measure highly *constitutional* '.[17] This was one of the ' blessed words ' of the period. The chancellor of the exchequer met the objection against proceeding at once by urging that ' a militia....has long been the wish of [Ireland's] best and most popular characters '. Even in 1797, after all that had passed, Castlereagh does not hesitate to express the view that of what he describes as the two ways of raising men that of the ballot was ' the most constitutional '. To see why the principle went through easily in 1793 is not difficult.

Some effect seems to have been produced by the suggestion, advanced by Hillsborough in the debate on 6 March, that ' the bill was only for a year '; ' any errors ', he added, ' that might exist in it could be remedied in the bill of next year '.[18] It is not clear exactly what his idea was; as it stands, the act is not limited

*Under the early commissions of array there was some compulsion.

in duration. Possibly he had in mind (and he may have explained this in his second reading speech which is not preserved) the annual pay and clothing bills which, on the model of the militia legislation system in England, became part of the Irish system. These acts provided, from year to year, the money for the pay of the militia. As each session came round therefore there was a new opportunity of legislation which could be used, and was in fact used 'to remedy errors' though on a limited scale. The first of these bills (33 Geo. iii cap. 33, clause 13) made an important modification of the recruiting law (see page 39); and the corresponding acts of subsequent years introduced other changes. In May 1794 a Dublin Castle official refers to this annual bill as 'the Hodge Podge bill'.[19] But there were limits to what could be remedied in this way and in each year up to the Union, bills to amend the principal act (1793) were brought in; some of these were, as will be seen, of considerable proportions. There was one other sense in which the militia could be said to be 'only for a year'; just as the pay was provided from year to year so the provisions for discliplining the militia (as well as the other military forces) required to be renewed annually; this was done through the annual mutiny act which corresponds to the Army Annual Acts of today. In 1805 Castlereagh said: 'The whole of the militia code is....in two bills: one containing the pecuniary part and therefore necessarily annual; the other perpetual and comprising everything else'.[20]

How far was the militia act (and the militia) regarded as perpetual at the time of its introduction? It is relevant to quote Castlereagh again: 'The first and principal militia act....passed in 1793....was drawn with a view to the immediate formation of that body; and the provisions of it were, in their form, in many instances inapplicable to any other state of things' and he mentions that 'the act provided for the returning lists of names for balloting for the militia at its first formation but not at any subsequent period'. It is shewn in chapter V that the surgeons were not originally chosen for other than a short period of 'actual service'. Though the bill was originated largely to meet an emergency it envisages the militia routine of peace conditions (i.e. annual trainings, permanent staff arrangements) as much as it does the conditions of what is, in contradistinction, called 'actual service'. This is still more true of the first pay and clothing act dealing with matters (e.g. hospital expenses during annual exercise; issue of pay during annual exercise; recovery of moneys, etc. etc.) which were in large part not actual during a period of lasting embodiment. The bill received the royal assent on 9 April but two months later, on 3 June, the chancellor of the exchequer was still not contemplating having to make continuous provision for the rest of the financial year : 'the expenses of arraying, he said, added to a month's pay....would amount to about £160,000, but as it might possibly be thought necessary to have them in service for a longer period than a month it might not be safe to estimate the whole of the expense....at less than £300,000 '. If this was the best forecast possible, in June permanent embodiment was probably little dreamed of during the discussions of March and it is no matter for surprise if the act took colour accordingly.

There is another reason for the act being couched as it was. It has already been indicated (p. 15) that Hillsborough moulded the Irish militia system, not on the Irish acts which had gone before (although these were probably studied) but upon the English law. The titles of the Irish bill* and of the English act (26 Geo. iii. c. 107, ' An act for amending and reducing into one act of Parliament the laws relating to the militia in that part of Great Britain called England ') were in fact identical, except for the regionally distinguishing words. But the latter was a true codification whereas the former reproduced little if anything of what was already in existence (viz. the act of 17 and 18 Geo. iii†).

The lord lieutenant's speech[21] proroguing parliament, on 16 August, discloses the trend of the government's calculations : he speaks of the bill as ' a measure which affords at present material assistance, and lays the foundation of a permanent constitutional force that has been found by experience in Great Britain of great resource in public emergencies '. That is to say that they contemplated a permanent but normally dormant force rather than one more or less permanently embodied ; the English act was on these lines and the Irish act which followed it as model naturally got the same complexion. The Irish act does not recite the existence of an emergency (although the English militia had been called out in the previous December) ; its first clause requires the governors of counties to ' cause to be trained....such persons and in such manner as is herein directed *once in every year* ', i.e. the militia routine of peace conditions.

It was some time before the militia of Ireland could throw off the semi-peace mould. The pamphlet published in 1767 had contemplated the officers, as well as the men, being chosen by ballot. This was not the system in England and it was not the system adopted in 1793 in Ireland. Had it been adopted, the force might from the beginning have had less of a peace-service

*An act for amending, and reducing into one Act of Parliament, the laws relating to the Militia of Ireland. All former acts were repealed by clause 115.

†This act of course contemplated quite a different force.

complexion and would have attained earlier to that modest measure of professionalized competence which, but only through the way of experience, it later attained. Its weakness was that it was officered by men who (in the higher commissioned ranks almost always, and in the lower commissioned ranks very frequently) besides their new military responsibilities, still had important county duties to perform, which neither their inclination, nor their interest, nor the public welfare allowed them to neglect. As the militia units became geographically deterritorialized, incompatibility between the two duties at once arose; and the military efficiency and value of officers may have varied with the extent to which they absented themselves from their county (and family) duties and stuck to the regiment. There was not of course incompatibility between annual camps of a month's duration (especially if held within the county limits) and adequate performance of county duties; and the original lay out presupposed temporary service and not perpetual embodiment. There is, in the many denigratory criticisms of the officers as a body, little recognition of these fundamental difficulties.

The act does not require previous service or military qualifications for officers other than adjutants. The property qualifications will be found in appendix I; the questions which arise are: how far they operated to exclude and how far they were enforced? There is little evidence on the first point. That unsuitable men became officers in the Irish militia, as in all other military bodies at that time, is certain. A merely money test without a close commanding officer's scrutiny could not prevent this. The property test was probably generally applied. The provisions of the act (clause 10) are precise and stringent. Nor was the application of the test left merely to the regimental authority. The clerk of the peace of the county has specific responsibilities: an account of the qualifications had to be transmitted every year to the lord lieutenant's secretary and copies had to be laid before parliament. In an important general court martial held in 1799 (see chapter X)[22] some facts about the effectiveness of the property-qualification condition emerge. The plaintiff says that his statement of qualification was duly delivered to the clerk of the peace on his being advanced in rank. Against the commanding officer various irregularities are alleged. A relation had been promoted three times since May 1798. 'On every promotion he must have certified under his hand that he possessed a sufficient qualification in property to hold the commission'. Doubt is thrown on his having in fact done this. It is also stated that 'on the formation of the regiment [the colonel] provided for all his relations even to his child at school [the lieutenant colonel]'. In September 1793 the father of a youth who had been appointed to an ensigncy in the Downshire militia writes to lord Hillsborough thanking him and he adds :[23] ' wherever he may be quartered he probably will have opportunity of pursuing his school learning (which his late illness has interrupted) and your lordship will, I am certain, allow him to take advantage of it '. In another case in the Donegal militia in 1814 a father asks for a commission for his son, stating that ' he is twelve years old ; 4 ft. 11 ; education and morals good '.[24] These cases do not perhaps suggest very scrupulous regard to the military needs of the regiment but they are no proof that the property qualification was not insisted upon in those two or in other regiments. An officer in the Downshire regiment, applying in January 1798 for a captaincy, tells his commanding officer : ' My qualification which I send to the clerk of the peace *by your direction* are as follows ' and he proceeds to set them out.

The statements of qualification of two afterwards distinguished officers of the city of Limerick militia are still in existence.* The first of these is Hugh Gough who was subsequently viscount Gough, commander-in-chief in India. The signature is youthful and immature ; Hugh Gough was at the time aged thirteen ; he may or may not have ' pursued his school learning ' wherever he was quartered but, with the property qualification he possessed, he was not prevented by youthfulness from being appointed to a commission. The other statement is that of Charles Vereker who won glory at Collooney in 1798. It reads as follows :—' I certify [the clerk of the peace is the signatory] that on the 16th day of May 1793, Charles Vereker of Roxborough in the liberties of the city of Limerick did deliver to me his qualification of which the following is a true copy, viz. I Charles Vereker of Roxborough in the liberties of the city of Limerick, esquire, do hereby certify that I am seized and possessed for my own use and benefit in possession of a real estate in fee in the lands of Roxborough situate in the parish of Cahirvella in the liberties of the city of Limerick which estate is of the clear yearly value of three hundred pounds sterling and upwards. Limerick the 16 May, 1793 '. This is addressed to the governor for the county of the city of Limerick.

The Irish militia was almost certainly an under-officered force ; the complements of officers are laid down in the act. For an eight-company regiment—which was the establishment of fourteen out of the thirty-eight units making up the Irish militia—the complement is : one lieutenant colonel commandant, one lieutenant colonel, one major ; for each company one captain, one lieutenant, one ensign ; a second ensign was allowed for

*In PRO. W.O. 68/59.

battalion companies of 100 men. For the grenadier and light companies a second lieutenant was allowed in place of the ensign and, if the strength was 100 men, a third lieutenant was allowed. The minimum strength contemplated for a company was fifty. The act permits the lieutenancies and ensigncies allowed to the companies to be occupied by surgeons, surgeons' mates, or battalion clerks; this often happened and it reduced the officer strength available to the company. As regards the double commissions of the surgeon and the mate, the Army Medical Board of Ireland[25] in February, 1800, stated that this doubling was normal and add that they believe 'this arrangement was adopted from economical views'. They condemn the plan of double commissions as unwise in conception and pernicious in practice, and add 'on service the joint discharge of the military and medical duties has ever been found impracticable and in the usual routine business of home troops we have never as yet met with a single individual who could act the part of the soldier and the surgeon at the same time without being good for nothing in the latter capacity'. Yet the Irish militia were not relieved from this weakness until after they had gone through 1798.

The adjutant (clause lviii) was restricted to the rank of lieutenant and, even when (in units of not less than six companies) appointed captain by brevet, he did not occupy one of the captain's places on the establishment. Like the surgeon and the mate the adjutant was not required to have any property qualification. These commissions were apparently regarded as something different and even perhaps as inferior. They were in fact often (see chapter XII) sold. The act is very specific (clause 63) in keeping the rank of captain free from admixture with other duties whether those of adjutant, surgeon, regimental or battalion clerk (who 'executed the office of paymaster') or quartermaster; the care of a company was a full-time occupation. The natural construction of clause 52 of the act is that field officers were additional to company officers: there is no hint of anything else. When, however, the units were formed the lieutenant colonel commandant, the lieutenant colonel and the major each occupied a captain's place in addition and in an eight company regiment the number of captains is thus not eight but five. This arrangement was no doubt also 'adopted from economical views'; the absence of expectation of a long embodiment and the low original strength of companies are probably also accountable. When in 1795 augmentation took place, and nearly 5,000 men were added to the establishment of the militia as a whole, no addition was made to the complement of officers; indeed the chancellor of the exchequer expressly said: 'The militia had been another source of expense; but....the augmentations in this quarter had been upon the least expensive scale, being not of officers but of men' (9 February 1795).[26]

The bill of course settled the number of men of which the force was to consist. The aggregate number was first mentioned on 5 February when Hillsborough moved for leave to introduce the bill.[27] 'The whole number of men he proposed to be 16,000, or, upon a rough estimate, 500 for each county in Ireland'. No explanation exists why this number was fixed upon as suitable. The 1767 pamphlet already referred to contemplated a force of 6,400 men divided between the four provinces as follows:—Ulster 1,800; Leinster 2,400; Munster 1,200; Connaught 1,000. This was said to be on a basis of 200 to a county. The act 17 and 18, Geo. iii chap. 13 contemplates a force raised by *companies*; the militia in any one county were to be not less than 100 and not more than 500 but a total for the whole country is not given. But the pamphlet, '*Consideration on the heads of a militia bill*'[28] contemplates a force of 12,000 men, or forty battalions of 300 men each, some counties having two battalions and some three. This had been the number contemplated by Mr Samuel Hayes (see chapter I). The *Dublin Evening Post* (17 November 1792) had mentioned 20,000 as being in contemplation; possibly correctly and *pace* the chancellor of the exchequer.

Hillsborough's explanation to the house of commons in committee (8 March) about the numbers is almost the only detailed statement proffered on the bill which remains on record. This figure had apparently remained blank in the draft, and keen interest was no doubt felt in what he was going to propose. He said 'he had formed his calculation from the best information he could collect and from what he conceived to be the most accurate documents, viz. the number of acres and the number of hearths in each county'. Allowing 5½ men to each 3,000 acres or 21 men to 1,000 hearths, he got the figures shewn in Appendix II. He added: 'What was very remarkable was that, notwithstanding the inequality of proportions as to acres and hearths in each county individually, yet when the whole numbers of men on each calculation were added, the difference between both was not one hundred, that on the calculation of acres being 15,655 and that on number of hearths 15,560'. He did not, however, explain why he took the rate of 5½ men and 21 respectively; the aggregate arrived at, approximately 16,000, obviously results directly from these proportions. It looks as if there were a prior decision to work up to an aggregate of that number. There was no debate or discussion on the matter. The actual number of men to be raised as set out in the act (clause 15) is 14,948; this excludes commissioned and non-commissioned officers. (See appendix VI).

Within fourteen days after the passing of the act the governors were required to appoint deputy governors. They were to be 'such proper and discreet persons' as the governors should think fit; they were to be 'living within their respective counties' and their names were to be submitted to and not disapproved by the lord lieutenant. They were to be twenty in every county 'if so many were found qualified'. The qualification was: 'to be seized or possessed' of property of the yearly value of £200 or to be the heir of some one seized or possessed of property of the yearly value of £400. They took the same oaths or made the same declarations as officers. They were to play an important part in the working of the act. They stood between the militia command and the civil interests of the county and taxpayer. With the responsibility incident on the county (which tended to become rather a money than a flesh responsibility) for providing the sinews (i.e. the men) the county needed to be protected against unjustified calls for replacements; and it was accordingly enacted that discharges of men become unfit for service required in certain circumstances to be covered by the certificate of a deputy governor and another man could not be balloted for in the room of a man so discharged until such discharge was confirmed at a subdivision meeting.

It is obvious that a deputy governor's execution of these duties might be challenged. A paper of instructions, probably a circular letter, addressed to a deputy governor of the county of the city of Limerick[29] informs him that his duties consisted in assisting the mayor (who in city-counties like Cork, Dublin and Limerick was the governor) in the militia ballot and in aiding him 'to enforce the act against such as are subject to it in respect of serving'. The document is quoted as closing with this sentence: 'their office [of deputy governor] in short may be termed militia magistrates; within their own jurisdiction, therefore, they are as much favoured as any magistrates can be in the execution of his duty, for if any person should be inclined to question their acts, the defence is made as easy as possible to them; it cannot be decided on by any other than a Limerick jury, and treble costs are to be given against the party complaining'. I have found no instance of the acts of a deputy governor being challenged but it seems probable that in the long period 1793-1816 this must have occurred.

The lists of deputy governors seem to have been quickly completed in most cases, though, where a regiment or battalion did not come into existence promptly after the royal assent date (9 April) this may have been due (not as regards the Kildare and Carlow—see next chapter) to difficulties in getting together an adequate list of deputy governors. Certainly not everyone was prepared to accept the office and in addition to apathy there was definite opposition. The usual biblical excuses for refusing public duty were forthcoming and some differed seriously on the essentials of policy. A letter[30] to lord Downshire may be quoted. The writer expresses regret that his sentiments respecting a militia establishment did not 'vibrate in unison' with those of lord Downshire. He continues: 'Having had the honour of a command in a volunteer corps for several years....of tenants of my own, I cannot think of abdicating a trust reposed in me by so respectable a body to join any new association by whatever appellation they may be styled'. He considers the old Volunteers 'as the natural guardians of our isle; besides, however eligible a militia establishment might prove, I cannot forbear entertaining doubts of its expediency in operation. England and Ireland are very differently circumstanced. What experience has proved and turned out favourably for the one country I think will not apply to the other. Volunteers, self-clothed and armed, never were known in England. In this country they have not only been known but repeatedly have obtained the thanks of parliament for the propriety of their conduct'. This is in part the typical diehard volunteer attitude which had been so forcibly expressed in the debates of 1785 and was still, with considerable vociferation, being expressed outside the walls of the Irish parliament while the debates were going on inside. In February the third Dungannon convention condemned the proposed bill as 'only having ministerial influence for its object' and as 'burdensome and totally unnecessary'. Individual Volunteer bodies staged similar demonstrations. Monaghan, and possibly other counties, instructed its parliamentary representatives to oppose the bill.[31] Many meetings—which also strongly advocated parliamentary reform—passed adverse resolutions. But gradually it seems to have become recognized that a militia was definitely coming. On 11 March, without waiting for the militia bill to become technically law, the lord lieutenant issued a proclamation against 'certain seditious and ill-affected persons in several parts of the north of this kingdom and particularly in the town of Belfast'.[32] There had already been in the previous December (see p. 11) the proclamation in Dublin which, though it had been careful not to name the volunteers explicity, had been directed against them. Hobart, writing on 19 March, says that 'the Dublin volunteers seem to have entirely given up the game' and he goes on: "Saint Patrick's day was the day fixed upon in Dublin and Belfast for a considerable show of volunteers, if not for a serious disturbance. The effect of the former proclamation in Dublin [8 December 1792] and the recent one in Belfast [11 March 1793] prevented the appearance of a single corps in either'.[33] The Belfast volunteers remonstrated to the government but ' the proclamation remained in force, and the Belfast volunteers obeyed it '.[34] Nothing is more surprising, especially in view of all the misgivings and, as it turned out, timidities of the Irish government than the unspectacular disappearance of the volunteers from the Irish scene. Belfast had been the place of their greatest strength. ' The question arose ', says a recent writer,[35] ' whether the Belfast volunteers would succumb and it was soon apparent that the answer would be in the affirmative. The *Northern Star*, commenting on the proclamation, recommended submission, for the sake of the general peace....Meeting with nothing but discouragement on every side, the volunteers were easily prevailed upon to discontinue their meetings, and before the end of the next month the familiar uniform was no longer to be seen in the streets. It was soon to be replaced by the red coat of the militiaman '.

III

Putting the Act into force

THE bill received the royal assent on 9 April.

On 6 March Hillsborough had said that 'the raising of a militia was a tedious business, of at least two months'. This was an optimistic estimate, as will appear. The government had not waited for the royal assent before starting the machine. Already on 4 April a newspaper[1] reports that 'preparations are making with great spirit by the gentlemen appointed officers of the militia in the southern counties of this kingdom; an event that, it is thought, will take place in the course of next month'. This suggests that the commanding officers at least had been nominated during March and that they had been vested with some authority to proceed in advance of legislative sanction. The list of the colonels appears in the *Freeman's Journal* on 27 April; in the Militia Successions book (Public Record Office) the lieutenant-colonel commandant's initial date is, in the case of most of the units, 25 April; this is also in some cases the date of all the officers but it is not in any case the date either of embodiment or of 'placing'—a technical term for placing on the establishment for pay.

While the officers were to be found by the lieutenant-colonel commandant (later colonel), the finding of the men was the responsibility of the deputy governors (see chapter II). The act allowed only fourteen days for these to be obtained. Though communications were surprisingly rapid, it must have been impossible to complete the action prescribed in so short a time. But many of the militia acts, even after the Union, seem to have been circulated, or otherwise made known to those concerned in the consequent administrative action, at an early stage. Before the royal assent to the bill, the governors had already indicated the preliminary steps to the deputy governors; for Donegal the list of these was already passed by the lord lieutenant on 24 April;[2] and in his own county lord Downshire was prompt. Enthusiasm overcame difficulties, and the original lists of deputy governors were in most cases prepared with no great difficulty, though later on, in consequence of some experiences of the year year 1793 and other circumstances, it was not always easy to fill up vacancies. To obviate any breakdown the act provided that the lord lieutenant should appoint deputy governors if the governors failed to do so. But there is no evidence that this was ever done.

Selection by ballot is so important a part of the act that a summary of the procedure prescribed must now be given, from which will be seen the nature of the machinery. This yielded results apparently unexpected, but it must be remembered in this connection that these provisions of the act had never been discussed in the house of commons, but accepted blindly, and in the ordinary course of 'keeping in step' with England, without much reference to possible reactions, and partly under an obsession of urgency.

Everything was to take place in public, with the fullest possibilities of criticism. The whole process takes the form of a series of meetings, general and sub-divisional. A county general meeting consisted of the governor or governors or any of them together with three deputy-governor at the least; a subdivisional of: the governor or governors, and deputy governors within the subdivision. The former were presided over by the governor; the latter by a deputy governor. A clerk was provided for each type of meeting: for the general meeting the governor appointed the clerk, and for the subdivisions the deputy governors.

This series of meetings began when the governor convoked the first general meeting. This was followed, if necessary, by further general meetings; in between were various subdivision meetings; the intervals to occur between these are in most cases prescribed by the act—with a resultant inelasticity which was probably found irksome in practice. The programme of a county's meetings from the convening of the first down to the final enrolling ceremony was as follows:

The first general meeting had to take place within fourteen days 'after the lord lieutenant....shall issue a proclamation for that purpose, requiring the militia of such county to be embodied'. The business of this meeting was :—

(*a*) to divide the county into such subdivisions as the governors shall think most expedient for carrying the purposes into execution;

(*b*) to appoint the first meetings of the several subdivisions;

(*c*) to issue orders to constables, etc., to return to the deputy governors at the places and on the days appointed for the first subdivision meeting 'lists in writing of the names of all men usually and at that time dwelling within their respective parishes and places between the age of eighteen and forty-five years'; these lists had to distinguish 'the respective ranks profession and occupation' and 'which of the persons so returned labour under any infirmity likely to incapacitate them from serving as militiamen';

(*d*) to appoint, 'if they judge needful', the time and place for a second general meeting.

The first subdivision meeting had to take place 'as soon as conveniently may be' and 'at farthest within eight days' of the first general meeting; its business was:—

(*a*) to enquire and select, out of the lists returned by the constables, 'the names of all such persons mentioned therein as are fit to carry arms', the enquiry and selection being made upon evidence to be given upon oath.

(*b*) to cause the clerk to deliver copies of the lists as prepared at the meeting to the constables to be affixed by them on church doors and other places where notices are usually published, with indication at the bottom of every list (i) of the day and place of the next or second subdivision meeting, and (ii) of the fact that persons who think themselves aggrieved could then appeal.

Nothing is laid down in the act as to the interval to elapse before the second subdivision meeting; its business was:—

(*a*) to hear any person 'who shall think himself aggrieved by having his name inserted in the lists or by the omission of any other name'; to direct the amendment of the lists 'as the case shall require'; and to direct the omission of the names of persons excepted by the act from serving if any such have been inserted;

(*b*) to appoint 'what number of men shall serve for each parish and place, within such subdivision';

(*c*) to return to the clerk of the general meeting certificates of the number of men in each parish or place specified in the lists as amended;

(*d*) to appoint the time and place for the third meeting, to be held within fourteen days.

The third subdivision meeting could obviously be held soon after the second as there was no displaying of lists or communication with individuals to be carried out in the interval: its business was:—

(*a*) to cause the number of men appointed to serve (item (*b*) of the business of the second meeting) to be chosen by ballot out of the list returned for every parish:

(*b*) to appoint another, the fourth, meeting to be held within fourteen days in the same subdivision.

(*c*) to direct the constable or other officer of the parish to give notice to every man so chosen to serve in the militia, to appear at the fourth meeting; the notice was to be individual, either delivered verbally and personally or left at the places of abode, at least seven days before the meeting.

At the fourth subdivision meeting those chosen by the ballot had to appear and take the oath; they were then enrolled. The constables attended and proved the serving of the notices. It was at this meeting, apparently, that substitutes were produced and, if approved by the governor or deputy governors, enrolled.

Notices of general meetings had to be, and notices of subdivision were in practice, given 'in any newspaper, usually published in such county' and therefore, so far as newspapers of the time survive, it is possible to follow the action taken in the different counties. A considerable number of notices of meetings are to be found, and, although the county authorities do not appear to have been furnished with any directions supplementing the provisions of the act, there is no reason for doubting that a serious effort was made at least to start the ballot machinery in all the counties.

After the royal assent (9 April) not much time, all the circumstances being considered, was allowed to pass before the proclamations requiring the militias to be embodied were issued. Two of these, affecting nineteen units, were issued on 20 and 25 April respectively.[3] Thus, before the end of that month, half the units had received the signal to start getting the men together. These were :—Dublin county, Dublin city, Kilkenny, King's county, Meath, Westmeath, Carlow, Leitrim, Longford, Louth, county of the town of Drogheda (20 April); Antrim, Cavan, Kerry, Londonderry, Queen's county, Roscommon, Sligo and Wexford (25 April). Four more, Down, Donegal, Monaghan and Wicklow, had their orders on 29 April; Armagh, Fermanagh, Tipperary, Tyrone, Waterford on 3 May; Limerick city, Galway, Mayo (north and south) on 8 May, and Clare on 13 May. Thus, within about a month, as many as thirty-three militias had been started. No doubt, therefore, could remain with anyone that the government was in earnest and the representatives of the various classes and, particularly, of those contemplating demonstrations, took note accordingly. The reactions which always attend innovationary legislation began.

Anti-militia sentiments, ventilated in the country, particularly in the north and among the Volunteer elements, during the preliminary discussions and also during the actual parliamentary debates, had not ceased to be expressed; and it is a tenable view that, had the scheme in the act been to raise the projected force by beat of drum methods rather than by ballot, the opposition would have been not much less. Political consciousness was greater in the north than in the south; it was there that, prior to the passing of the bill, criticism was most active. But after the bill had been passed specific disturbance, though not unknown, was not the method of manifestation chiefly resorted to in the north. Some assigned this to the possession of superior intelligence;[4] but lord Westmoreland,[5] writing on 5 June, refers to the 'north, having been dragooned lately, remains in sullen silence'. Violent manifestations did not appear until the making out of the lists began. So far as these can be attributed, not to peasant botheredness but to political mindedness, the engineering of them had probably been in progress all along. Without the irritation of the list-making there would not have been so much to fasten on; with it ingenuity in making trouble was not very much taxed.

The actual troubles were at their height in the month of May and lasted into June. What happened in a few cases is illustrated by an occurrence in co. Meath. Some 150 'defenders' surrounded Mr Hamilton Gorges' place at Kilbrew. He went to meet them and had a blunderbuss put to his breast. But he was popular and the majority of the raiding party did not stand for that sort of thing and stopped it. A parley ensued during which the men explained that they objected to being enrolled for the militia, which would oblige them, as they thought, to go to parts of the kingdom remote from their homes—which was, in fact, exactly what happened—to the distress of themselves and of their families. Mr Gorges humanely reasoned with them but it seemed to have no effect.[6] In other cases, on explanations being given, the men departed peaceably.[7]

This incident ended without violence but it was otherwise in some cases. An affair at Boyle, co. Roscommon (which, with Sligo, seems to have been one of the counties most disturbed), is several times mentioned in contemporary records. The house of a Mr Tennison was pulled to the ground by a large mob 'variously armed'. Soldiers were brought in and some persons were killed and some wounded. It is stated that Mr Tennison had brought this on himself by his activity in dealing with a mob; he was thought to have taken some men prisoners for opposing the militia. But it is stated alternatively that these Roscommon troubles were a protest against unfair returns made by several of the parochial constables and it is added that 'there are many instances where the whole stress has been laid on the shopkeepers and traders'.[8] In this case there seems no reason to doubt that Mr. Tennison's house was pulled down, but the origin of the trouble is a little vague. At all events this is not one of those uncritical general statements often made with little foundation in fact.

In other cases there were threats to individuals. There was an insult to lord Mountjoy near Swords;[9] and at Baltinglass, lord Aldborough, the governor of co. Wicklow, received a message from a 'formidable body' which insultingly invited him 'to come and choose among them such as he should think proper'[10] but there was no violence. Then at Clontarf, co. Dublin a Mr Commissary Weekes[11] is said to have only just escaped very rough treatment for attempting to take the names of the inhabitants.

Incidentally, this was a duty of the constables, but Mr Weekes, if he was a deputy governor, may have been involved somehow. Lord Thurles also received a letter ' threatening him with destruction if he should attempt to cause the militia of co. Tipperary to be embodied '.[12] The clergy did not escape attack. In co. Kerry, which was one of those most excited over the militia, priests are said—again in May—to have been ' hunted out on account of having made returns of numbers fit for the militia '.[13] The *Northern Star* also states[14] that in Kerry the disaffected people had ' nailed up the chapels from an idea that the priests are in the interest of administration '; later the Kerry militia was completed ' with great facility and dispatch '. In co. Wexford a priest was sentenced to be hanged.[15] Later, we learn that in early June, at Skreen in co. Sligo, the house of the parish priest (in which he was with two protestant clergymen) was attacked by a mob through resentment ' due to some evil-minded person having reported that he gave in a list of names previous to a ballot for the militia'.[16] There is an air of improbability, or anyhow, of sheer wrongheadedness, about these alleged incidents ; because it was no part of the duty of parish priests, or indeed of any clergy, to make out the lists of persons to go to the ballot. Still there is some evidence that in certain places the clergy did, indirectly though legitimately, take some small hand, but only to counsel their flock to comply with the law.[17]

The north was not exempt. The most troublesome and notorious incidents were in co. Down—the county of the ' father of all the militia in this country '. These were at Rathfryland and at Castlereagh and apparently created considerable impression in Ulster. In July the revd. Edward Hudson writes to lord Charlemont : ' lord Hillsborough's militia business goes on smoothly since the affair at Castlereagh '.[18] It may therefore be of interest to quote verbatim a contemporary account, noting that the incident (end of June) took place at an actual subdivision meeting and not on the earlier stage of the taking of names.

' The deputy governors assembled a little before 12 o'clock and immediately proceeded to business, a troop of the 17th Dragoons being stationed in the village merely for the purpose of preventing any disturbance of which some hints had been given ; and, before the examination of one appeal had been concluded, the guard at the door of the house was assaulted by several hundred persons throwing stones and one of the horses was actually knocked down. The house was immediately assailed by an innumerable quantity of stones, which drove in the sashes and the doors. At this very moment the remaining part of the troop were gone to an adjacent rivulet to water their horses and therefore that was the time taken to commence the meditated attack. But in a few seconds the whole troop formed and, the stones still flying in great numbers, made a charge upon the rioters up the hill, when several of them were killed and a great many dangerously wounded. On this being effected and those deluded people appearing to form themselves again in numbers of from 12 to 20 in a party, a sergeant was sent off to Belfast for a part of the 38th regiment and in a minute [sic] that regiment....marched from Belfast to Castlereagh, as also did a part of the train of artillery with two field pieces, with the utmost alacrity. But previous to their arrival peace was re-established. The deputy governors notwithstanding this disturbance, proceeded on and completely went through the business of the day '.[19]

A somewhat similar incident was threatened at Tulla, co. Clare ; two attempts to carry out the ballot there had been met with opposition by a rabble ; lord Conyngham collected a force ; then the opposition died away and the ballot took place ' without the smallest murmur or opposition '.[20] But the Castlereagh affair occurred not in some out of the way region but almost under the walls of more sophisticated Belfast. In June the *Northern Star* had claimed : ' In this neighbourhood where the measure (i.e. the militia act) is as unpopular as it can be anywhere else, the most profound tranquillity prevails—and why ? because the people are better informed than the southern peasantry and because they understand the difference between liberty and licentiousness '.[21] The *Freeman's Journal*[22] comments on the Castlereagh affair that opposition to the execution of the militia law was only the ostensible cause, ' the intent, purport and object of that law are perfectly understood throughout that extensive and populous county ' and assigns ' detestable party politics ' as the reason. Lord Hillsborough, it appears, was present at the meeting. His conduct is highly applauded : ' he evidently seemed most particularly aimed at repressing the ardour of the military on the instant that ardour became no longer absolutely necessary '.

But this military ardour was not always repressed. In May, 1793 the situation in Ireland was getting out of hand. There was fishing in troubled waters and some bloodshed at the hands of the military undoubtedly occurred. In that month at Lackan and Turrough, co. Roscommon, the soldiers fired on a mob assembled with intent to commit violence on those employed in enrolling for the militia ; seven were killed and sixteen wounded.[23] At Dingle, co. Kerry a mob attempted to enter the town by force to oppose the raising of the militia ; ten country people were left killed.[24] At Erris, co. Mayo, where some 1,000 peasants had assembled, thirty-six country people were killed.[25]

These are all specific statements and entitled to credence. On the other hand it is difficult to attach much weight to such general statements as the following : ' in the counties of Roscommon and Sligo above 10,000 of the common people are destroying the gentlemen's houses *and pulling down churches* ';[26]

or that 'There are few gentlemen here [i.e. in co. Roscommon] who have not been deprived of their firearms and compelled to swear that they would oppose the establishment of the militia'. Still, the Dublin Castle official, Mr. Cooke, writing semi-officially to London on 27 May, does characterize what was happening in Sligo and Roscommon as insurrection.[27]

The available newspaper and magazine evidence—there is little else to go upon—shows the same incidents repeated. It is of course possible that not all the clashes were reported in the public prints; on the other hand such spotlight incidents were already then, as now, welcome fare to the press. A reliable considered contemporary statement on this question would be of great interest, but it would probably have been impossible for it to have been made even by Dublin Castle. The authorities, so far as they were informed, appear to have remained silent. During the period of maximum excitement—from 30 April until the end of May—parliament was not sitting. On its resumption on 28 May several days passed before any notice was taken of the militia disturbances. Under modern parliamentary practice a government statement immediately on the resumption would have been almost inevitable; there were rumours that steps would be taken to abolish the ballot;[28] but the uppermost topic was the depressed state of public credit. A review of the year 1793 even suggested that 'the extensive failure of credit' had heightened the militia trouble.[29] But on 1 June one of the county Sligo members did mention the matter, without, however, making any motion; he spoke of 'ferment in this kingdom' but gave no hint of the extent. On 14 June the lord lieutenant states in his correspondence with Whitehall: 'I do not think we are at all likely to have any serious risings and I am in hopes many militia regiments will do good service very shortly but my opinion is not infallible. It is very different from many here'.[30] This is a little ambiguous, but the meaning is obvious.

On the extent of the 'ferment' the *Northern Star* is not perhaps an unbiassed witness but we may note its statement (issue of 25-29 May): 'It appears that a most extraordinary and determined spirit of opposition to the embodying of the militia prevails throughout the greater part of the counties in the south of Ireland. The counties where the greatest disaffection has been manifested are Roscommon, Leitrim, Sligo, Westmeath, King's and Queen's counties, Louth, Carlow, Wexford and Kerry'. There is now no detailed evidence which supports so sweeping a pronouncement; one other newspaper statement on 1 June refers to 'riot and disturbances particularly in the *northern and western* counties'.[31] Newspapers at that time obviously had not a highly organized news service. On the other hand rumour (i.e. inexact information) travelled fast. At Enniskillen a riot was reported to have taken place at the end of May in which ' some thousands ' assembled to oppose the magistrates of the county in carrying into effect the militia act ; a party of dragoons intervened ; seven rioters were said to have been killed, eleven wounded and a hundred taken. This appears in the *Freeman's Journal*, but in the same paper on 4 June this engagement is denied and it is stated that county Fermanagh is in a state of peace. Again the *Sligo Journal* gave two columns of accounts of anti-militia riots on 28 May but on 4 June the Sligo Association ask people to suspend judgment until a statement has been issued as the disturbances had been exaggerated.

Mullalla's *View of Irish Affairs* (1795) is fairly contemporary. He entirely approved of the militia act but, writing of ' riots and affrays ' which he alleges took place on the 1795 augmentation (see chapter V) and of the ' many of the ignorant and unfortunate populace ' who were then, as he alleges, ' put to death by the military ', states that ' on the first ballot for a militia in this kingdom *similar bloody scenes commenced* '.[32] There seems inadequate warrant for this particular piece of colourful eighteenth century phrasing. That there was playboyism, ferment and unrest, disturbance and violence and even more threat of violence seems established but that in May 1793 there was in Ireland a sort of carnival of bloodshed cannot be substantiated. One proof of this is that, however much some elements were infuriated, either on principle or from sheer ignorance, by the militia measure, and however much their opposition may have been manipulated, there is no evidence that the events of that month left in the popular soul any such bitter memories as remained after other episodes in Irish history. May 1793 is not one of the black months in that story ; it is not the first chapter of 1798.

The riotous assemblies cannot be attributed merely to ignorance and ill-information. Although soldiering was not repugnant to Irishmen of that epoch, undoubtedly there was some unreasoned aversion to military service as such and to what it was thought to involve. But the *Freeman's Journal*[33] will not allow that hostility to the militia project was the cause, certainly not the only cause, of the outrages. ' This ', it says, ' is all a farce—these mobs are heard to cry out liberty and equality ' and Mr Cooke on 6 June[34] notes that in Kerry a mob which broke into violence in Dingle used ' the militia as a pretext but declared also against tithes and taxes '. Analysing the position, in a semi-official letter of 27 May, Mr Cooke says : ' Militia may be the pretext but something deeper is at the bottom '.[35] A recent writer[36] supports this view. Amplifying his analysis, Cooke continued that he had ' real grounds for believing that a scheme for a general insurrection had been planned by the catholic committee.... We now see the relics of that scheme. When the catholics had hopes of gaining their ends without force they did not push insurrection.' A calm followed.

> The catholic committee then came forward with a resolution for parliamentary reform and government began arraying the militia. The catholic committee felt that they were not consulted on this militia and that commands were not given them. They grew jealous and they saw that if it could be well established government might gain great power against their future claims ....They have joined therefore with the United Irishmen to oppose it and have sent their emissaries through the kingdom.... This new insurrection was not in the least expected by the gentlemen concerned in the militia and the opposition was on the first endeavour to obtain a return of names.[37]

It is possible to over-stress the political side of these militia disturbances and to overlook that they were not peculiar to Ireland. It seems truer to say that such outbreaks were, in the eighteenth century, the more or less usual accompaniment of any innovation[38] and certainly of raising militia. In England, when in the autumn of 1757 Pitt's act reorganized the militia and instituted the ballot, there were serious riots in many counties;[38] the Duke of Bedford's house at Woburn had to be guarded by soldiers; at Biggleswade a mob of 1,000 persons demanded the 'tickets on which the men's names were wrote' and 'the petty constables absolutely refused to draw [the lots] as they said if they did they should subject themselves to be knocked on the head on their return to their parishes'[40] Something rather like rebellion followed.[41] There were also serious militia disturbances at Hexham in Northumberland in 1761 (42 killed and 48 wounded; 6,000 to 7,000 rioters);[42] at Boston, Lincolnshire, in November 1796, when the Yeomanry were called out; and at Chirk in Denbighshire, when 300 countrymen armed with clubs and pitchforks assembled and drove away the constables who were about to deliver the lists. Nor, as late as 1797, were the Scotch any less recalcitrant when Scotland's turn to raise a militia came. The lord lieutenant of Lanark refers to the 'violent, riotous and illegal resistance'; the solicitor general was of opinion that the act should be suspended and the lord advocate asked for English cavalry; the general in command also asked for more troops than he had; it was true, he said, that he had 20,000 volunteers but would they, he asked, do their duty well against fathers, brothers and friends?[43] There were very serious disturbances in several counties. At Jedburgh[44] 2,000 young men, each armed with a bludgeon, assembled and decided to oppose being drawn as militiamen. They got possession of the ballot lists and carried them off in triumph. Other meetings of a similar kind took place, and on a bigger scale, in some neighbouring towns. Opposition to militia, even to bloodshed, was not therefore a speciality of the Irish, as Fortescue[45] seems inclined to suggest.

The Irish newspapers contain frequent complaints of the people being left insufficiently informed and make suggestions for remedying this. If the reactions had been foreseen, effort to spread enlightenment would probably have begun earlier. No official step to forestall opposition by informed propaganda was taken before 22 May when the War Office, instructed by the lord lieutenant, issued a notice which recited that 'evil-disposed persons have endeavoured to excite the people to resist the execution of the militia law by false misrepresentation thereof'. It made statements on nine points calculated to be stumbling blocks. The last of these is as follows: 'No religious distinctions are made by the act; the officers and privates may be either roman catholics or protestants; and the free exercise of each religion is allowed'. This notice appeared in the *Hibernian Journal*, the *Northern Star*, the *Freeman's Journal* and probably elsewhere. Private enterprise joined in the effort to bring enlightenment. Grattan's[46] counsel when appealed to from county Wicklow was to promote the embodying and arraying to the utmost. An anonymous writer (possibly an official apologist) who calls himself 'Molyneaux' issued on 8 June[47] *An appeal to the peasantry of Ireland on the subject of a militia* in which he meets various objections one of which is that 'the militia is to continue perpetually embodied in the manner of the army'. He deals with this and then says: 'So much for the falsehood that the militia were to be kept constantly under arms'. He was no doubt writing in good faith and in accordance with government expectations at the time but in fact none of the units of the Irish militia were ever otherwise, from their first arraying down to 1816 (with two brief intermissions), than 'perpetually embodied'.

Another effort to counteract misrepresentations was 'a single sheet for the purpose of posting up',[48] as it was explained: these cost 11/4 a hundred; were called *Remarks on the militia act* and were on offer as early as 21 May. This and similar efforts no doubt had some effect, if they reached the right people, but more was probably attained by the explanations of the colonels especially when they already stood in some personal relation to those addressed. Anyhow, the fever quickly abated and its permanent effects and importance are insignificant.

Though there are alleged to have been 'resignations on account of the disorders, by gentlemen who had been appointed to command'[49] Dublin Castle seems to have remained unperturbed. By 11 June, Hobart writes: 'If the militia should turn out better than at first it seemed likely to do and which is by no means improbable ....'. On 14 June, as we have seen, the lord lieutenant was 'in hopes many militia regiments will do good service very shortly'. On 5 July, Mr Cooke writes semi-officially to London: 'We are going strong in numbers and we hope soon to have an additional force of militia. About 3,000 are called out but they are totally undisciplined at present and unprovided for duty. In a month we shall hope to get some battalions in forwardness'. Then on 25 July, Hobart says: 'Some of our militia regiments are already in great forwardness', and on 12 August, Mr Cooke: 'militia are coming forwards' and on 26 September: 'all quiet here and in a month or two I hope to send you good accounts of the militia'. By 14 November, Hobart was able to write to London: 'Everything is perfectly quiet. The militia as far advanced in discipline as could be expected for the time and likely to make very fine troops'[50]

The early part of the initial militia recruiting period is that which precedes the enactment of the modifying clause 13 of 33 Geo. iii. chap. 33 (see note at end of chapter and chapter II, p. 19). This bill only received the royal assent on 16 August, but it was in committee in the commons in June and through the lords in July and was probably at once brought into force. But in the period before and the period after, approved 'voluntary offering' differs only in that parliament had taken cognizance of what had already been going on. The Sligo member, Mr O'Hara, had put it (1 June) in this way:—

'In the counties where the militia had succeeded best a sufficient number of persons had voluntarily offered their service first and the ballot proceeded afterwards merely in conformity to the act, no man being afraid of the ballot when he knew there were substitutes sufficient. The experiment pointed out the relief the house ought to give. Let a short act be passed providing that where a sufficient number of persons offer their service voluntarily those volunteers should be embodied and that in such county there should be no lists made of the inhabitants and no ballot. Though this would not be a militia it would be easier to the county'.[51]

Under the letter of the law substitutes had always been allowed, without any limit; and anyone who offered himself as a substitute in effect 'voluntarily offered' himself. No record remains of the discussions on the new clause and it is not now obvious why legislation should have been necessary, but, as Mr. O'Hara's speech shows, the militia idea and theory were regarded as something specific; i.e. a 'militiaman' properly so called was a man who had been raised by ballot.

The advertisements in the newspapers of 1793, as well as the news columns, establish that the prescribed general and sub-division meetings must have been held, with possible exceptions, in all the counties which got their militias going early; there is some reason for thinking that the few which hung back a little (e.g. Armagh) did so in order to get the required men by voluntary means and so leave no balance to be made up by the ballot. At the fourth subdivision meeting all would go well if there was a plentiful supply of substitutes, whether normally or not normally procured, and if those summoned to attend at that meeting knew that this would be so.

The fruits of the going slow just mentioned are typified in the case of the militia of Limerick city, of which Major Ross-Lewin[52] (who began his military career in that unit) says: 'The Irish are a people naturally fond of the careless, chequered, errant life of a soldier; and, as one proof of it, my corps was *raised voluntarily in a single day*'. It seems likely that in this case there were no ballot proceedings even of a formal kind; the embodiment of this militia was ordered on 8 May and it was actually embodied on 8 June. The Queen's county militia, we are told (in 1793), were completed in ten days after the order for embodying;[53] a later account (October 1796) says 'in the short space of three weeks'. But, whether ten days or three weeks is correct, it seems improbable that there were any formal ballot proceedings. Both accounts agree that no bounty or 'advantage' was given to any man. Yet a third account says that the men were 'all volunteers' and that none were balloted for,[54] though this does not necessarily exclude the holding of the prescribed meetings, etc. It is also stated that at the embodiment parade thirty men appeared above the required number. If it were not for the three explicit statements quoted it might be thought that the men had accumulated slowly, because, though the embodiment order is dated 25 April, actual embodiment did not take place until September. The case of the South Mayo was probably somewhat similar. Lord Sligo, writing in 1803 about the second embodiment of this unit in that year, says: 'This is the third (*sic*) time this regiment has been completed from my estates and those of my nearest connections'. He also says in another letter of 1803: 'there can be no ballot attempted in these parts. It would produce a rebellion instantly'.[55] This regiment was raised on feudal lines.

The Carlow militia was one of those first ordered to be embodied (20 April). After some initial trouble the ballot proceeded harmoniously enough. There were some riots in mid-May in which colliery and quarry workers appear to have been concerned. 'Fathers to be taken from their families', was the outcry; why not try to get volunteers and do without balloting? A week later the 'designs of malcontents had been defeated by the publication of abstracts' (of the Act presumably) and recruits were offering themselves to the colonel in such numbers that he could raise the unit *without balloting*.[56] Nevertheless the prescribed procedure was followed and we have this account of what took place : 'On Saturday last [the date is 8 June] the ballot for the militia commenced here, when instead of any kind of opposition being given or the least appearance of discontent, the different parishes then appointed to be drawn came forward, cheerfully submitting to their lot ; one parish in particular, Myshall, whose quota amounted to no more than thirteen men assembled to the number of 200 and . . . .entered the courthouse when, after supplying the number allotted, [they] to a man voluntarily offered their services as substitutes in case any other part of the county should seem desirous of being excused '.[57]

In the case of Carlow there is no mention of bounties but where things went well there was often some lubrication. Of lord Doneraile, colonel of the South Cork, it is recorded :[58] 'he gives very liberal assistance to recruits '. From Roscrea (Tipperary) a report of 11 June says : 'The militia regulation goes on very agreeably here. This town, or rather this parish, has seventeen charged on it and the inhabitants have entered into subscriptions to raise them by bounty and send them in a body to headquarters ......recruits are to be had in abundance '.[59] This does not mean that balloting did not take place ; there are reports, both in June and in July, that the balloting was 'proceeding without incident '. This is the county where at the beginning lord Thurles had been subjected to threats. In county Waterford also things went well ; early in June there is a report from Carrick, half of which is in that county (see page 177 for a later ballot incident) : 'deputy governors balloted for militia ; no trouble and some volunteers '[60] But apparently this militia did not fill up adequately and the purse of lord Waterford who was the colonel came, under limitations, to the rescue : he 'by well-timed interference caused numbers to volunteer to fill the militia ranks '.[61] There had been a ballot in the city of Waterford on 16 August ; the report states that it was 'concluded by 6 p.m. ;" presumably it went well. The act authorized a separate city militia to be raised for Waterford, as it did for Dublin, Cork and Limerick ; though advantage was not taken of this provision the militia affairs of city and county seem to have been kept to some extent separate.[62]

Donegal is a county of scattered parishes. On the augmentation in 1795 (see chapter V) the aggregate quota was 185 ; this was furnished in money which was divided between thirty-four places. No wonder, therefore, that in 1793 getting the contingent was laborious. There is adequate information about the raising of this militia. The order for embodiment is dated 29 April but it was not actually embodied until 14 August ; the list of officers was approved on 13 July ; the list of deputy governors had been approved on 14 April and as early as 11 April the lieutenant colonel designate had been informed of his prospective appointment and told his commission would issue on proof that he had delivered his certificate of qualification. There must have been some delay over the preliminaries. On 2 September we learn that 'the greater part of the officers of the regiment are actually employed in a progress through a very extensive country to attend the ballot' and also that the colonel had been on a progress through a remote part of the county for the same purpose. The act provides that the lieutenant colonel shall be informed of the date of subdivision meetings but his attendance and still less that of the other officers is not obligatory.[63]

There are also two other first-hand, though not contemporary, accounts of the formation of the Donegal militia which are worth recording. One of the deputy governors says (1809):

> 'It was a matter very disagreeable to the people and met opposition in several places owing to the terror of balloting. My friend....joined me in opening a policy of insurance for five shillings for such as might be drawn by balloting. Several gentlemen soon after joined....in consequence subscriptions to a very large amount were received and handed over to the regimental purse out of which the regiment was chiefly completed and every individual placed, substitutes being found for every person as we engaged'.

The other writer, another Donegal gentleman, says (1807):

> 'When the militia was first embodied, heartily interested in the prosperity of the regiment, I formed a little society who insured against persons being drawn, for a small premium, by which we raised a sum that nearly recruited the regiment, which we gave for that purpose'.[64]

Insurance played a considerable part in the raising of the Irish militia. Fortescue[65] has written about this practice in relation to the British militia in the period after 1803, but does not mention that it was in use before that date. Yet Ireland in 1793 must have adopted the idea from English practice; one of the insurers states that his office (a general lottery office) is 'founded on similar principles with those in different parts of Great Britain'.[66] Adequate information exists about the raising of the Clare militia.[67] All the procedure of general and subdivision meetings was duly gone through. The first general meeting was held on 23 May (order for embodiment 13 May); at this meeting eight subdivisions were settled and the dates for the subdivisional meetings. The deputy governors at the same meeting unanimously approved of the idea of men being insured against being drawn to serve. The commanding officer, lord Conyngham, 'recommended that the premium be reduced so low as five British shillings saying he would make good any loss sustained thereby; in consequence of which books are opened at ....where any person paying 5/5 will be insured provided it is done before the day of drawing in the subdivision to which they belong '. Later, on 13 June, we are told that ' the embodying of the militia in this county proceeds in a manner which at once proves the civilization and good sense of the people ' and that ' volunteers continue to enter in such numbers and with such eagerness as to justify us in saying that balloting need only be resorted to for the purpose of fulfilling the requisites of the act '. When there was difficulty in one barony, Tulla, lord Conyngham, issued a statement that ' early in the business [he] declared his firm intention not to force any balloted man to serve in the militia against his inclination. His lordship was and is ready to provide substitutes for those who are amenable to the laws and who are not most fully able to provide them '. The ranks of the Clare militia thus seem to have been filled, (*a*) by men who accepted the luck of the ballot (which was duly held in all the eight subdivisions) ; (*b*) by volunteers, i.e. men who came forward without receiving bounty ; (*c*) by substitutes provided by lord Conyngham entirely at his own expense ; and (*d*) by substitutes provided through insurance.

In Donegal certainly, and in Clare probably, the insuring was a non-commercial enterprise.[68] But at Clonmel a company was formed ' to ensure people from militia service by providing substitutes in their room '. The rates were :—labourers 2/8½d ; working tradesmen and cottagers 5/5d ; and others 11/4½d. It is also stated that gentlemen and others gave their names to the public as security for the fairness of the scheme.[69] This seems to have been commercial : the promoters took the risks—and the profits. Clearly this was the case in Down from which we hear (in 1795) that ' the insurers have made a great deal of money and can afford to get good men '. In effect the insurers were recruiting agents : the phrase ' a man enlisted at Hillsborough by some of the insurers ' occurs in the Downshire papers ; this was as late as June 1798.[70]

Obviously the business was open to abuse. The three Cork units were not available for service until the middle of October 1793 and Richard Longford the commandant of the city militia writes (Nov. 1794) as follows about the insurers : ' I cannot omit the greatest nuisance I ever met with in my exertions to complete the regiment—I mean the lottery offices of Mr Harley and others at Cork. Unless the new act [i.e. the bill of 1795, see chap. V.] ' annihilates these seminaries for opposition and sedition we shall never carry on the business completely. They represented the measure as a delusive one to entrap the people and made it as black as possible on the part of government and the lieutenant colonels commandants, in order to induce everyone to ensure at their offices '.[71]

The business was most highly organized at Dublin. There however, though definitely a commercial undertaking, it does not seem to have been in bad repute and the numerous advertisements all mention the approval of the governors. There is no reason for thinking that the county, as distinguished from the city, had any great difficulty, though the earlier advertisements of the ‘ Original Militia Exemption Offices ’, as the concern was called, appeal equally to those who are or may be enrolled for one or the other.[72] Lord Mountjoy (who commanded the Dublin county militia) had started an exemption fund of his own before the subdivision ballot meetings began. ‘ The circumstances ’, it is stated, ‘ of every man from gentleman to labourer, were accommodated by the rates of subscription ; from those who could afford it half a guinea was required ; from those who could not afford more, 2/- was accepted ’.[73] The ballots were duly carried out, beginning at Swords on 2 July. The governors and deputy governors met at Bishop’s Tavern, Blackrock, to enrol balloted men on 27 July and by 22 August it was already said to be one of the finest corps in the kingdom. Its statutory complement (1793 act) was only 280 men.

The complement of Dublin city which had presumably opted for separation was 420 men. By 16 May the names had been posted on the church doors. Balloting for the various parishes took place on dates in the middle of June and in some cases were held in the parish churches : ‘ So great was the concourse, [at the church of St Mary] of auditors, that the governors deemed it prudent to give them the benefit of open air in the churchyard during the ceremony while they proclaimed the balloted names from a window on the south side ’. Another ballot, for the parishes of St Audoen, St Patrick, St Nicholas within and St John took place in St John’s church. The newspapers are facetious at the expense of the pawnbrokers ; the ballot for St Michan’s and St Paul’s is said to have been ‘ complimentary to their martial spirit ’ and in another account, to ‘ the bastard children of Israel, ycleped pawnbrokers ’. In St Peter’s parish it is said to have fallen ‘ heavy upon the sons of Galen. No less than eleven of these pharmacopolists were allotted ’ on one occasion. Again it is stated that in the ballot for the parishes of St Andrew, St Anne and St Mark (which took place in St Andrew’s church) the lot ‘ fell entirely upon respectable people ’, i.e. upon people of substance. There is mention of the lot having fallen in the parish of St Peter upon one judge, three barristers and nine attorneys and ‘ in the list were also two M.P.’s, several private gentlemen, one surgeon, two apothecaries, and, though last, not least in favour, two pawnbrokers ’.[74]

Most, if not all, of these would have been people who could afford a substitute and would have had no need to resort to the

'Original Militia Exemption Offices' which were run by Vincent Dowling and Co. But clearly many did resort there. This is what these insurers then offered to their clients :

> All persons whose names are or may be enrolled in the several parishes and districts....as liable to serve in the capacity of militia private soldiers for four years and who wish to avoid the risque of being allotted to such service in the event of a ballot or choice by lot are hereby informed that authentic policies are opened at the above officer for the purpose of securing to all persons who desire it exemption from the militia service by providing eligible substitutes in their room should they be chosen or paying their fine of £10 [i.e. the fine under clause 27 of the 1793 act] and preventing to them further trouble.

The premium for this was 'only three half-crowns, to be paid before the commencement of drawing in each parish or district'. They also offered 'as a further inducement to public preference ....a prize of twenty guineas to each of the persons last drawn in each division of county or city if enrolled in their books'. Possibly this indicates that other groups were engaged in this insurance business.[75]

Although in other counties volunteering was by then going on freely and had eased tension (on this see below p. 48) there is no mention of volunteers being received by the city though, as has been shewn, the county was taking them. No reason for this is stated but the idea possibly was—what we have noticed before—that of adhering to the pure militia idea. There were no disturbances in Dublin though balloting there was more extensive than elsewhere; its prolongation may have been as much responsible as anything for the bad name the ballot got. On the other hand, the attitude to it seems to have been one of curiosity regarding a new event in the city's social life. The meetings for enrolment (i.e. the fourth subdivision meetings) took place early in July. By 11 July it is stated that the city militia was completely embodied and in training.

If the Dublin city militia was indeed 'completely embodied', this could only mean that it had its full complement of 420 men. But in August ballots are again going on and it is stated that during these nearly one third of the 420 were balloted for. In the parish of St Andrew it was the sixth ballot held. On 3 September Dowling issues a notice warning the public that the 'ballot is not yet filled', and on 20 September there is a comment[76] as to the inconvenience caused to middle-class citizens, who, from not being apprized of the proceedings, are precluded from providing substitutes by insurance. But these August ballots apparently failed; on 28 October 'new returns are to be made forthwith of the inhabitants of the several parishes of Dublin to the governors in order to enable them to complete their ballots (for the quota), which, strange to tell, are not yet made up though above twelve successive ballots have taken place and more than two thousand men have been drawn '[77] The regiment was at Athlone and was reported on 5 November not to amount to 250 men, notwithstanding 2,000 had been drawn. At the end of the month the deficiency is somewhat lower, but preparations for a new 'general ballot' are said to be going on rapidly. By 31 December a new general ballot to provide 170 men to complete the regiment has begun; preparatory to this, fresh general returns of all persons resident in Dublin had been made out by order of the governors; to get the 170 men it was estimated that it would probably be necessary to ballot 5-600 names.[78]

Why had the original ballots been so unproductive? Apparently this falling away of the strength was not due entirely to 'inevitable causes', as a Dowling advertisement suggests. It seems probable that at the enrolment meetings, a very large number of exemptions were belatedly claimed and that substitutes, or at all events satisfactory substitutes, were not produced by many who otherwise had no plausible way of escaping service. The best general statement of what had taken place is contained in the *Hibernian Journal* (28 October):

> The frivolity of the various exemptions by persons in opulence to evade the expense of finding substitutes has rendered the operation of the act expremely oppressive on the working orders of society. Men of a thousand a year and from one thousand to ten thousand pounds property, when accidentally balloted to serve, have not blushed to plead exemption by being half an inch under size or a few days over age, a little weakness of sight or an annual rheumatic pain, when the lot of service or substitute has been transferred to a poor fellow with half a dozen children whose health and robust size has left him no other alternative but either depriving him totally of his protection and earnings or the means of bringing them food, in order to find a substitute.

There was talk of an amendment of the act in the next session, to render its operation more equal, but this did not happen. It was urged that 'age, infirmity or professional avocation' should not excuse 'men from finding substitutes who can afford the expense infinitely better than poor tradesmen on some hundreds of whom it has fallen'.[79] Though all this illustrates the hardships arising, it does not entirely explain how the reputed strength of 420 men in July had fallen away by 170 men in a few months.

The act of 1795 (35 Geo. iii. c.8—chapter 5) is an indication (clause 31) that many persons in various counties who had undertaken to insure individuals against serving in the militia by engaging to find substitutes for them or to pay the fine of £10 leviable by law, had failed to make good the said insurances; and a penalty was provided. But in 1793 no such complaint appears against Dowling ; and when the new ballots were coming on in December he comes forward with a new offer. First of all, he gives notice that ‘ his outstanding policies are now fully cancelled ’; he has ‘ abided the risk not only of the 450 names drawn on the first general ballot (i.e. that of mid-June) to which only he was pledged, but of above 2,000 names drawn in all ’. He intimates that ‘ he is now issuing policies at half a guinea each which secure complete exemption from the militia for four years ’. Under clause 25 of the act a balloted person for whom a substitute has been ‘ produced, approved, inrolled and sworn ’ is exempted from service as if he had served as a balloted man, which would have been for four years. He offered ‘ other policies at four British shillings which secures exemption only until the regiment is first completed ’. To holders of his ‘ former engagements a very considerable abatement will be made on the half guinea policies ’. At the beginning of January 1794 Dowling reinforces his appeal to the public by stating that seven hundred names may be drawn on the new ballot in order to get the 170 required and that ‘ ballots will also be necessary to fill up occasional deficiencies in the regiment arising by deaths, desertions and other causes ’. He urges that ‘ the risque is now much greater than it was apprehended even in the very first instance and that the difficulty of obtaining proper substitutes as well as the bounty to them have been enhanced fourfold ’. He also makes a special offer in regard to servants. ‘ Ladies and gentlemen may have the successive servants of their households (changing ever so often) perpetually exempted from the militia law, on paying the first premium only for the number first entered . . . . the policies issued in the names of the servants discharged will be transferred gratis to their successors if neither be previously drawn ’.[80] No account of the January ballots is available. We can only assume that the Dublin (city) militia at length obtained its complement in full or to a near figure. There is no more mention of Dowling. When parliament was opened, there were no debates in either of the houses about the Dublin or about any other difficulties, though, on 24 February in the house of lords, the lord chancellor seems to have refused to disclose the number of men embodied on the ground that it was not obligatory on the lord lieutenant to give this information.

Further efforts are to be noted in connection with the raising of the force. Some of these were expedients special to particular units. The Armagh regiment, which, though its embodiment was ordered on 3 May, was not actually embodied until 16 September, issued, on 5 January 1794, a reply to an anonymous paragraph, stating that it was complete to the present establishment ordered by government. On 10 December it had resorted to advertisement : they asked for about thirty stout young men, ' lads of character and height ', to complete the regiment. These would presumably come in as ' volunteers '; there is no reference to a bounty but it is stated that they would ' find it to their interest '.[81]

The three Cork units were, as stated, slow in coming into existence : the embodiment order in all three cases was not issued until 30 September and the date of actual embodiment was 15 October. The insurers were making offers early in May, with a qualification ' should the militia not be embodied '. The inadvisability of giving arms to people who were showing hostility was being urged. The county of Cork anyhow ' supported a large police establishment ' who were ' adequate with the aid of good citizens and the magistracy to preserve the peace thereof '.[82] The city was ' well supplied with constables and peace officers besides a strong garrison '. It would be better to appoint drill sergeants in every parish and give a premium to every person capable of bearing arms. There is report of a patriotically couched address[83] coming from high authority to some country gentlemen in the county regarding the necessity for a militia. The next thing occurring was the proclamation. Lord Kingsborough who was the commandant designate of the North Cork resorted to an original expedient ; he published a notice widely, not only in the Cork papers, offering the first 244 men coming forward for his militia a small farm in Munster at a reasonable rent during life on condition of residing there after the militia service was past ; candidates were to be protestants. We hear too of lord Bandon, on the day of balloting, in December, ' when anxiety was painted on each countenance '[84] having paid for twenty substitutes ; at the same time he also started a coalyard as an inducement and to help the poor. So diverse in all times are recruiting expedients.

Although, as stated above, the effect of clause 13 of 33 Geo. iii, chapter 33 was only to sanction what had been going on before, there is nevertheless evidence that the change then formally approved did in certain parts ease some of the tension. It is reported from Waterford (19 June) that a party beat up four men for the militia on that day ; ' this mode of procuring men seems to have entirely changed the terrific form of the militia act ; for notwithstanding that no bounty was offered twenty-five fine young fellows entered in the course of a few hours '.[85] But the volunteering amendment (clause 13) was not the only action taken by the government ' for the more speedy and effectual array of the militia '. Early in June there is reference to a bill ' which Mr Foster brought in under the idea of making the militia more palatable to the people at large '.[86] The house had resumed on 28 May, and leave had been given to bring in a bill 'to provide for the families of persons chosen by lot to serve in the militia'. (This became 33 Geo. iii. Chap. 28). Mr Foster, Mr Clements and lord Hillsborough were charged with the preparation of it. It did not pass without discussion and some amendment. Hobart, on the third reading,[87] defended it as 'a copy of the English act'; the 'parish applotments' he defended as 'not imperative' but as leaving 'the parishes at liberty to adopt them or not'. The 'cess or parish rate' was finally incident upon the parishes. The financial effect of subsequent legislation on this matter can be traced but there is reason for thinking that the *parishes* did not do much, in spite of the assurances of a member in the debate that "whatever applotments might be made for the purposes of the bill would be paid with cheerfulness'. Evidence of inaction of the parishes is that there are records[88] of large gifts of money by individuals for relieving the wives and families and also invitations (as late as September 1794) to gentlemen of property to make benefactions. The necessity for some organized action could not be disputed. At a later date the Irish militiaman was usually married; it was probably much the same in the earliest days; there is some but not much evidence of a policy of 'unmarried men preferred'. The social disruption caused in Ireland by the formation of the militia was considerable even though 16,000 men was a small proportion of the total population. Bray, for example, was crowded in September 1793 with the wives and children of Westmeath militiamen'. 'What a picture', is the newspaper comment, 'of distress of war in disturbing from their humble homes so many helpless husbands!'

A cause of hardship was that 'no aid from legal provision' was available for the families of substitutes. This point is stressed. 'The militia of Dublin in particular is almost completely filled by substitutes the greater part of whom are manufacturers and heads of little families who must necessarily be embarrassed by their absence'.[90] The Families act of 1793 did not in fact help very much to make militia service more palatable; it was repealed in 1795 when new provisions were enacted (35 Geo. iii. Chap. 2).* The whole subject of the wives and families of the Irish militiamen is treated consecutively in chapter XVII.

The main act (clause 102) provides that in cases where a county fails to raise the number appointed by the act, there was to be a fine of 'the yearly sum of five pounds for and in lieu of every private militiaman....directed to be raised' within the county and 'upon proof on oath being laid by any one or more governor or deputy-governor of such deficiency' a judge of assize could fine the county after the rate of five pounds and repeat the fine

*The 1795 act was 'for the more effectual support of the *families of militiamen*'.

annually so long as the deficiency continued. Resort to the provisions of this clause was ineffectual and rare. A case is recorded[91] where the county at fault was Wicklow. The official notice recites that several parishes or districts had 'declined or neglected to raise the number of men allotted for them' and records a resolution of the governors and deputy-governors that 'application be made to the court of King's Bench in the next Michaelmas term to have such parishes respectively fined the annual sum of £5 in lieu of each man deficient'.

Though for later balloting periods (1803; 1807-8; and 1809-10), there are some official statistics of the number raised and entered in the regimental records as 'balloted men' (principals or substitutes distinguished), there is no similar information as regards 1793 nor 1795 (augmentation). It is only possible to estimate roughly the extent of actual balloting. Later a practice either of balloting or of not balloting became established in different counties; some adhered to it even when they were left at liberty, and indeed were expected, to proceed otherwise. For 1793 the newspapers show that, in many counties, there was balloting though it was often piece-meal rather than systematic, e.g. in Kerry, where 'some parishes require no balloting'; and in Tyrone where 450 men were raised by the officers; 'remainder will be balloted men'. 'Balloting without incident' is reported from some counties. The reactions in Kerry have been referred to, but by 20 June the obsession against the militia was dying; by 9 July the colonel had certified his numbers as complete to the clerk of the peace; the privates, it is stated, were anxious to be employed immediately;[92] and later in the year the lord lieutenant was informed that the regiment had been filled 'with ardour and unanimity'. This is possibly a typical case.

In these ways, through these expedients and out of these birth throes, did the Irish militia come into being. On 21 January 1794 the lord lieutenant, in opening parliament, claimed that 'the law for rendering a militia in this kingdom effectual has been carried successfully into execution' and expressed his satisfaction to find that 'the people are at length fully reconciled to this institution which has already been attended by the most beneficial consequences in producing internal tranquillity and contributing to the general strength and force of the empire'. This is of course the official view and from its optimism some discount may legitimately be made. Plowden speaks of the 'great difficulties' which 'at first prevailed in raising the different regiments of militia'. It is as well to avoid exaggeration either way. Since then there have been many important social changes introduced by legislation in Ireland, as elsewhere. The common experience is that everywhere such transitions are attended by 'doubt, hesitation and pain '. Certainly the Irish social structure in 1793 exhibited the tautness and sense of complaint shewn by a rope when it first takes strain. But the introduction of the militia in Ireland in that year does not appear to have caused emotional disturbances to a more than normal degree. The absence of any marked parliamentary action points to the same conclusion, which is confirmed positively and negatively by newspaper recordings and by the general nature of official pronouncements. The general public came to have a good opinion of the militia and in fact became rather proud[93] of it. The view of Hobart on 14 November as stated to London has already been recorded. Anyhow, the militia was now in being.

33 *Geo. iii. Chap.* 33, *Clause* 13.

And for the more speedy and effectual array of the militia within this kingdom be it enacted ; that all persons who have heretofore voluntarily offered or shall hereafter voluntarily offer to serve in the same, and who have taken the oath appointed by law to be taken by persons ballotted to serve in the militia, or approved of to serve as substitutes, shall be deemed and taken to be militiamen, as fully and effectually to all intents and purposes whatsoever, as if they had been chosen by ballot, or receives as substitutes to serve in such militia, pursuant to the provisions of an act passed in this session of parliament, entitled (33 Geo. iii, Chap. 22) ; and all such persons shall be set down to the account of such parish as they shall respectively declare their intention or desire to serve for, and the deputy governors shall cause only such number of persons to be chosen by ballot out of the lists returned for such parish as shall be wanted at the time to make up the whole number appointed to serve for the same.

IV

The Militia in Being

The act of 1793 envisaged a normal annual training period of twenty-eight days and calling out for actual service of undetermined duration. It is of some importance to realize how quickly for the individual Irish militiaman the picture changed and that in the early summer of 1793 permanent embodiment for actual service tended to become the only prospect.

Already in early March a member[1] was saying in the house of commons that in England there were not many shades of difference between a standing army and the militia. The event was to prove that he was not very far wrong. The king had called out the whole of the English militia for actual service in December 1792; or, as another member put it, he had 'arrayed her militia to suppress the factious and levelling spirit that then prevailed'. The probability obviously was that Ireland here also would soon be 'keeping step'. On 19 March, the last day the bill was in the commons, a member pressed to be informed whether it was the intention of the administration 'to call out the whole or a part of the militia'.[2] This enquiry was not directly answered by the chancellor of the exchequer but he indicated that expenditure involved in a year's embodiment was not then contemplated.

After the adjournment, on 3 June, the chancellor announced 'the expense of arraying, added to a month's pay' but added 'it might possibly be thought necessary to have them in service for a longer period than a month'. The official notice (p. 38), by referring pointedly to the limitation of service to twenty-eight days in time of peace, went to remove any impression of impending continuous service; and the apologist 'Molyneaux' scouted the idea that 'the militia is to continue perpetually embodied in the manner of the army'. he called it 'fabrication of the basest falsehoods'. Nevertheless the chancellor, on 20 June, obtained assent to a resolution granting funds for the pay and maintenance of the force for one year. Either the general situation deteriorated fast during the month of June or the government decided to be on the safe side in the provision made; up to the 20th ten units had been actually embodied as distinct from being placed under orders for embodiment. Anyhow the house surrendered its financial control over the duration of service when it accepted the chancellor's resolution. The lord lieutenant, in proroguing parliament on 16 August, did not go beyond saying that he had 'thought it proper to call forth a very considerable portion of the militia'. By then some twenty-six units had been 'called forth'. The lord lieutenant did not say so but in fact all prospects of an engagement importing for the individual merely a twenty-eight days annual outing were gone. Upon the largely peacetime militia framework, which the 1793 act presented, gradually became superinduced an altered framework. Castlereagh's remarks on this point are quoted in Chapter XV. The Army Medical Board of Ireland (to whom are due many useful general comments on the Irish militia) in 1800 referred to 'the peculiar frame of our militia which from being originally organized for a local purpose (which was also non-continuing) are now wanted for general service'[3]

What aspect, then, after its formation did the militia present? What was its religious composition? From what classes were the men drawn? What social changes did permanent embodiment involve? How was the militia distributed over Ireland and on what principles was this settled? These are some of the questions which this chapter seeks to answer.

The only parliamentary debate of importance on the militia during 1794 took place in the house of lords on 1 March. A return of strength had been asked for and granted and the debate was a request to the lord lieutenant 'to order the counties not as yet embodied forthwith to raise their complement of militia and that the defective regiments do complete their number with all convenient speed'. The reference was to Cavan and Kildare. Cavan had had the order to embody on 25 April 1793 and earl Bellamont had been designated colonel in the original list; it is not clear why no action had been taken unless it was that disturbance in the county made this impracticable. A newspaper report of 20 June says that the governors met to arrange the ballot; the meeting was surrounded by 900 armed persons; the names for ballot were partially taken down; the list was then demanded on the threat that, if refused, the house would be burned and those in it destroyed; the list was given up and the crowd, after looking at it, dispersed. The Cavan militia was embodied in March 1794, i.e. shortly after the house of lords debate. It had not originally been competent to the lord lieutenant to defer the raising or embodiment of the militia in any county but this power was conferred on him by the Pay and Clothing act of 1793*. Colonel Keating was originally designated to command the Kildare militia but he did not take up the post. Then, as the duke of

*33 Geo. iii. chap. 33, clause 15.

Leinster complains,[4] it was ' hawked about ' without being offered to him'. Finally, shortly after June 1797, the battalion was embodied, with the duke of Leinster at its head, without any difficulty. When the militia bill was in the house of lords he had, as stated in Chapter II, raised a technical point; he appears to have been in substantial and not merely polemical opposition to the government, and this, coupled with the fact that Kildare was a rather unruly county, probably accounts for the delay in getting the Kildare militia out. Thus in March 1794, eleven months after the passing of the act, there were these two county units still unembodied.

In a despatch[5] to London of 14 January the lord lieutenant reported that ' the militia are about 10,000 strong and are becoming fit for garrison duty and purposes of police but could not well be relied on against a disciplined enemy without the intermixture and aid of a body of regulars ' and on 1 March Mr Cooke wrote that ' if the country were true the militia alone [i.e. unaided] could protect but alas there is not a county where internal force is not necessary to preserve the peace '. When an address intended to stimulate the lord lieutenant was not agreed to lord Aldborough registered a formal dissent[6] in which he quoted the ' last returns ' as being 9,949 effective men which is practically the lord lieutenant's figure of about six weeks earlier. Mr Cooke, in the letter quoted, also said that ' the militia is ordered to be completed '. A return[7] for 24 March gives the effectives (without the Cavan and Kildare units) as being 10,342 rank and file and the number wanting as 3,606. By the end of June Cooke reports[8] ' about 12,000 rank and file effective and well armed and about 10,000 well disciplined ' and he adds that they behave well. In the March return only the Leitrim, Longford and Carlow are shown as having no men wanting; Limerick city, Drogheda, King's county and Queen's county have only insignificant deficiencies; while Wexford, Galway, Cork city and Cork north have an everage deficiency of 300; on the other hand Cork south, and at least a dozen others, show a deficiency in the region of 100. The duke of Abercorn refers[9] (23 April) to ' the infant establishment and system of an Irish militia '. The force was indeed young but it went on growing. Next year (Feb. 1795) Fitzwilliam[10] gave an effective strength of 13,366.

There seems to have been difficulty in arming the force. On 19 October 1793, the Ordnance office in Dublin stated that:

> Such has been and are still the demand [i.e. for arms] for the regiments for service abroad that the Board cannot venture to say when it will be possible to supply the militia regiments in the north....So soon as the Board can send a proportion of arms to each regiment they will do it without waiting for such a number as will complete their establishments.[11]

Lord Downshire would most probably have had arms for his regiment as early as anyone if they were to be had ; but even he was compelled in December 1793 to obtain authority to buy up arms ' from the owners in the province of Ulster '; presumably volunteer firelocks still in the hands of old volunteers. This was humiliating, and the result must have been motley, if he succeeded in getting arms from this source—about which there is no record. When the Antrim passed through Belfast on 7 August en route to their temporary headquarters at Carrickfergus they all had uniform but only 50 had arms[12], and the Kerry on parade at Killarney on 20 August had no arms[13]. When arms became available special escorts were necessary to get them safely to their destination.

The clothing, which had to be provided by the colonels, caused less difficulty and the progress of the force was not retarded by deficiency ; this was made in Ireland even if the arms were not. We hear that ' the manufacture of 16,000 sets of cloaths has wrought a very happy change in the woollen branch in the Liberty '[14] (Dublin) and at the end of May the woollen manufacturers were said to be fully occupied for some time to come. The wool fairs at Mullingar and Ballinasloe were also expected to benefit. This was one of the first economic results of the institution of the militia. Somewhat later the Army Medical Board reported that the militia was ' well clothed '. As regards accoutrements, on 19 April the Board of Ordnance invited supply of 16,000 sets of cartouch boxes and belts, 1600 slings for musquets and slings for bayonets, as well as 1600 swords for sergeants and drummers and 640 drums, carriages and cases.[15]

After the provision of the officers (the commissions of most of whom are dated in April or May) the important matter was to get together the adjutant, the noncommissioned officers, the corporals and the drummers ; these had to be obtained before any assembly was allowed, or possible. Incidentally, the n.c.o.'s and the drummers formed part of the number to be balloted for. In some instances at least the adjutants seem to have been formerly warrant officers. Possibly one of the most successful of these was Captain Kay of the Armagh. He had been sergeant major in the 23rd Fusiliers, which regiment happened to be quartered in Armagh at the time the militia was being raised. ' His character and appearance led to his being appointed adjutant to the young regiment and, being in fact the only drilled soldier in it from the colonel down, he soon had the management of literally everything and may be said to have been colonel, paymaster, quartermaster and adjutant all in one '.[16] He was a Lancashire man. There is a letter[17] in which the colonel of the Donegals is thanked by a regular officer ' for appointing our sergeant-major as your adjutant'. In the early days of the Irish militia there are not infrequent offers of adjutancies of militia for sale as well as inquiries from would-be purchasers, and no doubt sales often took place. The practice does not seem to have been officially stopped until 1804. (see Chapter XII).[18]

It is probable also that a certain number of the sergeants, corporals and drummers were obtained from line regiments and that some of these too were non-native. Each unit seems to have been required to send in to the adjutant general a return of the sergeants, corporals and drummers then in the regiment who had served in the Army. Many units had none. To meet this difficulty the line regiments in Ireland were instructed to lend n.c.o.'s etc. to assist in drills or to receive men for instruction.

Nevertheless the force was almost entirely Irish in composition even if some of the n.c.o.'s were English. Trade in England was not good at the time the Irish militia was starting, and at the end of May, 1793, there is a report of young men from Cheshire, Lancashire and North Wales arriving daily in Ireland for the purpose of enrolling in the militia owing to lack of employment in the weaving, dyeing and hardware trades.[19] But there is nothing to show that they were taken or that the inflow continued; probably it was discouraged on both sides of the channel. In an official notice of August 1793 about deserters from the Meath regiment one is described as an Englishman born in Birmingham. It does not seem to have been expected that there would be non-Irish in the militia; returns on this point were not required in the early period but later this information was regularly given at the half-yearly reviews. In the Armagh regiment just after the 1803 embodiment out of 552 only two were non-Irish; in the same regiment in June 1807 out of 840 there were 834 Irish, two English, one Scotch and three foreigners; these last were probably in the band. Some of the bandmasters were contimentals and in the ranks of the bands it was common (and not in the Irish militia only) to have one or more men of colour. The Tyrone militia had these and there is extant a description of their resplendent uniform. The Armagh also had one. But on the whole non-natives were few. Later during service in England local recruiting, i.e. of English, was permitted.

To what extent were the private militiamen drawn from the peasant or from the artisan class? The best evidence on this is furnished by the Army Medical Board of Ireland. In a report of March, 1796,[20] they give a comparison, based on the monthly reports from August 1795, of the incidence of disease in the militia and in the fencibles serving in Ireland. The comparison is much in favour of the militia. The fencibles are said to be 'mostly mechanics from unhealthy parts of Great Britain or from unwholesome sedentary trades ', whereas the Irish militia is said to be composed ' of stout men in the prime of life drawn almost entirely from the Irish peasantry, inured by labour in the fields to every vicissitude of climate and of season '. A later report (March 1801) says that : ' a majority of the soldiers has certainly been drawn[21] from the peasantry who are acknowledged to be as stout and as hardy a race of men as any in Europe '. But not everyone held the view that the force was in the main of peasant stock. In December, 1796, the Duke of York in correspondence with Pelham, expresses the opinion that the Irish peasant had a distaste for quitting his home and that ' almost all who enlist are manufacturers [i.e. artisans] and inhabitants of the town '.[22] The commander in chief was possibly only echoing what he had been told by Pelham who had conducted a limited investigation[23] on the point by obtaining a return from the militia regiments in garrison in Dublin. He does not say how many of these there were at the time but they were probably nor more than four or five. He does say, however, that they came from the different provinces of Ireland and he found that two-thirds or three-fourths of each regiment were ' manufacturers and mechanics '. He concludes that the militia were chiefly of that class. This is just about eight months after the Army Medical Board had said exactly the contrary. Other evidence is scanty but some of it supports the estimate of the duke of York. The Dublin city were said to be manufacturers ; that is what one would expect. But in the Donegal militia one would perhaps have looked to find the peasant element predominating ; yet in 1802, when the Linen Board offered looms to disembodied men (see page 166) and returns of the number of linen weavers in each regiment were asked for by the Board, the Donegals returned (in August) the names of 185 men ' of the Donegal militia that is linen weavers '. On the other hand, lord Sligo, already quoted, on the same occasion says of his Mayo men : ' men bred to drive ploughs and dig lands however well inclined do not become soldiers in a moment ';[24] those of whom he speaks were clearly not manufacturers or mechanics.

The official communiqué which the lord lieutenant issued in May 1793 (see p. 38) emphasized that under the act officers and privates might be either roman catholics or protestants, and that the free exercise of both religions was allowed. How far in fact was the force, in its selection and composition, open indifferently to men of both religions? In November 1792 his majesty's confidential servants in Ireland specified, through Lord Westmoreland,[25] a protestant militia as being one of the chief points upon which they insisted. In the house of lords on 11 January, 1793, Lord Darnley put the problem as follows : ' if the militia is to be composed exclusively of protestants, it is likely to raise bad blood between them and the catholics; if left open to all *and consequently composed principally of catholics* would this be prudent etc.'. But, as stated, the act did leave it open. The ballot could not differentiate. Bounty offered would also operate in the main indifferently as between adherents of the one religion or the other. But promises to possible recruits could be so worded as to facilitate differential treatment of catholics and protestants, as e.g. in Cork where volunteers to serve as substitutes were advertised for at a bounty 'proportioned to their size and figure'.[26] A higher bounty might conceivably have been offered to either catholics or protestants. It is to the credit of the colonels that, so far as is reported, only one, lord Kingsborough, did anything of the kind. He published in October, under the heading 'encouragement to protestant volunteers' the offer of farms referred to in Chapter III. This was commented on adversely at the time as 'not altogether liberal' and as not consonant with 'the benign intention of the sovereign which had for its object a generous fraternity of his people'.

Technically, there was nothing to deter a catholic from serving. Exclusion of catholics from a commission in any county unit might have so operated but actually did not. Possibly in few counties did men offer for service in such numbers that a colonel could, even if he would select or reject on religious grounds; indeed the militia could not have been manned, as anti-catholics pointed out, unless a large proportion of catholics were accepted. In November, 1792, Westmoreland had stated the problem thus: 'I do not know how far a militia will be practicable; the great difficulty with me is to find the men; the labouring description except in the north are chiefly catholic'.[27] Accordingly we may take it that catholics predominated in the ranks in at least the proportion of catholics in the population generally (which was three to one). No statistics are available; it is improbable that any were ever collected. In September, 1793, in the Clare militia of about 250 privates, all were catholics except five.[28] In the north Mayo, in December, protestants seem to have predominated slightly.[29] A generalized newspaper estimate in August 1793 was that at least two-thirds were catholics in every regiment;[30] and a later newspaper estimate was that at least three-fourths of the militia were catholics.[31]

The officers however were usually protestants. Plowden says: 'although catholics were rendered capable of serving [i.e. by the act] no catholics officers were appointed: this marked reprobation of all gentlemen of that communion so directly in teeth of the act, diffused a general diffidence amidst the lower orders and it was found necessary to appoint several catholic officers before the militia corps could be completed'.[32] Contemporary evidence does not quite confirm the sequence of events suggested. The speaker, Mr Foster, is praised for having, notwithstanding his opposition to catholics, appointed to commissions in the Louth militia 'indiscriminately both catholic and protestant gentry, as they appeared best qualified for it by character and situation'.[33] It is also stated of him that the 'conduct of none has been more strongly marked by liberality of sentiment', which implies that others did not show such broadmindedness. Lord Westmeath 'with his usual liberality of sentiment'[34] appointed a catholic as his second in command. Lord Muskerry, who commanded the Limerick county militia, is also praised for his 'laudable spirit of religious toleration'.[35] No doubt there were other similar cases. All the same the majority of those appointed to be colonels—and the government at the time received marked praise for its list of nominations—were protestants and it seems probable that these in turn would have offered the commissions in their gift largely to their protestant neighbours. But this was not by any means universal; the commandant of an unnamed unit in the south is reported to have nearly two-thirds of his officers catholics and to have thereby 'conciliated the lower orders'.[36] The important lead on this matter given by the bishop of Cork in the house of lords (see Chapter II) will be recalled. His expectation that it would be difficult in many countries to officer the militia with protestants was no doubt based upon some knowledge of the facts and these facts must, in the event, have had the weight which he anticipated they would have.

The Clare militia, as stated, was a unit in which the privates were almost exclusively catholics and the officer exclusively protestants. But this is what took place at Drogheda[37] on Sunday 22 September 1793, 'lord Conyngham ordered them (the militia) on parade shortly before noon and made them march to mass with drums beating and fifes playing and two officers to inspect their good behaviour. When mass was over they returned ....attended by multitudes who thanked God they lived to see this age of liberality'. There are other similar records and there is no doubt that the spectacle of the catholic militia proceeding with bands etc. to mass impressed observers at the time very favourably; some protestant observers seem to have been taken a little aback but the general attitude seems to have been of marked approval. It is not clear how far, if at all, catholic chaplains were appointed either in mixed, or in pre-dominantly catholic, regiments. Later the catholic authorities objected to soldiers being required to attend the protestant parade Sunday service before being free to attend mass. Part of the objection raised by the English militia colonels to Irish militia coming to England was probably connected with the religious question and something similar may have influenced the king when he put a veto on Irish militia units being brought to serve in Great Britain (p. 147).

Note was taken (p. 27) of the unspectacular disappearance of the volunteers from the scene, That force was mostly middle class whereas the militia was in conception, and probably quite largely in reality, mainly a peasant force officered by country gentry. It was therefore antecedently improbable that many ex-volunteers would be found in the militia ; the middle class being even more disinclined to leave its own home place, and its business associations, than the peasant class. The militia was definitely a new departure. The volunteer organizations faded out of sight ; to a small extent only do they seem to have demonstrated against the militia after the act was in force. At the end of May, 1793, there is the following:[38] 'the awkward squads of Sunday soldiers calling themselves volunteers, who were sometime since legally disbanded occupy themselves at present as orators against the militia. Every barber's shop, fourpenny ordinary, and petty alehouse rings with murmurs of those crestfallen heroes against a militia law which compels them to risk becoming constitutional soldiers'. This presumably refers to Dublin. There is a report from Sligo[39] of the volunteers assembling on a beat to arms occasioned by some apprehended trouble, and they also gave help in a riot at Balinaford five miles from Boyle, early in June. The same thing no doubt happened, as it was natural it should, elsewhere. This was not action hostile to the militia. In the north there was some assembling of the ex-volunteers, but at the end of July, lord Hillsborough in formed[40] Dublin Castle that it had been exaggerated. In September a volunteer review was planned at a village ten miles from Belfast.[41] Appararently it did not take place, but a force of about 400, which included the Fermanagh militia and regular artillery, cavalry and foot, marched out at 5 a.m., without beat of drums, to deal with the situation. In the west the Ennis volunteers, who had had a grand field day on 16 April, passed a resolution on 5 May, that it was useless to meet further but that they would continue associated. On 20 June the officers of the Clare militia were 'elegantly' entertained at dinner by the Ennis volunteers.[44] The general upshot is that the transition from Volunteers to militia was reasonably smooth and that the personnel of the two forces was different and distinct.

The government, having got their militia force, had to plan its distribution with due regard for the requirements of internal order and ready availability for employment against invaders if need should arise. Grattan and others had put contra-invasion as the first duty ; but at Dublin Castle (' we trust lord Howe will keep us from invasion; and we shall be able to keep ourselves from insurrection '[43] Dec. 1793) the militia was conceived of as a police force rather than as an army. The character of the different units—northern or southern, country or town origin—had also to be considered. General Dalrymple (who was subsequently in charge of the Bantry operations) puts the distribution problem well (Sept. 1795):

> To quarter the corps of national militia properly requires a considerable share of knowledge of those who command them and, if the disposition of them is made with judgment, quiet good order and great advantage will follow. They are not at all to be distributed without selection. Some will do very well in garrison that would be the cause of eternal difficulty if put into cantonments.[44]

But however imminent invasion might be, the militia in its early days was not and could not be fit for field service against trained troops. Meanwhile the problem of internal order was more acute, and it is therefore not surprising that for some time little attention was given to anything else.

The earliest 'routes' are for billeting in the county; this is the formula sent to the Armagh: 'a route for billeting the Armagh militia at Armagh or such towns in the county as you may judge expedient until further orders'[45]; others were no doubt similar. In the case of the units embodied early their location would be to some extent determined by the uncertainty which still existed about the duration of their embodiment. Then the wishes of the colonels had to be considered. General Cuninghame, the commander in chief, asks lord Downshire where he wished to be quartered: 'my wish is to accommodate your lordship in everything but will be responsible for nothing where government is concerned';[46] and he enumerates 'eighteen towns unoccupied by militia'. Later, in November, lord Downshire was told he could settle with the colonel of the Sligo militia 'now on march to Newry' whether his regiment should be quartered there. A desire expressed by lord Gosford that the Armagh should be 'permanently stationed at Dundalk'[47] was passed to the commander in chief for consideration. But deference to the regiment's wishes could not continue indefinitely. The units had to be placed in accordance with some defence theory or plan and, apart from this, scraps* with other regiments (regular, fencible, or even militia) or with the civil population, resulted in some places becoming, at least temporarily, impossible for certain units. The location of the various units, as from 29 August, 1794, was published officially[48] (see appendix III); this seems to

*This is not to say that relations with the civil element were not in general harmonious for the militia; the complaint of the authorities would rather have been that they might become dangerously intimate.

show that Dublin Castle regarded the force as then reasonably established.

Quartering units at a distance from the county of their origin became almost at once the accepted policy, before the question of disposition to repel an invader received any serious attention. For this there were two grounds, The first was discipline. It was held that training would go on more efficiently at a distance from the influence of the home county. It was not alone what Castlereagh,[49] in speaking later about the departure of the troops for Bantry, called 'Mr Whiskey'—the tendency of friends and relations to be continually treating the men—but the absolute necessity of concentration on the stark military job in hand. 'The most effectual method to discipline these bodies' runs a contemporary statement,[50] 'is to remove them from whence they were raised, as it secures more attention to duty'.

This particular reason of course did not hold equally good after the initial period of formation and organization. But it was seen almost from the beginning that of the two functions of the militia the quasi-police duty was going to bulk the larger and was going to be easier otherwise than against their own fellow inhabitants of town and county. Close attachments with the surrounding people would make policing difficult, if ever it should become necessary; and, if such close attachments with the people were going to lead to corruption (which in 1797 became a nightmare with the Irish government), then units might become utterly unreliable. These considerations were the second and main reason for the quartering policy adopted and they also explain its permanence. The authorities did not want the militia to be too friendly with the people. Quartering therefore away from the county of origin, and in quarters changed frequently, became the rule. 'To prevent attachments' [such as had apparently developed in the northern counties by the autumn of 1793] 'from being formed between this constitutional army and the people seems to be the reason for so frequently shifting their quarters....mutual goodwill and affection between an army and a people can never be an object of fear to any minister but him who intends to use that army as an instrument of oppression'.[51] But a purely military reason was also pleaded; it was called 'a salutary measure as habituating them to some of the more active duties of a standing [sic] army and accustoming them to that variety of situation which is more incident to the military life than to any other. From hence local attachments lose their hold on the mind and a degree of alertness is acquired which is alike useful and necessary'.[52]

The Irish militia became veritably a nomad force; before the end each regiment had completed an odyssey. One result incidentally was that wherever the militia came prices rose. There is complaint about this even in August, 1793.[53] Another result was that some counties seem almost to have forgotten the existence of their regiments; one regiment complains, at the disembodiment in 1802, that they are 'as little thought of *as when they were* 200 *miles from the county*'.[54] It would probably be no exaggeration to say that during the whole period from 1793-1816 hardly any unit spent any substantial time in its own county except at embodiment or disembodiment. Extra-county quartering must also have aggravated the problem of absence of officers (with or without leave) from their units. This became a perennial source of trouble, leading to drastic orders, and severe disciplinary action. For those who genuinely had county duties and calls—many pleaded them who had none—reconciliation of these and military duty would have been easier if their units had been quartered in or near their counties. Another aspect of the quartering question was the breaking up of the units into scattered detachments. But there was little of this at first; the list of quarters in August 1794 shows many of the units not divided at all. Such dispersion as occurred in the early days of the force was prejudicial to the initial training and there is a bitter protest, early in 1794, from an officer to his absentee colonel about 'our being hacked about in this manner'.[55] This splitting up of units will be illustrated in chapter VI.

Undoubtedly the policy and practice of quartering men at a distance from their native counties complicated the recruiting problem; it was something which the plan of the act had not contemplated; with units far away from the county it must have been difficult for the deputy-governors and the clerks of the peace to keep records which would show correctly how their liability to the regiment (i.e. for the production of men) from time to time stood. In 1796 the adjutant of a regiment, quartered at Loughlinstown, sends his muster roll to the colonel (who is not with the unit) for the clerk of the peace 'in order that he may settle his ballot book';[56] this class of document no longer survives. The accepted quartering practice must also have accentuated the tendency to extra-county recruiting; an attempt was made to check this by legislation in the year 1797. The county arrangements and the county finance were based upon a county liability to produce the men and after 1795 the allowances to wives and children were also a county liability (see chapter XVII). Notwithstanding all this the extra-county quartering persisted. Castlereagh indeed suggested (1807) to Wellesley, then chief secretary, that 'if the regiments were sent for two months into cantonments within their own counties advantage would result in obtaining men': the regiments might by this means be raised to their full standard during the winter ; the Londonderry would soon be complete if sent to Londonderry and ' several of the officers of the regiment being deputy governors would be enabled to give additional activity to the civil proceedings under the militia act '.[57] This suggestion was of equal validity at any time after 1793. What actually happened was that recruiting parties of substantial dimensions were sent from the unit into the county concerned—which of course reduced the number of officers available for regimental duty ; alternatively there was in some cases resort to extra-county recruiting.

Dublin was a capital city with a court and ' Dublin duty ' was for the militia one of the chances that the ' route ' might bring. ' The troops employed in Dublin garrison ' (i.e. within the city, not just in the vicinity as e.g. at Chapelizod) received an extra emolument (abolished in 1801) commonly called ' city pence ',[58] Dublin meant more ceremonial : guards of honour for judges, lining the streets on the arrival of a viceroy, attending him on formal occasions—the Londonderry provided the band when lord Camden in April 1795 laid the foundation stone of Maynooth College[59]—and at reviews in the Phoenix Park. It meant that the uniforms must be in good order if a fine show was to be afforded. The militia seem to have appeared to advantage on these occasions. In October 1793 General Cunninghame had told a unit that ' it is not at present intended that any militia shall come on Dublin duty '; they had not as yet in all probability been got into parade ground trim. But in July, 1794, the lord lieutenant ordered the militia[60] (fifty men from each regiment, as it seems) to come to Dublin to take over garrison duty from the regular troops who were thus set free for service on the continent. Apparently they exhibited an ' uncontrollable tendency to riot with the regulars '[61] and they were sent away. But this difficulty could not have been more than temporary, for there were nearly always militia in Dublin garrison throughout the period. Pelham had many words of praise for them : ' I saw a very fine regiment reviewed close to my garden wall [i.e. in Phoenix Park] this afternoon ', he says in June 1795 ; and in April, 1796, he gave breakfast to a large party ; ' the review .... was altogether the finest sight I ever beheld ....the garrison consisted of three very fine regiments of militia and a regiment of cavalry ....certainly no regiments ever marched better and with more air than they did '.[62] The militia brought a new note of gaiety into life in the provincial towns, with their half-yearly reviews and other parades ; and even in Dublin we hear, as early as May 1793, of militia colonels in militia uniform attending the lord lieutenant at the Castle and to the house of lords, and of crowds of militia officers at the Castle ball on St Patrick's eve.[63]

It is not out of place to devote some space to these matters of ceremonial. The eighteenth century was pre-occupied—perhaps too much—with the pomp and circumstance of the military life. Quite early colonels were canvassing to have their regiments denominated 'royal' or 'Prince of Wales'. At least a dozen applied either directly to the sovereign through their noble colonels or through the lord lieutenant for this favour. To some of them it was accorded; others assumed that by the act of making application they became entitled; while others again received a reply only after a long delay. In 1803 the military authorities in London investigated the position and at the end, in 1815-16, only three Irish militia units (Down, Limerick co. and Meath) were recognized as entitled to be designated 'royal'.[64] The present point however is that in 1793 the colonels gave great attention to the matter.

During that year and the following there were many ceremonial presentations of colours. Usually the expense of providing these was borne by the colonels from their own purses but, later, the lord lieutenant ascertained that in England a set of colours was furnished (or an allowance of £18 10s. 0d.) given in lieu to each regiment of militia once every twelve years. We know that lord Downshire had a bill for £70 10s. 6d. for regimental colours in 1793.[65] These were presumably the 'truly superb' colours ceremoniously presented to the Down regiment at Youghal in May, 1794, on this occasion, when he addressed his regiment 'in an animated speech of some length' and of admirable sentiments; the chaplain 'delivered a truly feeling and excellent discourse, impressive of loyalty, subordination and the professional duties of a soldier which was listened to with profound attention'; and 'at night his lordship gave a splendid ball and supper at the Mall rooms and the private men of the regiment were regaled in their quarters with strong beer, etc.'[66] These ceremonies seem to have been not infrequent: the Wicklow militia in November 1793 received 'two beautiful pair of colours presented by their colonel',[67] and we hear of another presentation where 'the men were all dressed in new clothing and made a truly martial appearance' and 'the privates were most hospitably regaled by their colonel'. In October the Dublin city militia had 'their two stand of colours (agreeably to military etiquette) presented to them by the 13th Dragoons' at Athlone.[68]

On these occasions 'the number of spectators was immense' and the bands of the regiments played. The act of 1793 allowed two drummers to a company but if the commanding officer wanted to keep up 'a greater number of drummers than two per company, to be employed as fifers or musicians....and shall be willing to defray the expense of such additional drummers' he could have any number he pleased. The colonels took advantage of this permission. They vied with one another as much perhaps in turning out an impressive band as in turning out an efficient regiment. References to such and such a band as the 'crack' band of the militia service are not infrequent; and we may remember that 'the band of the Fermanagh militia, *at that time the most celebrated in Ireland*' was expressly brought up for Mrs. Rooney's ball.[69] No drum-major as such was allowed by the act but the colonel could appoint a drum-major from the drummers. Advertisements are fairly numerous for trained musicians for this appointment; the additional remuneration over and above the drummer's pay of 8d. per day, was found by the colonel. He also provided the instruments, which were costly, as appears from extant accounts.[70] Payments for these seem often to have been much delayed, with consequent complaints. The clothing of the bandsmen was usually splendid and was another heavy charge on the colonel: there is a full and rather startling account of the very magnificent uniform of the band of the Tyrone militia about 1810, but equal attention appears to have been paid to the dressing of the militia bands in the earlier period. The drum-major or bandmaster performed functions other than musical; in the Westmeath he was also quartermaster (and lieutenant), and in the Down in 1796 when the adjutant became paymaster, the bandmaster, who objected to being addressed as 'sergeant', desired to have the adjutancy and was prepared to give the previous adjutant whatever the colonel might think proper.[71] The disciplinary functions of the drum-major and drummers are described in Chapter XIII.

When, as often happened, regiments or battalions or portions of either, came together in quarters or in camp, disputes were liable to arise over precedence. This was an old difficulty. The pamphlet of 1776 before referred to states that it had caused great confusion in England during the last war and urged that 'the ascertaining of rank by ballot' was absolutely necessary. For troops getting the 'route' so continually as did the Irish militia, and finding themselves in garrison now with this and now with that unit, precedence was of practical importance in such matters as choice of quarters. An unofficial announcement in August, 1793, of the ballot ordered for this purpose by the lord lieutenant says 'silly competition will be averted and chance determine what pride never could'.[72] The English lord lieutenants had had a ballot for this purpose in March; that for the Irish militia took place at the Treasury Chambers in Dublin and a proper person attended on behalf of each county and city in Ireland. The order of precedence thus determined is given in Appendix IV and remained unchanged throughout the period with one exception. When the Drogheda battalion was (from 1 May 1797) incorporated in the Louth regiment their number of precedence[24] was set free. The Queen's county (No. 25) tried to jump the 24th place; without authority they had the clothing changed so as to show '24';[73] but this was disallowed and the vacant number was, on the division of the Down regiment into two battalions, assigned to the south Down battalion. It is outside this story, but it is interesting to note than in 1833 the English, Irish and Scotch militias all drew together for precedence. For determining 'precedency in the line' as between regiments of fencibles and militia it was ordered (8 Nov. 1794) that priority of being raised should be the deciding factor and that all the regiments of militia should be considered as raised from 8 August 1793;[74] the date of the ballot for precedency. But next year, apparently because the militia continued embodied and also, probably, because the colonels agitated, the matter was reopened, and it was decided that during 'the continuation of the present war' the militia should have precedence over the fencibles.[75]

Organization of the force went on steadily through 1794, but, early that year began what was always so obnoxious to the colonels—the disturbance of their units by the withdrawal from them of part of their personnel. In February, orders were issued for twenty-four men from each regiment to be formed into an artillery company and taught the use of ordnance.* Detachments consisting of an officer, sergeant, corporal and twenty-one privates, were sent to schools of instruction, at Chapelizod, Belfast, Limerick and Kilkenny. Parties for instruction made up of detachments from six or seven units selected apparently so as to bring together northern and southern corps, attended in succession. The intention was to train a detachment from each unit. When the detachments had been trained and had returned to their units, two light guns were issued. When the Tyrone regiment had a grand field day at New Geneva on 17 June the light guns were on the field and those in charge of them are reported as 'admirably trained'. It is not clear how far the colonels had to keep these trained gun detachments separate and distinct. This artillery work is part of the picture of the Irish militia in 1794 and it illustrates that erosion of their units, sometimes temporary and sometines more permanent, which vexed the colonels unceasingly.

In 1794 also began the transfer of militia personnel to the line. At first this was done on a small scale, limited possibly to young officers; but it became afterwards a permanent, and unpopular, feature of the annual routine of the Irish militia. Later the practice was to ask the units to furnish volunteers

*There is evidence that before this some units had been practising cannon exercise.

and, as an incentive, to promise ensigncies in a given proportion. On this first occasion, which was that of an augmentation of the regular artillery, the lord lieutenant announced a desire to recognize ‘the good conduct of the militia of this kingdom’[76] and his willingness to recommend militia officers for commissions in the Royal Artillery. The total number of junior officers lost by the regiments in this way was twenty-one. Each had to raise ten men. It is not clear whether these were obtained from the militia unit, but as steps were taken about this time to prevent drain of militiamen to the line, the men probably had to be got from outside.

On its first formation each unit received a letter of instructions from the adjutant general and also one from the quartermaster general. The former stated amongst other points that the regiment's agent (a functionary allowed by the act to the unit when it was drawn out into actual service) would receive a book of ‘Standing orders, by which the Army in this kingdom is governed’. This—probably the same in range as the ‘Standing orders and regulations for the Army in Ireland’ issued in 1794—contains a miscellany of royal and viceregal warrants and of general orders. It must be remembered that, though these military units had some guidance from such ex-regular officers and non-commissioned officers as they contained or had lent to them, nevertheless they were essentially a new creation and consequently had serious problems of organization. Not all of these were successfuly solved, particularly in the case of units which started with a bad tradition. This helps to explain the unevenness of the militia in military value (discipline, cohesion, etc.). In the case of one unit its steadiness during 1798 is specifically ascribed by one of the officers to the influence of the ex-regular adjutant which it had had from its embodiment.[77]

The general ‘standing orders of the kingdom’ referred to were supplemented by regimental standing orders. Those adopted by the Armagh militia were copied into its original regimental order book. They may well be a copy of the ‘Standing orders for regulating the discipline of a regiment of militia’ produced by captain George Vallancey in June 1793 as a private enterprise,[78] and are printed here as appendix V.

A book of rules and regulations relative to field exercises was also issued to each newly-formed militia unit. Before the first review by a general officer the men were to be proficient in marching past the general, forming into line, manual exercise, platoon exercise, firing by companies, advancing in line, firing by wings, retreating in line, firing by battalion, advance, open ranks and general salute. Commanding officers were specially enjoined not to go too fast and they were recommended also to keep the numbers at first called out down to the 'manageable' figure of thirty per company.[79] At a review at Cork in August 1794 of one of the Limerick regiments and of the Downshire, we are told that there was a 'variety of manoeuvres and firings', that 'the firings consisted of sixteen rounds, by subdivision, grand division and battalion' and that 'each round conveyed to the ear the report of cannon'. These reviews created considerable popular enthusiasm; that just mentioned is reported as arousing 'inconceivable admiration [in the people attending] in having witnessed two regiments, composed of our countrymen, the guardians of our lives and liberties, called forth for national service, exhibiting such state of military perfection and excellence in so short a time of training'.[80]

The appearance at this time (December 1793) of the Queen's county, is described in a letter written from Portarlington[81] when the battalion was on the point of leaving the county for its first station (Monaghan). 'From an idea formerly annexed to militia' the writer had been led to expect an 'irregular, half-appointed and undisciplined rabble', but he found the Queen's county by 'no means inferior (in appearance) to that of any veteran regulars which I ever met with, in point of personal consequence and acquired uniformity'. He praises the grenadier company, and says the flank companies are well chosen and 'at the moment' does not remember to have seen a battalion superior: 'juvenile active soldiery which we would expect equal to a weight of real service'. Then he mentions that 'they discharged a number of men last week that exceeded their complement'. 'The colonel', he says, 'never omitting attending all drills and parades, under every disadvantage of weather'. Many of the officers had 'seen a great deal of active duty'. The inhabitants of Monaghan may promise themselves 'from the excellence of their behaviour, collectively and individually, much pleasure from the regiment's residence amongst them'. There were other similar complimentary descriptions; of the Antrim: 'young able-bodied men, who already exhibit a very martial appearance (March 1794); of the Tipperary (same period) 'fine robust fellows'; of the Longford: 'a very respectable corps', and 'of soldier-like appearance'; and of the Dublin city (at Cavan, August 1794): 'men all new clothed and clean as bridegrooms'. A newspaper report from Carlow of one of the August reviews, says: 'The regiments of militia here, compared with regulars from Great Britain, have the most decided superiority; and as to the efficient appointment of the men there is no degree of comparison'.[82] We must allow something for county patriotism. We may remember Bob Mahon, Charles Lever's major in the Roscommon, who said : " No, no ; give me the native troops '.[83] This was, no doubt, the attitude of many at that time and afterwards. The English generals, however, who were their extra-national leaders—no militia colonel ever rose or was likely to rise to any extra-regimental situation—had a different approach. Military organization above the regimental unit was anyhow rudimentary in those days.

But there is another side to the picture. In August 1793, on the occasion of one of those frequent orders to all officers to rejoin their units, a newspaper[84] warned the militia commanders that they would ' soon discover that they have not engaged in an holiday army but in one where they are to expect real service '. The absence of officers without leave was in fact already causing difficulties ; the first general court-martial for the trial of any person belonging to the militia was in a case of this sort.

In a general debate in February 1795, it was urged that in the year 1793-4 there had been abuses.[85] The member for Wicklow alleged that ' in raising the militia....the most obvious and oppressive frauds were practised on the people ', and recommended the ' adoption of fencible regiments raised by the bounty of government....as a measure infinitely preferable to a militia by means so partial and oppressive to individuals and so odious in the practices of its operation '. Another member suggested a committee to investigate. Mr Bagwell (Tipperary). Sir Laurence Parsons (King's co.), and others traversed these allegations, and the proposal for a committee was rejected. The debate is notable for the intervention of the hon. Mr Stewart, (the future lord Castlereagh) who dealt with the abuses which in his opinion really *did* exist : discharging men who were perfectly fit for service to give them an opportunity of enlisting in a marching regiment ; officers in marching regiments holding commissions in the militia ; and the issue of money for clothing in excess of the actual numbers. Irregularities of this sort were certainly not confined to the militia, and they appear venial enough when the standards of the time, administrative and otherwise, are taken into account. Of all large-scale organization problems of those times it must be remembered that they did not become capable of being efficiently handled until modern communication facilities and appliances became available.

The Irish Militia, 1793-1816

V

Augmentation

LORD Fitzwilliam arrived in Dublin on 4 January 1795, and on the 22nd opened his first, and last, Irish parliament. He found it necessary at once to give personal attention to military and defence matters. Parliament had not met since 25 March 1794. During the year the country had been generally quiet, and throughout it there was no mention of possible augmentation of the militia. But Fitzwilliam's activities since his designation as viceroy had stirred up expectation and even created hopes—emotions which led to some political discontent. But economic conditions were improving; harvests had been very good: so that the general situation did not of itself call for increased military expenditure. Yet in his speech Fitzwilliam spoke of the 'awful present situation of affairs'—and his correspondence harps on this point—though he did not indicate that any additional force was to be raised. As early as 15 January however, he proposed to Whitehall a 'measure necessary for the internal peace and tranquillity of the country....the establishment of a yeomanry cavalry',[1] and he continued to press this strongly as the second item, after catholic relief, in the programme of his administration. 'We must have a respectable staunch army', he writes on 28 January, 'were it only to keep a disaffected rabble in due obedience'. On 23 January he was 'preparing a considerable force, consisting of militia [Sligo] and light cavalry' to send to co. Cavan and its borders. The journals of the house of commons print (27 January) an estimate for increasing the militia by 4,300 men. On 28 January, Fitzwilliam looked upon it as 'not only practicable but easy' to increase the militia to 20,000 men. On 3 February, Grattan, in his speech proposing a grant for the British navy, appealed to the house to 'assist the augmentation of the militia'. In committee of supply on the 9th, the chancellor of the exchequer said that 'it had been objected that [the militia companies]....on an average contained no more than fifty men each' and notified a decision to make an aggregate addition of 4,886 privates. This programme had apparently been formulated by Dublin Castle before the session began, possibly even before Fitzwilliam came upon the scene at all. The necessity for filling out the companies could of course easily be justified on purely military grounds, apart from any specific anticipation of either disorder or invasion. There was considerable discussion about the militia on the 10th, but it did not touch the matter of the augmentation nor the reasons for making it.

By 1795 the Irish government had been able to observe the working of the act of 1793. Their experience, though it was to be widened subsequently under the stress of invasion or threatened invasion and of continued internal disquiet, already pointed to the necessity of some alterations ; and, apart from augmentation, the principal step taken in 1795 was an amendment of the original militia act. This new act acquired importance as establishing definitively the standard of contribution in men, or alternatively in money, required from the counties. There is no evidence of intra-county agitation on the size of the quotas, though the parliamentary journals contain two petitions from the city of Drogheda germane to this.[2] The relative size of the burdens imposed on the different counties remained practically constant throughout. Nor have I found, except in one case (page 104), record of any outburst of irritation at the assize meetings, although militia affairs were constantly on the agenda. A tendency to regard the augmentation men as on a different footing of permanence to the men of the original establishment was finally disposed of by the act of 1798 (38 Geo. iii. chap. 62) which provided that the original establishment of 1793 and the augmentation of 1795 should ' be deemed and taken to be one and the same body and shall hereafter be kept up and maintained by the same provisions and regulations '. The augmentation of 1795 was thus a permanent fundamental augmentation: the counties* became financially liable for the maintenance of an increased number of rank and file per company.

The 1795 act (35 Geo. iii. chap. 8) is ' an act to explain and amend [33 Geo. iii. chap. 22].' The recital specified that an augmentation of the militia was necessary and that the main act required to be altered and amended in many parts. It was presented very early in the session, on 24 February, by three members of whom Grattan was one. In the case of subsequent similar bills—there was an amending and explaining bill almost every year to 1800—the procedure seems to have been to appoint a committee of members, probably members with special know-

*The subsequent augmentations were different, and will be dealt with as they occur ; generally speaking, they were not at the charge of the counties, and were not compulsory—at all events not after that of 1805.

ledge of the militia and its needs, as soon as the session opened, and to draft whatever new enactments were thought necessary as a result of the previous year's experience—well in advance of actual legislative consideration.

Whatever idea or hope there may have been originally of the militia being disembodied after a short period of 'actual service' must by now have been abandoned. The provisions of the original act as to the strength of the units had probably come insensibly to be regarded as 'inapplicable to a state of things changed since 1793'. The bill of 1795, for which the government took full responsibility, provided for an increase of the companies to a strength of 70 rank and file. Even this did not satisfy Mr Stewart[3] (lord Castlereagh to be) who proposed that the committee should be empowered to receive a clause enabling the lord lieutenant to increase the companies, in case of emergency, to 100 rank and file. He stressed the need for more complete defence and deplored the lack of energy and urged the advantage of augmenting the militia rather than the regular army. The former, he said, was more easily recruited 'as it was more speedily disciplined on consequence of the superior skill and discipline of the subalterns of the militia over those of the regular army'. His proposal involved a further augmentation of 8,190 men and it is clear that he wanted it, if he could get it, at once. The government opposed on the ground that it would 'be time enough to attempt a still further augmentation when that which was already voted should be completed'. But authority was given to the lord lieutenant for discretionary increases and this power was often used afterwards. It was claimed, however, at the time that the clause [authorizing discretionary increases] did not 'go to warrant the raising of men to the proposed extent by militia ballot but to enrolling men recruited by bounties from government'.[4]

The act, like the original act, sets out in detail the exact future standard composition of each of the 38 regiments and battalions.* For the six ten-company regiments it provides 764 men; for the fourteen eight-company regiments 612 men each; for the twelve six-company battalions 460 men. These amount to 32 units; besides them are those with an abnormal composition; the Down with ten companies and 916 men; the two Mayo battalions with seven companies and 536 men each; the Kildare and Carlow battalions with five companies and 384 men; and finally the Drogheda battalion (which was joined to the Louth in 1797) with three companies and 232 men. These remained

*See Appendix VI. It is impossible to reconcile the various references to the aggregate number by which the force was increased.

the standard establishments for which the counties were responsible : at the disembodiment the number of arms to be maintained was fixed on these numbers and when the units were re-embodied in 1803, it was to these strengths. The future standard composition of each company is left at : 65 privates, 5 corporals (together 70 rank and file), 4 sergeants, and two drummers ; there were, in addition, two staff-sergeants and two pipers for each regiment or battalion.

'The discretionary power during the present war still further to augment the militia' for 'the more effectual defence of the kingdom' was subject to conditions : (i) such augmentation was to be by enrolment of 'such volunteers as shall offer to serve during the continuance of the present war' and who subscribe the oath contained in clause 16 (see p. 16) ; (ii) the strength of companies was to be limited to 100 rank and file with the usual proportion of commissioned and noncommissioned officers ; (iii) no additional company was to be added to any battalion or regiment*: (iv) the warrants directing augmentation were to specify the precise number to be enrolled per company.

This discretionary power might have been refused if its exercise was to involve additional expense for the counties. But this was obviated by the provision that such augmentations should consist of volunteers. That the counties were not liable for filling discretionary additions to the standard establishment was not very explicitly stated, but the intention was apparently made clear verbally when the bill was before the house. Later, in 1798, it was thought necessary, for the removal of doubts, to enact that liability for the 1795 augmentation stood on the same footing as the liability for the 1793 establishment. At the same time, it was then enacted specifically that the intention of the 1795 act was that 'the men so enrolled [i.e. as volunteers] in addition to the establishment of the militia, as then fixed at 70 rank and file per company, should be raised and kept up without any charge being made on the counties whatsoever'.

The act of 1793 (clause 103) had imposed, in respect of every private man deficient on the number appointed to be raised in a county, a fine of £5 annually 'so long as the said deficiency shall continue'. This fine was charged on the county funds and charges to meet it were presented at assizes in some counties, even after the act of 1795. Thus in 1797 Londonderry[5] 'paid the regiment (as required by act of parliament) as a fine of £5 a year for every private man deficient in said regiment....£905'. There are similar records in the case of other counties.

*When the Carlow and Kildare were increased from five to six companies in 1797 this was by statute.

'To facilitate the raising the necessary number of men with all convenient speed' and in order to provide 'for the relief of persons balloted' the act of 1795 made new provisions and introduced a new system of fines. In future a sum not exceeding £6, derived from a parish cess levied at a parochial vestry, might be paid 'to any balloted man for his serving' or to a substitute. Alternatively £6 per man, in respect of each man to be provided, might be handed over by the parish straightaway to the county treasurer for transfer to the stockpurse of the regiment. As regards fines, 'not sooner than the fourteenth, nor more distant than the twenty-ninth day after the passing of the act' a special sessions of the peace was to be held 'to enquire into the execution of the act' (clause 13). Where it appeared that the whole number specified in the act had not been enrolled, nor the £6 per man, which was the alternative, paid to the treasurer, the justices could direct the treasurer to levy off the subdivision, townland or parish concerned 'a sum after the rate of £10 for every man which shall be wanting at the time'. The money to be paid to the stockpurse of the unit. The payment of this £10 fine discharged the county's liability for the continuing £5 fine and ended the obligation of finding a replacement necessitated by the discharge, death or desertion of any man who had been 'procured by bounty out of the stockpurse fund of the regiment' to fill a vacancy in respect of which the £10 had been paid. Similarly, a parish which had found its men by the £6 or parish cess method, was under no obligation to provide a replacement in similar circumstances.

Illustrations will show these provisions in operation. In Donegal we have this: "Cash paid the stockpurse of the Donegal Militia from the parishes [here follow the names of 34 parishes] in lieu of one hundred and eighty-five men, being their proportions of the augmentation of the regiment, at the rate of £6 per man'.[6] In this case there was no balloting; throughout the county there was resort to the parish cess method of providing the men. The parish of Forkhill co. Armagh (like others, no doubt) had difficulty in finding the sum required of it. A munificent lady stepped in and provided it: and for this she had an address of thanks presented to her.[7]

Here is a sample of the other way of meeting the county's obligation, from the city of Limerick:

'Paid the colonel the sum levied at spring assizes 1795 for 192 men (the augmentation of the said regiment) at £10—the sum of £1,920'.[8]

In several cases the sums entered as paid by counties for the augmentation are not multiples either of £10 or of £6. Presumably in these cases the colonel raised the men and certified to the county authorities what it had cost him. In many cases no payments are recorded. While this might *prima facie* point to a fairly wide use of the ballot, it might just as well indicate that the levies were *parochial* : as such they would not be included in returns of *county* expenditure. However, before the ballot is dealt with, the position in which the volunteer was left by this act should be briefly stated.

The emergency provision (clause 13) in the pay and clothing act of 1793 (see p. 51) was repeated in the similar act of the next year ; it contemplates those who might have ' voluntarily offered '* —either as having previously taken the oath prescribed for the balloted man or the substitute, or as taking these oaths if they voluntarily offered themselves after the act. But the act of 1795 contains a new formula of oath which a volunteer might choose as an alternative to the oaths prescribed in 1793 for the balloted man and the substitute. By this alternative formula he undertook to serve ' during the continuance of the present war with France '—a stiffer obligation than that of the balloted man and equivalent in effect, though differently stated, to that of the substitute. The obligation to find a *replacement* for the volunteer was explicity imposed on the county, whether the vacancy arose by death, discharge, desertion or expiration of term of service.

The men obtained for the Donegal, Armagh and City of Limerick regiments through the financial methods explained would all have been ' volunteers ' (or at all events ' enlisted men ', as they seem subsequently to have been called), and would have counted in diminution of the number to be got by actual ballot. But balloting could not be done without ; indeed some still regarded it as the right and appropriate method of getting men and as truer to the theory of a militia. The act of 1795 indeed put the responsibility of getting the men required almost completely on the colonels : it said, in effect : ' Here's the money ; go and raise the men yourselves '. But at a cabinet on 5 February there had been a discussion as to whether the ballot should be dropped and the additional men obtained by bounty. The decision was apparently to continue it and to introduce changes designed to make it work better than it worked in 1793. An initial general meeting was still prescribed, but the four subdivisional meetings of the original act were now telescoped into two which, with the general meeting, are concentrated into a maximum seventeen days from the date of the passing of the act The period of parochial agony was thus shortened. New grounds of exemption were admitted : a man was exempted if

*The term ' volunteers ' is used for the first time in clause 20 of the act of 1795.

he had not goods worth £10, or if he paid less than £5 a year in rent, or if he had more than three children. The actual machinery of the ballot was greased by providing that constables, for 'their great trouble and loss of time in carrying the act into execution', should receive specified fees for which the collectors of revenue, and not the county, were to be responsible. This act does not amend verbally the 1793 act (i.e. it does not cancel words, sentences and clauses, and substitute others) but simply states the new procedure with the implication that it is to be read with and supersede the old where there is a difference; there is a general statement that all regulations in the former act of 1793 regarding persons drawn by ballot, except those specifically altered by the new act, are to continue in force.

Notwithstanding these changes the ballot where it was used did not in all cases go smoothly. But, so far as one can now form a judgment from the scanty and almost entirely newspaper evidence available, Mullalla[9] is not correct when he says:

> In consequence of a ballotting for the augmentation of the militia that took place this session, riots and affrays ensued in various parts of the kingdom, and many of the unfortunate populace, in the conflict, were put to death by the military.

In the first place, in many counties there was no balloting, the obligation being discharged in money. Secondly, only a few disturbances are reported though the probability is that most of those which did occur got into the newspapers. On the other hand, it is the fact that in 1803, when the Irish militia was being re-created, there was disinclination to rely on the ballot. The act of December 1802 (43 Geo. iii. chap. 2) recites that the 'mode of raising men by ballot has not been generally adopted in Ireland'. It was as much the delay incident to balloting as consequential disturbances which in the main determined the method then employed (see chap. XI). In 1803, Dublin castle was guided principally by the experience gained in 1793 and 1795. How far did the experience of 1795 come into the picture at all and what did it amount to?

The act had not contemplated dawdling procedure. Co. Down balloted promptly, without apparently considering any other method. 'The last drawing for the augmentation...and filling up the deficiencies' took place on 2 April[10]. For co. Longford, lord Granard—on the date the act was passed (24 March), called a meeting for 28 March 'for the purpose of fixing the days for balloting and alloting the numbers of men each division and subdivision are to furnish'.[11] On 12 March the commander-in-chief understood that 'many of the colonels of militia have taken upon themselves to complete their regiments without waiting for the return of the militia bill from England'.[12]

The Down balloting passed off without disturbance ; to some extent submission to the act was obtained by giving a pledge not to take ' men with families that might be a charge to the parishes they were to serve ',[13] but the insurers, who were operating again, complicated matters as regards this pledge. In early February there is the report that ' the augmentation for lord Donoughmore's regiment is going on with nearly the same success as the regiment was raised, being now nearly complete '.[14] But as regards Longford the lord lieutenant reported to London (28 May) that ' lord Granard had been opposed in enforcing the militia laws and was obliged to have recourse to arms ' [15] and there is a further report that ' six of those rebels who . . . . compelled lord Granard to take an unlawful oath were killed at a militia ballot in Ballymahon . . . . and twenty were committed to Longford gaol '.[16] It is no doubt to these incidents that Maria Edgeworth refers in a letter of 11 April : ' The raising of the militia has occasioned disturbances in this county. Lord Granard's carriage was pelted at Athlone '; and in another letter of 20 April : ' There is a whirlwind in our county, and no angel to direct it though many booted and spurred desire no better than to ride it '.

The other county which is known to have balloted is Westmeath. Here there was undoubtedly considerable trouble. On the day appointed ' deluded country people ' to the number of about 2,000 ' assembled from various parts of co. Westmeath *and co. Longford* ' to oppose the balloting at Five Mile House.[17] A neighbouring magistrate expostulated but to no effect ; they demanded the ballot-bag in order to burn it. The magistrate had the foresight to assemble a strong party of his neighbours ; at length he gave them the word to fire on the mob which had already started stone-throwing. Nine are reported to have been killed and a great number wounded. The military then came up but the mob had already been dispersed. ' The governors proceeded to ballot, when the business was concluded impartially and strictly conformable to the wholesome laws of the land '. At Ballinalack.[18] on 10 April, the day appointed for the ballot, a mob of about 700 assembled and ' threatened destruction if they proceeded in their business '; the Limerick militia, quartered at Mullingar, intervened and the mob fled, when presumably the balloting was gone through. The upshot is that balloting is known to have taken place in three counties—Down, Westmeath and Longford—and that there was violent opposition in Westmeath. Simultaneous trouble in Roscommon was agrarian[19] and had no connection with what was going on in Westmeath and Longford ; but that the causes of discontent were not kept in watertight compartments is evident from the fact that at Five Mile House the cry ' no tithes ' was raised, as well as the cry, ' no militia '.[20]

Apart from these disturbances, the augmentation (orders for which apparently went out on 26 March) was not, in a recruiting sense, very successful. Several parishes in south Cork had not complied with the act by the end of April.[21] On 4 May lord Doneraile 'earnestly requests the friends of the south Cork to bring forward as many substitutes as possible on 11 May'. On 17 June Camden[22] told London that 'the augmentation ordered to the militia has not hitherto been attended with the expected success'. Early in the year there had been reason to suppose[23] that individuals had 'assisted themselves in raising their regiments [i.e. various semi-regular units then approved] by the militia'. This, so far as it was going on, had no doubt been stopped. In the autumn Drennan writes :[24] 'I should imagine that the militia has not served government as essentially as it hoped. Indeed the people may now, I think, leave it to itself and it will die a natural death or a voluntary one'.

In a memorandum[25] written in September 1797, Pelham claims that soon after lord Camden's arrival in Ireland at the end of March 1795, there was a great move forward in military activity and efficiency: a large increase of generals on the staff, an augmentation of force, a medical board and general hospitals established, and finally, camps formed. As early as November 1792 a newspaper forecast[27] of the nature of the coming militia bill contemplated a force 'to be practised in all military exercise and evolutions and *habituated to the service of a camp*'. Though some units may have been in camp in 1794—and even in 1793—the systematic encamping of the militia did not begin till 1795. In fact Pelham laments in April 1795 that 'now at the eve of a third campaign'* Ireland was 'without any single measure of preparation for the defence of the country'.[27] A pamphlet of 1795, among many strictures on the defence position in that year, notes that 'our army consists of disjointed corps, unused to the system of acting in great bodies....manoeuvres in great bodies are unknown to our troops'.[28] In 1794 the force was still only in a raw state and probably, until the year was well advanced, only partially armed; in 1793 it was not more than inchoate. Camping could hardly have been effectively started before 1795.

Camden, in a despatch of 17 April,[29] told the duke of Portland that he was contemplating three encampments (near Dublin, Southern and Northern) and that he had asked for camp equipage for 20,000 men. The barracks of Ireland could accommodate 8,000, and as the peace establishment after 'the disembodying of the militia and other reductions' would not exceed one quarter of the war establishment he recommended temporary barracks or

*'Campaign' then meant 'camping season'.

huts in which the troops could be cantooned during winter. Obviously the ultimate duration of the war was not then foreseen. In a despatch[30] about a month later, he urged that, as a considerable part of the troops in Ireland was to be encamped during the summer, it was necessary to create a commissariat and a medical staff; he proposed a medical board which should superintend all hospitals, general and regimental, and to which the surgeons should report weekly and monthly. The Army Medical Board was formed in June 1795.

The newspapers during 1795 are full of the movements of militia units to and from the camps. Most important of the camps, by reason of its nearness to the capital, was that at Loughlinstown, also known as Lehaunstown and as Brennanstown. There were also camps at Clonmel (Ardfinnan), at Belfast (Blaris), and at the Naul. The Naul and Loughlinstown were estimated to take 4,000 each and Ardfinnan and Blaris 7,000 and 8,000 respectively.[31] 'These camps will render the militia of Ireland, as it ought to be, completely efficient for actual service, by discipline and inuring them to the field'.[32] This was the object, obviously necessary if the militia were to be able to cope with external enemies as well as with internal disturbers of the peace.

Of the camp at Loughlinstown, as it was in June 1795, there is a contemporary description:

> The camp consisted of the Westmeath, Downshire and Drogheda militia and Perthshire Fencibles. The camp formed a half circle and extends from Loughlinstown to Brennanstown. The corps drew lots for their stations, by which the Westmeath has the right wing, the most pleasing and comfortable situation, by Loughlinstown Groves, and the Downshire the left. The rest are in the centre. None have wooden booths as yet but the Westmeath, and those they got by chance in drawing lots. These wooden booths are made to contain an officer and thirty-six men each, in which at one side are their berths in two ranges, tier over tier, that contain their beds, and are strong and staunch enough to resist any kind of weather.' A market is held at the camp. The first was on Monday 22 June and it is to be continued on every Monday. Great encouragement is held out to the country people to come to it with provisions, and an officer's guard is to be always stationed at it that nothing but the fair business of buying and selling to the satisfaction of all parties shall take place.[33]

This camp appears to have opened on 1 June. The Londonderry arrives at a later date under their colonel, the right hon. Thomas Connolly, after he had entertained them[34] at his country seat at Castletown en route. Such paternal and almost patriarchal regalements given by the colonels to their units illustrate the relations between commanders and commanded; these relations appear to have been cordial though this did not prevent punishments which now appear almost savage for breaches of order and discipline.

The marquis of Downshire was residing at Dalkey and lord Westmeath was camping with his regiment; of the latter we are told:

> He is a martinet in military tactics, having early made it his study, and being an expert officer during the time the Volunteers of Ireland were under arms.[35]

Two further pictures of the Westmeath in camp may be given: 'How much the comfort of a regiment depends on the humanity and public spirit of the commandant' is illustrated by the action of the 'noble earl who is colonel who reflecting on the present high price of provisions bought a number of fine sheep, had them killed, and the mutton (equal to that which fetches 6d. a pound in the Dublin markets) sold to the soldiers of his regiment at 3½d. a pound'.[36] The other is equally paternal:

> Sunday last, after church parade at Lehaunstown, the earl of Westmeath, assembled his regiment, read over the articles of war making some pointed remarks explanatory of particular articles, but when he came to that regarding profane cursing and swearing, his lordship, in a laudable and animated manner, exhorted them against so heinous a crime, adding that such of his men as were detected in the commission of that abominable vice should be punished.[37]

Lady Emily Stewart (not yet lady Castlereagh) helped to organize balls and 'public breakfasts' for the amusement of the camp. The officers 'made a subscription for the building of a temporary assembly room and other apartments there. Two individuals were preparing to build one there on speculation, but the officers of the camp took up the business themselves for the purpose of having it erected to their own taste and to be under their own regulation'.[38] These were no doubt the 'New Rooms' where the dances of which we hear were held. The lord lieutenant visited the camp on 24 June and reviewed the Downshire, expressing[39] 'his highest pleasure at the adroitness with which this formidable corps went through their martial evolutions'. There was also a grand review by the lord lieutenant at this camp in August[40] and 'all the spectators felt confident that should the enemy pay their shores a visit they would at least receive a warm reception from the loyal Irish militia'. It is expressly stated that Roman catholic chaplains had been appointed by the order of the lord lieutenant for all the regiments of militia encamped at Loughlinstown'.[41]

A contemporary poem[42] about this camp illustrates a point of view and may be quoted in part:

> While Defenders encrease and extend through the realm
> The clearheaded pilots who sit at our helm,
> With wisdom and forecast their actions to stamp
> Send soldiers to quell them—shut up in a camp.

Thus for no use the nation is put to great cost
And in foolish encampments much treasure is lost;
But soon the projectors will be forced to vamp
The scheme of protecting the land—in a camp.

Life in the other summer camps was no doubt much the same—apart from the prestige and the stir of the Dublin propinquity. That at Clonmel was at Two Mile bridge and in May it was announced that the following militia regiments were to be encamped there: Antrim, Donegal, Dublin, Galway, Leitrim, Mayo (south), Monaghan and Waterford. Ardfinnan does not seem to have opened until the latter part of July. Eighteen wagons and forty cars laden with camp equipage were sent from Dublin.[43] The lord lieutenant was visiting this camp when the September mutiny in Cork took place (see page 85). The camp at the Naul was open from early July. There is a description of a church parade there of the Sligo; and the lord lieutenant visited this camp also and reviewed the troops. It was broken up at the end of August and the regiments there were transferred to replace regular regiments ordered abroad.

The Naul camp was only temporary, but that at Blaris (Lisburn) continued for some years and became the quarters of the 1st Light Battalion. It was formed as from 21 July on which day the Limericks who had been in temporary billets in Lisburn marched in. Another camp was at Carleton Moor, near Hillsborough, where the Dublin city were concentrated in August from their scattered cantonments at Dundalk, Newry, Rostrevor, Kilkeel and Portadown. This camp had been formed in July; it was also known as the Maese or the Maze camp.

Although Blaris became a more or less permanent station, there is no evidence that it or any other canp, except Loughlinstown, remained occupied during the winter. Possibly the huts had not been yet provided. The 'wooden booths' for Loughlinstown were provided quickly. 'About 130 carpenters are employed each day and the whole of that business will soon be completed'. Loughlinstown continued to be occupied throughout the winter: in December we hear that the men there are very comfortable[44]—the booths being covered with canvas and coated with paint; with a stove in each and coal from Dunleary port and turf from the mountains. On the other hand we hear in October that the wooden houses are 'sadly complained of and to make them weatherproof the expense will be great; the commander-in-chief says he will never consent to withdrawing camp allowances while the troops remain in the field'.

The importance of camp training lay in the preparation it was calculated to give for field operations against an invader, should these become necessary. How far it was successful in consolidating the regiments and ' inuring them to the field ', we have no reports. A newspaper of 14 August states that ' it is thought the troops at Lehaunstown are not yet sufficiently manoeuvred to hazard their public exhibition of [sic] a review by the lord lieutenant or general officers '.[45] There is no official list of the units which were encamped this year. In May a circular had gone round telling them ' to prepare to take the field on the shortest notice ' and the majority seem to have had at least a short period of camp training. It may well be that the alacrity of the militia response to the Bantry call owed something to the camp experience of 1795.

Camp training was of less value as a preparation for the second duty of the militia. In 1795, as the verses quoted above claim, 'defenders were increasing and extending through the realm '; the work of the militia in their regard was no longer prospective, like encountering foreign foes, but extremely actual, and many domestic scraps and fights occurred in this year. In May, an ' engagement ' took place in Roscommon between

> a part of the Londonderry militia and a body of three thousand defenders wherein the latter had fifty men killed and a great number wounded and taken prisoner. The militia on their march were fired at first by the insurgents and in turn completely emptied their cartridge boxes of seventeen rounds per man against their assailants. The unfortunate wretches fought with savage fury for a time but feeling their utter inadequacy to withstand the cool bravery and steady discipline of the militia they soon dispersed and endeavoured to maintain themselves by firing in parties from behind hedges and walls but they were followed by a party of the militia who completely routed them.[46]

At the end of December 1794 there is the following from Newry:

> ' A numerous body of armed defenders appeared near Portadown. The Royal Dublin militia stationed there under captain Giffard turned out. Towards night the insurgents approached the town, the militia going out to meet them. They fled, pursued all night. The next day the militia came within range of them at a place called Mullavalla where they had burnt some houses. The defenders fired from concealment in a wood but again took to flight. Seven were captured and committed to prison by Mr. Obins, a magistrate who accompanied the militia '.[47]

The last point, in view of the difference of opinion which arose later between Camden and sir Ralph Abercromby, is to be noted.

There is hardly a month of 1795 in which some similar incident is not reported. Sometimes the defenders attacked ; sometimes the initiative in attack was with the militia who were sent to disperse gatherings. Thus in July : ' A party of the Fermanagh militia came up yesterday from the camp at Lehaunstown and were marched off to co. Kildare. In every place where these miscreants called defenders violate the laws there will appear a military force immediately to punish their nefarious conduct '.[48]

The number of defenders concerned in these affairs is probably somewhat exaggerated in the contemporary newspaper accounts from which the above details are taken.* But on some occasions the militia engaged had a few killed. The service was obviously not pleasant, and quite a number of the regiments went through this baptism of fire ; yet in no case does there appear to have been any disposition to refuse service. General Dalrymple, in command at Belfast, reports to Dublin in September : ' In all the circumstances that have yet occurred the behaviour of the regiments of militia has been excellent, and nothing can be more ready than they are to come to blows with the defenders, if they can be found. Discipline has put an end to a disposition, some time since visible, the desire of carrying things beyond the point requisite and cool obedience has succeeded '. And : ' The conduct held by the regiments of militia has been firm and obedient and that of good soldiers ; they are ready enough to do their duty '. He also states that ' great pains is now taking to debauch the militia soldiers. At Lurgan two houses supply them with drink gratis '.[50] Camden reported[51] to London at the end of May that ' on all occasions the militia have behaved with the greatest spirit and shewed the most loyal attachment to his majesty's government '; and Pelham (19 June), adverting[52] to a comment[53] by the duke of York on the spirit of mutiny amongst the militia in England and to the execution of Oxfordshire militiamen, says : ' The militia in this country have behaved very well '.

A letter in the *Dublin Evening Post* on 17 September, said that since their formation they had ' invariably acted with that soldier-like prudence and intrepidity, mixed with a manly humanity, which has ever distinguished the sons of Irishmen '. Sometimes the proceedings against the defenders were rather ridiculous—as when a magistrate ' mounted four privates of the north Mayo militia on his carriage horses and with three other gentlemen ' rode after them.[54] But it is none the less clear that to be a militiaman was not all a rollicking life. There are several accounts of attacks on individual militiamen, some of a particularly cruel character ; in December, for instance, a Fermanagh militiaman, stationed at Prosperous, was murdered by a defender, being cut down with a scythe ; and in September a soldier of the Meath militia was shot through the head by a woman in Skibbereen and we are told that the soldiers would have sacked the

*In later times the numbers said to have been at various O'Connell meetings are accepted as rather inflatedly reported.[49]

town as a reprisal, had it not been for the intervention of their officers. But things were happier on other occasions ; the Kildare militia in November earned thanks for their help at a wreck off Arklow ; there were 113 passengers on board but they were 'safely landed in small boats with long ropes tied to them, drawn by the privates of the regiment, above mid deep in water'.[55] In December the Westmeath are warmly praised for their efforts in extinguishing a fire at Newry.[56]

This picture of the duties for which the militia were used may be supplemented by the story of another incident. It was decided this year that the line regiments numbered above 100 which had been raised the previous year should be drafted. Many of these had been troublesome in various ways, but that was not the cause of their suppression, which was a measure of general policy. The drafting led to mutiny both at Cork and at Dublin. At Cork the men of the 113th and part of the 105th took up a position outside the city and assumed a threatening attitude and General Massey had to assemble a considerable force. The lord lieutenant was at the time (September) visiting Ardfinnan camp and he immediately detached three regiments of militia to proceed to Cork ; when informed of their mission they 'gave three huzzas and were ready to march in less than an hour afterwards.[57] It is also stated that General Massey sent for the Louth, Meath, King's County and Roscommon regiments, in addition to the regiments despatched from Ardfinnan. At Cork, 'the mutineers were drawn up on one side of the Mall, apparently prepared for action ; while the loyal militia formed on the opposite side'....The pause was 'terribly awful'. General Massey directed 'two field pieces to flank the mutineers....the matches to be lighted and the militia to load'.[58] The mutiny at Dublin in the 104th and 111th regiments caused the intervention of the Downshire and Londonderry militias.[59] Pelham expressed[60] satisfaction that 'the militia of Ireland have had another opportunity of proving their loyalty'. The *Cork Gazette*, *Northern Star* and a Dublin paper published what was regarded as 'a false and malicious libel against the regiments on duty at Cork during the mutiny', and legal proceedings in the Court of King's Bench followed.[61]

The desired Medical Board was constituted in June 1795, and an attempt was made to improve the medical service in the units. The original act had not prescribed any medical qualification as necessary for those commissioned as surgeons ; it did not require them to have any property qualification ; it did not exclude surgeons of county hospitals from eligibility ; and, finally it allowed or even contemplated the holding of a lieutenant's commission in addition. The Medical Board has left on record[62] a strong criticism of these double commissions (see page 23), but the anomaly—an obvious impediment to medical efficiency in the units—was not removed until it was abolished by the act of 1798. It was reasonable enough that a county medical officer should be the surgeon of a county regiment so long as the militia was normally intended to assemble only for a short period of training within the county coundaries; but service within the county had almost at once become the exception rather than the rule, and a surgeon could not be in two places at once. Accordingly, the act of 1795 provides that 'surgeons of county hospitals or infirmaries' are not capable of serving. The same act prescribed that after 1 November 1795 a surgeon must be 'certified by the Royal College of Surgeons, after due examination, to be properly qualified in like manner as surgeons are required to be certified'. In consequence we find the surgeons of the Wicklow and King's County Militias taking out certificates with the Royal College. A surgeon who has passed his examination offers to dispose of his commission; he states that 'it now brings in £200 a year clear of all expenses' and that 'to prevent trouble the lowest sum that will be taken is £500'.[63] In another case a 'regular bred surgeon, member of the Royal College of Surgeons' offers 'a moderate douceur to any gentleman willing to resign or likely to be precluded under the late act of parliament'.[64] The day was passed for 'surgeons attached to militia regiments not brought up to the profession and not having passed any examination' and of whom it had been said that 'some of them keep apothecary's shops and only join their regiments for reviews, etc'.[65] The militia may have been joined by some in a spirit of picnic but it had speedily become a very serious business, as surgeons who had not made the discovery earlier quickly realized in 1795.

VI

The Year 1796 and Bantry

To whatever degree of field efficiency the Irish Militia had been brought as a result of the 'campaign' (or camping season) of 1795, little progressive addition to it was made in the year 1796. In October 1795 Camden had given orders for the ground at Loughlinstown camp to be taken for another year. 'If we have', he said, 'an encampment next year there cannot be a better place and if there is a peace the forfeit for non-occupation will probably be trifling.'[1] In November of that year, in a despatch to London, in which he refers to the voted strength of the militia as being 22,369, officers included, he alludes to the contingency of events taking place before January, 'which might give a nearer probability of peace and put all danger from invasion away'.[2] Pelham, in June had written about the 'army which we are setting on foot as if the war was beginning instead of being, as I hope it is, near its conclusion'.[3]

Any such hopes of peace had passed away before the next spring. The smaller provision for camp training in 1796 did not arise from any such optimism. It was the internal situation which governed the disposal of the militia. On the 21 March, Camden, in a despatch[4] to Portland, said : 'There will be fewer in camp as the state of the country will require larger distribution in quarters'. The programme allowed for three militia units being in garrison in Dublin, which was not of course field training; for three at Loughlinstown ('near the capital for its protection'); for three at Ardfinnan camp, near Clonmel ('the properest position for a reserve in case any attack should be made on Cork, Waterford or Limerick'); and for three at a northern camp, which was Blaris. It would be interesting to know how far this modest programme of camp training was concurred in by the military authorities. We know that Camden and Pelham did not put much store by their military adviserrs. Two expressions of Camden's opinion may be quoted : 'We have often', he says[5] in July 1796, writing to Pelham, 'agreed that not much dependence is to be placed upon our generals'; and again, also to Pelham, in October 1797 : 'I am sure that in many parts of that profession [i.e. the military] a man not bred to it can judge as well as one who has been so educated'.[6]

The considerations affecting distribution of the available military force have been stated (chapter IV). By the spring of 1796 demands for protection of individual properties (the object, as some apparently thought,[7] of having a militia) must have poured in, and, as between the two inherently somewhat incompatible functions of the militia, there was, during the first part of the year 1796, a definite switch over from contra-invasion preparations; the course was again decisively altered in the autumn; this year was mainly one of preoccupation about the internal situation.

Continuous knowledge of the distribution of the militia, in the pre-Union period,* is unfortunately not available. In the list of quarters printed in appendix III the majority of the units are concentrated and, where they are split up, they are not very much so; though it does not follow that even then (1794) the units were not providing many small subaltern's or sergeant's detachments to outlying places. A statement[8] of the summer quarters of the troops in Ireland for 20 June 1796 shows how the militia units were in a great many instances split up. The Downshire was a twelve-company regiment; its headquarters and ten companies were at Drogheda; one was at Navan and one at Balbriggan. But there were the following detachments:—at Swords, Rateath, Lusk, Malahide, Dunshaglin, Westpanstown, Collon, Torphecklan, Slane and Parsonstown; six of them were in charge of a subaltern and the others of a sergeant; all had a sergeant. The country covered by the regiment was fairly populous and its communications were presumably good for the time. But where the towns and villages were dotted more thinly, the effects of scattering would have been more pronounced. As yet neither the adjutant nor the surgeon were allowed anything for the upkeep of a horse for their public duty; in some cases the mate (or, as he was afterwards called, the assistant surgeon) was sent with a detachment when it was of sufficient size. The Tipperary, a ten company unit, was similarly dispersed. We have the rather plaintive remark of a commanding officer of the Downshire in August: 'The regiment is greatly scattered but I hope to keep up their discipline notwithstanding'.[9] The authorities—to be fair—did not distribute the militia solely according to what was politically important: barrack accommodation and even supply exigencies would have a good deal to do with it; uncertainty as to the probable duration of the war seems to have checked expenditure on construction.[10]

The Irish militia had scarcely a chance of getting disciplined before being thrown into the hurlyburly of domestic strife. Some commanding officers aimed at segregation. In November 1794

*For the post-Union period it is continuously available.

an officer of one of the Cork units says : 'I have.... as much as possible detached them [i.e. the men] from having any intercourse with the town or country '.[11] But this rather monastic ideal was impossible and essentially undesirable. Still splitting up impeded training, and made the men, who were from the people and of the people, more amenable to the influence of the current opinions which were flowing so strongly. These movements would include what are spoken of as corrupting influences. During 1796 the militia became more and more the objects of general suspicion; by being split up they would mix more amongst the people than if they had been segregated and kept continuously under the influence of their officers, or had been concentrated under barrack conditions. If the Irish militia are to be judged rightly, standards applicable to regular troops living under the conditions normal for such troops should not be applied to them.

What may be called the officer-absence problem was now acute. Two aspects of it have been mentioned (chapter II) : under-officering and the double call of the regiment and the county. 'Almost the whole of my officers', writes a general in the south in July 1797, 'are anxious to get away to the elections'.[12] The assizes, before which county militia business came, occurred twice yearly. Leave seems to have been given almost as a matter of course. 'I obtained leave on the old plea of attending the assizes', writes[13] a field officer in 1810 ; it might have been written any time from 1793 ; and it is clear that the assizes were made a pretext. They were occasions of much merry-making—the officer quoted speaks of 'bacchanalian orgies'. It was a change from the dullness of the military routine ; and the 'scramble for the public money' which took place afforded legitimate excuse for the attendance, in the militia interests, of those officers of the county regiment who were grand jurors. The county called also in another way. The colonel of the Londonderry, Mr Conolly, was in November of this year, very insistent for the return of lord Castlereagh (then still Mr Stewart), to regimental duty at Limerick. In county Down it was electorally touch and go ; 'the true motive [i.e. of his delay in leaving] is the fluctuating state of the tenantry', writes[14] Mr Stewart (19 November) to his wife, and, in another letter (15 November) : 'I really feel that I can do more good here than on parade at Limerick'. Mr Conolly continued impatient and Mr Stewart then wrote to lord Camden about what he should do. This illustrates the perplexities of a high-principled officer with a sense of responsibility, and there are cases of a conflict of call where the families of officers were isolated and in danger ; in some cases officers in this predicament, unable to obtain leave of absence, without further ado tendered their resignations.

Still there was much reprehensible abuse and officer-absence was a grave handicap to the units as military formations, with definite and important national tasks before them. Complaints by generals are frequent : 'I think the captains of - - - - - ought to be obliged to attend', and 'Captain - - - - - of the - - - - - has never been at quarters since the assizes'. There were, however, other less admissible causes of absence than attendance at assizes nor did this excuse apply in the case of the regulars and fencibles amongst whom absence from quarters was also frequent in that period in Ireland.

It was a crying scandal. Appointment of the Irish militia officers was, subject to the lord lieutenant's veto, within fourteen days, by the colonels ; but no provision had been made for displacing them when once appointed. This year it was enacted that the King, without initiative from the colonel, could from time to time as he might think fit, signify 'his pleasure....to displace all or any officer of militia' serving in any battalion or regiment ; and this remained the position at all events until 1804, when Hardwicke[15] defines it clearly in a despatch to London. In June 1796 Camden[16] submits the displacement of two militia officers for absence without leave and similar submissions regarding fencible officers were numerous this year. The trouble continued ; e.g. a submission of the following October contains the names of three regular officers, eight fencibles and eight militia officers. Enforcing supersession does not appear to have improved matters and Camden[17] speaks (October 1797) of 'the difficulty of enforcing the attendance of militia officers' as rendering the force less to be depended upon. On 21 December 1796 a 'standing' order stipulated that an officer joining his regiment after being reported absent without leave should be put in arrest and his case specially stated for further instructions.

The colonels also, it would seem, were less assiduous, as time went on, in attendance with their regiments. In November 1796, Camden tells[18] Downshire that he is 'among the few who give the exertion which is so necessary in these times'. It is difficult to generalize. We find lords Loftus and Louth present[19] at Ardfinnan camp during the summer months of 1796 with their units. In another case it is expressly recorded that the colonel was almost always with his regiment. It was to the colonel, lord Portarlington,[20] in camp at Blaris, that the Queen's county (October 1796) made their offer to serve his Majesty in any part of the world or in any manner. These instances go to show that the militia did not, generally at all events, lack leadership from their colonels, though it may often have been administrative and from a distance rather than instructional and on the spot. Some indication of the varied matters the militia colonel dealt with may be useful. In most cases, like many of his officers, he was performing other public duty, and could not easily give undivided attention to his militia charge (see chapter VII, p. 114). The existing papers of one or two colonels show them dealing with these among other matters :—complaints and representations (memorials) on a variety of matters, some anonymous and some through the regular channel (commanding officer) and some even from sergeants and privates direct ; applications for commissions and for companies ; adjustment of quarrels between officers ; applications for adjutancy, bandmastership and surgeoncy ; currency troubles (shortage of money) ; regimental accounts and general supervision of paymaster ; relations with agents ; quarters ; applications for discharge from n.c.o.s ; clothing questions (a very big matter and one on which the colonel could lose, or gain, a good deal) ; adjutant's reports ; lists of, and reports about, recruits ; courts martial, etc., etc.[21]

The causes which tended to keep the colonels more and more at their county duties were also compelling the authorities to meet requests for home-protection detachments. Demand for these grew and it was the need to produce at all events the sense, if not the reality, of security, that led to withdrawal in part from the militia of quasi-sedentary protection functions and the transfer of these to a new force, the yeomanry. The need for this force might have been less insistent if the gentry had had less unfavourable views about the militia. Camden wrote[22] to Portland on the 24 August 1796 : 'The suspicions which the gentry entertain of the militia, even were an invasion not to take place, has induced great numbers to wish to associate for the preservation of their property and to form corps of yeoman cavalry and infantry....all under commissions from the Crown'. He said that he would not be able to delay his encouragement of 'associations of this nature many days longer'. They were to be 'guarded as much as possible from assuming the appearance of Volunteers'.[23]

Camden had been under pressure since mid-July to take this step. Probably earlier than this the attorney general, Beresford, the speaker, the chancellor, and sir John Parnell were for the measure,[24] which, as noted, had at the beginning of 1795, been advocated by Fitzwilliam[25] and rejected by Whitehall. But Camden did not readily accept the view that the new force was inevitable. On 6 August, he admitted to Portland that it was the opinion of the five officials just named, that, to oppose internal disorder and threat of foreign invasion, Ireland had 'an army composed of nearly 19,000 militia certainly as fine and for the most part as well-disciplined troops for the field as can be produced in any country'.[26] But he himself had felt doubts about some of the militia. The fencibles* were 'neither sufficiently numerous nor powerful to give much confidence if it is denied to us to repose it completely in the militia'; and he ends by dwelling on the extreme dispersal of the military force generally, and says that 'the number of cantonments could not be much diminished without danger to the public tranquillity'. He then asks for authority for raising yeomanry.

In London there was hesitation in acquiescing. Camden after his despatch of 6 August, again wrote on 28 August, and in that despatch, made the further point that 'we cannot place much confidence in the militia on account of the religious opinions of many of them'. The previous year Downshire had, as we have seen, written to Hobart in India in a different sense about the militia. During the Rebellion year evidence is wanting of the militia having refused service because they were required to act against co-religionists and it seems very possible that Camden's alarm was, though explainable, unfounded; he was no doubt expressing an opinion which many held.

On the 30 August it was decided[28] to raise yeomanry. The preamble of the act† (37 Geo. iii. chap. 2), shows what it was intended to achieve in the Irish defensive system. This recited that further exertions had become necessary for the defence of the kingdom and for the preservation and security of the lives and properties of his Majesty's subjects therein; the word 'yeomanry' is not mentioned—in a letter of 17 October lord Camden calls it 'the County Cavalry and Infantry Bill'—nor 'defence', apart from the preamble; there is provision for arms, accoutrements and clothing to be issued, and pay under certain limitations, to 'any of his majesty's loyal subjects' who shall 'voluntarily associate and enrol themselves....under officers having commissions from his majesty or from the chief governor' for the protection purposes named; it is an act 'for encouraging and disciplining such corps as shall voluntarily enrol themselves'. Further than this it does not go; the form of the act and its not giving a title to the force, suggest that there was the deliberate intention to avoid the appearance of setting up a defence force which would be a rival to, or to compete with, the militia, or recall the Volunteers of the pre-1793 period.

*Fencibles (mainly raised in Great Britain, though some were raised in Ireland) (*a*) had their commissions from the Crown; (*b*) were for general service, not merely for service in the country where they were raised; (*c*) were not raised through county machinery and the counties had no financial responsibility whatever in regard to them. Fencible corps from Great Britain (mainly Scotch) were in Ireland in 1798.

†Announced in lord lieutenant's speech on 13 Oct; second reading 15 Oct.; concurred in by lords, 25 October.

Other defence ideas were floating about. Grattan,[29] at one time (1794) had contemplated independent volunteers 'attached in some manner to the militia', but this plan 'might occasion an interference and rivalry with the militia'. Another scheme put forward was for the addition of a second battalion to each militia regiment 'to remain as nursery in their respective counties'. Lord Ormonde[30] proposed to government to raise a corps of cavalry 'to be either annexed to his regiment of militia or to serve in any other manner'. The doubling[31] of the militia was also talked about. The Irish government had to walk somewhat warily about the yeomanry. We find Camden[32] telling Downshire what line he should take at a meeting and pointing out to him that the meeting's decision would be a precedent. But the creation of the new force, as it was formed, apparently caused no resentment in militia circles; it appeased some of the old Volunteer stalwarts like lord Claremont;[33] and there was no trouble. Furthermore, the yeomanry and the militia seem to have lived on good terms with one another, though on some occasions, the newer force got more limelight. Militia officers, in fact, themselves had commissions in, and in some cases raised, troops of yeomanry. The two became more or less complementary to one another. While the organization of the yeomanry remained simple, that of the militia became more complicated.

The purpose in view in the formation of the 'Yeomanry' was (24 September) officially stated;[34] it would become necessary in the event of invasion, or under the well-founded apprehension of it, to concentrate the regular and militia forces of the kingdom by withdrawing them from the dispersed cantonments into which they had been scattered by the disturbances. This is the idea of the militia as a contra-invasion force. Lady Sarah Lennox, who was in close touch with military circles, writes[35] (3 September) that that was 'the first moment in which government have allowed there is any danger'. She reviews Ireland's military situation and refers to the militia in the following terms: 'The militia are about 33,000 [*sic.* query 23,000] nominal men, very many regiments exceedingly well and carefully disciplined, some remarkable fine bodies of men, others not so showy, but equally active and spirited. Some regiments are supposed to be disaffected but many of these reports come from the shameful neglect of the officers chiefly composed of 'Irish Buckeens', the worst sort of animal in the creation who neglect or never know his duty, but wherever the officers attend the regiments are excellent'. Before the end of August Camden had been talking of the necessity of the army being drawn together 'to act in larger bodies than it has lately done'.[36] but it does not appear that any action was taken. There were reports that the formation of small camps throughout the country was contemplated ; that the south-west coast[37] was to be lined with troops and batteries to be erected on every spot commanding harbours ; and also that orders had been issued for changing the inland quarters of the army to cantonments nearer the coast.[38] But the hurried rushing of the militia to the south when eventually, in December, the crisis arrived, suggests that few precautions had been taken in advance. On 10 September the following militia regiments were at or near Cork : Galway, Roscommon, Dublin county, Sligo, Leitrim and Meath.

Attention was given in that month to the idea of organizing battalions from the militia light infantry companies as a measure to meet invasion. Both Pelham and Castlereagh were interested in this and the matter went so far as the nomination of a general[39] to command the projected concentration and a scheme was prepared.* Nothing had in fact been done towards bringing the light companies together when the Bantry crisis supervened. But lord Carhampton (24 December) seems to have contemplated some separate action by what he calls ' the light troops ', and the light companies of the Dublin garrison (possibly regular and militia) were put in movement towards the south.

General Robert Cuninghame who had been commander-in-chief in Ireland since the institution of the militia had been asking to be relieved, and Camden had represented,[40] in September, that to deal with invasion a more active commander-in-chief would be wanted. After several other names had been considered lord Carhampton was appointed with commission from 10 October. Before his arrival Camden had raised with London the desirability of requiring all officers to join their regiments ' at the present crisis '. This action has an odd ring. It was early September and the public danger was admitted. But no doubt Camden feared causing alarm. In London it was thought necessary to refer the matter to the King who minuted :[41] ' Undoubtedly here all officers have been attending the whole year and not allowed to be absent without special leave being given. It seems that the same rule would at all times be right in Ireland .' So (23 September) all leave of absence was cancelled.

At this time the men in the ranks were probably beginning to look forward to their release which would be occurring, for large numbers of them, at various dates in the next year. Notwithstanding this, and probably in ignorance of it, the English authorities, in the autumn, conceived the plan, which was to become a fixed idea, of getting for the Line bulk supplies of recruits out of

*For the story of the light companies and the light battalions in the Irish militia see chap. X.

Ireland. The suggestion, with this object, of some sort of parochial levy was rejected by Pelham as impracticable, but it seems to have occurred to him[42] that the time-expired militiamen might be the solution of the English need ; how the militia units would be filled up again is not mentioned. Pelham had apparently gone on the basis that a big exodus of time-expired militiamen was impending, but the miscalculation was recognized[43] and the matter left over till the next year.

But there was on this point much general misconception and the idea that 'the militia act was expiring '[44] was shared by Sir John Moore, and has been countenanced by Lecky and others. The view which had currency was that the force (i.e. the institution as apart from those who gave it body) came to an end, abruptly, at the expiration of four years. But four years from what date ? From the date of royal assent to the act ? This certainly is not in the act. The different units came into embodied being from different dates, and, within the unit, completion of the four (and five for volunteers and substitutes) years enlistment periods of one man and another, occurred at different times according to the date of each man's attestation. This theory of four years' duration and then 'dead stop ', unless fresh legislation provided otherwise, is shewn to be erroneous by the fact that the act by (clause 41) provides for the commanding officer, in the case of 'every man whose time shall be within four months of expiring ', approaching the man to find out if he is willing to continue in the service and 'for what price or sum he will continue '. He is to make this approach six times every year, i.e. on the first day of January, March, May, July, September and November. There is therefore ample provision in the act against the militia institution dying off through absence of flesh and blood, and the enactment on the point applies specifically to the case of militia units embodied and serving outside the county. What was not provided was the money necessary to finance 'continuance in the service' when it was to take place on a wholesale scale and when its necessity was not merely a regimental but a national matter. It was not dealt with next year, without the intervention of parliament.

Lord Carhampton does not appear to have made any substantial rearrangements of the troops ; general orders of 12 November indicate that the more complete organization of the yeomanry was awaited ; the announced policy of concentrating the militia (and regulars) and locating them on the coast had not been carried out before the Bantry 'sudden call ' came. But Carhampton was active in giving special training to the troops of the Dublin garrison and to those at Loughlinstown. He practised them in night operations and in meeting daybreak alarms and surprise attacks, and in repelling landings.[45] Shortly after his arrival, he reviewed three militia regiments and a fencible unit and the order of review was gone through with a steadiness 'not to be excelled by any army'.[46] This was followed by an elaborate sham fight and manoeuvres. The next month there was another field day and sham fight and experiments were made with an improved type of wooden huts which on emergency could be converted into bridges for crossing small rivers.[47] He organized the kingdom (26 October) for military purposes into five districts. On 12 November a comprehensive order dealt with :

(*a*) arrangements to enable the several regiments to move with the utmost celerity and when collected to act together without confusion ;

(*b*) general regulations for the march of the Army when collected.

That these 'mobilization instructions' had been digested in the few weeks which elapsed is improbable. There were irregularities on the march of the troops from Dublin to Bantry and the duke of York strongly censures one of the generals.[48] But Carhampton had scarcely had time to make himself felt before the military and militia organization of Ireland was exposed to trial.

Anxiety about a possible invasion had become intensified in September. By 13 October it was sufficient to cause parliament to be assembled ; in his speech[49] from the throne the lord lieutenant said the enemy intended making a descent upon Great Britain and Ireland. About Christmas mere diffused apprehension changed into acute realization of an imminent coup. The dispositions for meeting this, as compared with those in force at the beginning of the year, had been improved to the extent that the yeomanry had been instituted. This should, but not immediately, increase the readiness of the militia to proceed on contra-invasion duties. An abstract of 'measures taken and arrangements framed [or formed] for defence of the kingdom'[50] (endorsed September 1796) shows steps taken : supply of 30,000 blankets and of camp equipage for 33,000 infantry and 8,500 cavalry ordered ; increase of store of gunpowder to 10,000 barrels ; depôts of biscuits and oats to be formed at Clonmel, Bandon, Galway, between Athlone, Banagher and Portumna, Omagh, Hillsborough, Newry and Dundalk, and contracts for supply to be entered into without delay ; ovens to be constructed at Athlone, Birr and Omagh ; tents to be provided at the various places named ; and finally contracts to be entered into for supplying the various garrisons with three weeks' provisions. But how far all these measures had been put in hand, and the necessary organization set up, is doubtful and it is probable that, when the crisis came, improvisation was the rule.

Adequate information about the placing of the troops is not available, but it was not as a counter-invasion measure that the six militia units, mentioned above as being at or near Cork on 10 September, had been moved to that part of the country ; they were already there in the month of March when serious alarm had not yet begun to be felt. No additional militia (or indeed regular troops) had apparently been moved into the threatened district before the Bantry crisis came swiftly over the western wave. Then all was bustle and movement, almost from one end of Ireland to the other. There was no such large scale simultaneous militia movement until the (first) demobilization in 1802. Then we hear of the people of the countryside flocking down to the roadside when bodies of troops were passing. That was idle, if legitimate, curiosity. But now there must have been acute concern and even alarm. Much was at stake. When, in an agricultural and pastoral country, the cattle[51] are to be driven from their habitual grazing grounds to where they can browse more peacefully then indeed the heavens must be beginning to fall. And a crisis so home-thrusting is one thing in summer, but in a winter bitter almost without precedent, such as was that of the year 1796, the sense of peril must have been the more sharp and searching.

The first step in consequence of the arrival at Cork of an express from Bantry was to move, on 22 December, the militia and other troops, of the garrison to the west.[52] The Armagh, which, after spending the summer at Ardfinnan camp, were apparently at Mullingar, also seem to have moved west. All these troops left in high spirits.[53] The yeomanry—not yet on permanent duty—took over garrison duty in Cork, and a curfew (10 p.m.) was imposed.[54] The Louth, Westmeath and Londonderry militia were also set in motion from Limerick. Castlereagh has left[55] a vivid picture of the departure of the latter. They were 500 strong ; their detachment from Tarbert did not join them until they had reached Mallow ; the first day's march on 24 December was to Bruff over mountainous country ; the weather was 'charming, a little cold'. 'Mr Whiskey', he says, 'had done a little mischief in our ranks but upon the whole for a first day's march (taking leave of sweethearts and parting with the inhabitants who brought spirits in quantities to them when they were chilled on the streets waiting for stores which they never received) we did fairly well'. 'The men are in great spirits and very much afraid that the Navy will run away with their credit from them'. Then from Mallow on the 29th : 'Our men are grown impatient but I believe there is very little hope of their being indulged with anything except marching'.

Other troops were following the Londonderry on the same route. General Dalrymple had (27 December) beween Cork and

Bantry the following :—Galway, Wexford, Londonderry, Leitrim, Waterford, Sligo, Roscommon, Westmeath, Meath and south Cork.[56] This list does not include the Armagh nor the Dublin county and the Louth which are recorded as having marched respectively from Cork and Limerick. The Wexford had spent the summer at Ardfinnan and had afterwards gone to Loughlinstown camp ; the Waterford had reached Cork about mid-November but had apparently been kept back when the first contingent left for the west. About the south Cork there is fuller information. A mounted orderly reached their headquarters (probably Ennis) in great haste with a message that they were to set off for Cork at once. It was a very long march. ' For eight-and-forty consecutive hours ', an account runs, ' they were never off their feet. They had no time for sleep, or even to dry the wet clothing which clung round their half-numbed limbs '. This march became a legend in the regiment. Before they had started their colonel had directed that their queues should be cut off to save time and effort in stiffening and powdering. But when they were paraded the morning after their long march, ' Where's their powder ?" gruffly enquired the general, to be met by the colonel with the justifiable retort : ' By God ! general, 'tis in their pouches ; and 'tis there it ought to be in such times as these '.[57]

The contingent sent from Loughlinstown and Dublin marched off ' with the loudest acclamations of joy '[58] on Christmas Day. In it, besides ' a fine park of artillery ', and ' forges for making red-hot balls ', were included the Kildare, Clare, Donegal, Limerick city and Wexford. The total of this contingent is given as near 3,000 men.[59] They marched upon two roads in unconnected columns and were to be followed by other corps from the northern district which were to form the reserve. Although little is known of the movements of individual militia corps, there is official record that thirty-one—the names of which are recorded[60]—of the thirty-eight units, were ' moved to the southward part of the kingdom '; grants were approved for this number in respect of baggage and allowance to wives. Others (e.g. the Tipperary at Londonderry) were directed to hold themselves ready to march at a moment's warning.

Of these the Downshire were lying at Drogheda. They had had a general warning to stand by which had been issued on the 24th. Writing before dinner on the 25th to lord Downshire, the commanding officer says that ' the regiment shall be ready the moment they are called upon '. He is distressed that the assistant surgeon who will have to go with the regiment ' has not a single instrument fit to make use of ', and he begs that the surgeon may be ordered to join instantly ' and to provide the proper instruments adding that ' he will have plenty of use for them if the French stand '. After dinner, he adds a postscript that the route has arrived and that he will march in a few hours ; ' the drums are now beating to arms '. He had been hoping to get over Christmas quietly. There is a glimpse of the celebrations ; ' the men have all got their balances, and that, with the season, sets the whiskey a-going among them, but we have had no riot or any bad behaviour to signify '.[61]

The voice of the man in the ranks of the Irish militia can unfortunately seldom be heard. Possibly not a large number were literate.* It is not therefore surprising that little written by the militiamen to their homes should be any longer extant. But there is this rather pathetic note that a Downshire militiaman, before leaving for Bantry, wrote[62] to his mother, dating it ' only two o'clock in the morning ' from Collon :

> We have just received an express route to march to Bantry Bay near Cork. The French are landed there and we are going to face them. Do not be fretting at this. God is on our side and he will conduct us through all dangers. Keep up your spirits as I will mine. Wherever the Downshire boys goes they strike terror into the enemy. Farewell, my dear mother, I have not time to say any more but pray for the safe return of your affectionate son till death.

The Downshire, as also the Queen's county, did not in fact get beyond Dublin where they were detained for garrison duty.

The crisis subsided as suddenly as it had come. It had evoked great alacrity and soldierly response on the part of the militia, almost all of which were launched suddenly from their quarters on laborious marches at the Christmas season and in weather of unexampled bitterness. The Londonderry regiment were kept waiting for stores which they never received. The Longfords had to march without blankets which had been despatched from Dublin, but were delayed owing to the canal being frozen. Other regiments probably had similar experiences.

Not very much had been done in advance by the authorities for the troops. The order of 12 November[64] says :

> As soon as orders shall be given for assembling the army, it will likewise be expected proper persons to be sent (sic) from the Commissaries department to the towns on the great roads within 20 or 30 miles of the place appointed for the army to collect, who must be instructed to provide bread, straw, cattle and fuel for the supply of the different corps on their march, and to render every assistance in their power to the officers sent forward by the regiment to prepare accommodations.

How far those who were to perform these difficult duties had actually been appointed is doubtful. Camden, in a despatch of

*In 1813 the Armagh had 66 men who could read and write, and the officer who records it,[63] seems to think, even at that date, this number was creditable.

10 January, speaks[65] of the meat provided by the Commissary in many places not having been consumed, owing to the private hospitality offered. But a commanding officer seems to convey that his unit ‘ had not had any commisarys or supplyd any rations except some whiskey ’;[66] and the system, whatever it was, can hardly have been efficient. There was, however, by an order of the adjutant general on 25 December, a special issue of spirits—to meet the severity of the weather. This seems to have been limited, in terms, to the men ‘ upon their route ’. Later from Bandon, there is the report : ‘ The troops [i.e. in quarters] are very well fed, plenty of good beef and potatoes daily and now here and some other places they receive, as I understand, a glass of spirits. Sick we have none ’.[67] It seems the case that little sickness resulted from the exposure on the march and afterwards in the improvised quarters for which barns and also churches were used.

In the main, the system at this crisis, and afterwards, was that each unit was left to provide for itself ; the troops had to live on the land and on the people of it, legitimately, if so it might be, and often illegitimately, when hunger would not be denied. It is hardly fair, therefore, to take a very strict view of some acts committed which were oppressive and indefensible. There was no higher military formation and practically no common services. What could the officers, who are much blamed, do ? We have seen (p. 81) a colonel himself buying for his men carcasses of meat in the Dublin market. Nothing of course like this market would normally be available.

It is probable that, if the officers failed to concern themselves about the messing of the men, it would be from inexperience rather than carelessness or inhumanity. It was of course not a question of moving from station to station at each of which there would be a contract for the supply of bread and meat. What seems to have fallen to the officers was not merely supervision of messing, and hearing and investigation of complaints, but catering on a more or less large scale ; and this, certainly was not always done. Consequently the men sometimes, as we know, went hungry. Difficulties were increased for everyone when there was a shortage of currency[68] in the places where the militia were—another reason accounting in some cases for arbitrary exactions of food.

Pelham, writing in September 1797, expressly says that the publicans did not furnish meals for the soldiers on the march as they did in England, though on the route between Dublin and Cork, during the Bantry crisis, the inns seem to have been open at all hours of the night.[69] It is not difficult to picture the plight of the relatively inexperienced militia regiments during these few hectic days. But people of all classes enthusiastically set themselves to help. 'Every cottage', says a newspaper,[70] 'shared its last potatoes with the troops and every hand was busy in erecting cabins for protecting them against the most violent rain and storms we ever remember'. This refers to Cork, where 'the heart and hand of the people were in the common cause'. The yeomanry were everywhere on duty, and gave help in various ways. Kildare was on the route of the western column marching from Dublin; here a fund was started, with an appeal to the opulent inhabitants, for 'relief of our brave defenders', whose shoes, stockings, etc. were already destroyed without their having the power of replacing them.[71] Footwear was a great difficulty. Pelham mentions having ordered an agent in Cork 'to buy up all the shoes in Cork' before any combination could be established.[72] At Carlow, which was on the route of the eastern column from Dublin a committee provided accommodation for the troops; large collections[73] were made to provide necessaries, and people voluntarily brought in food from the country. At Naas several of the inhabitants left their houses in order that the men might be lodged, and where no straw was available for the horses, brought 'grain unthreshed out of their haggards and gave it to the soldiers'.

In Dublin a printed bulletin[74] of the news, was distributed within an hour of its arrival. But the city remained perfectly quiet. 'Notwithstanding the holidays and consequent idleness of the lower classes of people, there has appeared no disposition to riot. The better and upper classes betray no marks of fear or alarm'.[75] Still the sudden moving of the militia left distress behind. An allowance however of 4d. a day to the wife of each non-commissioned officer, drummer and private was authorized on 25 December. They were not allowed to march (as they normally did on change of station) with their husbands. At Loughlinstown, on the sudden departure of the troops, 'upwards of 1,000 females, the wives and children of the soldiery, remained behind and in apparent want of food and support. When the lord lieutenant heard of this, he ordered them to be supplied with bread and necessaries'.[76] In Limerick[77] a considerable sum was subscribed in one day for the wives and children of the militia. In 1794, the ladies of Ireland had had a flannel drawers fund for the soldiers (which the wits of Dublin said testified to their abhorrence of '*sans culotte*' principles) and this winter of 1796 a flannel waitscoat fund was started with a distributing depôt and Lady Camden at the head.[78]

It was the same everywhere—one of those moments perhaps rare in Ireland, when all were working together in harmony and with one purpose. The threatened invasion, as in the case of the Great Armada in 1588, was defeated largely by the elements;

afflavit Deus et dissipantur; the troops, cordially aided by the people,[79] were lying ready to co-operate; the French, we are told, had not 'the most distant chance of getting assistance from the inhabitants'.[80] There is no record of anything like refusal to march.

'At the sound of invasion, the generous spirit of native loyalty filled the hearts of all men, and returning kindness seemed to have extinguished all bitter recollections. All wounds were healed: all grievances consigned to oblivion: we tendered our lives and fortunes to protect those of even the most prejudiced amongst them....I saw the peasant and the peer, the parson, the proctor and the farmer, all mingling together in the ranks, and breathing one common resolution, that of repelling the invader. All lent or tendered their horses and their cars to draw the ammunition, the artillery, and the baggage of our army. Who does not remember, that the poorest amongst us, in that rigorous season, gave their beds, their butter, the milk of their cows, their all, for the refreshment and support of our marching troops? They carried the firelocks and the knapsacks of our fatigued soldiers; they cheered them with songs and smiling welcome and their mirthful alacrity presaged, and truly, the speedy discomforture of invasion'.[81]

The Lord Chancellor expressly stated in the house of lords (January 1797) that, from Dublin to Bantry, not a single man had deserted.[82]

On this high note the year 1796 ended in Ireland.

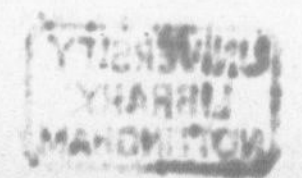

VII

The Year 1797

In the year 1797 the centre of political strain tends to get established in the north of Ireland, where, in internal affairs, problems group themselves separately to such an extent that the authorities in Dublin, in their efforts at maintaining domestic order, come to recognize the military forces there as constituting in effect a 'separate army'. Already in January the duke of York,[1] who seems to have maintained a close interest in the military affairs of Ireland, comments that Lake had a harder job in the north than Dalrymple in the south; and throughout the year the bulk of Pelham's military correspondence is with the generals in the north—Knox (Dungannon), lord Cavan (Londonderry), and (principally of course) Lake. In this correspondence the Irish militia are a preoccupation; the *Northern Star* is a thorn in Lake's flesh; and the *Press* (first published in Dublin in September 1797) is firing at the militiaman such questions as 'did you enter into the service of government for the purpose of murdering your countrymen?' On the other side, the term 'rebellion' is used as applying already to the conditions existing in Ulster in the summer and autumn of this year. General Knox, an apostle of 'Thorough', even in April, puts forward[2] a paper giving 'the regular gradation of measures which appear to [him] to be necessary to subdue the province'.

Parliament early turned its attention to measures to keep up the strength of the force. A special committee (on which Castlereagh and Foster were the leading spirits) was appointed (3 February) 'to enquire into the present militia laws'. A few days later it put forward a series of ten resolutions.[3] In the previous session Pelham had introduced two bills which made no further progress; one for regulating the mode of selection by ballot and the other for amending and consolidating into one the different acts relating to the militia.[4] These ten resolutions probably reproduced the substance of Pelham's first bill: they deal exclusively with the ballot machinery. A new general ballot was one of the two ways available of renewing the strength of the force and it was no doubt necessary to have this machinery in order in case it was needed. Anyhow, the militia purists (of whom Foster was one) would not willingly have let it fall into desuetude. In fact, during 1797, the ballot was very little resorted to at all, but the revised provisions for operating it in the militia act of this year are lengthy; they are stated to supersede the provisions of former acts.

Actually, the militia-renewal problem was tackled not by use of the ballot but through re-enlistment. On the same day that the ten resolutions referred to were accepted a committee of the whole house presented a separate set of eleven resolutions;[5] both became embodied (i.e. so far as was technically necessary) in the militia act. Four made provision for militia families (see chapter XVII) and five others dealt with re-enlistment. The proposals were: re-enlistment before the current attestation period expired, to serve during the present war and for two months after; a bounty not exceeding three guineas if time shall expire before 29/9/97 and not exceeding two guineas if between that date and 24/6/98; expenditure incurred by the collectors to be 'reimbursed by the county'. Dublin Castle issued a circular to the units on 9 February; this was based directly on a relevant financial resolution and dealt with the prospective outflow in 1798 as well as with that to take place in 1797. The estimated cost of these re-enlistments was: for 5,000 due to go before 29/9/97, the sum of £22,750 and for 3,000 to go before 24/6/98, the sum of £10,237.[6]

How far did the men in fact accept re-enlistment? As already indicated, there was no breakdown involving recourse to the ballot. The inference is that re-enlistment took place on a wide scale. But there were hesitations. In the Downshire regiment there was a feeling, as regards the treatment of the families,[7] that men in other corps had got something which was denied to the Downshire. The grievance operated as a deterrent to re-enlisting; the commanding officer wishes to God it was over 'for at present we have nothing but drunkenness and debauchery which it is impossible to prevent without putting a stop to the whole business'. The lord lieutenant insisted that the regiments should be kept complete, and when in the Armagh the men lord Gosford wanted refused to re-enlist he was then informed that 'the regiment must be completed from the county in the manner directed by the act of parliament'. Whether this happened does not appear, but in the Downshire there was recourse to the ballot. At the end of September there was the longest assize[8] known in the county, and there were complaints about the charges presented for the militia; this feeling had come out in debate in the house of commons.[9] Castlereagh was one of those present and, after some plain speech, 'was asked to explain some parts of the last act', but he replied with much *sangfroid*[10] that, as he had hoped lord Downshire would have been at the assizes and have taken the measure upon himself, ' he had not made himself master of the subject so as to venture an opinion about it '. Lord Downshire's agent, who reports this incident, which is an interesting sidelight, thought that Castlereagh did not want to take up the gauntlet on behalf of certain regiments which had in general opinion been guilty of unsoldierlike behaviour.

By the 1 October the lists of names in co. Down had been gone through and the drawings were about to begin. By November, about 100 ' drawn men and substitutes ' had been sent off to the regiment. The commanding officer[10] states that the county still owed the regiment a number of men and that he was going the round of the county again ; the last drawing was to take place on 20 November and following days at seven places. The first round had gone off without a repetition of the troubles which had occurred in 1793. The commanding officer said ' there never was a finer sett of fellows ever joined ', and Downshire's agent says : ' I attest them every day—strapping dogs in general '. On 26 November, there were ' still enough men owing us by the insurers and parishes to complete, which we will get '.

This goes to show that county Down was extensively balloted and things went harmoniously, but one cannot conclude that balloting was in this year common. Lord Downshire was one of the militia purists[11] and he preferred rather than otherwise to have a ballot ; but this attitude was not general. There is however an almost complete absence of newspaper references to ballot proceedings or to re-enlistment. The Dublin city[12] in July were advertising for ' loyal and spirited young fellows ', promising privates ' every comfort and accommodation from the attention of their officers ', and dwelling upon the provision made by parliament for the families and upon the recent increase of pay (p. 111) ; it was also pointed out that the privates were ' in a much better situation than most classes of working tradesmen ', but at the end of April, a draw had taken place in several of the parishes of Dublin.[13] Details of the sums presented for militia purposes at county assizes still exist ;[14] they show in several instances large expenditure on reimbursement of re-enlistment bounties. In these cases it may be accepted that the personnel was renewed by continuance rather than by reprovision. In many cases other means probably had to be used. The two methods available have been described in chapter V, viz. the voluntary assessment by parishes of themselves, in the sum of £6 for each man apportioned on them or the forced levy of £10 for each man. Illustrations were there given of the operation of these arrangements in 1795. In 1797 those methods of meeting the regional liabilities were again freely resorted to, and, so far as this was done, the ballot was not used. In addition there was still the liability of the *county*, as distinct from the subdivision parish or townland, to the (continuing) fine of £5 annually in respect of each continuing deficiency. (for Londonderry case, see chap. V, p. 74).

No returns are now available of the progress or aggregate result of the re-enlistment operation, but there are no laments about its having been a failure. Such newspaper references as are to be found point the other way. The general evidence is that no appreciable difficulty occurred; the strength of the militia on 1 February 1797 is given as 18,219, and on 1 February, 1798, as 22,917. Beyond the addition of one company in each of the Kildare and Carlow battalions the total establishment of the militia remained for the year ending 31/3/1798 what it had been for the year ended 31/3/1797.

But the recruiting effort of 1797 was not limited to re-enlisting, or, alternatively, raising new men—to fill the standard establishment. In a despatch[15] (January) reviewing the position after Bantry, Camden announced his intention of augmenting 'those regiments of militia which are complete within 10 men of their complement, to 100 men per company'; and the Journals[16] show an appropriation of £113,425 for augmentation of 147 companies or 4,704 persons (i.e. one lieutenant, one sergeant, thirty privates per company). In debates during February both Grattan and Castlereagh supported the augmentation. It appears to have been the first 'discretionary augmentation' under the act of 1795 and to have been applied in 18 units.[17] There is no return of the results but Tyrone and Monaghan were quickly completed to the full 100 men per company;[18] other counties are known[19] to have carried it out. It was financed on a grant of 3 guineas a man from public funds;[20] the parliamentary assurance, given in 1795 (chapter V), that discretionary augmentations were not to be at the cost of the counties was at this time renewed.[21]

Early in January 1747 the commanding officer of a militia unit writes:

> 'We have had a wonderful escape. Such conduct damps us all, and, if not changed, must destroy the country. The generals have expressed their opinions very openly and had a memorial ready to publish in case of the French landing to clear themselves for not being able to make any resistance. Everyone here [Birr] is of opinion they will attempt another invasion; if they they do and we do not beat them the fault will not rest with the soldiers'.[22]

Recriminations usually follow all military episodes like that of Bantry. In the city of Cork there had been consternation[23] at the idea that the authoritues might abandon the city and make the great stand at Kilworth, but the city's committee on invasion were generous in praise of the 'good order, alacrity and ardour that pervaded and animated our regular and militia forces ', and they trusted this would ' recommend them to the particular favour of their soverign '.[24] But this favour was not forthcoming for the militia on this, nor on any subsequent occasion ; and when, later on, it was suggested by Cornwallis that some indication of royal interest would be a help,[25] the suggestion fell on stony ground. It appears that the duke of York, at the instigation of lord Moira, contemplated sending thanks for the ' military perfection ' to which the militia commanders had brought their regiments and their laudable attention to discipline.[26] But the nearest the force seems ever to have got to royal favour was the Prince Regent's description of the south Corks—the ' long Corks ' as they were nicknamed—as the finest Irish regiment he had seen. This was, however, at a much later date, in 1813.

Reaction after Bantry was not unnatural. The militia had not been blooded as they had hoped to be ; and they made a relatively tame return to their old quarters and to that emptiness of military routine which then, as at other times, afforded favourable ground for the spread of ' dangerous ' ideas. At Dublin Castle the lord lieutenant took stock and, without delay, drew morals. A general order (24 January) (which was based on a letter[27] from the lord lieutenant to the commander in chief) begins by expressing thanks to the ' generals, officers and soldiers who marched with so much alacrity towards the enemy ', and refers to ' the late sudden call '. It also says that his excellency desires that ' the army may be formed into brigades and that each general commanding a brigade may remain constantly with it ', and explains why he should do this, i.e. to get the regiments together. It makes no specific reference to the militia. There are some caustic words on the officer-absence difficulty : ' by hastily joining his regiment in a moment of threatened danger ', [many officers had gone off from Dublin on the 25 December to join ; some had failed to do so]' an officer may indeed save his own character from reprehension but, as the returns of officers present with the regiment on the 1st and 14th of the month were intended to ensure his continuance at quarters all the intermediate time, being present merely on those two days is a palpable evasion of the order. Even the bravery of the soldier, unless amenable to orders and on every occasion under control, is more likely to turn to his own disadvantage than the public good '. This in tone is a little akin to Abercromby's notorious general order of 26 February, 1798 (see page 117) and recalls Wellington's castigations.[28]

On the same day was issued an order for the assembly of the light infantry companies. Simultaneously, or shortly after, there was issued a distribution of the troops into groups or brigades. Both measures were, at first at all events, unpalatable to the militia colonels : there is mention of a ' considerable indisposition on the part of some of the militia colonels to the idea of brigading the army ', and to ' some of the colonels talking a most mischievous language '[29] about detachment of the light companies. The opposition to the latter was not, however, carried as far as objection to a similar scheme was carried by the English militia colonels who, in 1799, represented that ' the pride of the county at large, at whose expense the regiment was raised, is mortified by the transfer which, in destroying the distinct existence of the regiment, annihilates with it the merit of comparative excellence '.[30] Previously the insistence of the English colonels had caused reference of the matter to the law officers of the crown who did not support the contention that detaching the light companies was illegal. One colonel however persisted that if his flank companies were ordered away he would provoke a court martial. This opposition was in the English militia but it illustrates a difficulty which was continually arising in the Irish militia, i.e. difference of view between the militia colonels and the administration. Both Camden and Cornwallis were quite aware of the necessity for ' managing ' a force like the militia.[31]

The ' brigading ' probably made little difference to the militia. The idea of ' supplying the experience in the militia colonels and interior economy in the regiments of militia by brigading them under general officers ' which Pelham later (September)[32] described as the object, was scarcely realized. The units comprising brigades were never exercised together. Camden, in October, said of the troops in Ireland : ' They are now brigaded but without system '.[33] Indeed, it seems probable that, for the units, being brigaded amounted only to having a different address to which to send the periodical returns of the 1st and 14th of each month. Pelham made a tour in August. He was very disheartened : he found ' a determined opposition to the introduction of any kind of discipline or system ',[34] and, reported[35] to the lord lieutenant that he had gathered from the different generals that the militia regiments were very much neglected by their officers ; that the accounts were in general ill-kept, that the men were mostly strong and active, obedient to the orders of the generals, though they did not much regard their regimental officers.

The general order of 24 January required ' each regiment to send its system of regimental orders and economy to the adjutant general's office from which a judgment may be formed of the different degrees of attention which have been paid to the regiments and a uniformity of discipline established for the future '. This was probably an embarrassing requirement. One commanding officer writes to his colonel and asks[36] what answer he shall give 'about our standing orders and system of discipline and interior economy'. There is nothing to show either that the statements required were in fact furnished, or that, having been furnished, they were examined and new regulations, either particular or general, issued. Other measures taken early in 1797, and presumably regarded as giving effect to lessons learned, were the issue of two light six-pounders to most of the militia units, arrangements about horsing the guns, and the detachment of about 320 sergeants, corporals and privates to the regiment of artillery 'to do the duty of gunners'.[37]

Most, if not all, of the military measure taken after and as the result of Bantry, were directed to the contingency of invasion. But the trial which was coming was to be primarily from within and was less easily provided against. Pertinent is the question: could the contingency of a well-organized insurrection have been competently met in advance at all and were the military authorities at the Royal Hospital—an English staff acting through an almost exclusively Irish instrument—the people to grapple with a problem essentially more political than military? What was going to happen was to depend upon factors normally beyond the ken of the commander-in-chief. Had it been a question of invasion being certain, or almost certain, for some practically certain date, the Irish militia, and other forces available, might perhaps have been prepared for it intensively. And it is probable that the officers of the force would have responded; a difficulty in military training is the unreality of what may never come at all and the sense of this.

A militia officer in January 1797 recorded his opinion that 'having spirit enough to meet the enemy in the field is by many people thought sufficient for an officer; in my mind it is the least part of his duty'.[38] Not all the militia officers were of this opinion; and many of them had, as we know, legitimate distractions arising from other spheres of public service. Preparation for the certainty of an invasion might have been possible, if difficult; but preparation against what would come, if it came at all, suddenly and inconsequently, was, in an ordinary military sense, impossible. The military authorities in Dublin can hardly be blamed if actually there were few and insufficient preparations in advance for the insurrection of 1798. Whatever was done—and it took the century old form of collecting, under threats, the arms in the people's hands—was done mainly in the unruly north. But it was not in the north that the brunt generally, and the insurrectionary brunt in particular, came. The generals in the north made their views perfectly clear: their specific was to clear out all the Irish militia units and substitute fencibles;[39] some of them would even have confined the choice to English fencibles because they feared

Scottish fencibles might have had too much sympathy with the Presbyterians.[40] But the Irish government could not move the militia about freely in the way the generals would have liked; they had to reckon with the views of the colonels and they had not then the case which they were able to urge in the summer of the next year for asking reinforcements from England.

Beyond the calling in of arms—manufacture of *pikes* could still continue a thriving industry—no precise steps were taken to meet insurrection on a wide scale. There do not seem to have been any special dispositions of the militia units. Those which had been strung along the south-west coast remained there. At the time of the great sedition incident in the south-west in June (in which regular units were also involved)[41] the militia units which were at and near Bandon were the Westmeath, Galway, Meath, Dublin county, Sligo, Roscommon, Limerick county, Wexford, Fermanagh, Leitrim and Waterford—eleven units or nearly one-third of the whole of the militia. This militia concentration was of course contra-invasion provision and in accordance with the policy adopted when the yeomanry were instituted. But maintaining so large a force of militia in those relatively remote regions, where they were left with ample time for dabbling in politics and dallying with those who were there to work upon simple souls, was not a contribution to coping with the internal troubles which were coming. The rest of the militia was scattered about in different parts, primarily on home-protection duty, much as it had been before the yeomanry was instituted. The Tyrone, in October, were at Tarbert, but had detachments at Killarney, Castle Island, Tralee and Dingle; for a review these were not brought in; that shows the degree of their detachment.

Grumblings in the militia about pay conditions seem to have been rarely heard. During the early part of the year 1797, apart from the satisfaction or otherwise of the militiaman with the amount he received, payments of what, under the existing scale, was due must have been often in arrear. There was a banking crisis in both the north and the south. Carhampton[42] on 2 March, reported that ' some of the regiments [in Cork] are absolutely at this moment without a shilling subsistence '; and in June, generals Lake, Nugent and the earl of Cavan were all in want of cash.[43] General Loftus (9 June) reports from Cork that the Wexford were without the money to discharge billets and to pay money due to officers; the Roscommon and the Waterford were to move the next week, and he hoped that the necessary funds would be available. Here was obviously the possibility of discontent. The Spithead mutineers in April had demanded better conditions of service, i.e. fair wages, decent and sufficient food, etc.; and in the month of May, suddenly, the pay was increased. In Ireland no overt demand followed this concession though this was represented to Pelham as a probable consequence by general Knox. Pelham realized that treating differently the British and Irish soldier made for sedition. In June the Irish parliament voted over £250,000 for augmenting pay ; the infantry private henceforth was to get 1/- a day and the subaltern officers an additional 1/- a day. A speech of the lord lieutenant referred to this as a 'judicious augmentation....which must render their situation [i.e. that of the regular and militia forces] highly comfortable' and as being 'at once a seasonable and honourable acknowledgment of their steadiness and loyalty'. The duke of York in London was pleased that action had been taken before discontent shewed itself and had thus appeared a voluntary act.

Prior to this step being taken there is no symptom in the militia of general or organized bread-and-butter discontent, though such feeling is more or less endemic in all military as well as other organizations and attempts had in fact been made to work it up. There is a leaflet[44] headed 'Dublin Garrison' and dated Dublin, 29 April, which after a temperate statement about 'difficulties the soldiers have laboured under from their low pay' and reference to the 'very severe garrison duty' in Dublin and the assertion that they 'the soldiers of the garrison of Dublin are not inferior to any body of men in loyalty to our king and country', announces a 'stay-in' strike—the determination 'to remain in our present quarters until [our moderate and just claims] are settled to our satisfaction'. Finally every regiment throughout the kingdom 'is urged to assist in obtaining this just and reasonable demand'. This Dublin lead was from and to the army generally in Ireland and not specially to the militia. The leaflets were distributed in Cork, and also in Sligo, where they produced a demonstration of loyalty in the market-place on the part of a portion of the north Cork militia. In one of the court martials (see next paragraph) evidence was given of militiamen being taken into a house and asked if they were 'going to stand out for a shilling a day, as all soldiers were going to do'.[45]

But for meeting an insurrectionary outbreak what mattered was not so much pay conditions or military proficiency as the morale of the units. As regards military proficiency, the Irish militia could hardly, in the nature of things, be anything but a rough soldiery, but there was no corresponding bar to the exhibition of courage and steadiness in the task for which they had suffered themselves to be enrolled. Throughout 1797 the political situation kept deteriorating. It was a year of strain and mutinies. Much has been made of the mutiny incidents in the militia. In some four or five of the regiments, men were, after court martial, sentenced to death. Correspondence of the period refers to widespread seduction and perfidy in general terms such as these employed by general Lake on 30 April in a letter[46] to Pelham : 'I have every reason to apprehend that all [sic] the regiments of militia have vast [sic] numbers United ' (i.e. sworn as adherents of the United Irishmen). But, although in England and in certain circles in Ireland there was almost ghoulish satisfaction in propagating news of sedition incidents, no such incidents are on record anywhere in connection with the majority of units. Reports were often started which rested on little foundation. Pelham records someone's ' strong suspicion of disaffection in some of the militia regiments and particularly the - - - - -'.[47] Investigation showed that the allegation against the regiment was entirely unfounded. Lord Cavan, who commanded at Londonderry, formally contradicted[48] in the London newspapers, grossly misinformed accounts, attributed to him, reflecting on ' the conduct of that highly honourable, loyal and disciplined body of men—the militia of Ireland '.

Throughout 1797 there was in progress a struggle for the soul of the Irish militia. The contention was between Irishmen and Irishmen and not between Irishmen and aliens. To a large extent, as will appear, this predominantly catholic-mauned force held the keys of the situation. The private soldiers, as already shewn, were plied with drink in the public houses which they frequented. In leaflet and in the columns of the press, they were the targets of the written word ; they were targets also of the whispered word.

What were the reactions to all this and how did it leave the militia for the imminent troubles ? There are two tests : what was the showing made in 1798 and what is the positive evidence of the reactions in 1797 to the sapping and mining of ' loyalty ' which continually went on ? The former point will be dealt with in the next chapter. On the latter there is no evidence that ' seditious ' efforts held back the re-enlisting though the time-expiring men must have been under pressure in that sense. Probably the militiaman did not read to any great extent such papers as the ' Press ' the possession of which is stated by a ' non-commissioned officer ', writing in that paper under that pseudonym, to have meant ' very little short of a thousand lashes '. They were not, however, by any means ignorant of the currents of opinion. In this year 1797 there were numerous demonstrations of ' loyalty '. In Ireland, as in England, introduction of ' seditious ' handbills into barracks was at this time not uncommon. At Fethard on 16 May, the drummers and privates of the north Mayo and Limerick city light companies, in a reply to one of these, expressed their detestation and horror, and another reply, signed at Waterford on 19 May by the sergeant major of

Limerick county at the desire of the sergeants, corporals, drummers and privates, expresses horror of such diabolical schemes; their determination to bring to punishment 'any person presuming to tamper with our loyalty in any shape whatever; their offer of a reward of 20 guineas to any person who shall make known and prosecute to conviction any traitor so offending'. There is a manuscript record still existing which sets out that the n.c.o.'s, drummers and privates of the 3rd light infantry battalion published 20 May a declaration of their loyalty and offered a reward of 25 guineas 'to any person who shall bring or cause to be brought before the commanding officer any persons guilty of endeavouring to alienate and delude the friends of the people and army from their allegiance'.[49] On 10 May, the n.c.o.'s, drummers and privates of the Antrim, on parade at Dublin, offered a reward to any soldier for private information which would lead to discovery. It was not mainly the militias of the north which made these demonstrations; a large majority of the whole number are recorded as having asserted in this way their sentiments. The resolutions passed were usually on the same lines and most of them in the month of May.

One may speculate how the apparent unanimity came about. To some extent it may have been a case of 'keeping step with England', because there also these resolutions seem to have been passed.[50] Very similar unanimity was shewn later in the year in making contributions to the fund for the widows and orphans of the men who fell under lord Duncan, and, next year, to the fund for carrying on the war. Usually these contributions were of one or two days' pay in the case of the lower ranks. These combined demonstrations were possibly made under some pressure from the officers; if this were the case, it need not be reckoned to their discredit, more especially as the general criticism of them is that they influenced their men too little rather than too much. There was a militia officers' club which had meetings from time to time. At these a common course of action on current points of interest would no doubt be arranged. But individual regiments could hardly have been under much centralized pressure. Sometimes the suggestions for a demonstration of loyalty are known to have come from the rank and file; and in several cases it was in terms limited to those ranks. Importance was at the time attached to these manifestations: *à propos* the resolutions passed by the Tyrone and Londonderry in garrison at Limerick it is remarked that they 'should do away with the idea broached by incendiaries that no dependance could be placed in case of danger on the Irish militia'.[51] There was nothing hole and corner about these actions: they were in fact definitely a challenge: for instance the north Cork, as already recorded (page 111) 'publicly declared their loyalty in the market-place of Sligo '. All the units which formally declared themselves—and it seems probable that practically all did—thus tied themselves, if pledges meant anything, to a certain course of action in eventualities daily becoming more definite.

Some of the colonels, however, had searchings of heart at the way things were going. A full record[52] exists of the doubts and difficulties felt by lord Bellamont, colonel of the Cavan. His main trouble was the proclamation issued by general Lake in the northern district (13/3/1797). The Cavan had passed two years ' within the narrow compass from Newry to Carrickfergus '; he had pressed for it to be moved ' upon the general principle of preventing the consequence of habitual social intercourse in a disturbed country '; and now he had to act in execution of a proclamation to the legality of which he could not subscribe. Obviously lord Camden's only course was to accept his tendered resignation. But the incident illustrates both the difficulties inherent in the problem of quartering the militia and also the even greater difficulties for a lord lieutenant arising from the dual position occupied by the colonels : lord Bellamont in his letter of resignation, says that ' constant attendance at headquarters would have been to [him] the highest indulgence if [his] necessary attention of matters of more extensive and more pressing public concern had not rendered [his] absence from the regiment indispensably necessary '; he had in fact been absent since August 1795. He had not necessarily exercised preference wrongly ; in 1799 lord Granard was told officially that ' his parliamentary duty is paramount to every other consideration ',[53] but holding the office of sheriff was not considered sufficient reason for an officer to take leave of absence. There was in May a report that Mr Conolly (Londonderry) and also lord Ormonde (Kilkenny) and lord O'Neill (Antrim) had resigned their commands but in each case there was a *démenti*.

The Monaghan were one of the militia units which in 1797 had some of its men shot. This was a strong regiment and had a good reputation. Its history illustrates so well the virtues and defects of the militia units that it is worth giving. It is a story of high spirit and energy, or, as it might conceivably be put, occasional or even habitual *trop de zéle*. They had been quartered in Belfast, the centre of political free thought, from June 1796. In the May following they were in trouble. At a parade specially called, seventy men came forward[54] and declared themselves sworn United. Four were convicted by court martial and were, with great solemnity and publicity, shot on 16 May ; the rest were pardoned by the lord lieutenant. This was announced to them on parade by Lake when they declared themselves contrite ;

'they would give the French a drubbing whenever they met them'. On 1 June Lake reports that the people of Belfast are trying to get the Monaghan militia sent away, but he is against this 'as the Monaghan are determined to keep the Belfast people in order', and, a few days later, he tells Pelham 'they have this town in complete order and are most useful and much to be depended upon'. Still, a few days later, Pelham is remarking to Lake that 'our friends the Monaghan' were a little too active over public houses; he is no doubt passing on a complaint which someone had dropped into his ear. Previously, in May, the Monaghan (not acting alone, as most accounts suggest, but together with 'a large party of the artillery')[55] had, acting apparently upon orders,* wrecked the offices and destroyed the type of the *Northern Star*. They probably knew that this was desired by Lake: he had in fact, on 16 April, written to Pelham: 'May I be allowed to seize and burn the whole apparatus?'[56] But the Monaghan had a reason of their own for not liking this paper: it was considered to have corrupted men of the regiment and done damage[57] to its reputation; it had, not surprisingly, refused to give publicity, in the form it was submitted, to the resolution of loyalty which they had passed.

In London the government were apparently, towards the end of the year, expecting attack from the opposition upon the conduct of the army in Ireland; and Camden sent to ministers a report about what he calls 'the supposed atrocities which have been practised by the military'.[58] The affair of the Monaghan and the *Northern Star* is one of some half a dozen incidents (only two of which concerned the militia) on which he comments. In referring to it he says: 'To have severely punished the soldiers when they were required to act with spirit would have been very dangerous'. He acknowledges the 'dreadful state of the country' and he urges that this 'made it indispensable to take strong measures and to employ the military without waiting for the forms attendant on their acting in quieter times'. Pelham[59] tells a correspondent that he believed that 'no army ever behaved better under similar circumstances' and that 'no army was ever placed in exactly the same situation'; and Camden says: 'In the sort of warfare we have carried on, it is wonderful that so few real grievances were to be complained of'.

That Abercromby should replace Carhampton as commander-in-chief, had already been decided[60] in London by the beginning of October. Carhampton had taken badly a general report on

*The sergeant major of the Monaghan declared to the young men in the office when the military first entered it—there were two attacks—'Don't blame me, boys, for what we are going to do; we are only executing the order of our officers'.

the state of the army which Pelham had made to the lord lieutenant after a tour in the south during August. His knowledge of Ireland was greater than that of most, if not all, of the other generals, but he was not seeing eye to eye with some of the more thoroughgoing of them about the militia. General Knox's ' sack the lot ' policy, not acceptable to the government, has already been referred to. In a letter of 19 April[61] in which he comments on the difference between the powers granted to general Lake and full martial law, he remarks that ' lord Carhampton does not seem sensible of the dangers of employing the militia in the north ' and says that hardly a day passes that does not bring him an account of the Dublin city militia regiment having become United. ' But lord Carhampton ', he proceeds, ' will not believe it '. Early in May Carhampton reversed an order of general Knox that the parties of militia at Charlemont fort (sent there to learn the gun exercise) should go back to their regiments. He was disposed to accept the avowals of ' loyalty ' which were (as already stated) at this time being generally made by the militia ; general Knox complains (14 May) that ' lord Carhampton says that the militia in general are to be depended upon '. The event shows that Carhampton read the militia more accurately than did general Knox. This makes it interesting to speculate how things would have turned out if the former had remained in the chief command. His apparently greater understanding of the militia did not mean that he was himself inclined to half-measures with insurgent elements. His conduct when he had gone to ' pacify ' Connaught is is evidence of this and in May 1797 he ran a near risk of being killed : as a result of a plot against his life two men were put to death.[62]

On 2nd December, sir Ralph Abercromby was appointed commander-in-chief. The question, for the purposes of this book, is whether the effect of his famous pronouncement has been to create a fair picture of the Irish militia and whether the action which he took made the Irish militia better, or worse, for meeting insurrection and invasion. His military experience and his proper passion for military order were great but did he contribute anything to the treatment of the problems which had inveterately perplexed his predecessors? These he diagnosed under three heads : (*a*) yeomanry only to be employed for duties of police, so as to release the troops ; (*b*) detachments to be gathered in to regimental headquarters and army concentrated as far as possible so as to be ready in case of invasion ; (*c*) military, when inevitably employed in aid of civil power, to observe the bounds of legality.[63] Abercromby pressed for these not hitherto unadvocated reforms but he was not in Ireland long enough, even if he had the temperament and the right instinct for approach, to carry them into effect.

Did he then contribute anything, through personality, to build up the morale which he seems to have considered (and in a situation undoubtedly confused and difficult, probably was) dangerously low? This is mainly a matter of his words and not of his actions, because, in a few short months, personality could not, in the then conditions, have much direct impact. His main activities consisted of a tour in the south and then of a tour in the north. In between these on 26 February 1798 he issued the order which is what, so far as Ireland is concerned, is recalled by his, historically, justifiably famous name.

The order as issued—the last three paragraphs are usually omitted*—is printed as appendix VII. Carhampton's order issued after Bantry (page 107) may be considered more scathing. But, in addition to criticism, it had something in it to edify the morale: it recognized *some* merit and it caused no furore. Two things are to be noted about the Abercromby order: its terms cover *all* parts of the army in Ireland; and, secondly, what it says has in later times been generally quoted as a stigma attaching exclusively, or, at all events, peculiarly, to the Irish militia. But for 'licentiousness' the generals, as Abercromby states, had responsibility. It is not unfair to say that what the militia (and other troops) were the generals had made them, or allowed them to become.[64] In action such as that against the *Northern Star* they did not simply act on their own initiative. It was not the case that generals were in number insufficient for the necessary supervisory duties. Lord Buckingham,[65] writing in July 1798, says there were then 43 actually serving in Ireland (even though he says that he believed they were 'the worst in Europe'). It is however necessary to remember that the great county magnates who were at the head of the militia corps were perhaps not very easily controlled. They were prone to regard their colonelcies as a sort of personal freehold and as an inviolable appanage of their county state. As territorial magnates they did not suffer generals very gladly. Some of the letters sent to them from Dublin castle are rather cringing in character. The dual authority seems a weakness of the militia system as developed in England, and, afterwards, in Ireland. But still, whatever criticisms may be fairly made of the colonels, generals had ample powers and it is not fair simply to put the strictures of Abercromby by as not to their address at all and to attribute all the trouble to the original sin of the Irish character.

The terms of the order cover not only the militia, but also the regular troops and the yeomanry. Reference to it will show that the only particular part of the army mentioned is not

*e.g. in lord Dunfermline's Life of Abercromby, 1861.

the militia but the regular cavalry (dragoon regiments). When the order was issued, the big people in Dublin quickly took sides; most of them ranged themselves against Abercromby, but not all. Chief amongst those who did not was Pelham. A detailed exposition of his attitude exists in his papers.[66] From this long document what is relevant here is that, in enumerating instances of licentiousness and want of discipline that have been brought to his notice, he sets out, in the first place, details of the irregularities which had occurred in the cavalry. Six regiments of cavalry assembled in camp at the Curragh were found to be 'perfectly ignorant of the new excercise'; there were 'irregularities in most of these regiments with regard to the feeding and buying of horses and the application of the savings upon these two heads'. Of one of the cavalry regiments he records that '365 horses were lost or died in the course of two years, notwithstanding that no glanders or epidemic disorder appeared to have prevailed in that regiment'. Another cavalry regiment was 'reported to be unfit for service'; in the same regiment within the same period 216 men died or deserted. Then he sums up (the document was intended for the duke of Portland, the secretary of state): 'I should think that if your grace gives credit to the cases I have mentioned you will agree with me in opinion on the state of the army and it will be unnecessary for me to detail the numberless irregularities in the regiments of militia'.

Normally, the expectation would be that regular troops should provide a standard for auxiliary troops. On Pelham's showing they did not at that time in Ireland. The word 'licentious' must not be read in a modern setting. It was then a common *epitheton ornans* of the word soldiery, and was often applied almost indiscriminately to all soldiers. That regular troops did not set a standard for the non-professionals would have shocked Abercromby then as it shocks military historians today.[67] Arguably it was an error of judgment to have launched his rather petulant epigram* at all. His contemporary, lord Bridport[68] knew a better way. Writing to Pitt about the Spithead mutiny, he says: 'I have always considered peevish words and hasty orders detrimental, and it has been my study not to utter the one or issue the other....I think it wiser to soothe than irritate disturbed and agitated minds'. No one can say that in Ireland in the winter 1797-8 minds were not both disturbed and agitated. Regrettably, the epigram was allowed by Cornwallis (who, incidentally,[69] said that Abercromby had been 'exceedingly wrong-headed') to become stereotyped as of sole application to the

*Running in Abercromby's mind may have been what lord North said of a list of generals placed before him: 'I don't know what effect they have on the enemy, but, by heaven, they frighten me'.

militia. His letter to Pitt[70] of 25 September 1798, may be quoted: 'A militia.....which Abercromby too justly described by saying that they were only formidable to their friends'. In modern times the sort of thing which is found is: 'his famous general order that the militia were far more dangerous to their friends than to their enemies'.**

Sir Ralph Abercromby continued in office as commander-in-chief, in somewhat embarrassed isolation, until the end of April. We need not stigmatize his action as 'incredibly foolish';[71] it is at least fair to say that the effect of it was rather to depress than to raise the morale of the militia. His order 'was universally circulated by the United Irishmen amongst their friends as an encouragement to them to proceed....and certainly no better encouragement could have been held out to them',[72] and a correspondent of Henry Dundas writes of his orders as 'calculated to invite the enemy to attempt the conquest of the island by holding out to him the prospect of an easy victory'.[73] The beginning of entirely overt insurrection was close at hand. This being the position the months of Abercromby's period of command can only be regarded as largely wasted.

**This is from the biography of Abercromby in the D.N.B., which also makes the inaccurate and inconsistent statement that 'the garrison of Ireland consisted nearly entirely of English and Scottish militia....'

VIII

Rebellion

ABERCROMBY was somewhat inclined to make light of the possibilities of grand scale rebellion. Camden in a letter[1] to Pelham (apparently of date April) says :—' he describes the rebellion as less formidable than we have in general construed it to be but this is an opinion which his political tenets which he professes very strongly, urge him to give, in order to justify his orders and his subsequent conduct and he knows not the extent of the conspiracy'. If Abercromby's general view of the prospect was as stated and if anyhow the steps that could be taken were limited, it does not surprise that during the early months of the year 1798 there was, in military circles generally, a spirit of 'business as usual'. Applications for leave from senior and other officers were still numerous.[2] In mid-April it was still proposed to hold next month the Maze[3] (co. Down) races; and the spring assizes were duly held.[4] Even later, what Burke calls 'the cramps and holdings of the state' were not seriously loosened. Beresford, Commissioner of Revenue, notes (1 June)[5] that 'what is most strange and extraordinary.... the revenue rises every week in a degree unknown' and again (11 June) 'the revenue is still rising at the rate of £20,000 a week'.[6]

The outflow from the militia of 9,000 time-expired men to take place down to June had been provided for in the 1797 session; after June there would be further outflow. Now it was a question of about 4,000. But Pelham did not, in a general statement on army matters on 1 February, refer to prospective loss of strength at all. On the other hand, he announced an increase of the militia establishment from the figure 22,698 at which it had stood since April 1796, to 26,634.[7] On 1 May Castlereagh explained the administration's proposal for dealing with the outflow of time-expired men; these were on the same lines as previously and were adopted the next day. The report of this speech[8] contains no explicit reference to the special circumstances of the time. The strength of the militia seems to have gone up from 18,219 on 1 February 1797 to 22,917 on 1 February 1798, and it was still only 22,356 on the same date in 1799.[9] If the augmentation of establishment was effective and if the outflow of 4,000 was prevented by re-enlistment, the strength should have increased ; on the debit side would be any loss arising from deaths in action. County returns[10] include charges for re-enlistment, most regiments probably re-enlisted their time-expired men more or less as completely as on the previous occasions. At all events, a circular was issued on 9 May[11] offering, to those entitled to discharge before 24 June 1799, a bounty and stating the duration of the re-enlistment period.

The militia strength during the year 1798 is obscure. No instructions for the increase of establishment can be traced. County machinery certainly did not break down entirely. Levying of money at the assizes for reimbursing re-enlistment bounties seems to have proceeded much as usual. But though at the end of August the Clare militia (and probably other counties likewise) had recruited heavily, no recruiting in the early part of the year when the trouble was brewing is recorded. The strength at which the force entered on the fighting was under 23,000 ; some confirmation of this is casual press references to 22,000 as the strength.

Another military step taken was an order (26 Feb.) that all officers should rejoin from leave. But this was a not infrequent order, though, even at the beginning of 1798, it was not unnecessary. General Hutchinson in the west urged the commanding officer of a militia regiment to mention to his colonel the urgent necessity for captains to rejoin their regiment ; he wanted them back before 11 February or others appointed. Camps were to take place generally throughout the kingdom ; Colonel Handfield, the new commissary general and an efficient officer, was indefatigable in preparing for them. There is no evidence of the militia or other troops having been redistributed. In April, the country was becoming very disturbed and the yeomanry were consulted about coming out on permanent duty[12] so as to admit of the concentration of the regulars and the militia. Some time in that month for the first time—previously they had only been employed as escorts and piquet guards at night and on such-like duties—the whole establishment (15,000 cavalry and 21,000 infantry) was placed, though possibly by degrees, on permanent duty and so remained in May and June ; they then returned to a normal occasional duty basis, but were again out on permanent duty after the affair at Castlebar (27 August).[13]

These early months of 1798 were the period in Ireland of widespread general contributions ‘ towards the exigencies of the state ’.[14] Newspapers commented that the soldiers were more forward in making these than were the clergy. The latter were possibly less subject to influence and pressure than the former. The contributions of the militia units (as well as of individuals, officers and men) were handsome and few stood out. A not unusual contribution from the non-commissioned officers, drummers and privates was seven days' pay. No doubt there was the pressure normally arising from a general impulse. It has been explained earlier how clannish the militia-men were. It was generally a case of '*mens omnibus una sequendi*' whether a comrade was being attacked by hostile elements, when there was certain to be a rally to form a common front of resistance, or whether it was a question of volunteering for service outside Ireland or of re-entering the militia service after the period, in 1802-3, of disembodiment. There was a cohesion not purely the product of county neighbourship (though the honour of the county may have been a factor). At the least, these contributions like the 'loyalty' resolutions, of 1797 (chap. VII), are evidence of what spirit animated the militia on the eve of the rebellion. If witness of another type may be quoted there is Abercromby's letter (Bantry, 28 January). 'I have often heard of disaffection among the militia; it may perhaps exist among a few individuals; but it cannot exist to any considerable amount. My inquiries have been unremitted in this particular'.[15]

The *Sun* newspaper incident, with other things, illustrates the susceptibility of Irish public opinion to attacks on the prestige of 'the native forces'. This newspaper, published in London stated, (6 April): 'It was yesterday reported that some of the Irish militia regiments had joined the rebels. This is extremely likely to be true'. The Irish house of commons took notice of this and on 16 April it was resolved,[16] *nemine contradicente*, that 'the said publication is a false, scandalous and malicious libel'. A further resolution urged that the printer and publisher of the libel should be prosecuted. A Dublin castle official's comment (9 April)[17] on the matter was: 'individuals of different corps have been misled, but in general, as regiments and detachments from regiments, it is not possible for them to have conducted themselves better'. In May 1797 there had been in London newspapers 'unfounded paragraphs' relative to the militia, which lord Cavan (who commanded in the north at Derry) had contradicted, adding that the militia of Ireland were a 'highly honourable, loyal and disciplined body of men'. (See page 112).

The foregoing illustrates the reactions of official circles to attacks on the loyalty to constituted authority of the force. But nothing is more difficult than to assess what, in this immediate pre-rebellion period (as well as in other periods), the people generally were thinking of their brothers who were bearing the government's arms. Had the militia in fact (being, as seems established, preponderantly catholic) lost touch with the people from whom it was recruited? In whatever 'military severities' (Thomas Addis Emmett's phrase)[18] there had been, the militia had clearly been called upon to take a part. At the same time, they probably had an asset, even at this time, of general popularity based upon much human helpfulness in various ordinary vicissitudes of life, constantly shewn by them.

What appeared in the '*Northern Star*' (Belfast) and in the '*Press*' (published in Dublin; and eventually suppressed) is perhaps evidence rather of the attitude of the leaders of the United Irishmen than of that of the ordinary people. They, as is well known, had given[19] an assurance to the French Directory that the Irish militia would join the French if they landed in considerable force. Naturally therefore, if the United Irish leaders were looking to the Irish militia as almost the corner-stone of their scheme, they would hardly at the same time be vilifying* the force. They in fact went somewhat further than this. In November 1797 it was thought that there was a scheme that the militia should be sent to England and be replaced by non-Irish troops. This policy was thought to have emanated from the English ministry. It was met by the *Press* with: 'We do not want to part with our militia', and talk of 'robbing us of our militia'. A considered article on 30 November appeals against the suggestion: 'Will [Ireland] in time of impending danger deprive herself of her natural protectors?....Will you Irish soldiers embodied for the defence of your country consent....to this transportation? Will you abandon your country, your wives and your children to hold their liberties and their lives at the will of strangers?' The general tone is not that of disgust with the militia as the result of outrages nor of suggestion that they were an undisciplined soldiery which was bedevilling the wretched peasants. Certain regiments are, it is true, criticized, and reference can be found to 'an immense military force, too seldom restrained by discipline or law' and to 'officers frequently deficient in prudence and experience and studiously exasperated against the people'. But other comments seem to show that this was mainly, if not exclusively, to the address of the English and Scotch troops, who, it is suggested, would not 'come here to be trifled with'.[20] It was possibly realized that interchange would promote the policy of a union between Great Britain and Ireland. But the real underlying motive probably was the hope (which had apparently become a conviction) that, in case of insurrection or invasion, the militia would, *en masse*, be found at the disposal of those who were against the régime.

With the small amount of special preparation that was, or could be, given to it, and with general expectations in regard to it

*A paper marked 'Memoir delivered to the French government by Dr. McNiven' (PR.O. Home Office 100/122), endorsed as probably written previous to rebellion in 1798 speaks of the Irish militia as 'the finest and best disciplined of the British Army'.

as just described, the force was tumbled higgledy-piggledy into the turmoil of declared insurrection. No attempt will be made here to describe the series of scraps, mêlees, affrays, guerilla fights and general encounters which, with all sorts of minor hostilities, in a military sense make up, what is called the Irish rebellion. 'Partial battles and skirmishes', says sir Jonah Barrington,[21] 'were incessant but general engagements were not numerous'. The fog of war rests on the whole rather confused medley of heterogeneous clashes; and will perhaps always do so. The whole campaign, if the word can be used with propriety at all, was rough and tumble warfare—a complete antithesis of a general-staff-planned series of operations. It was far rather in the nature of a *sauve qui peut* of the existing régime. There was no time for anything but the immediately next step. Individual bodies of troops were necessarily thrown largely upon their own resources, though there were some who put blame on the action, or inaction, of the generals.[22]

The fighting in the months of May-July was essentially irregular fighting. In appendix VIII will be found a list of the engagements, big and little, between 24 May and 12 July; the actions between 22 August and 26 September are separate and arose from invasion as distinct from insurrection. It will be obvious how scattered they were, and, by consequence, how exacting were the physical demands they made upon the troops. For any bodies of fighting men transport is vital. In Ireland in 1798 marching was almost the sole method of getting about. Cars, it is true, were also used. Bishop Percy, in a letter[23] of 8 June, says :—'Our jaunting cars have been found extremely useful in conveying the soldiers through the country with the greatest expedition. Four are drawn by one horse; and, changing horses, they clear 50 or 60 miles in a day. What an advantage this gives them over the slow and fatiguing march of English infantry....A hundred and twenty-five cars convey thus 500 men'. But, in spite of the bishop's testimony, this cumbrous form of cavalcade, severe for the horse, can hardly have been resorted to very often. Of the use of cars in the ordinary way there are several pictures. On 4 June part of the Cavan militia set out for Wexford. 'About 30 noddies, the like number of jaunting cars and about 12 or 14 coaches were pressed for their conveyance'.[24] On 27 May the Cork city regiment marched from their barracks at St. Stephen's Green: 'Every vehicle plying on the Blackrock road and various other quarters were pressed for the service of the military, in order as well that their progress may be accelerated as that they should arrive at the place of their destination fresh for active duty'.[25] On 7 June a further part of the Cavan militia (with Durham fencibles) left 'for the country' and 'near ninety coaches and curricles were impressed for this essential purpose, among them some carriages belonging to the gentry.'.[26] For the engagement at Arklow (9 June) militia, and other troops no doubt, were rushed out from Dublin just in time to fight and 'the drivers of the hackney carriages which had conveyed them saw the battle from the hills'[27] as they returned to the city. Another account says that on this occasion 500 carriages were pressed in Dublin for the use of the troops.[28] There was undoubtedly at various times, even when it was not a matter of life and death, a good deal of high-handed action over the pressing of cars, and complaints occur.

But cars naturally were not always available in quantity and for the most part movement was by foot-slogging. What the Irish militia did in meeting the challenge of 1798 cannot be appreciated without some idea of the exhausting marches they performed. Later in 1805 an English observer comments[29] upon the superior marching capacity of the Irish soldier and quotes an English officer as stating that 'on a march the native troops of Ireland have frequently preceded the English by one mile in four miles'. However this comparison may be stated, prodigies of marching were undoubtedly performed and the fatigue resulting had important effects on fighting capacity; especially was this so in the case of the Castlebar action. In the Bantry alarm, as has been seen, some terrific marches occurred. In both parts of the 1798 operations these were frequent. Thus an officer of the Londonderry says[30]: 'The battalion of the regiment had a great deal of harassing duty to perform in marching always by night to attack the insurgents....It was no uncommon thing to march 30 miles during a night and day and, although we were frequently wet and dry during the times we were from camp, I never, through the entire insurrection, missed an hour's duty and I was only 17 years old'. At Kilcullen (two attacks on 24 May) sir James Duff told the Dublin city militia who begged to be employed that he did not want to harass men who had 'already marched 90 miles in 3 days'.[31] In June there were operations in Queen's county in which the Downshire were concerned and in which they did very good service. 'The spirit of the men', we are told,[32] 'was such that, after having marched from 7 o'clock in the morning of Monday till two in the morning of Tuesday, they resumed their march in two hours and with the assistance of cars went eight miles to the field of battle'. There are many other instances recorded of long marches; this was a side of military training in which the militia had hadlarge experience and this stood them in good stead.

Although for the campaign against Humbert efficient supply arrangements were made, for these earlier 'operations' no such arrangements as a rule either were or could have been made. The trekking commandoes of militia, and of yeomanry, had to help themselves to supplies on which they could lay hands. There are no records, as in the case of the Bantry marchings, of the people aiding the moving troops with supplies, although they no doubt did so, in the measure of their sympathies. To bodies of men which had lived at free quarters* it no doubt came natural to appropriate what they wanted for their very support. After it was all over, some claims are to be found in official records preferred against units which had appropriated, and without making payment, cattle or other things, sometimes when they were on the way to market for civilian consumption. But this need not shock greatly ; it is inevitable, and not only in Ireland, in times of tumult. So far as it happened, it would tend to create some bad blood and to conduce to irregular or—to employ the word which has been so freely bandied—' licentious ' conduct and indiscipline ; it is important because of its connection with the question of the relations which existed with the common people.

The theoretical difference of function as between the militia and the yeomanry tended to disappear under the acute stress. The yeomanry did not remain restricted in their range of action to the neighbourhood of their homes ; there were of course cavalry and infantry yeomanry ; the former, being mounted, could, and did, operate away. The report of the Secret Committee 1798 speaks of them as ' sharing all the hardships and dangers and performing all the duties in common with the King's regular and militia forces ',[33] though Lake (in his general order of 11 June, draws a distinction between the ' army under his command ' and ' the gentlemen of the Yeomanry corps '. In so far as the rebellion was a religious conflict, there was probably more ' *odium theologicum* ' in the ranks of the yeomanry ; it is described as ' a religious animosity that was nearly fanatic '.[34] The militia were, to the extent of about 4/5, catholics.† The general charges against them, in fact, seem mutually destructive : that they were treacherously hand-in-glove with their co-religionists and at the same time committing outrages against those co-religionists in their capacity of rebels. It seems therefore inherently probable that their attitude was, in the main, more restrained. In their odysseys around Ireland they had come into

*Troops at free quarters were compulsory non-paying guests with coercive duties, probably as a rule, but not necessarily always, unwelcome.

†The ' paper found....in the possession of Mr. Sheares '. (Secret Report 1798, p. 208 ; reproduced in facsimile) speaks of ' aristocratic yeomanry '. The conclusion I have come to, after reading documents and records of the period, is that there was a *class* as well as *religious* antagonism between the yeomanry and the people, while, between at all events the great majority of the militia and the people, there was neither.

contact with all sections of their fellow-countrymen and the writer of an anti-catholic pamphlet[35] published in 1799, notes, in regard to the catholic militia, that ' by shifting often from one place to another, their minds were enlarged '. Recent writers seem to attribute the savageries which are by one side called ' atrocities ' and by the other ' reprisals ' predominantly to the yeomanry; and Cornwallis, in his general order[36] after Ballinamuck (p. 141) expresses his acknowledgments to them ' for their not having tarnished [their] courage and loyalty....by any acts of wanton cruelty towards their deluded fellow-subjects ',—a reference which was taken as an insult[37] by the yeomen. It is perhaps fair to interpret his qualified and tactless commendation as indicating non-materialization during the invasion of what he may have been told had happened in the rebellion part of 1798.

The employment of the militia and yeomanry, with little or no differentiation of function, illustrates how much had to be left to improvisation. There had been few regular troops in the country at the time of the outbreak. It was a matter of all hands to the pumps; much had to go by the board. An officer of the Sligo regiment present at the Vinegar Hill engagement (21 June)—one of the few stand-up fights—recalled the circumstances attending his actual military debut shortly before that action. ' A sergeant entering the schoolroom at Sligo where he was attending at his lessons, saluted and notified the adjutant's request that the youthful ensign should forthwith join his regiment. The schoolboy, thereupon flinging his books at the head of his pedagogue, rushed out of the classroom cheering for the army '.[38]

All these circumstances—want of preparation, guerilla nature of fighting, transport difficulties, march fatigues, absence of supply arrangements, general improvisation of attack and defence arrangements—naturally tended to break down normal discipline which, in September of this year, Castlereagh[39] described as having suffered, in the case of ' the native army, particularly of the native militia....from the irregular service in which the troops have necessarily been engaged '. The militia were auxiliary and not regular troops; the influences of 1798 made them irregulars. They could hardly have been anything else and achieved what they did achieve. Though general references to malpractices and severities are plentiful, examination of the ' State of the country papers: 1796-1803 ' at Dublin castle does not provide support for sweeping allegations. There is probably no collection of official information still in existence by which the general accuracy of such wide allegations can now be tested. Mr. Elliot, under-secretary of state writes[40] on 28 July: ' The army is still, I fear, in a sad state of disorder and the troops have been guilty of great outrages in the course of the rebellion '. This must probably be accepted as a generally correct statement. In July 1797 the revd Edward Hudson, writing to lord Charlemont,[41] speaks of ' various abuses of power that are exercised in different parts of the country ' and adds : ' that there was a necessity for a vigour beyond the law, I am perfectly convinced, and I am also that it has been attended with many good effects. But in many, too many, instances, it has been carried to the most shameful excess '. This statement was no doubt even more true of 1798. That the militia, and still more perhaps the yeomanry, took easily to the highly unconventional warfare which prevailed can hardly, however incomplete the first-hand materials for a generalization now available, be doubted. Discipline and parade ground excellence were to much 18th century opinion almost synonymous and the Irish militia kept with difficulty the mould even of this the then accepted norm of military virtue. What, however, is here in question is something more than ineligibility for the description ' parade ground soldiers ' which was how, we are told, dominion troops during the great war of 1914-18 sometimes summed up the British soldiers with their clean and neat uniforms and their boots and buttons shining. But before independent responsibility for ' methods of barbarism ' is rhetorically fixed upon the militia, or upon any of the military forces (regular, fencible, yeomany) then in Ireland, what must be remembered is that primary military units (battalions, regiments, companies) are not principals but *instruments*.

How then did the militia, in the opinion of contemporary opinion, acquit themselves in the rebellion period ? There are various opinions on this. The marquis of Buckingham, who was in Ireland at the head of his Buckingham militia in 1798-99, speaks, at the end of July, of the yeomanry and militia having ' saved the country '[42*] but these forces had ' certainly made it pay most severely for this protection '. The *Freemans' Journal* speaks of their ' bravery and unshaken loyalty ' and a correspondent of lord Downshire writes (3 July) to him as follows : ' It must be a pleasing reflection to your lordship to find that the militia have behaved so universally well notwithstanding the great pains taken to seduce and calumniate them '.[43] The archbishop of Cashel (31 May) wrote to lord Auckland : ' It is right to say that all our denominations of soldiers—regulars, militia and yeomanry —have behaved extremely well '.[44] Mr. Alexander on 26 June writes to Pelham from Londonderry of the militia on the whole having acted so steadily and having been so highly praised in the late ' *certamina belli* '.[45]

Beresford writes on 11 June : ' No troops on earth have behaved better than our militia and yeomen, whenever tried, the

*This was the opinion of Lecky—quoted in chap. XVIII, p. 282.

roman catholics as well as the protestants '.[46] On 8 July, Dean Kirwan, preaching in the presence of the lord lieutenant a sermon for the benefit of the widows and children of the militiamen and yeomen who had been killed, spoke as follows :—

> To the militia of Ireland I likewise pay a feeble tribute. What an example have they presented of steady and incorruptible loyalty ! What regiment has not evinced itself worthy of our utmost confidence ! And who shall presume again to tarnish with the unjust breath of suspicion the honour of an Irish soldier ? Placed in the most delicate situation, too uninstructed to feel all the sacredness of the cause in which they were engaged ; connected by innumerable ties ; by country ; by class ; almost universally by sect ; perhaps, in numerous instances by blood and consanguinity ; such the unhappy people to whom they were opposed ; they yet marched to the contest, not with dejected brows, but with highcrested spirit, and everywhere came out of it adorned with the wreath of superior valour and unstained, so far as I could learn, with a single instance of defection....let us study, on all occasions, to make them feel and enjoy the greatest of all rewards, that of being numbered among the saviours of their country.[47]

The foregoing are unofficial opinions and from the words of the preacher, though he is highly relevant, some discount is perhaps to be made. Official opinion is not less favourable. William Pitt writes : ' The contest has at present (31 May) existed about a week....the troops of all descriptions behave incomparably '.[48] General Lake writes : ' Nothing ever behaved better than lord Gosford and the Armagh ' (27 May) ; ' you will see by the bulletins that the militia have behaved most uncommonly well ' (30 May) ; and ' the militia of all descriptions have behaved uncommonly well (3 June).[49] Elliot, on 1 June, speaks of ' the highest spirit and intrepidity and most inviolable fidelity '[50] of the troops ; and another Castle official wrote the next day : ' Our militia, even the King's county, have all behaved very well '.[51] Castlereagh writes to Pelham on 8 June, i.e. just after the battle of New Ross (5 June) in which men of nine regiments of militia had been engaged, that ' our militia soldiers have on every occasion manifested the greatest spirit and fidelity, in many cases defective in subordination but in none have they shewn the smallest disposition to fraternize but on the contrary pursue the insurgents with the rancour unfortunately connected with the nature of the struggle ';[52] On the 12th he says that ' the conduct of the militia and yeomanry has, in point of fidelity, exceeded our most sanguine expectations. Some few corps of the latter, and but very few in that vast military establishment, have been corrupted ; but in no instance has the militia failed to show the most determined spirit. In this point of view, the insurrection, if repressed with energy, will have proved an invaluable test of our national force, on the disaffection of which our enemies either actually did, or professed, very extensively to rely '.[53] The next day he writes to Pelham : 'The experience we have already had of the Irish militia has completely dispelled all our apprehensions as to their fidelity, and must remove every jealousy on the part of England in employing them in Great Britain '.[54] Camden praised the troops generally but with reservation : 'Whenever our troops have had opportunities of meeting the rebels they have behaved well but their wildness and want of discipline is most alarming, looking as we must do to a more formidable enemy '.[55]

These opinions were mainly expressed in private correspondence. More public utterances might perhaps be subject to some discount. Camden in a despatch to Portland, said the 'militia have had opportunities of evincing their steadiness, discipline and bravery which must give the highest satisfaction to his majesty and inspire the best-grounded confidence in their exertions should they have a more formidable enemy to contend with.'[56] In the British house of commons in a speech from the throne the king (5 July) said : 'I cannot too strongly commend the unshaken fidelity and valour of my regular, fencible and militia forces in Ireland '. General Lake in his order of 11 June, in which he specifies the 'trying engagements' which had taken place up to that date (i.e. Naas, Kilcullen, Tara Hill, Kildare, Hacketstown, Rathangan, Mount Kennedy, Carlow, Newtown Barry, Ross and Arklow) and differentiates them from 'many other smaller actions' (for these see appendix VIII) describes the whole as a 'very rapid succession of gallant actions.' Of all the militia units two-thirds seem to have been engaged in one way or another—some more, some less seriously. Those stationed in the more remote parts of Munster and Connaught (which were a small part of the whole) did not take any part in the rebellion fighting. But some were engaged for some part of time almost every day. Of these the Antrim regiment was one : they fought on 24, 25, 27 and 30 May and inflicted defeats at Baltinglass, Hacketstown, Killthomas, Ballinrush, Newtown, and Mount Kenny, and on 1 June they met rebels at Ballycanew.

Many of the colonels took the field with their units. Two lost their lives. Lord Mountjoy, who had originally raised the Dublin county unit, was killed in the critical fight at New Ross ; he was the only officer who fell, but several were missing. 'When we stormed their [i.e. the enemy's] post', says Major Vesey, the second-in-command, 'we found his body mangled and butchered in a most horrid manner '. In the attack on Antrim (7 June) lord O'Neill received a dangerous wound of which he afterwards died. At Vinegar Hill (21 June) colonel King of the Sligo was wounded but he recovered. Lord Kingsborough, the colonel of the north Cork militia (see page 48 for his recruiting activities) was captured by the rebels with two of his officers while sailing from Arklow and was imprisoned in Wexford for four weeks. Lord Gosford also, the Colonel of the Armagh militia almost lost his life on two occasions at Naas whither his regiment had marched from Dublin just before the outbreak and where they were engaged in the first action which took place in the Rebellion.

IX

Invasion

DURING the interval between the rebellion and invasion phases of 1798, ordinary routine in military administration seems to have been re-established. Castlereagh on 27 July, introduced yet another militia-amending bill. This was reported with amendments on 13 August. It is obviously the bill which would have been brought in if the rebellion had never taken place : it makes amendments in the law which current experience indicated as necessary and is in no way relevant to the remarkable events through which the country had been passing. It is curious, among the agitations of the time, to come upon this order (30 July), ' as the powdering is very prejudicial* to the hair and apt to create vermin, the troops are in future only to wear it twice a week, on Sundays and Thursdays '.[1]

Had the troubles of 1798 been finally over when the insurrection was suppressed, the effort that the militia had made (subject to whatever qualifications as regards excess of correctionary zeal) and the loyalty they had undoubtedly shewn might have remained unobscured and the answer to the question which the dean of Killala had put (' Who shall again presume to tarnish with the unjust breath of suspicion the honour of an Irish soldier ?') would never, in the sense that he had put it, have had other than a negative answer. But the troubles were not over. Though this force had carried out not unsuccessfully, at the climax phase, their contra-insurrection duty—no fraternizations, no refusals to march, no white feathers†—they had still to face the contra-invasion test. Camden, as we have seen, did not think that the ' more formidable enemy ' would be so successfully dealt with but he had ' best-grounded confidence '. He might have had in mind what had happened at the end of 1796 (chapter VI) and might have expected, though the situation had since deteriorated, that, given competent leading, such credit as Bantry had brought would have been retained or increased. Before the rebellion phase was over, his successor, Cornwallis, had arrived in Dublin (20 June) and seems to have brought with him not only an anti-

*But see chap. X, p. 157.

†The question of desertion in 1798 (rebellion) is dealt with in chapter 9.

Irish mentality (' I fear that the levity of our countrymen teases him ',[2] said lord Clare 1 August) but also some prejudice against militia.[3] In spite of the views expressed by many persons of weight about what the militia had achieved, Cornwallis' correspondence shows no recognition of any credit due nor perception of what dean Kirwan had called their ' most delicate situation '. On 8 July he tells Portland ' the Irish militia .... could not have behaved worse ' and at the end of September he writes of ' their repeated misbehaviour in the field '.[4] The question arises : what, if anything, happened during the second phase of 1798, which could justify this attitude. It may be that Cornwallis arrived in Ireland with the policy of the Union so definitely implanted that he unconsciously tended so to use events that they ensured to the materialization of that policy. Castlereagh held that it was ' of importance that the authority of England should decide this contest '.[5] Cornwallis would hold this just as strongly. Outside the purely military sphere the militia magnates were, in Cornwallis's eyes, an over-influential element in the country ;[6] within that sphere, they had been to viceroys a thorn in the flesh ; to a viceroy who combined the supreme political and military functions these politico-military bigwigs may well have been doubly an annoyance. The course of events promoted the end to which Cornwallis seems to have been working.

During the period from August to September there were three engagements in which the militia were concerned : Castlebar, Colooney and Ballinamuck.

Humbert landed at Killala on 22 August. Next day the Longford regiment at Ennis (whose colonel lord Granard was with them) were ordered to march to Gort. They started, about 400 strong,[7] on the 24th, and, at Gort, two instructions were received from Galway; one from general Hutchinson directed them to march to Castlebar, the other from general Trench directed them to march ' in the direction of Hollymount in the county of Mayo '; both despatches urged expedition; general Trench added that Hutchinson had moved forward and mentioned his statement that ' the French were both feeble and rash, and that a prompt attack was much to be wished for '. Later, another despatch directing an advance to Oranmore, was received. This place was reached after dark. Next morning yet a fourth order, from general Hutchinson, instructed the regiment to march to Castlebar ' with all possible despatch, by pressing horses, cars and carriages, wherever found, to convey the troops with speed and to avoid harassing the men more than absolutely necessary '. The regiment, having pressed horses, cars, carriages and other conveyances, reached Castlebar at 11 p.m. on the 26th. They had covered

80 miles in three days. They bivouacked in the street and are described as 'broken down with excessive toil'.[8] The other militia regiment which was in the Castlebar affair was the Kilkenny.* They had been marched in to Castlebar from Loughrea (55 miles in 2 days) where they were joined on the afternoon of the 25th by their colonel, lord Ormonde. The Kerry militia marched from Galway to Castlebar (47 miles) in two days and were immediately, with some regulars, detached by Hutchinson to Foxford, ten miles away. This force—about 800 men in all—was not in the Castlebar affair.

The force hastily got together comprised, in addition to the two militia regiments, the following:—the skeleton of the 6th Foot; some regular cavalry (6th Dragoon Guards) who arrived about an hour before the Longford; some Royal Irish Artillery, with four six-pounders and a howitzer; some Galway yeomanry; and detachments of the Frazer fencibles, the Prince of Wales' fencibles and of lord Roden's fencible cavalry regiment. The scratch force (some 1,700 men)† thus rapidly brought together and drawn from more than 10 units obviously could have had no cohesion whatever. The concentration within striking distance of an enemy was a military proceeding which was, with evident reference to Hutchinson, condemned by Cornwallis in a general order issued on 12 September.[9]

Of the two roads from Ballina to Castlebar, the lower was patrolled, and the other, being regarded as impracticable, was neglected. Humbert made a feint advance by the lower road, but his advance proper by the other. Early on the 27th, Lake and Hutchinson learned that the French were upon them. For their being in this predicament the troops, whether militia or others, cannot be held to blame. But even for the seasoned troops in the force, such as the regulars presumably were, their leaders had provided a testing situation. For inexperienced troops who had 'never yet seen a regular enemy'[10] or indeed a shot fired in anger, advancing was one thing, but to retire steadily under heavy fire required troops inured to warfare. That the troops ranged against Humbert's tried veterans were not so inured was of course within the knowledge of Hutchinson, and of Lake. The case of the Kilkenny colonel and his officers—the

*This was an eight company regiment, at this time of strength of 70 per company. It is stated, though this seems erroneous, that only four of the companies of the Kilkenny were marched to Castlebar.

†I am aware that a larger figure is often given; there are also references to a force in reserve. But it seems to me clear that about 1,700, or less, is the number with which Hutchinson planned to meet the attack to which '*he exposed himself*' (Cornwallis) and that it was with this number that he actually met them. See articles by present writer (The Government Forces engaged at Castlebar in 1798) in *Irish Historical Studies*, vol iv. No. 16, and (Jobit-Fontaire-Sarrazin) *Ulster Journal of Archaeology*, vol. 10, parts 1 and 2, 1947, p. 115.

Kilkenny were in the first line—is that, while their regiment was displaying great steadiness before the enemy, an aide-de-camp arrived with an order that they should retire. After consultation with two other commanding officers, lord Ormonde declined to act upon the order. After the Kilkenny field-gun had at the second round done some execution, a second aide-de-camp from the general came to lord Ormonde with a peremptory order that he should retire and a threat of punishment for disobedience of orders. Retirement was then, apparently, commenced and the troops fell into disorder. One or two criticisms made by Humbert are on record and he appears to have told major Alcock, an officer of the Kilkenny, that he 'could not at all understand the tactics of the English generals in seeking to retire their first line at such a moment, as, had they been left in the position three minutes longer, the French must of necessity, from their comparative weakness as to numbers, have retreated'.[11]

The foregoing account is of course from the Longford and Kilkenny side but there seems no reason for doubting its substantial accuracy. It is reasonably claimed by the Kilkenny regiment,[12] that if they 'reaped no laurels' they had 'no occasion to blush more for the result of the fight than any other regiment engaged therein'. A general panic undoubtedly occurred. On this Lake's biographer[13] says: 'For the panic that followed no explanation need be attempted, for panics are unexplainable'. A yet higher authority, Napoleon, has said: 'The bravest armies have all in their turn been seized with panic'. The mounted troops seem to have galloped off the field; the Dragoon Guards, without the loss of a horse or man, were some of them, it is stated, at Athlone within thirty-six hours.[14] The infantry (mainly the militia) were left submerged. There is some sense in the alleged statement of a private that it was not they who retired from the enemy but the rest of the army from them.[15] The historian of the Longford regiment denies explicitly that men of the militia regiments went over to the French *during* the action, but in the subsequent confused proceedings many were made prisoners and willy-nilly joined the enemy not from deliberate treachery but to save their lives.[16] Next year (September) Cornwallis, writing to Dundas, says: 'Two regiments of militia and one of Scotch fencibles....did at Castlebar *run away for many miles* from a very inferior French force, carrying terror and dismay through the whole country'.[17] As regards the italicized words, whatever in fact happened at Castlebar, the two Irish militia regiments could not (*a*) have gone over *en masse* to the enemy—a charge often made—and also (*b*) 'run away many miles'—apart from the fact that in both regiments considerable numbers are known to have been killed fighting (see p. 143 for numbers killed by gunshot).

They had not horses and could not save themselves by flight to Tuam or Athlone ; and the Longford men at any rate could not, after three days of strenuous marching, a few hours' bivouac in the street and a fight under impossible conditions, have had much kick for anything. Little supported as the militia were by their generals or by the regulars (who should, as Fortescue admits, have been counted upon to set an example) nevertheless under lord Granard's leadership, they made a fight at the bridge at Castlebar of which Humbert says that " he had not seen a more obstinate engagement, even in La Vendee ';[18] one of his officers, Toussont, makes a similar statement.

The fog of war still shrouding these proceedings would have been dispersed if Cornwallis had thought fit to have an enquiry. Lord Granard impressed on him that ' no enquiry could have been held on my military conduct which I should not, for myself and my officers, rejoice at '.[19] Lord Ormonde no doubt took up the same attitude. What was thought of the Longford regiment by people conversant with their recent record may be inferred from the fact that next year (March) the high sheriff and grand jury of county Clare formally put on record their thanks to the regiment for their services in the county during the rebellion.'[20] Camden, but with the desire that the Longford and Kilkenny regiments should be broken, seems to have expected Cornwallis to hold an enquiry.[21] It was probably refused because it might have been ' embarrassing to administration ' and ' injurious to His Majesty's service in times like these '.[22] Cornwallis probably realised that what would be in question in any enquiry would be not so much the conduct in impossible circumstances of the rank and file of part of two militarily unpretentious Irish militia units as the prestige of England, its generals and regular forces. He could not but know that to expect from militia (whether English, Scotch or Irish) a high regular standard—if there was at that time such a thing at all—was out of reason. He has left on record the opinion that Hutchinson, to whom more than to Lake is attributable the blame for what has recently been called ' a British defeat of some interest ',[23] was ' no general '.[24]

The early newspaper accounts (1 September and 3 September) stated that the Kilkenny had behaved ' with great gallantry ' but ' when the account [i.e. the account let out from official sources] of the rout at Castlebar became known a howl of execration followed every officer and man who had been engaged in that unhappy affair. Every case of individual merit was ignored, and the broad fact that a British army had been disgracefully beaten by an inferior force of French was alone recognized. From that day to this [1894] no attempt has been made to arrive at the real facts, and statements of the wildest description have been accepted with unquestioning belief'.[25] When a considered official statement was put out* it was promptly criticized as tendentious, in fact if not in intention, and by what it omitted as well as by what it stated. This was in a pamphlet[26] which (following in the same year) made the points that the author of the *Impartial Relation* evidently was not a witness of the attack at Castlebar; that the map attached to the pamphlet failed to give the road over the mountain by which Humbert's troops actually came 'though it is noticed in every common publication of the kind before it'; that the surprise to which the troops were exposed is burked; that the statement that the troops gave way without any apparent reason, in spite of the efforts of their generals and of all their officers, ignored the general's order (that 'the Kilkenny regiment do retreat'); that it was only on the receipt and repetition of this and not before, that the men 'were ordered to the right about'; that even then, they retired for some space 'with great regularity, then halted and came to their proper front'; that the number of those who deserted to the enemy, in the Kilkenny, did not exceed five and was not the 'greater part of 43';† and that the statement about the desertions from the Longford regiment may be presumed to be equally exaggerated. The writer of this very temperately-worded pamphlet goes on to say:

> That a single individual in His Majesty's service should....desert.... can never be too much reprobated, but to magnify the extent of a crime so disgraceful to the army and of so much importance to the country, is as unwise as it is unjust, and will by the judicious be considered as a price too great for a shield to cover the mistakes of any man whatsoever.

He then makes the point that, whatever desertions there may have been, after the actual fighting, that cannot be

> 'adduced as a *cause* of the defeat which our troops had *previously* met with.

*See '*Impartial Relation of the Military Operations* which took place in Ireland in consequence of the landing of a body of French troops under General Humbert in August 1798 (by an officer who served in the corps, under the command of His Excellency Marquis Cornwallis) Dublin, 1799'. This not entirely accurate narrative has been attributed to Cornwallis himself but is now considered to have been written by lieut-general (as he became) sir Herbert Taylor who was lord Cornwallis' military secretary at the time of the events. The published *Taylor Papers* (1913) make no reference to this, and I have ascertained from the editor and owner of these papers that in the papers not included in the published volume there are no references to the Castlebar affair.

†The figures given in the 'Impartial Relation' were :—

Longford. Killed :—1 sergeant and 23 rank and file. Wounded :—9 rank and file. Missing :—1 captain, 1 lieutenant, 1 ensign, 1 staff, 8 sergeants, 146 rank and file.

Kilkenny. Killed :—12 rank and file. Wounded :—2 sergeants, 10 rank and file. Missing :—1 major, 1 lieutenant, 43 rank and file. (See also p. 143).

These figures are quoted from Lake's report which is dated 27 August, i.e. the evening of the affair. The two militia regiments, it is to be noted, had six officers missing; the 6th Foot had five officers missing, but it is not alleged that these officers 'deserted to the enemy'.

Disaffection was in no instance whatever discernible among the men either prior or during the action ; on the contrary every one seemed anxious to receive orders and to discharge his duty. Their fault was an impatience not uncommon to young troops ; their misfortune want of skill in its direction.

It is always easy, for those who consider themselves loyal and patriotic, pharisaically to launch charges of disaffection. The Irish militia having, as has been demonstrated, been loyal in all the uneasy and troubled fights against their own kin in the rebellion, the probability is against the truth of the Castlebar allegations which have now been passed on from one book to another. Generals have admittedly often been unjustly made scapegoats. But this seems a case of '*quicquid delirant reges, plectuntur Achivi*'; Cornwallis, in pursuit of the Union, seems, in current phrase, to have 'cashed in' on the Castlebar affair. He apparently argued that the 'desertion' of the Irish militia regiments should show the gentry that England alone could protect the country. It would be in this sense that (as Barrington[27] said) 'the defeat of Castlebar was a victory to the viceroy'. Earlier, in June, the King appears to have viewed the rebellion as of utility to the idea of Union[28] and it may be that Cornwallis had been inoculated with that view before he left England.

The next engagement with Humbert in which the militia were concerned was Collooney. The Essex Fencibles and some yeomanry were in it also but the main force was Limerick (city) militia[29] and the officer in command, to whom Ireland awarded laurels, was colonel Vereker. After Castlebar Humbert had headed north-west with Ulster as his general destination and Sligo as his immediate goal. At this town the Limerick city were stationed. Dispositions to meet this move by Humbert do not appear to have been made. Lord Ormonde is reported[30] to have always maintained that 'if they had no generals that day Humbert would have been signally defeated at Castlebar, notwithstanding that his troops were hardy and well-tried veterans....and his opponents raw and untrained militia and fencible levies'. The absence of any general at Collooney realized this conception of a satisfactory fight. Collooney is about five miles to the south-west of Sligo and the route to be followed by Humbert, who had with him the whole of his recently successful force, was through the pass at that place. Here Vereker, with his three hundred or so men, and with good military judgment, took up his position and 'although he retreated without his guns, the loss he inflicted on the enemy was most serious and discouraging'[31]. This opposition caused Humbert to abandon his design on Sligo. On this occasion the militia engaged were well led ; 'I met', said Humbert subsequently, 'many generals in Ireland, but the only general I met after all—was—Colonel Vereker '.[32] Though the *Impartial Relation* concedes that the officers and men of the Limerick city regiment behaved most gallantly and suffered considerably, it attaches no importance to the fight. But Irish opinion applauded Vereker's success. The city of Limerick gave a piece of plate for the officers' mess and medals for the non-commissioned officers and men and later fifty guineas was voted for the purchase of a sword of honour. How the imagination of Ireland was struck by this piece of military enterprise may be seen from a speech of lord Plunket :[33]

> I mean him [i.e. lord Cornwallis] no personal disrespect ; but this I must observe, that whilst the military lord lieutenant was in the field, with an army of 60,000 [*sic*] to support him, history will have it to record that we are indebted to a gallant Irishman (Mr. Vereker) at the head of about 800 native troops, for having withstood the enemy, and prevented the capital of Ireland from being entered in triumph by a body of not one thousand Frenchmen.

There is rhetoric here ; Colooney was not a Thermopylae ;[34] but it was a creditable action and there is something in the underlying criticism.

For the third and decisive phase of the invasion, Cornwallis had in fact, as Plunket suggests, got together a substantial force, though very much less than 60,000 men. To the Shannon force Cornwallis assigned the following militia units : 1st and 2nd light battalions ; Downshire ; Armagh ; Antrim and Louth. This selecting of northern units strikes as curious in view of a statement by Cornwallis's military secretary under date 21 August that disaffection in the militia was ' confined in great measure to the northern regiments '.[35] Lord Castlereagh appears to have recommended the Downshire and Louth to Cornwallis.

In the order of battle of Cornwallis' army on 2 September,[36] general Hutchinson (who had been allowed to retain his command) had a brigade composed solely of militia :—Antrim (546 men) ; Downshire (633) and Armagh (215). Later general Lake was given command of a force drawn mainly from Cornwallis' force (which was about 8000 strong) but partly from the force of general Taylor which was joined at Boyle by general Lake on 3 September. This force of Lake's consisted of cavalry and two infantry brigades ;[37] in the first of these was part of the Armagh militia and part of the Kerry militia (which had been in the command of general Taylor at Boyle on 1 September) and in the second the 3rd light battalion. The infantry also included fencible but no regular units. Of tbe three fencible infantry units, only one, the Reays, had been in Cornwallis' army as set out in the order of battle of 2 September. The two others were the Northamption and the Prince of Wales' fencibles, probably drawn from the force of general Taylor. Up to the last moment before despatching Lake with his special force on the pursuit of Humbert, Cornwallis was still sifting his troops. He was naturally not taking any chances. Castlebar was probably already as much graven inside his heart as Calais inside that of Mary Tudor.[38] He had started by preparing for fighting on the large scale, with organization into brigades, and an adequate system of supply, so lacking for Bantry and so demoralizingly absent in the rebellion period. But Cornwallis as a commander and his force as an instrument were more unwieldy than Humbert and his force; and it was necessary to detach a force for more mobile movement.

So Lake went off with the troops named. His report, dated Ballinamuck camp 8 September, begins by referring to 'four days and nights most severe marching'.[39] At 2 a.m. on the 5th his force was on the march and in full pursuit of Humbert. That night, it is recorded, his men ate the dinner which had been prepared by Humbert's troops for themselves. On the 7th at daylight Lake made another circuitous and harassing march. During the nights of 7th-8th they were again on the march. 'When they came in sight of the enemy they had marched 56 English miles without halting: the men were falling asleep on their horses as they rode and the poor infantry were almost fainting as they marched'.[40] In the fight which ultimately brought Humbert's enterprise to a close the troops actually engaged were by a further act of selection or by accident of routine,[41] two militia units (i.e. the 3rd light battalion and part of the Armagh militia). The light battalion consisted of the light companies of the Dublin (city), Armagh, Monaghan, Tipperary, and Kerry. Lake appears to have accepted the suggestion of the men of some of these companies that they should be allowed to mount behind[42] the Hessians, Carabineers and Roxburgh dragoons and thus get into the thick of the fight. As it turned out the Armagh had the luck of the day. Of the five companies of the light battalion the Armagh were on the left and as the battalion moved left to come into contact with the French that company was upon them first; the Armagh regiment itself (i.e. such part of it as was present; how much is not certain) was moving parallel and at a little distance. In the fighting which seems to have been spirited but not prolonged the French colours fell into the hands of a private named Toole, the regimental servant of one of the Armagh officers.[43]

A recently published outline of British military history, though it mentions the French landing at Fishguard in 1797, makes no reference to the Irish rebellion of 1798, with its 'miniature French invasion and a British defeat of some interest', i.e. Castlebar. It has been noted[44] that a battle honour was awarded for the

Fishguard affair—the only one, it seems, for an operation in the British Isles—but not for Ballinamuck. Cornwallis would probably have regarded this as politically inexpedient. His general order, issued from his headquarters near St. Johnstown on 9 September, merely recognizes in general terms the 'zeal and spirit which has been manifested by the army' and 'the perseverance with which the soldiers supported the extraordinary marches which were necessary to stop the progress of the very active enemy'. More than this, except the equivocal reference to the yeomanry (see page 127) he does not say. His military secretary shows disappointment at loss of credit they had promised themselves; he complains that 'the Downshire went 8 miles out of their way. This delayed and drew after them a whole brigade and obliged us to wait some time for them. Otherwise we should have cut in on the French before Lake overtook them'.[45] Pelham however wrote to Castlereagh on 13 September: 'I heartily rejoice....that the Irish troops distinguished themselves so much'.[46] On 30 September Cornwallis is talking, as has already been pointed out, of the 'repeated misbehaviour in the field of the militia.

Irish opinion did not take Ballinamuck like this. Lord Charlemont's correspondent, the revd. Edward Hudson, wrote to him on 17 September: 'I am delighted with the Armagh boys charging the heroes of the continent so gallantly. It will, I think, inspire our militia with confidence in themselves, by showing them that a good thrust with an Irish bayonet can overset one of those little heroes who call themselves invincible'.[47] A correspondent of lord Downshire says: 'The character of the militia which the Longford has stained is restored. The Armagh charged with the bayonet most gallantly. There was a brigade of light infantry made up also of militia'.[48]

Saunder's Newsletter[49] commented as follows:

> The bravery of all our soldiery was beyond praise; the Armagh militia in particular did not fire a single shot, but rushed upon the enemy with fixed bayonets in such a style as to astonish the veterans of the army of Italy. If it were possible to enhance the singular good fortune of this glorious victory, it would be done in the recollection that (though we owe every gratitude to our generous fellow subjects of England and can never forget their voluntary assistance, not only offered but given to us in time of danger) the day was gained by our own Irish soldiers.

Other press reports of the period are similar. In the debates on the question of the Union, it was emphasized by Plunket, and probably by other anti-Union speakers, that the Rebellion was was "substantially put down"....by native valour and native honour, before any reinforcement had arrived from great Britain.[50]

Though the rebellion and the invasion were largely separate, and raised different problems, it would be a mistake to over-compartmentalize. Insurrection and invasion reacted the one upon the other; and, when the latter was disposed of, the insurrectionary fever had not gone out of Ireland's system. Humbert's landing had caused a rising in Connaught. The Kerry and also the Armagh militias seem to have been employed in dealing with it. An Army Medical Board return[51] of the distribution and strength of the militia on 1 October show both these two units, with strength respectively of 650 and 582, as then stationed at Castlebar. In the west were also :—Antrim (834) at Galway; Down (905) at Tuam; Longford (622) at Athlone; and at Moat, about 10 miles south-east of Athlone, were the 1st and 2nd light infantry battalions each with an effective strength of 1050. All the other militia units are outside the then storm area, except that there are several units in the home counties near Dublin; five were in Co. Kildare. In Dublin itself there are no Irish militia but seven of the English militia battalions (out of a total of thirteen such units then in Ireland). In the Irish militia as a whole the 'total number of effective men including non-commissioned officers and drummers' is 28,543. The Monaghan (822) are still at Belfast and the Tipperary (1047—the strongest unit) are at Londonderry and the 3rd light infantry battalion is at Enniskillen. The following record of the peregrinations of the Clare militia will show how one unit at least—and it may not have been singular—was moved about during the year 1798; they were at Fermoy in January and thereafter at Waterford, Clonmel, Fermoy, Waterford, Wexford, Ross (in June), Fermoy, Waterford, Fermoy and Stradbally, Maryboro', Doonane, Baltinglass, Stratford, Davidstown and Doonane.[52]

The return alluded to gives the number of militiamen non-effective from various causes as 1,296. This figure added to 28,543 makes up 29,839, as the strength at which the militia stood on 1 October. This number is surprisingly large, especially as it must take account of men killed in action. It is considerably in excess of the voted establishment (26,634—see page 120) and it is not clear how it can have been reached. The Army Medical Board (1 October)[53] speak of the effectives (i.e. of the whole force in Ireland) having increased by 9,116 in September. Some of these must certainly have been militia. There had been the re-enlistment but this was strength retained and not strength gained. On 1 April the Down regiment was 28 above the establishment.[54] The Clare militia which as stated on page 121 had recruited heavily and in excess of establishment were officially reproved for having continued to recruit after the issue of an order on 11 July. The Meath regiment which had suffered heavily was filled up again at the expense of the colonel. It therefore seems possible that the colonels simply went on recruiting on their own authority and that this is the explanation of the very high strength existing on 1 October. No other explanation is available. For 1 February 1799 the strength is given as 22,356. The drop to this figure from 29,839 on 1 October 1798 is also unexplained.

In 1801 the Army Medical Board[55] gave the number of those killed in the fighting as 512, exclusive of officers. They stated that this figure had been ' precisely ascertained by comparing the medical reports with the returns transmitted monthly to the adjutant general's office '. It would not appear possible now to get anything more reliable. For the officers less information is available, and there is no centrally compiled return. The number killed hardly exceeded twenty. Of the officers and n.c.o.'s and men who were killed and wounded between 20 August and 20 September, i.e. during the invasion fighting, there is an official report (by the Army Medical Board);[56] the numbers are as follows :—officers : killed 1, wounded 7 ; n.c.o.'s and privates : killed 2, wounded by gunshot 63, punctured 2 (this is the term used in the return). It is to be noted, in justice to the Longford and Kilkenny regiments, that of the 63 wounded by gunshot 22 were in the former regiment and 20 in the latter. It is also to be noted that this return states the number of killed and missing in the ' county of Mayo ' for the Kilkenny as 58 (i.e. 32 missing and 20 killed, and for the Longford as 114 (i.e. 92 missing and 22 killed). There is no definition of ' missing ' (but see note on p. 137). The militia units to which the figures apply were, besides the two named, the Armagh, Downshire, Kerry, Limerick (city) and the 3rd Light battalion.

It cannot be said that the militia had lost heavily. But many of the units, and not merely those which had taken part in the western operations, were completely exhausted with the severe strain. They had, at the least, lost a large amount of equipment and personal property. There is a very complete picture of the plight of the Downshire, in a series of letters from major Matthews, the commanding officer, to lord Downshire.[57] On 11 July he writes : ' We are almost naked and many of our men are in foraging caps '; he doesn't know what answer to make to the general officers [who were possibly worrying for review conditions to be re-established] : ' the light company is so bad from the service they have gone through that they have scarcely the remains of a red coat or a regimental cap '. He wants new watch coats and asks lord Downshire to sanction these. ' We will find it almost impossible to get our men to stand out at night without their cloaks '. On 2 September things are still bad : ' the regiments to the right and left have watch coats. We have none and the weather is very bad. Many have new clothing; we are almost naked '; if notice had been taken of his requests ' we should now have been in better order for service [they were then with Cornwallis' army] and not so much taken notice of as we are '. In October he had apparently been reproved and replies (14 October): ' Many of your men are in French coats and many in the coats of the Longford [men] which they found at Killala, one of which is worth three of yours.... We have more French caps than English ones now in the regiment '. No doubt there were difficulties in supply; the idea of procuring clothing from England was not approved by the authorities; but the same officer had said to lord Downshire in November 1797: ' I am sure the regiment ought not to be an expense. On the contrary it should be worth a thousand a year '.

The records[58] are full of applications for indemnification of losses incurred by units during the rebellion and the invasion. It is interesting to note that both the Longford and the Kilkenny regiments, in spite of the adverse attitude initially taken by Cornwallis, were indemnified and there is record of a grant of £31 10s. 0d. to captain Armstrong of the Longford for a horse lost while he was endeavouring to rally the regiment on the bridge at Castlebar on 27 August. Many regiments represent that they had lost all their baggage; in other cases all the regimental cash had been lost; blankets were missing on a large scale; the French had got ' the medical apparatus '* of the Kilkenny on entering Castlebar; and there was wide need for the replacement of such articles as sergeants' pikes and swords, sword-belts and sashes, drums, bayonets, firelocks, scabbards, slings and packs. These claims seem to have been dealt with on a fairly liberal scale: £60 was the amount normally paid to officers for baggage lost. Captain Swayne was killed at Prosperous on 24 May. A complete list exists[59] of the things for which indemnification was claimed by his executors. This is possible a unique list of the ' kit ' which a militia officer took around with him. It includes, in addition to a plentiful supply of articles of uniform, three regimental swords but no mufti, eighteen shirts but apparently no underclothing, one ' bed and suit ' but no specifically night wear except six night caps (and the eighteen shirts). There are of course many other articles and the executors were paid the sum of £264 9s. 4d. There is no evidence that such liberal treatment was given to any other officer but the circumstances of captain Swayne's death had been as moving as anything which occurred in the whole tragic and memorable procession of the events of the year 1798 in Ireland.

*The fine quality of this when it was taken to Paris caused a sensation. See *Analecta Hibernica*, No. 11, July 1941, p. 53.

X

The Years 1799-1801

Interchangeability; and line volunteering

After the rebellion no one seems to have contemplated abolishing the militia. But it was not yet over when there begins to appear frequently in official, and also in private, correspondence an idea which, in the sphere of defence policy, was to remain, as an object of Irish aspiration and discussion, long without realization—like emancipation itself. Both, though in different degree, seem to have been regarded as essential parts of the Union policy taken in wide sense. About emancipation much has of course been written; of interchangeability of the militias of the two kingdoms little notice has, however, been taken. But after the rebellion, Ireland saw it as an important object of policy. By Irish publicists it continued to be so regarded until it had became realized. The king was probably initially responsible for the non-realization of this interchangeability, as he was for the prolonged cold storage of the more important policy of emancipation.

Perhaps the earliest, and certainly the most explicit, expression of opinion on interchangeability is in a letter[1] from Castlereagh to Pelham dated 13 June, 1798:

> I hope that Mr. Pitt will not let slip this opportunity of making the militia of both countries what it ought to be—an imperial force for the defence of the Empire at home; whether the militia of one country should be lent to serve in the other except in case of actual rebellion or invasion may be a question, but there can be none that when either country is visited by one or both of these calamities the service of every soldier should be at the King's disposal. I think the measure would in appearance as well as in fact strengthen our connection and the experience we have already had of the Irish militia has completely dispelled all our apprehensions as to their fidelity,* and must remove every jealousy on the part of England in employing them in Great Britain should the occasion call for their service. It might be sufficient to legalize the employing such regiments out of their own kingdom as shall voluntarily offer their service, until the expiry of the present term of service of the men but hereafter every militiaman to be attested to serve in Great Britain or Ireland under such restrictions as might be thought consistent

*'and the experience....Great Britain' already quoted, p. 130.

with the main object. *We* should gain security by the measure at present, but the day may come when the plague may have spent itself here and when England may experience the same struggle.

Two days before Camden tells Pelham that ' nothing would so effectively secure [the safety of the country] as the exchange of militia regiments '[2] and on the 12th Beresford urges on Auckland that it is perhaps the only opportunity ' of obtaining a law which ....would go further to secure the connection between the two countries than any other that could be made....a law which should make the militia of both countries the militia of the empire and subject to be employed in either kingdom '.[3]

An unofficial correspondent of Pelham writes to him on the 25 June : ' we are all highly pleased at the idea of exchanging a certain number of militia between the two countries '.[4] It would seem that the idea was considered to have become practical politics ; it was in some sense perhaps considered ' a lesson of the war '. But there is no evidence of its having been at that time put officially to Whitehall ; if it was put there is no sign of any response. Possibly ' interchange ' was regarded by Cornwallis, when he came on the scene, as having been prejudiced by Castlebar. English militia were, in the summer of 1798, taken to Ireland to help in the rebellion. But they came after the brunt, and, though they remained through the invasion period, were not called upon to do much. They felt *dépaysé* and wanted to get back, sooner than they were allowed. They probably did not take kindly to potential periodical expatriations and the powerful political influence of their colonels was no doubt exercised then, as it generally was, against innovation of practice.

The Irish militia on the other hand seem to have actively wanted to get sent to England. There had been sporadic individual offers earlier ; one or two units claim to have been the first to volunteer for England ; the Dublin city apparently offered in 1796, as did the Queen's county. But the first ' wave ' of volunteering *by units* came in 1799. There is some talk of repaying the indebtedness to the English militia for their assistance in 1798. But the offers were also manifestations of desire to stand well with English opinion, similar to that which had probably inspired the demonstrations of 1797 (see chap. VII). There is no list extant of the units which offered, but offers were numerous during the early months of 1799 and in many cases enthusiastic. Roscommon's offer is stated to have ' originated entirely with the men '. In another case it is explained that ' the offer is not by acclamation (the consequence of drink) but by the individual signature of the men '.[5] Several of the offers are signed by the sergeant major on behalf of all ranks. The Queen's county again (April 1799) offered stating that ' both officers and men have wanted the blue cockade*....you will therefore be so good as to insert in our address Europe in the room of Great Britain '.[6]

A bill which stimulated the volunteering enthusiasm was introduced on 3 April (39 Geo. iii. chap. 31). It empowered the king 'for a time and to an extent to be limited' to accept services voluntarily offered, and to be utilized in Great Britain or elsewhere in Europe. The act recited that the employment of English militia in Ireland had led to the greatest benefits and referred to the 'ardent and affectionate zeal' evinced for 'his majesty's service and for the general interests and security of the British empire' and to the king's desire to 'avail himself of his distinguished proof of the attachment and public spirit' of his Irish militia. So much of any act or acts as prohibited carrying Irish militia out of the kingdom was suspended so far as concerned 5,000 men.

The Irish militia had originally been created as a national force for purely Irish purposes. At that time no one remotely dreamed of the force being sent, either in whole or in part, out of Ireland, any more, perhaps, than anyone would ever have contemplated this for the Irish Volunteers, its predecessor. Indeed, when the force was being formed, one of the bogeys which operated on the popular mind seems to have been the fear of being sent abroad. 'Molyneaux' (see p. 38 chap. III) denounced the idea as an 'audacious untruth'—as it was—and the relevant provision of the act (clause 92) that 'neither the whole nor any part of the militia....shall on any account be carried or ordered to go out of Ireland" was the first of nine points emphasized, in reply to the 'evil disposed persons' who had 'endeavoured to excite the people to resist the execution of the militia law'.

Cornwallis' correspondence with Whitehall shows that the offers of the Irish militia units caused some embarrassment. They were not wanted in England, it appears, for home defence.[7] But Cornwallis thought that it was politically useful that some of the units should be sent to Great Britain: 'If two or three regiments were to be sent to England in the course of the summer, and taken notice of by the king and duke of York, it would have a good effect'.[8] This however did not commend itself to the king who minuted on a despatch: 'I can by no means encourage the idea of any of the Irish militia coming to Great Britain; it would with reason offend the English militia; some going to Jersey, Guernsey or North America might be countenanced'.[9] Cornwallis could only acquiesce. In June 1799 the King's county embarked, at a strength of 760 privates, 285 women and 259

*See also *Freeman's Journal*, 2 April 1799. 'Cork 26 March. This day officers, n.c.o.'s and men, Westmeath militia, hoisted the blue cockade in token of their willingness to serve in Europe'.

children[10] for Jersey and in August the Wexford, with over 460 women and children, for Guernsey. They remained for a year. Both regiments gave satisfactory service. By what criterion they were chosen is not clear. In April 1797 general Dalrymple had wanted the Wexford to be moved from Cork and encamped. 'I am sure' he said[11] 'both its principles and discipline will suffer a change for the better by this movement'. But this was long ago now. They were also prominently involved in the disciplinary trouble at Bandon in May of that year (see page 110) and two of their number had been solemnly executed. The King's county had apparently been in bad official odour early in 1798 but had acquired considerable merit in the action at Newtownbarry on 1 June. They were a predominantly catholic regiment.

In June the employment of the two regiments 'on actual service', i.e. on something more than garrison duty was suggested. Cornwallis thought this 'would infuse a spirit into the militia in general here, and would flatter the pride of the country'.[12] But it received cold water and on 3 July Cornwallis writes: 'I find that the measure of employing some regiments of Irish militia is not likely to be approved on your side of the water and shall therefore say nothing more on the subject, but I cannot help thinking that you lose an opportunity of obtaining a more efficient force than can, at this moment, be procured by any other means'.[13] For the moment this was the end of any idea of interchangeability, or of service outside Ireland. There is no evidence that the former was ever put officially as a policy by Dublin to the English ministers but, since the suggestion of receiving Irish militia regiments unilaterally was unwelcome to the king, there was obviously no chance for interchangeability unless some change of attitude took place.

The need for troops in Ireland after Humbert had been disposed of in 1798 was not much lessened. Invasion alarms continued. In October of that year the 3rd light battalion were at Athlone;[14] and a whole series of moves to meet the contingency of the French landing in Galway bay was arranged. Similar orders, and new march regulations, were again issued in the spring[15] and again in October 1800 and in May 1801. In the first of these three schemes,[16] which provided for a moveable and for a stationary force in each military district, only five militia regiments were included in the former category which comprised the troops to be immediately moved in the event of an enemy's landing; the stationary troops were those which could be collected in four or five days. In the October 1800 scheme also,[17] only five militia units were included; the lord lieutenant explained that the militia had within a few months given 12,000 of their best men to the regulars and contained large numbers of raw and undisciplined recruits.[18] In the year 1799 the militia units were probably not entirely reconstituted after the gruelling and material losses of the previous year. The scheme[19] of May 1801 included eight militia units among the ' moveable ' troops ; these were the Leitrim, Antrim, Cavan, Louth, Roscommon, Fermanagh, Londonderry, and lastly the Tyrone which alone had been included in both the two previous schemes. But in addition to these county units of militia there was included (as in the 1800 scheme) the militia corps d'elite consisting of the four (as there were now) light battalions* of which Cornwallis and everyone else seems to have had a high opinion.

May 1799 was in fact a time of special apprehension as regards invasion ; in 1803 this was given as a reason why the volunteering offers of 1799 had not been accepted. The French fleet were reported to have sailed from Brest on 26 April. On this alarm the whole establishment of the yeomanry were again placed on permanent duty.[20] At this time there were still 3 officers, 6 sergeants, 1 drummer, and 58 rank and file of the Limerick city militia who had been taken prisoners at Colooney and were on parole not to fight the French ; their case caused perplexity and was discussed between Dublin and London.[21] Cornwallis intended himself to direct any operations which might take place. On 3 May a very important court martial (see p. 158) assembled in Dublin. Fourteen militia commanding officers composed this court but on 6 May the lord lieutenant ' in consequence of the Brest fleet being at sea and an attempt at invasion being expected, directed that all officers should at once repair to their quarters '[22] and the court was broken up accordingly.

The corn harvest of 1799 failed ; the use of flour for the hair by the troops was consequently discontinued until further orders and they were authorized to give assistance in digging the potatoes.[23] But the Brest invasion scare died down. Before it had done so the British government had, in March, raised with Cornwallis the question of procuring for the regular regiments man power from the Irish militia. They did not want units ; they were ' perfectly strong in point of home defence '; they understood that the militia corps were badly officered ; but they would like to be ' permitted [by the Irish parliament] to fill up our regular regiments '[24] from the Irish militia. The duke of York had for some time been casting covetous eyes towards Ireland, the traditional ' *officina militum* '. What the reaction of the Irish colonels would be was clear from their attitude to the separation from them of their light companies (see p. 108). Cornwallis

*In the 1800 scheme the strength of these was taken as 2,500 ; in that of 1801 as 3,050.

was at first rather unresponsive: 'it was the opinion' he said (6 April) 'of every person with whom I ventured to converse on the subject that it would be dangerous even to agitate the measure under the present circumstances of this country'. The colonels 'would cry out that they are to be crimps and drill sergeants for the army'.[25] If it had to be done he would have liked it done without legislation. A parliamentary discussion might be too outspoken. He sought the advice of the chancellor. For a little time the view prevailed[26] that, as the augmentation of companies from 70 to 100 men had been (under the act of 1795) discretionary, consequently the disbanding of an excess 30 in each company was also within the lord lieutenant's discretion and—so ran the inference drawn—men so discharged could be utilized for the line (of course, if they volunteered) without specific parliamentary sanction. All this is interesting as showing how nervous even a relatively strong viceroy was of the militia colonels.

But at the end of the year, in deference to the insistence of the English ministers, it was decided to bring parliament together specially. What was contemplated was obviously a new departure in the use of the force and it seems plain that to proceed without consulting parliament was inadmissible. On 15 January 1800 Cornwallis, in a speech from the throne, expressed the king's confidence that the zeal and loyalty of the militia would be prompt and conspicuous. On the 20th[27] Castlereagh introduced resolutions. Cornwallis had previously assembled the colonels of militia and 'met on the whole as good-humoured an acquiescence in the wishes of government as could reasonably be expected in the present situation of things'. Lord Downshire was the only person who showed any violence on this occasion'.[28] The first of the three resolutions provided that it was expedient at the present conjuncture to permit not exceeding 10,000 to enter the line as volunteers, and laid down the numbers which were to be provided by each regiment. The aggregate of these was 11,209. The house reduced these figures all round; thus counties with an original quota of 440 (e.g. Antrim) were given a quota of 344; those with a quota of 304 (e.g. the three Cork regiments) one of 232; and so on. The total of the amended quotas was 10,041. The second resolution provided bounties of 12 guineas for general service volunteers and of 8 guineas for volunteering to 'serve in any of His Majesty's forces in Europe'. The last resolution, conforming to the government's promise that the men should be replaced without expense to the counties, provided a bounty of three guineas for the recruits to replace. The then effective force of the militia was stated by Castlereagh to be above 22,000.[29] An ensign's commission was offered for every 40 men volunteering for general service and for every 60 for limited service in Europe.

This made a motive for the junior officers to bring pressure to bear on the men.

'The militia business was stated in parliament today', writes Castlereagh on 18 January, 'and acquiesced in with much good humour....several of the opposition colonels....behaved very handsomely'.[30] He admitted quite frankly that transferring militiamen 'for the purpose of being employed on foreign service was certainly not coincident with the original principle on which they were raised'[31] and he paid many compliments to the zeal of the militia. One militia colonel complained that the government policy was 'taking away the flower of the trained militia troops and filling up their places by raw levies'. But Cornwallis had done effectively his work of persuasion and the resolutions passed unanimously, on the 20th; the next day all the necessary circulars and documents (which had already been printed) were sent out and parliament dispersed on the understanding that a bill would be introduced on the resumption to give statutory effect to the resolutions. This, when it was produced (8 February) was in the main a recruiting measure but it also provided in the customary way 'for amending the law relative to the militia of Ireland'; principally, in this sphere, it dealt with the division of the Down regiment of twelve companies into two battalions of six companies each; this was stated to be 'expedient for the general service of the militia'.

Cornwallis urged[32] the colonels of militia to be with their regiments during the recess of parliament so as to promote the obtaining of volunteers; not all responded. He complains that some officers 'prevented their men from turning out for the line by very improper means'. On 4 February, men were coming in fast and almost all for general service; this was in spite of a muddle in London which 'sent over parties from regiments for restricted service, in post-chaises two months ago, at a most enormous expense, and those of the regiments for *general* service named by the duke of York had not yet arrived'.[33] He goes on to say that 'our whole militia during this period of volunteering is in a state of perfect confusion'. It is worth noting this; when, later, volunteering became an annual event it also became an annual period of saturnalian indiscipline, as we shall see. By 28 February Cornwallis felt that the drafting of the militiamen had gone almost far enough: 'I shall', he says, 'put an end to that business and re-assemble the light infantry battalions on the 10th of next month. We have obtained 6,300 men almost all for general service, and shall probably get 1,000 more'.[34] By 1 February (1800) the strength of the militia was already down to 14,970, as compared with 22,356, and 22,886 on the same date in 1799 and 1801 respectively.

To sum up the results of this first* line recruiting effort, the aggregate number eventually obtained was over 8,000 ; the exact figure is a little differently given in different returns but there is no doubt that it somewhat exceeded 8,000. Twelve regiments produced their (amended) quota ;[35] several others came near it and, of those which had a quota over 400, both the Tipperary and Tyrone produced over 400 though not quite the full number. Some got nowhere near the number required. Cork north was lowest with 38 out of a quota of 232, Limerick city had 70 out of 174, Kerry 93 out of 232, and Wexford 92 out of 290. The Wexford colonel unsuccessfully asked[36] that, in consideration of their having given service in Guernsey, they might be entirely excused. Apparently at first five line regiments had been designated to receive the volunteers for general service ; these with the numbers they actually obtained and the places of assembly, were the following : 1st battalion Royals (Newry—776) ; 13th Foot (Charlesfort—625) ; 54th Foot (Limerick—895) ; 64th Foot (Belfast—851) ; 68th Foot (Trim—2246).[37] Later, it would appear, other regiments were appointed to receive general service volunteers. One of these was the 85th Foot. The then adjutant-general in Ireland constituted himself a recruiter for that regiment which had been his own, by sending out a circular[38] to the militia colonels requesting them to use their influence on behalf of his late regiment which in consequence seems to have done very well. Of the 54th Foot is is stated that ' in the spring of 1800 the regiment was ordered to Winchester but, before leaving Ireland, it had obtained so many volunteers from the Irish militia....that a second battalion was ordered to be formed '.[39] Of the 68th Foot the regimental history says : ' In the beginning of the year 1800 volunteering from the Irish militia took place and the 68th received about 2,600 (sic) men. The regiment then embarked at Warrenpoint.'.[40] Almost an army. This was the favourite regiment with the Irish militiamen ; practically all the volunteers given by the Dublin county (253) and the Kildare (199) and the Leitrim (218) went into it. The Cork city, out of 232 volunteers, gave 231 to the 85th Foot, and the Tyrone, out of 406, gave 353 to the 1st Royals. Later in 1804 the Roscommon, when volunteering as a unit, claimed that ' five officers and near 300 men did actually serve....in the glorious expedition to Egypt '.[41] They had, in 1800, given 210 volunteers, out of a total of 249, to the 54th Foot. At the end of March *Saunders Newsletter* states that ' regiments about to be augmented by recruits from the Irish militia are said to be selected for an expedition '. The baptism of fire was not to be very long in coming. Three of the line regiments—13th Foot, 54th Foot (1st and 2nd battalions) and

*The next did not come until 1805

27th Foot (2nd battalion)—which had received Irish militiamen were included[42] in the force which sir Ralph Abercromby had in Egypt in 1801 and with which he achieved so much fame. It is stated that of nearly 30,000 men assembled in the early summer of 1800 on Netley common for foreign service the flower were from the Irish Militia that had then for the first time been allowed to volunteer for the Line. Contemporary Irish newspapers[43] state that more than 5,000 Irish officers and men took part in the engagement on 8 March and that in his despatch Abercromby greatly commended the bravery of those men who were drafts from the Irish militia. No special mention of the Irish militiamen is to be found in Abercromby's official despatches. He may have semi-officially made some express commendation—an '*amende honorable*' for the stain which his general order had been the means of fastening upon the force.

Steps were also taken in 1800 to bring into the line men who had deserted from the militia. There is, apart from anything that took place at Castlebar, not much about desertion in the newspapers or correspondence of 1798. At all times of course and in all military forces a certain number of men trickle away. 'At no time during the war', says an historian,[44] writing of Pitt's difficulties in 1804, 'was it an easy task to obtain soldiers, for the privates were subject to savage punishments and their comforts and well-being were shamefully neglected'. Similar causes would account for difficulties in retaining them. These difficulties were perhaps operating in Ireland during the year 1798, less, rather than more, than at other times; on such evidence as there is, desertion was, in that emotionally critical time, smaller in amount than it was in (say) the years 1803-4,* 1811 and 1812, for which years there are some figures available.[45] Garrison ennui of course produces desertion but there was probably little of this in 1798. For that year there are no figures, only—what is much more easy to produce—statements. In February 1799 there was a comprehensive debate[46] in the Irish house of commons on this matter. It was then sweepingly alleged that from several militia regiments during the late rebellion large proportions had gone over to the enemy. The remark that this was notorious was greeted with cries of 'No, no!' The speaker mentioned specifically the King's county, Longford, Antrim, 'and some other regiments (not specified) including one of dragoons'. Castlereagh repudiated wholesale charges, recalling that the Irish militia were native troops 'actuated by local prejudice and warm feelings for their country', and said that 'if the means perpetually and sedulously used to seduce them were considered the defection was

*1,450 desertions. This was the period just after the re-embodiment.

not in the proportion alleged '; he also said that when he considered the uneducated state of the men he wondered more did not desert. The members for the three counties animadverted upon and also colonel Longfield for Cork spoke in defence of their county units. For Longford sir Walter Newcomen said that the Longford militia were ' not 300 strong on that day in the field ' (i.e. at Castlebar); that 170 of them stopped the progress of the French for a considerable time ; ' had they been supported they had prevented the taking of the town '; and he urged strongly other points in their favour. The member for Antrim, admitting that some men of the Antrim regiment did desert, asserted that these had been enlisted in co. Wicklow ; this was presumably prior to 1797 in which year extra-county enlisting had been prohibited, though it may have occured in spite if the prohibition.

Next year on the 1800 militia bill the committee were instructed to receive a clause instructing the lord lieutenant to pardon militia deserters on their surrendering themselves or voluntarily enlisting into the regular regiments. A proclamation was accordingly issued which recites that there were ' several deserters ' from the militia who might be induced to return to their duty. The fact that this action was taken indicates that there was a real mischief. There are no official statistics as to the number who sought pardon but newspaper reports are[47] to the effect that in the month of May there were a body of not less than 120 deserters from the militia, well-armed and disciplined, who committed daily and nightly outrages upon the well-affected people of co. Wicklow. There are no reports of any other similar gangs. This Wicklow gang (to which no doubt other than ex-militia desperadoes resorted) was not easily dispersed (see below, p. 157).

The desertion problem requires to be approached with an adequate sense of proportion. A writer who examined in 1898 the (then available)* statistics affirms that ' in 1797 when disaffection was supposed to be most rampant ', the average desertion from the Irish militia on the one hand and from the line and English and Scottish regiments on the other, was exactly equal ; ' conceding ', he says, ' the fact that regiments lose most men when stationed at or near their native places, it works out most creditably for the militia '. In a previous year, 1794, he finds that the desertions from the English and Scotch regiments in Ireland were six times the number from the militia. He further states that the ' deserters from the regular troops and the English and Scotch fencible units were always in excess of those from the militia '. His general statement is as follows :—

*See *Guide to the records deposited in the Public Record Office of Ireland* (1919). Herbert Wood, p. 216 ' Deserters Registers and Papers concerning 1777-1838 '.

When and how the continued statements as to the untrustworthiness of this body originated it is impossible to say, except that the persistent belief of the United Irishmen to that effect and the absence of any contradiction has caused the idea to become stereotyped. Down to the present day these statements are made, and every argument upon the period starts on this assumption. Yet not one fact worthy of consideration is brought forward to justify such a charge. All we can gather from the official returns which are above the imputation of partiality leads to an absolutely opposite conclusion —that these men were a credit to their country from no matter what point of view they are judged, inasmuch as having sworn to do certain duties, they manfully did them under the most extraordinarily trying circumstances.

He also says that the steady augmentation of the force was 'a curious process for a government to pursue if they really thought they were training only veiled insurgents'.*

Cornwallis' intention of reassembling the light companies has been mentioned (p. 151). These had been sent back in February 1800 to their regiments for the volunteering. The previous year there had been complaints from Dublin to the units of the unfitness of the men sent from the militia regiments to serve in the light battalions and there is evidence that the colonels were not sending to the light battalions their most suitable men and were sending men who were not properly found. Cornwallis however was very much in earnest about the light battalions and, when the companies were sent back, he had kept up the staff establishments of the corps at Athlone and Ballinasloe. But if the colonels were to send back their men it needed a stimulas. This was administered in March by Cornwallis ordering immediate reassembly; he was confident that the colonels would 'forward this very essential object by every exertion in [their] power'. It is not clear what happened. Some of the colonels probably fought a dogged rearguard action and procured some stay of execution. After some months Cornwallis issued yet another order for immediate assembly, and also ordered that an exact description of each man sent to the light battalions should be forwarded to Dublin 'to prevent the impositions which have been sometimes practised by changing the men after they have been approved by the general officers commanding'.[48] On 1 September when the strength was 1,500 rank and file, he held an inspection at Athlone. A contemporary account[49] says that they were reviewed in one corps and that 'notwithstanding that the ground was extensive they were so numerous as not to admit their being formed in one line'. Cornwallis expressed 'the highest satisfaction at the steadiness, precision and exactitude with which this most respectable corps performed all its movements and operations'. He also

*These quotations are from articles (unsigned) which appeared in the *Irish Times* in May 1898. The author's name is, I am informed, not ascertainable.

attended the evening parade and the next day ' all the battalions marched out of Athlone about two miles where on very uneven and broken ground they again, in the presence of his excellency, went through a variety of movements, advancing, retreating, charging and countermarching, etc.'. The order he issued before leaving Athlone spoke of the ' high state of discipline of that distinguished brigade '. By November all the companies had come in; they were then formed into four battalions, and the strength was 2,800. This had increased to 3,369 rank and file by June 1801 and it was then anticipated that the strength would soon reach 3,800 or 38 companies of 100 men each.[50]

There seems no doubt that this body of militiamen reached a high state of discipline and efficiency. Brigadier general W. Scott* who was in command was a remarkable trainer of troops. A militia officer[51] who was with the light infantry at Athlone and elsewhere has called general Scott ' an excellent drill ' and he says of his system that ' while based upon the mathematical precision of the Prussians it exhibited all the rapidity of French movement—that rapidity introduced by Napoleon..... Our brigade was well-qualified to have met the French in this style of movement '. Another interesting comment on these militamen, derived from the same source, is the following: ' I must say that he [general Scott] had a troublesome set of Pickles to manage as need be. In fact Pickleism was assumed to be the privilege of the light bobs. Nothing short of a cat or a monkey could compete with many of them in feats of activity '. Mental qualities, intelligence and activity, distinguished the light infantry men (colloquially ' light bobs '); the physical qualities of good stature and of being well set up characterized the grenadiers (colloquially ' tow rows,' while the battalion men were ' flat foots '). A letter[52] written by lord Sligo in 1803 brings out another important point. After stating that some 4,000 men had been brought to ' a perfection as nearly approaching troops of the line as possible ' he says that the men who had:

> ' rendered this service to the Irish militia had benefitted the whole country in proving that a detachment from every regiment might live together as one corps; that men from every town and village might be assembled together without affray; whose politics and religious opinions had made them hate each other; and that they had been governed with that impartiality that justice that regularity that wherever these men settled there was hopes (if not positive proof) their cabin and their conduct proved they once belonged to the light brigade '.

Notwithstanding invasion alarms, the two years in Ireland after the rebellion year, were, as regards active military duty,

A Sketch-map of the Castlebar *terrain* by this officer is reproduced in the *Journal of the Society for Army of Historical Research.* Vol. 26, 1948, No. 107.

comparatively calm. In 1799 a camp was held at Monkstown (co. Cork) but the abatement of the invasion scare, for the moment, and increasing internal tranquillity caused the plans for encamping other units to be altered. Rebels still remained active, more particularly in the Wicklow mountains. Dwyer was their leader and the duty of pursuing them there came to be known as 'Dwyer hunting'. In October 1800 we hear of[53] the 'arduous duties of officers lately employed and to be employed in the Wicklow mountains during the ensuing winter and spring'; they are described as 'harassed by constant patrols, without a market and deprived of the ordinary means of comfort which other officers upon home service usually receive'. Each field officer received an extra payment of £30 and each captain, subaltern and staff officer of £20. There are also records of payments to soldiers employed in these mountains 'in search of outstanding rebells'. This search was still going on in the winter 1803-4 though in the meantime the Wicklow military road and the barracks had been built. In one of these latter Dwyer was held prisoner before he was taken to Dublin. This pursuit was the principal active military duty of those years; there was comparatively little general disorder such as there had been in the pre-rebellion period or during the period of Defender activity in 1795. The militia units consequently enjoyed a relatively quiet time. 'Now that provisions', writes a lieutenant colonel to his colonel in October 1801, 'are become so reasonable* and our pay so good, I think it will be an advantageous way of disposing of a very small portion of it by wearing powder when on guard and on Sundays and Wednesdays; it adds much to a soldier's appearance in point of dress, exclusive of the comfort of cleaning the hair'.[54] The authorities at this period seem now to have been prepared to let the regiments become settled down in one quarter, and, when the disembodiment came in 1802, many had been uninterruptedly in one place for as much as three years. What was said of them when they eventually moved away from a quarter was often on the lines of: 'the polite and social manners of the officers have engaged our friendship' and 'the good behaviour of the privates has merited highest approbation', and it was in the glow of such compliments that many of them went to their disembodiment.

During the years 1799 and 1800 Union was a general pre-occupation and the travails which preceded it were hardly likely to go through without the militia getting involved in political controversy. This had not happened before, though lord Blayney in 1797 had expressed the view that the 'militia are all politicians'.[55] The person who now got himself irretrievably impli-

*Extra allowances (discontinued, however, in October on account of the abundance of every sort of provisions) had been issued 'during the late scarcity'.

cated was no other than the 'father of all the militia', lord Downshire. A pseudonymous letter to government from one 'Jeffery Foresight', from Carlow where the Downshire regiment were lying, suggested that if a corps of militia were to be allowed to 'petition against and reprobate the government who pay them there was some danger of a second part of the concerto played at Castlebar'. Enquiry swiftly followed. A petition against the Union had, it appeared, lain at the quarters of the commanding officer for signature and most of the officers signed it; and another copy had lain at the adjutant's quarters and had been signed by as many non-commissioned officers and privates as there were in the regiment—if not by more. Lord Downshire was removed from the command of the Down militia and also from the governorship of the county and his name was erased from the list of the Privy Council. British ministers would have liked to take even more drastic action. This was in February 1800.[56]

In 1799 the city of Dublin militia had been under the fierce light of publicity. The Sankey-Giffard general court-martial (see p. 149), the proceedings of which were published as a substantial pamphlet[57] in 1800, disclosed irregularities. In 1800 no militia unit was more in the news than the Downshire. There was, first of all, the trouble just mentioned. Then, as from 1 April, 1800, it was divided into two battalions. There had been little alteration up to then in the county structure of the militia as laid down in the original act except the incorporation, as from 1 May, 1797, of the small Drogheda battalion of three companies into the Louth regiment.

The alteration of the structure of the Down regiment was stated by Castlereagh,[58] to be due to unwieldiness; with companies of 100 each the total strength would be 1,200 privates; few barracks were equal to accommodating this number; there had already been with this regiment too much breaking-up into different cantonments and command devolving upon junior officers; and in 1793 the property basis, in regard to the assignment of militia complements had been miscalculated for county Down. The opposition urged that increase of patronage for the government with a view to their Union policy was the guiding motive and that the proposal was 'directed to the vexation of a distinguished and virtuous nobleman who preferred his country to the minister'. A division was insisted upon and showed seventy-five in favour and 26 against.

On the first day of the new century came the Union, and, like many other great historical transitions of wide bearing social and political, it came quietly, without surface disturbance. Nor did Mother Nature take any large scale elemental notice of the Union being accomplished. The stars did not

‘ with deep amaze
Stand fixt in stedfast gaze ’.

Men had ceremonial observances. It was an age of *feu-de-joies*—three royal birthdays, the royal coronation, the accession, king William III’s birthday, king Charles’ restoration, the Gunpowder plot, as well as the Irish rebellion (23 October) and the not infrequent victories on sea and land—all of these had to be celebrated by the troops in Ireland by the creation of noise. On the initial day of Union a royal salute was fired. The ensigns, armorial flags and banners, altered as prescribed by the lord lieutenant, were hoisted. The militia and other troops were all under arms.

Matters military had not bulked largely in the Union debates. Interchangeability seems somehow to have got overlooked. Later, in 1803, Hardwicke represented to Whitehall that there was no gentleman or colonel of militia who did not regard the want of it as a defect in the Act of Union ; if they had foreseen, in 1799-1800, that there would afterwards be objection to permitting interchange they would have pressed for a clause in the Act of Union.[59]

Nothing new came into being, pat as from the day. Fortescue[60] says that ‘ the union of Ireland with Great Britain contributed enormously towards the simplification of our military affairs at large ’ and suggests that from 1801 the military picture became entirely changed. But the ‘ periodical lists of promotions and vacancies, ’ to which he alludes as ceasing, still continued to be submitted from Dublin by the lord lieutenant. On 29th December 1800 Cornwallis[61] was ‘ inclined to believe that for some time at least it will be proper to have a War office here ’. In the list of charges for ‘Army Extraordinaries ’ for 1803 appears[62] an extra charge in respect of the ‘ great increase of business in the military department of the Chief Secretary’s Office ’. Hardwicke, who resented being deprived of the lord lieutenant’s military patronage, opposed the centralizing tendency of Whitehall. He insisted that ‘ local knowledge, information and control gave a better means of forming a correct judgment of the characters of individuals and state of affairs in Ireland than could be obtained at a greater distance ’. ‘ Whatever ’, he said, ‘ may be the state and condition of Ireland at some distant period of time it is now too soon to consider it on the footing of an English county ’.[63]

If for regular troops the Union may have involved administrative changes, for the national militia it seems to have made no difference except that legislation concerning it (which still continued abundant) was a London and not a Dublin function. Even this, however, is subject to qualification : the militia bills were for a long time, if they were no longer debated in a Dublin parliament, still drafted in Dublin castle. In connection with the disembodiment and re-embodiment (see next chapter) draft bills appear to have been taken over to London by the attorney general. Another draft bill was sent over in 1805 and the consolidation bill which sir Arthur Wellesley introduced in 1809 (p. 239) was also worked out and prepared in Dublin.

Many militia notabilities entered the first Union parliament and their duties there took those who were colonels still more from their regiments and accentuated the field officers' absence difficulty, which had always handicapped the Irish militia. The parliament in London gave early attention to this problem. The Irish parliament in its last militia amending act had increased the number of captains and thus relieved the field officers. But the act of 1801 * was for ' increasing the number of *field officers* of the several regiments of militia in Ireland '. It was explained that ' the number of officers in the Irish regiments was too small in proportion to the number of men '. Castlereagh subsequently justified these additions by reference to the augmentation of the year 1800, but an Irish member put his finger on the spot when he pointed to the fact that ' many of the field officers were members and would be obliged to attend their duty in parliament '.[64]

The increased establishment of officers consisted, in the case of units of eight companies and upwards (21 in number) of one additional lieutenant colonel and one additional major and, in the case of units of seven companies or under (17 in number), of one additional major. Additional officers were to have the property qualifications as laid down and were to be appointed by the colonels or lieutenant colonels. Some of the extra officers were provided from ' axed ' officers of the Royal Irish Regiment of Artillery.[65] After the re-embodiment in 1803 the Irish militia re-started with the 1795 establishment and, of course, a reduced cadre of officers. The English militia had had its field officers augmented in 1798.

Reference has been made to the ' augmentation of 1800 '. Castlereagh had apparently suggested increasing the militia units by way of compensating the colonels for having their units drained for the line. Augmentation and tribute of volunteers became parallel processes. On this occasion the idea seems to have been to get the new-levied men into the units in advance of the efflux; and the augmentation was announced (October 1799) before the details of the volunteering had been settled. Possibly to avoid trouble prematurely with the colonels, the augmentation was announced as having the object of equalizing ' the establishment of the regiments and battalions of militia with respect to the strength of their companies '. This was a discretionary augmentation and no expense fell on the counties. The colonels were to

*41 Geo. III. U.K. chap .6, royal assent 24 March 1801.

'make all practicable exertion and dispatch in completing this augmentation'. It is not recorded how many men had been obtained by the end of the year but they did not come readily. An order of 2 January 1800 refers to the 'event of any colonel being unable to complete the augmentation'. The units were at one and the same time trying to get (and, when got, trying to absorb) additional men and carrying out the volunteering programme which had come into operation at the end of January. No wonder Cornwallis (4 February) found the whole militia during this period of volunteering to be in 'a state of perfect confusion'.[66] By June 1801 the force was 'half composed of recruits from twelve to one months'. Of the units, by about this date, only 21 were augmented[67]; the dates of augmentation being complete (i.e. as certified by the general) range from February 1800 to April 1801. In October Cornwallis describes the force as 'incomplete' and the completion of the light infantry brigade is known to have hung fire because of the slowness with which the regiments fed it; the strength was then 25,412; and the establishment 28,424;[68] on 7 August the effectives had only been 18,118 and over 10,000 were then wanting.

Important light is thrown upon the state of the militia at this time, with reference to strength, by the report of the Army Medical Board dated 1 June 1800.*[69] This shows that, in 35 battalions or regiments inspected in April and May of that year, 1,546 men in all, drummers and non-commissioned officers included, had been rejected, and were presumably discharged. Of these 202 were 'children or boys' and undersize; the remaining 1,344 are classified as: old, feeble, or worn-out; general bad health; chronic disease producing incapacity for active service; lame, diseased or deformed limbs; incurable ulcers on legs of long standing; and ruptured. The inspection did not cover the Wexford and King's county which were in the Channel islands nor the light infantry companies at Athlone and Ballinasloe nor some 730 sergeants, corporals, drummers and privates who were absent either on leave or on duty. The total number of diseased and unserviceable men in the force was estimated at 1,600. During the four years preceding June 1800, as a result of special applications of the Army Medical Board, some 1,590 men had been discharged as labouring under incurable ailments; and this was independent of double that number at least estimated to have been got rid of, on similar grounds, subsequent to the annual regimental reviews by the district major-generals. In March 1801 the Board were able to report that during recent

*Valuable information is obtainable from the reports of the Army Medical Board, when available. Unfortunately there is no complete set.

years 'a vigilant and laudable attention had been paid to the treatment of the militia sick and in May 1802 the 'medium annual mortality' had fallen substantially.

During the greater part of 1801 the inhabitants of Ireland at large suffered greatly from famine and fever. A Castle official reports that the commanding officer of the Kerry militia had told him that his regiment 'were reduced to a state of feebleness, from inaction. They have only oatmeal and water to live upon'. They were at Rathangan, in the neighbourhood of Dublin. These conditions may have predisposed the militia towards serving, if they could, outside Ireland. Then again the monotony of militia service in small towns and on command in small detachments (which probably accounts for many desertions as well as for the scraps between different units and different religious persuasions) may, irrespectively of the bad conditions prevailing, have been at this time and at others a motive towards volunteering for England.

In 1801 there was another volunteering (by *units*) wave. Whereas the suggestion of volunteering as indidividuals originated from England, the interchangeability idea and simple unilateral England-wards volunteering as whole units had been put forward from Ireland. The second volunteering wave in 1801 was initiated from England, taken up keenly in Ireland and then frowned down by official England.

Some time in July a semi-official letter[70] from the War Office in London mentioned 'the immediate apprehension of an attack upon England' and desired the means to be prepared of sending from Ireland such force as could be spared. The commander of the forces in Ireland, with the assent of the lord lieutenant, in a private letter asked the colonels of militia 'whether they would volunteer their service into England for the immediate defence of that part of the United Kingdom'.[71] This produced a remarkable response; 32 militia corps volunteered; and the chief secretary urged: 'there never could be a more favourable opportunity for entering upon what I shall ever think the truest measure for cementing the Union, namely, an interchange of militia service'.[72] But by Pelham, now secretary of state, this was not well received; that England should be beholden to Ireland apparently did not go down well; and the lord lieutenant was told that this volunteering was a 'measure upon which the King's servants in England should have been consulted before it was undertaken'.[73] Pelham spoke of 'the illegality and consequent difficulty of carrying the measure into execution'. This was presumably a reference to the lapsing of the powers under the act of 1799 or, if they had not lapsed, to the large and unauthorized scale (beyond the 5,000) of contemplated transfer. The lord lieutenant replied that he had thought the exigency justified the acceptance of the offer and that he had been unaware of the illegality. He had, in order to make the volunteering a success, issued special regulations making 'a suitable and proper provision' for the wives and children of the militiamen who volunteered; from an endorsement it would appear that Pelham felt that the king's approval to these regulations had been obtained over his head.[74] Nothing was done. Disembodiment was coming into the picture; by the time this came no units of Irish militia had been 'carried out of Ireland' other than the Wexford and King's county.

A picture may perhaps usefully be given here of the make up of a militia unit as regards age and height of the men, just at the period before disembodiment. A return was called for on these two points in January 1802. The assembled statistics arising from these reports are not available but these are the figures for the Donegal[75] and Armagh[76] regiments respectively :—

	Donegal	*Armagh*
men of 5ft. 10in. and upwards ..	96	103
men of 5ft. 5in. and under 5ft. 10in.	654	510
men under 5ft. 5in.	141	6
	891	619

Out of its 619 men the Armagh had 46 who were 6ft. and upwards and the Donegal had 19 out of 891. The ages were as follows :—

men upwards of 40 years ..	17	8
men of 40 years	38	12
men of 35 years*	38	30
men of 30 years	160	71
men of 25 years	310	146
men of 20 years	213	238
men of 18 years	115	110
men under 18 years	—	4
	891	619

It would have been interesting if the figures for a southern unit had been available. In March 1802 the aggregate strength was 25,106 and there were wanting 3,394. The average effectives for 1801 had been 25,936.

*'And upwards', presumably, in this and the next four lines. The figures are as given in the returns.

XI

Disembodiment and Re-embodiment

In the middle of November 1801, if not earlier, Hardwicke raises the point : should the clothing which the militia would ordinarily receive on 25 December be issued—in view of possibilities? The commander of the forces thought that if the force remained embodied for but a short time after the 24 December—the clothing renewal date—new clothing would be required, as in several regiments clothing had been worn considerably longer than it was supposed to be serviceable. To do nothing was not justifiable and it was decided that the clothing should be provided but delivery of it postponed.[1] The official disembodiment letter ultimately issued in May 1802 shows that the clothing due to the men on the 25 December 1801 had been 'delivered in pursuance of the general Regulation'.

In October 1801, recruiting, and re-enlistment of men whose four years of service was expiring, was stopped. About the same time lord Pelham put to the lord lieutenant the following point :—

'The reduction of the Irish militia requires much consideration ; it occurred to lord Pelham when in Ireland that some mode of gradually reducing that establishment would be necessary in order to anticipate the public inconvenience, and possible private distress to the individual militiaman, to be expected from the sudden disembodying of the Irish militia according to the rules followed in England ; and he had intended to employ them upon the roads, canals, and other public works, allowing such of them as could find employment for themselves to go home. If the system of building places of strength should be adopted the militia could not be better employed than on those works ; the officers and noncommissioned officers should be kept up and military discipline preserved, so that they might not only be employed upon the footing of military working parties, but in case of internal civil commotion be called upon in aid of the civil power. If the principle should be approved of, an act of parliament enabling the militia to renew their services upon these terms would be necessary and in the act provision might be made for their general reduction at the discretion of the lord lieutenant'.[2]

This document is endorsed by the duke of Portland : 'the subject is so new to me that I cannot hazard any opinion upon it but generally I should incline to think the Irish militia an establishment highly desirable to be abolished'—a view which he had stated formerly in 1799. There is no trace of any attention having been paid to this, perhaps not very important, expression of opinion. No other reference at this stage to abolishing the force is traceable though, if that was to be the policy, here was the opportunity—as was indeed pointed out in the debates at Westminster in 1803 (see page 178).

That it was not taken deserves to be noted. Before the Union, the Irish parliament was in control, though not absolutely, and it is perhaps hardly to be expected that it would have allowed abolition. The force was popular. It assisted, as already pointed out, civilian effort on numerous occasions, in subduing fires and in dealing with other emergencies such as shipwrecks. Its frequent reviews, inspections and military exercises were resorted to eagerly; and its colourful presence, and its not infrequent escapades in the streets, gave gaiety to the Irish towns. We hear, for instance, of the Clare militia band, quartered in distant Londonderry, entertaining on Sunday those northern citizens on their mall with music. This was in the early days, but the popularity seems to have continued. Wherever the militia battalions and regiments were quartered for any lengthy period, they normally received warm votes of thanks, and, in some cases, the officers were given pieces of plate. All this, however, was the Irish aspect which did not necessarily look the same, and after 1800, across the channel. But Irish susceptibilities in regard to its militia were obviously considered. The British military authorities however did not lack experience of disbanding military formations; the regiments of foot from 101 to 128 were summarily disbanded in the nineties and the fencibles in 1801; and undoubtedly, if there had been any serious opinion in favour of disbanding the Irish militia (which would have required legislation), that course might have neen adopted. But this did not happen. In February 1802, Addington reviewed[3] Irish business and took account of the disembodiment problems, but the report of this review makes no mention of possible abolition. England was not going to abolish *its* militia; and the general policy was for Ireland to be kept in step with England.

Hardwicke, in January 1802,[4] gave symmetry as one reason for having a militia in Ireland, though he had more substantial, if not military, arguments. It tended to induce many of the leading country gentlemen to look continually to the crown for the honours and emoluments belonging to the command of regiments, 'the possession of which will naturally incline them to give local support to the King's government'. Also it brought the gentry of Ireland into closer touch with the lower classes of their countrymen; it made for closer relations between protestants and roman catholics 'whose religious animosities will, it is hoped, in consequence abate'. On the other hand, there was the danger arising from 'arming so large a body of the people amongst whom so considerable a proportion are roman catholics, whose sentiments and actions have heretofore been too frequently in hostility to the British connection and government'. He took the opportunity of pressing the idea of interchangeableness which (if the services of so great a military force were retained) would 'obviate mischievous consequences'. The mutual intercourse arising from an interchange would be an excellent thing politically. On these rather than military grounds, he seemed prepared to contemplate retention of the militia; but without interchangeableness the political objects could not be attained. His military advisers thought that 'in a pure military point of view, to recruit in Ireland for the line without raising a militia, would be highly expedient'.

Pelham's idea of an act to provide for special employment of the militia did not entirely drop. Hardwicke agreed with some measure for *gradual* disembodying, either retention by law of a proportion of the force for a certain period after the signing of a definite treaty of peace and their employment on public works whether military roads or fortresses, or any other plan thought expedient by ministers.[5] A bill was drafted which was to be called 'An act[6] ....to continue the services of the respective regiments of the militia of Ireland for certain public purposes therein recited'. The preamble of this stated that it was highly expedient 'to employ a certain portion of the officers, non-commissioned officers and private soldiers....in the construction of works for public purposes and in assisting if the occasion shall require the police and magistracy....and whereas it is proper to encourage the private soldiers of the militia to re-enlist for the above-mentioned purposes'....The project of such an act got, however, no further than this draft.

Mr. Foster,[7] the late speaker of the Irish house of commons, whose opinion on militia matters always carried great weight, and whose brains Hardwicke had been advised by Pelham to pick, was against the policy expressed in the draft bill but thought that the militia might be offered employment on approved public works, *after disembodiment*. He also suggested that it would be advantageous to employ a certain number in the woollen industry. In December 1801 the trustees of the Linen and Hempen manufacturers decided that 1,000 linen looms should be without delay made against the time that the militia might be disembodied.[8] The colonels were asked to send in returns of those of their men 'who are likely to be established on the disembodying of the militia in situations for weaving or to whom the grant of a loom might be a probable means of obtaining such a situation'. In the case of one northern regiment the return sent in exists; it gave 'the names of 185 men that is weavers'. In January 1802 the Linen Board apparently authorized £4,000 for the purchase of looms to be distributed amongst the privates; a certain number were to be allotted to the colonel of each regiment to be disposed of at his discretion at the time the men were discharged. Other similar efforts to help militiamen on discharge were probably made. The colonels in some cases no doubt provided agricultural work on their demesnes—not all the militia were 'manufacturers'—and those who in 1793 had been promised farms as an inducement to come in (see page 48) may then have been invited to take up the promises. The duke of York, and also Mr. Foster, advocated enlisting to the line prior to disembodiment; the king supported[9] this, but nothing was done. After disembodiment there was a limited amount of line-enlistment but this was not under organized arrangements.

By the end of April the militia were in their counties, and the official view in Dublin was that 'the situation of the regiments on the eve of being disembodied required more than ordinary vigilance and attention. The sooner the disembodiment is effected the better'.[10] There was, of course, much merry-making. The reception of the Limerick city seems to have been tumultuous. This is how it was described in 1827:[11]

> They halted at Woodford, the seat of their venerated colonel Gough, who entertained his companions-in-arms, from whom he was about to separate, with an elegant repast laid out in tents on the lawn. They entered the city amidst the ringing of bells and the enthusiastic acclamations of their fellow citizens, marching to their own tune of "Garryowen".

There was also enthusiasm in other counties. The best first-hand account is from Armagh:

> At length the hour came and the month of May 1802 saw all Ireland alive with regiments and companies on their march to their respective counties.... As we approached Armagh the friends of the men began to meet us in considerable numbers.... The greatest trouble on the march was in preventing their mistaken kindness from bringing the soldiers into disgrace by giving them liquors.... Our arrival in Armagh was the signal for all manner of gaiety. The gentry of the county flocked in and we were fêted and dinnered and suppered. We....gave a grand ball.[12]

From another county there is a slightly different story; the field officers and captains gave a dinner at which sixty, including a bishop and three ladies, were present. But there is this wail:

> This is the second time the regiment was polite to the gentlemen of the county, yet they have scarcely deigned to acknowledge us, and every other regiment has been welcomed home by addresses from grand juries, and other little civilities. The Donegal regiment is as little thought of as when they were 200 miles from the county.[13]

What was the feeling of the men at being disembodied? The officer already quoted says the disembodiment was a period

> looked forward to with pleasure by some of our men but far from agreeable,

I believe, to the great bulk of them.... In fact, very few men, after having made a fair trial of the comforts of a soldier's life, can sit contentedly down to the labours and privations of ' life in a cabin '. Two hours on his feet at a time as a sentinel are very different from five or six at the bottom of a ditch or even behind a loom.

And again :

Of the soldiers some were pleased at getting home but the greater part regretted the loss of their regimental comforts. It was curious to see them taking leave of their firelocks. One grenadier, I heard, as he pitched his into the store, exclaim : ' There ye go darlin' an' be' jabers I'd know the crack of ye in a thousand '. Some enlisted into the line before they were half an hour discharged, thus gaining two days' pay for the one, a feat of knowingness for which they took great credit to themselves.

Enlistments into the line of disembodied militiamen are stated not to have exceeded five hundred.[14]

The peace of Amiens had been signed on the 25 March, and the lord lieutenant advised that the regiments could not be kept together after the signing of the definitive treaty of peace for a longer period than two months. This had reference to the ' two months after ' provision in the attestation oaths. On the 5 May were issued three documents[15] drafted by the law officers of the crown in Ireland : lord lieutenant's warrant ordering disembodiment ; letter of thanks from the lord lieutenant for the services rendered ; and a circular letter setting out the technical details of the disembodiment. There is at this time a remark by the lord lieutenant on the ' want of precision and consistency in the existing militia laws '.[16] Without doubt, there was much difficulty and legal discussion. Before the disembodiment, on 1 May, the rank and file strength was 24,882 and 3,618 were wanting ; there were 1,493 sergeants and 633 drummers. The officer strength was 1,040 and the staff (paymasters, adjutants, quartermasters, surgeons and assistant surgeons) amounted to 175. There were at the time 449 rank and file on furlough.[17]

Some of the men to be discharged were let go previous to the march of the regiments to the place where they were to be disembodied.[18] This goes to show that there had been extra-county recruiting. The settling of the accounts and the discharges seem to have proceeded with reasonable rapidity. The colonels had been warned from Dublin ' to prevent any unnecessary protraction of this business '. In the case of one regiment it is stated that ' all the companies except two made frivolous complaints and advanced a variety of unreasonable demands ' but that all these claims ' were refuted to the satisfaction of the general '.[19] The men seem to have ' persevered in their good conduct to the last moment they held their arms ' and no disturbances occurred. There was some trouble about the clothing. The militiaman and his clothing were not easily parted ; we know that, at a later period, the men's coats were, when worn out, passed on to their wives to be cut down into clothing for their children. The Limerick county nearly mutinied at the disembodiment because they were not permitted to take their great coats which the government alleged they required to clothe the naked soldiers returning from the Peninsular. The Tipperary also gave trouble when they were refused their clothes. But lord Hardwicke had, early in April, suggested to Whitehall that the men shall be allowed to carry away their clothing ' as a boon from his majesty ', which he said was the usual practice.[20] This seems to be a reference to the English militia disembodiment precedent of 1783—which was admittedly being followed. Possibly the men, who probably had no garments except their uniform, and no money, had, by action they took or threatened before Hardwicke moved, led him to make his proposal. Anyhow, the circular[21] adopted his formula and the men were allowed to carry away ' for their own use as a boon from the king ' not only the clothing which had been issued new on 25 December 1801 (and was due to last until 25 December 1803) but also their ' watchcoats, now in wear, which have been paid for by the public '. This did not apply to those sergeants, corporals, drummers and fifers who were retained on the disembodied establishment but it did apply to the non-commissioned officers ' who were not to be continued '.

The number of those to be retained was less than the embodied establishment and, selection consequently had to be made ; this was a matter for the colonel's dicretion. ' Consideration was paid to the credit and contentment of the permanent staff, as also to the foundation of a future....regiment. Some who wanted discharge were held to serve '. In one regiment a number of corporals applied to be discharged ' having small farms and habitations in different parts of the kingdom '; several also applied ' whose families were settled in America '. In making new appointments proper attention was paid ' to the people who have taken a part with the regiment from its establishment '. Another point a colonel was asked to settle was whether the non-commissioned officers on the disembodied establishment should be permitted ' to wear their hair in short queues instead of clubbed as formerly '.[22]

But there was a far more difficult disembodiment problem. The militia had been augmented at different periods ; men had been re-enlisted from time to time ; and as a whole they were then ' held under attestations of various descriptions '. This was perhaps due to some irregularity,* which is easy to understand,

*The returns mentioned in the next sentence contained no numbers for the Kildare regiment against which is : ' enlisted for no limited period '.

in the attesting of the re-enlisted men and the men raised on augmentation.[23] The final returns showed, out of a total number of 23,770 privates, 16,866 under engagement to serve during the war *and two months after*. The proportions varied considerably as between one unit and another : while in the Galway the whole of the privates (788) were eligible for discharge under the 'two months after' covenant, in the Donegal only 148 were eligible out of 949 privates, and, in the Wicklow regiment, only 63 out of 689 privates.[24] This matter evidently exercised the pundits. In an existing memorandum, there are references to 'an injudicious deference to the dictum of Mr. Foster' and also to 'Mr. Foster or any others proficient in political logic'.[25] Mr. Foster was almost certainly against letting any man off his unexpired service, and this was the view on which the relevant paragraph of the disembodiment instructions[26] was drafted. This runs as follows :—

> Those men whose period of service is not expired are to be particularly informed that, in conformity with their oath and engagement, they are liable to be called out, in case the militia should be again embodied before the expiration of their service, or to attend any assembly of the regiment, for the purpose of training or exercising, in time of peace.

This did not settle much : for instance, what and when was the date of expiration of service of this man and that ? Dublin Castle was no doubt inundated with queries. About a fortnight after the issue (5 May) of the demobilization instructions, reference was made to the Law Officers : 'to report what number of militiamen are entitled to their discharge'.[27] The actual report made is not available, but it was sent to London. It must have proved impossible to devise a formula which legally would hold water and at the same time be a plausible simple explanation, comprehensible to the peasant mind, as to why nearly the whole of one regiment could be finally discharged from all obligation for further service and why nearly the whole of another should have to be retained still liable. Had not peace, after all these years, been signed, and had they not all had so much more than they had reckoned for in 1793—those now somewhat far-distant days ?

On 19 May, the adjutant general's office issued a notice (Dublin Gazette) saying that all the men of the militia regiments

> which are, or shall be, disembodied (except permanent staff) are fully discharged from their respective corps and are at liberty to return to their several occupations without being liable to be called on again for the service of the militia under any former engagement, or to enlist in His Majesty's forces, as they shall think fit.

As this notice was issued the day after the law officers' opinion was given, it seems probable that it embodies what they advised.

At Westminster it caused something of a parliamentary storm. The cabinet seems to have been called together to consider what steps should be taken. They did not agree with the view taken in Ireland. But Hardwicke (7 June) stressed 'the doubts entertained in regard to the legality of holding any of the men of the Irish militia after they were disembodied' and referred to the 'other strong circumstances of policy and expediency which rendered the publication of [the adjutant general's] order highly necessary'.[28] In another letter[29] he says that the 1793 act had only been 'acted upon as a measure of war and is hitherto unknown in this country in a period of peace'. The men had been raised during war and for war service, and did not in general appreciate that peace service (without pay) was involved; this had not been explained to them. He also said that the majority of the colonels were for the course taken. A motion was made in the house of commons for a copy of the order, but withdrawn. Criticism of the wholesale disbanding arose again in the militia debates of 1803.

There was not, it became realized, much to be done but to regularize the action taken in Dublin, and this as quickly as possible. The notice in the Dublin Gazette was speedily supplemented by a bill (royal assent, 26 June 1802) which declared that all should be discharged and be entitled to the 'same immunity from further service as if [they] had served the full time of their engagements'. Nothing could have been more thoroughgoing. At the same time an indemnity not exceeding two guineas a man was authorized 'to the several counties and places in Ireland which may incur any expense in consequence of the discharge' of men who by their attestations were legally bound still to serve. The statutory undertaking to indemnify was contingent: it came into operation 'whenever it shall happen that any county....shall be called upon to provide and shall accordingly have provided any man....' in room of men specially discharged who had been legally bound to serve for a further period. If the militia should not be re-embodied the undertaking would not have effect. As stated above, the disembodiment seems to have been carried through without disorder.[30] A general order, issued on 22 May, which refers to 'the soldier-like and very handsome manner in which the militia have been disembodied', may have been a compliment to the generals and to the generous treatment accorded to the men by the government, but the men seem also covered.[31]

Accordingly the militia departed: the officers to their demesnes and estates and the men to their cabin homes. The number of the latter restored to civil life, some 25,000, was not perhaps so very large, but large enough to create possibilities of certainly individual, and, possibly in some areas, wide-scale distress. Of this, however, there is at present forthcoming no evidence, and it may perhaps be taken that, whatever there may have been, it did not amount to very much. In point of fact the limits of a good long holiday had hardly been exceeded before the call to the colours came again. How far it was responded to, more or less generally, by the same men who in 1802 had been disembodied, will be discussed presently.

Early in November 1802, Castlereagh addressed a 'most secret' semi-official letter[32] to Dublin, urging that 'in the present state of things it may become necessary for the security of Ireland to raise a militia without loss of time'. Ireland must be weak and exposed till she had an efficient militia. That mode which would raise it most speedily had great advantages; recruiting it rather than endeavouring to raise it by ballot commended itself. 'Any attempt to procure funds from the counties must protract the operations till the next assizes and even longer before it could be collected;....money should be advanced by government, to be repaid by the counties'. He thought balloting was calculated to excite more feeling in the country than it was perhaps wise to encourage at a moment of weakness and that it would not be generally successful in all the counties. Enlistment, 'though certainly objectionable on general militia principles', interfered less with the general recruiting of the army. If the militia was raised by bounty, competition with the line could be controlled but competition for substitutes put up the price too much above the amount of bounties offered for the Line.

On 11 November Hardwicke was officially instructed that the militia of Ireland was to be set on foot with as little delay as possible; it was left to his discretion 'to proceed by ballot or by such other means, according to the provisions of the different militia acts, as the time and state of the country may render most expedient'. His advisers agreed that raising by ballot would be impracticable; they favoured Castlereagh's method but the law officers urged that the lord lieutenant could not authorize the colonels to recruit; it should not be done in the teeth of the law unless the emergency was sufficiently strong. The three regular modes of raising men (i.e. by ballot, by substitutes, or by parish volunteers) must be tried first, before resort was had to the fines on parishes provided for under existing powers. All other extraordinary powers (i.e. for receiving volunteers) given by the last acts, had, in the opinion of the attorney general and of the lord chancellor, expired with the last war.[33]

The Irish Government had not been aware that the political position was considered so critical. They pointed out that *emergency* recruiting unaccompanied by an order for immediate embodiment, would be no good, and recommended getting a parliamentary sanction which method would give ' safe useful effective results '. They proposed, with a view to a new general (i.e. codified) militia act,[34] to consult with certain of the militia colonels and take their ' private opinion on the simple question : whether, in case of emergency, the balloting system could be carried into execution with effect or whether it would be right to apply to parliament for a power to recruit '. Meanwhile, they would have everything in readiness for calling out the militia, and, when the power to recruit had been obtained, would then begin that as a matter of course.

In April 1802[35] Hardwicke had been occupied with the idea of revising the militia acts ; these later he described as ' so numerous, so complicated, and so much at variance with each other that it is very desirable to reduce them into one general act '. In August 1802, the law officers in Dublin had been requested to prepare the draft of a bill for ' repealing the existing militia laws '.[36] This is certainly not a bill for abolishing the militia but for codifying the law relating to the force—in fact what is referred to later as a ' bill for the purpose of establishing a general system for the militia, similar, so far as the circumstances of the two countries will permit, to that which was adopted for the English militia by Mr. Yorke's act of last session '[37] (42 Geo. iii, chap. 90). It was always intended that such a bill, before being finally put through, was to be submitted to the Irish militia colonels and they were informed (24 November) that the bill would be ' printed and circulated and the second reading deferred until after the recess, so that the gentlemen of this country may have full opportunity of considering it '. Then they were told that it would take too much time ' to carry through parliament, in the manner proposed, a bill of such extensive detail containing so many regulations* hitherto unknown in Ireland '[38] and that it was now contemplated to authorize the lord lieutenant, whenever the numbers required were not forthcoming within a limited time, to direct men to be enrolled by bounty. At the same time it was notified that it was not intended to ' abandon or delay the intended plan of bringing forward a general militia act on the principles explained ', but the risk must not be run of ' depriving Ireland of the advantage of an effective militia that may be ready to be called out and exercised early in the ensuing year '.[39]

The attorney general for Ireland ' who really understands the subject ' was in mid-November in London with a draft bill[40] which the law officers had been asked for in August and which had been mentioned to the colonels. But the peace was precarious

*i.e. assimilations of the Irish to the English militia law. (42 Geo. iii. chap. 90).

and the Irish pre-peace militia had been almost completely dissolved. Recollections of what had happened in 1793 suggested the greatest possible speed ; and then there was ' the difficulty of framing a new and permanent system in time to furnish an effective militia for the service of the ensuing year '. This was the situation which had to be expounded at Westminster in order to justify summary methods in preference to pressing on with a general bill, under which, as was contemplated by Hardwicke before things became critical, the Irish militia could be called out for ' annual exercise ' in the spring. What we may call the ' speedy enrolment ' bill was presented on 3 December. It recited that it might be ' expedient that the militia of Ireland should be forthwith enrolled ' and that ' the mode of raising men by ballot has not been generally adopted in Ireland ' and that it might be ' attended with inconvenience ' to proceed by ballot only. It directed that the colonels should be ordered to enrol volunteers. The necessary money, not exceeding £40,000, to provide the bounties was to be advanced by the Treasury. The bounty given was not to exceed two guineas for each man enrolled ; they were not to give more than that sum ' nor any other largess, bounty or reward '. The money advanced was ' to be raised on the counties ' but it was reaffirmed that the counties were not to be liable to pay in the cases specially provided for in the act of 1802 (see page 171). On November 30 a committee of the whole house had been set up ' to consider of the militia laws of Ireland.' But the next day the house was recommended in the name of the king, to make provision for ' filling up vacancies in the militia of Ireland '. Thereupon the advance of £40,000 mentioned was authorized and the ' speedy enrolment ' bill was rapidly passed (royal assent 17 December). This did not mean that the contemplated general bill was entirely dropped. It was printed, considered and amended but eventually ' not proceeded in '. (See chapter XIV).

Speedy administrative action seems to have been not unusual ; often the draft militia bills had been communicated beforehand to the militia colonels. This was, to have been done as regards the general militia bill and when in 1809 sir Arthur Wellesley introduced its lineal successor which passed as 49. Geo. iii, chap. 120, he emphasized that the sense of the country gentleman in Ireland had previously been taken (see page 238). At the end of 1792 the Irish government had consulted leading personages before introducing the original militia bill. This shows recognition by the viceroys that they must take the Irish territorial magnates with them in their militia policy, if they wanted things to go reasonably smoothly. After the Union the Irish country gentlemen could, and in certain cases probably did, exercise influence at Westminster over the lord lieutenant's head and perhaps against the line which he had officially taken.

In the case of the re-embodiment of 1803 there were two stages : first enrolment and then embodiment. This had been so in 1793 ; and two stages were again necessary in 1803 because the pre-peace militiamen had been let go. Enrolment was quickly started. The earliest enrolment warrants are dated 3 January ; there were many others in that month and most of the remainder followed in February and March. By 21 March, thirty-one regiments had had orders to enrol. Some of these, however, though they had received the enrolling warrant (e.g. Armagh, N. Down, Kildare and S. Mayo), had not, by the time they got the embodying warrant, started enrolling men.

There is ample evidence that the pre-peace men came back on a very large scale.[41] In the regiments quartered on re-embodiment in the Cork neighbourhood, there was in May a round-up to discover sailors who had enlisted in the militia to avoid being pressed for the Navy. Only two were found ; they had before the disembodiment served in the regiments they were found in ; and it is expressly stated that 'they returned to the regiment as soldiers that before belonged to it '.[42] An officer who has been quoted, says that a number of the former regiment rallied round its colours again as well as others who, though native of the county, had been serving prior to the disembodiment in the regiments of other counties.[43] Of the north Mayo there is similar report. The men of this unit had said on being disembodied that they would to a man fall in again if it became necessary.[44] Of the Carlow it is stated that it was composed of above one half of the men lately discharged and that the same was no doubt the case in every other part of the kingdom with the result that there would be 'a very large body of disciplined soldiery at the very first embodying '.[45] The numbers not so supplied were also, it seems, quickly forthcoming ; on 26 March 'numbers[46] are still flocking to be enlisted in the city and county of Dublin regiments '. Hardwicke reported 16,770 men[47] enrolled by 19 May and this indirectly confirms both that the pre-peace men came back in good numbers and that, so far as these did not fill up the cadres, they were readily supplemented by new enlistments. The taste for the military life is one that clings. Another moral drawn by the newpapers of the period is that the treatment accorded to the rank and file by their officers—of whom the bulk* seem to have continued to serve on the re-embodiment—must have been good or so many would not have come back. Some came back without taking a bounty or at a bounty less than the 2 guineas

*Comparison of 1802 and 1804 militia lists.

authorized. Thus co. Fermanagh took 61 men at £1. 2. 9 (Irish), and Limerick county 92 at the same figure.[48] The small sums 'presented' at the Lent assizes of 1803 by other counties, show that they got their men cheaply or had not to pay bounty to many. Co. Monaghan, however, 'presented' at the summer assizes of 1803 the large sum of £1,285. 7. 6. for the militia. This regiment had a high establishment, and, though large numbers came back, it probably had to pay high sums for those it had to enlist, as was certainly the case with the Armagh (see below, page 177).

The proclamation ordering the re-embodiment is dated 15 March 1803 and the reason for it is stated to be 'the preparations carrying on in the ports of France and Holland'.[49] It was to take place under warrants to be issued for that purpose by the lord lieutenant. Probably, though this is not certain, the re-embodiment date was the same for all units, viz. 25 March. The first general return[50] available shows the number of rank and file on 1 May as 12,319 (7,631 wanting) and the number of sergeants as 829 and drummers 451. By 1 October the numbers had reached 18,315 (wanting 1,651), 1,147 and 636 respectively. The numbers went down as well as up; during June-August, 773 were discharged and 574 deserted. Re-embodiment was gradual and by companies. 'The plan of embodying the militia by companies is so evidently judicious', some official remarks. The Londonderry, which already had by 15 March, 390 men, was able (25 March) to call up seven of its companies and apparently another three in a separate batch on the same day. Castlereagh was of course a potent influence in that quarter and he is found, on one occasion, giving a personal guarantee that some contemplated measure would go well in the Londonderry, and also in the Galway. Normally the corps were assembled a little less promptly. Thus the Armagh was embodied—five companies individually on different days between 25 March and 3 April, and the remaining three companies on 20 May. This is more typical. Each company was embodied at the strength of:[51] 1 captain, 1 lieutenant, 1 ensign, 4 sergeants, 5 corporals, 2 drummers, and 65 privates.

The speedy enrolment act had somewhat ironically said that to proceed by ballot only 'might be attended with inconvenience'—a euphemism according to Fortescue, as already noted (see chapter III) for 'violent disorder'. Hardwicke (July 1803)[52] speaks of a 'general prejudice against balloting in some counties of Ireland from want of experience of its fairness both in principle and practice'. An early return (end of March) speaks of the Longford and Louth as 'regiments which are to be raised under acts of parliament passed antecedent to the present session'[53] and also specifically as 'raised by ballot'. Mr. Foster was colonel of the latter and a militia purist. At a conference with Hardwicke in January 1802 about militia matters in general he said ‘ raising a militia by parochial ballot was by no means inapplicable to Ireland ’.[54] There is, however, record that there was ballot in other counties. In April 1804 the house of commons[55] were given, in reply to a request for a return of the number of balloted men serving in the Irish militia regiments on 1 November 1803, the numbers serving in the Carlow, Longford, Louth, Down (north and south) and Waterford militias ‘ being the only corps which, on the embodying of the militia in Ireland, *received balloted men* ’. The phrase italicized is slightly ambiguous but there is newspaper record of county militia meetings in some of these counties. There is also a specific statement that Belfast was balloted in 1803 and one of the insurers in that city at a later date admitted that he had come down badly over his insurance operations in that year (see page 223). But this may have been balloting under the Additional Forces Act—a different matter. A published contemporary diary of a resident in Carrick-on-Suir. shows that both the balloting and the recruiting systems were in operation in that town which was and is partly in co. Waterford, partly in co. Tipperary. This says : ‘ on the breaking out of war again in 1803 militia was once more embodied. The response in men (eighteen only) not however being equal to the exigency, a second call or ballot was made, when thirteen additional men were secured. In co. Waterford the levy was met by subscription and not directly in men as in Carrick ’. Another earlier entry is : ‘ Militia re-embodied in February 1803 [sic]. The ballot for that purpose took place at Lynch's schoolroom on Monday February 20, to ballot for 18 men for the parish of Carrick ’.[56] Some difficulty apparently arose in co. Longford ; there was a reference to the law officers of the crown on 27 September 1803 ‘ on difficulties which have arisen with reference to balloting the parish of Maskin alias Edgworthstown ’, but there is no record of what the difficulties were.

But relatively expeditious though the 1803 re-embodiment was, the filling of the ranks was not achieved without a raising of the two guineas originally offered. On 15 March the permissible bounty was increased (43. Geo. iii. chap. 33. 7 April 1803) to four guineas which was to be paid as the lord lieutenant might direct. He was authorized to make this increase within twelve months of the passing of the original act. It is difficult exactly to reconcile this provision with the facts as recorded in an Armagh document which is a complete list of all the men enrolled between 25 March 1800 and 25 March 1805.[57] In this, between 25 March (i.e. earlier than 7 April) and the month of August, about 440 men had been enlisted and had received a bounty of £3. 8. 3 (three guineas); after August the bounty paid is as much as £5 and £6. On 5 March 1803 the adjutant general in Dublin bewails the adverse effect on recruiting for the line of the high bounties given by the militia. 'The militia', he says[58] 'was to be raised by enlistment at a low bounty'. This had been departed from 'and it is now left optional to lord lieutenants of counties to ballot the men. *A considerable number* have done so and are giving ten guineas for substitutes instead of two guineas for volunteers as originally proposed'.

In a full-dress debate at Westminster on 16 March on the report stage of the increased bounty bill, the merits of a militia system were strongly challenged by Mr. Windham. He was 'unfriendly to the system adopted in England, still more to that adopted in Scotland, but to that of Ireland unfriendly to the highest degree'. All the work of man could not bring the militia to that state of perfection which the regulars possessed. Mr. Elliot (see page 127), now in the house of commons, argued that the constitutional mode of obtaining a militia was by ballot; if there could not be a ballot then that was an argument against the establishment of a militia. When he was in office in Ireland the militia was not only embodied but encamped; 'it would therefore not have been a very safe measure to have proposed at that period to dissolve it'; now it was disbanded and the question was of its revival. Almost all the other speakers (including the secretary of war and Castlereagh) supported the militia and the report stage eventually went through without a division.[59]

Two more points about the re-embodiment. The Army Medical Board, which had always been a stern critic of recruiting methods, reported (1 July) that the staff surgeons who were employed in inspecting the militia had been careful and that they hoped for better sick returns for that force;[60] they emphasized, however, their view that 'neither our barracks nor our regimental hospitals are so large, so numerous or so well-constructed as the present emergency undoubtedly calls for' and they regret that 'more was not done during the late short interval of peace'. General Fox, who had succeeded sir William Medows as commander of the forces, also represents that 'the deficiency of barrack accommodation has not only delayed the march of the militia out of their counties and thereby retarded their improvement in discipline....but prevented concentration to points where they should be'.[61] In July there are payments of considerable amounts to the militia regiments to enable them 'to defray the expense of baggage on the intended change of quarters'.[62]

XII

The Years 1803 to 1805

Invasion Threats

On 19 May 1803 lord Hardwicke gave directions for embodying the whole of the militia ; in a short time he expected every regiment would be almost completely enrolled, to the 1795 establishment.[1] An officer concerned says of the spring months of that year : 'once more the clang of war ran thro' the land ; the rattling drum overpowered the voice of traffic in fair and market and the work of recruiting proceeded merrily'. By July his corps had mustered 'strong enough for field movements' and he had 'selected a very nice light company'. Clothing however was wanting, save forage caps of white cloth bound with red, 'so that a more motley crew can scarcely be imagined'. They had reckoned upon remaining in their county until their equipment was fully completed but this expectation 'was upset by that strange event known by the name of Emmett's rebellion'. There was 'marching and countermarching of regiments, half-raised, half-drilled and unequipped'. The route arrived suddenly. 'Great was the fuss in consequence from one end of the county to the other. High and low, rich and poor were all more or less interested, and mighty was the flocking....of the fathers and mothers and wives and children, each and all of them doing as much as in their respective powers lay to delay and embarrass our preparations'. A wrong day for the march was given out and the unit actually marched the day before and thus got off with fewer drunken men than we expected under the circumstances'. Their first day's march was 'a very long one for a half formed corps, being a distance of 22 Irish miles, making 28 English'.[2] This was however almost nothing compared with a march of 48 miles achieved at the same time by a Scotch fencible regiment.

The foregoing experiences of a particular militia unit may well have been those of others. Licking the unit into shape followed. The same officer refers to recruits 'who could not without harsh means be induced to learn the full and entire mystery of pipe clay and heel ball'. The colonel was 'an anxious and unsparing martinet '.* But 'the spirit of exertion in the way of polishing led before long to the regiment being one of the best pipe-clayed in the service '. This particular regiment was, with three others, detailed for 'Dwyer hunting' (see page 157.) A party of the Monaghan captured Dwyer's second in command 'for which they were well rewarded '. Militia were not much used in actual connection with the rising (on 23 July); this was localized to Dublin. It was stated in the press that the Cavan 'were the first called upon at the late important crisis to defend the metropolis '.[3] General Fox, brother of Charles James Fox, who was now commander of the forces and who is said by a modern writer[4] to have had an attack of nerves over the outbreak, thanked all the troops in the garrison of Dublin for their 'zeal, alacrity and spirit' and enjoined the avoidance of any acts of severity or violence 'beyond what the faithful discharge of their military duty shall render indispensable '.

In September the light battalions were again set up. If the militia colonels had thought that, on the re-embodiment, that light infantry business would be forgotten and drop, they were disappointed. This time there were six[5] battalions organized in three divisions. The order constituting these new battalions is not available but a complete set of the pay-lists for all of them exists. These do not afford much information. No active service came to the light infantry during the period to 1806 when the organization was discontinued and their service was, apart from their innate gaiety (we have a reference to the 'merry hearted light bob'), even dull. A light infantry commander, writing later, says they were between two stools and that the captain 'had the onerous duty of endeavouring to please two masters', their immediate commander and their militia commanding officer. The cohesion obtained in the light infantry battalions is evident by the fact that the 1st (which in its composition reproduced the old 3rd) volunteered, during the 1803-4 volunteering wave (see below page 182), *as a unit* whereas, in other cases, light companies volunteered only if they might go with their own regiments. The end of the light infantry experiment in the Irish militia will be dealt with in the next chapter ; here the reassembling of the centralized formation comes in as one of the contra-invasion measures of preparation which were taken in the latter part of the year 1803.

At this time fear of invasion was again rampant. The preparations made were many. In August pontoons were being built at Dublin Castle to be sent to Athlone for use on the Shannon in case of invasion. Flying artillery were ready. Athlone was

*This word was then less pejorative.

in a high state of defence. Carts for commissariat purposes were imported from Great Britain. During August the strength of the yeomanry was increasing fast; every little village near Dublin, we are told, had a corps. On 13 August the establishment was increased from 48,000 to 60,000 [6] Grattan made an offer to raise a corps. In September the lord lieutenant reviewed them and they were—for the fourth time[7]—called out on permanent duty. It is stated in the press that by this time there were in Ireland 50,000 men who a month previously did not know the use of a firelock. By November, again according to the press, there were some 200,000 men under arms in the country. Signal stations were erected between Berehaven and Cork harbour. The building of the martello, or Corsican, towers between Bray and Balbriggan was begun. There was also talk of turning Howth head into an Irish 'Gibraltar'. The Wicklow military road was completed and a chain of barracks built on it. The Royal, Islandbridge, and Pigeon house fort barracks in Dublin were also built about this time, as well as many in country parts.

To descend in the scale, the question of the provision of flannel jackets for the troops—a recurring symptom of anxiety—was again raised; in October commanding officers were ordered to provide each man with an 'under flannel waistcoat'.[8] Finally, in county Cork inspectors were at work taking inventories of all stock, alive or dead, in the possession of farmers, for possible removal or destruction in case of invasion.[9] Hardwicke, early in August 1803, pressed for reinforcements of regular troops, pointing out that the 'militia of Ireland will be exposed to all the arts and seductions of the enemy' and, luridly but gratuitously, picturing the 'dreadful situation in which the country would be placed if our militia or any considerable part of them were to fail us'.[10] He was told (30 August) that 10,000 men would be sent from England within a few weeks. But a fortnight later he is pressing again. In December he was told that a force of 3,000 was being held in readiness in north Britain to go to Ireland in case of invasion.[11] By January 1804 the position had apparently eased as the force of 3,000 in Scotland was then moved elsewhere and Hardwicke was so informed.[12] On 19 October 1803 a general fast had been held in England and Ireland.

General Fox, reporting[13] to the lord lieutenant on 15 August 1803, spoke of the militia as 'newly raised and but now moving out of their counties'. He contrasted them with what he called the 'tried and steady national militia' existing at the time of the late peace. Their number had reached 16,504. Barrack accommodation, as already stated (p. 178) was deficient. In September the old question of applications for protection and the resulting dispersion of the troops was discussed. Fox says this dispersion was 'highly prejudicial to the militia, a part of the army formed only within these six months' and that it 'exposed them to be seduced from their allegiance by the disaffected'.[14] In December lord Cathcart, who had succeeded Fox, and made the usual tour of inspection, on returning spoke of 'the fair progressive state of the militia'.[15] That was about as much as could then be expected. The material of the force would appear to have been more carefully selected than before.

The year 1803 saw a new 'wave' of volunteering by units. That of the year 1801 had been in effect initiated from England; this of 1803, which was almost torrential, seems to have had its origin in Ireland. It is strange that, when the Irish authorities were asking and the English were promising reinforcements from England, any initiative should have proceeded from either side the effect of which would be to denude Ireland of any portion of its organized force; if however what was going to happen was an exchange and not a unilateral movement, this criticism does not arise. Hardwicke had in fact, when asking in August for reinforcements, suggested passing an interchange of militia bill; in urging, as he did in September, acceptance of the offers, he advocated 'the interchangeableness of the militia service'. In a previous chapter (p. 146) the strong views held by persons of standing about the absence of provision for interchange have been stated, as they were represented by Hardwicke. 'The means of intercourse', he said, 'which interchange would afford between the middle and lower orders of the people would tend to produce a spirit of conciliation and goodwill[16]'—an argument frequently used in support of interchangeability. He asked that the first six or eight regiments of the Irish militia to volunteer their services to Great Britain should be accepted conditionally for twelve months, and that an equal number of British militia should be sent over to Ireland. The regimental officers and the other ranks probably offered their services in the spirit of adventure or under the influence of their seniors and certainly without any ulterior sociological or political motive. In 1801 one of the south Cork who had been asked to volunteer for England had replied 'to be sure, I will volunteer to England; it will be like going from the kitchen to the parlour'. It was high politics which was the rock on which the volunteering wave ultimately spent itself.

One of the earliest offers, that of the north Mayo, was specifically suggested by the interchangeability idea.[17] But there is nothing of this in any of the other offer-letters, several of which refer to the offers they had previously made. The north Cork approached their commanding officer with the offer of service and each man's name signed to a roll for that purpose'.[18] The Dublin city said it was the third time they had offered. The colonel of the Roscommon observes that his regiment was the first to offer 'last war' and also that five officers and near 300 men did actually serve.... in the glorious expedition to Egypt.[19] One or two commanding officers took the opportunity to work off their annoyance that their light companies were separated from the regiment;[20]—which they said precluded them from including the light company in their offer. Several light companies offered separately both from their parent regiment (or battalion) and from the light battalion to which they belonged. The returns[21] ultimately (April-May 1804) showed 769 officers, 1456 noncommissioned officers and 15,460 rank and file as having volunteered. A nickname, or opprobious epithet, 'blackbelt' seems to have been applied to those in the different regiments of militia who had declined to volunteer for England.[22] These were not numerous. Though stress was laid on the volunteering being voluntary, it was probably no less or more a matter of choice than it would be for an English public school boy to stand out of the Officers Training Corps. Most of the offers were for any part of the United Kingdom; one (from the Meath) was for any part of Europe; the Sligo, defiantly, offered 'for any part of the United Kingdom where the enemy shall dare to show his face'. There was some, but not much, stipulation about the wives and families being cared for. The Knight of Kerry attached a semi-official '*cri de coeur*' to his offer of the Kerry:

> 'there is a reason which may not have occurred to government for removing the Irish militia to England, that is to separate them from their wives who are, in case of actual service, really a pest to the regiment and tend very much to damp the ardour of the men. Of course their families in such cases should be provided for. This reason applies to the Kerry militia with particular force from the extraordinary number of wives among our men. I should wish for a general divorce, not to extend however to officers'.[23]

The offers were formally acknowledged from London as having been laid before the king and accepted as marks of loyalty and attachment to his sacred person.[24] These fine words probably aroused no exaggerated hopes. Hardwicke had, as already stated, urged acceptance of the offers. But apparently they caused some difficulty in London. Hardwicke seems to have had no reply to his September despatch, and, for several months, no instructions on the offers. In Whitehall ministers were gravely preoccupied, amid general embitterment of party relations, equally with defence questions and with their own possible demise.

Finally in February (1804), probably on instructions, Hardwicke sounded[25] such colonels and other principal officers of the militia as were in the neighbourhood of Dublin on three points:

raising 5,000 men by draft of 20 per company, for the line; augmenting the militia; and volunteering by units. After reporting on this conference he was told[26] there would be a bill to accept the volunteered services of the militia in England—to the number of 8,000, and to augment the force to the same extent.[27] Acknowledging this, he again presses (9 March) his views about general interchangeability of the militia of Great Britain and Ireland. Different gentlemen of the country had urged the measure in the most convincing and impressive manner, and he was sure it would be received with unanimous concurrence; and he urged carrying it into effect with the 'despatch which is consistent with its importance.'[28] The decision finally conveyed was that the king proposed to accept for England 8,000 militia—when his message to parliament was delivered on 26 March the figure had risen to 10,000—and to augment the companies from 70 to 100 men. To Hardwicke's urgings about interchange the reply was that ministers entirely concurred in his opinion as to the benefit which the public service would receive from the services of the two militias being extended but retrospective legislative provisions would be required to give this effect; parliament could not take such a step 'consistently with its good faith and the terms upon which the existing militia has been raised and called out'.[29]

This means that on general grounds the policy of interchange was not found politically practicable. The king's opposition to the Irish militia coming to England (see page 147) had obviously been got over. But at a meeting[30] the lords lieutenants of English counties and members of parliament with commissions in the English militia emphatically condemned the policy of 'reciprocal service'. At this time therefore interchange of militia, though it found favour in Ireland, made no progress in England. Neither of the bills introduced (acceptance of offers and augmentation) actually dealt with it but there were references to it in the debates; one member thought the offers bill would 'go to recognize the principle of an interchange of militia'.[31] Fox seems to have urged that the opposition was not caused by considerations of personal inconvenience to the English militia colonels but from the conviction that such an interchange was contrary to the constitution of the militia system and to the spirit as well as to the letter of the Act of Union.

What the two bills provided for was as follows: the first (44 Geo. iii, chap. 32), after a highfaluting patriotic preamble, suspended, in respect of not exceeding 10,000 men, those provisions of the militia acts which prohibited the carrying the Irish militia out of Ireland; it was to be explained to the men that volunteering was voluntary; and finally there was exemption of the counties from liability 'to be drawn' to replace any non-commissioned officer, drummer or private who might die, desert or be discharged whilst serving out of Ireland (royal assent: 3 May). The augmentation bill, which was considerably the more important, became law the same day (chap. 33). The augmentation authorized (i.e. to not exceeding 100 per company) was only what had been authorized in 1800 without legislation—under the discretionary power given in the act of 1795. New powers were presumably held necessary because the pre-Union powers were considered to have lapsed. The men taken were to be volunteers (' such volunteers as shall offer to serve ') and they were ' to be considered to all intents and purposes militiamen ' and their families eligible for relief as such. Another important provision, for the counties, was that they were not to be charged with filling vacancies under the act, ' it being the intention . . . . that the men so enrolled in addition to the establishment of the militia of Ireland should be raised and kept up without any charge being made on the counties whatever '. If counties were not to be responsible for the cost of raising, it would appear not to matter so much to them if the men were recruited at large, i.e. outside the county. But, as stated, these volunteers were to be eligible for relief for their families and this made them a county interest; it is in fact provided in the act that they should be enlisted by the colonel within their respective counties and be ' usually resident within such respective counties '. Finally it is provided that the augmentation shall continue ' only during the present war '. This is the statute most frequently referred to in the years following and it remained unrepealed until it became incorporated in Wellesley's co-ordinating act of the year 1809.

The debates on these bills are directly interesting from the Irish point of view and indirectly from that of high politics. Fox raised a point which seems to have been a real bogey at the time. It was being put about that the Irish militia in England would become liable to ' the corporal punishments of the articles of war, for abstaining from the protestant or attending their own worship '. On the offers bill, he suggested a clause[32] to prevent the catholic soldiers who should come to England from being compelled to attend protestant places of worship. But this does not find place in the act. Other points made were that Ireland could not spare so large a portion of ' her natural means of defence '. The old point—that the Irish militia would fight better in England than at home ' as they would not be opposed to their near relations '—was duly stated. On the other hand Mr. Yorke, who was in charge of the bills, ' observed that the rebellion in 1798 had been put down by the militia of Ireland who had in that struggle encountered difficulties equal to any that any other troops in the world had to contend with ';[33] and Castlereagh ' bore testimony to the loyalty and valour of the Irish militia in the year 1798 when every exertion of treason and every artifice of treason were used to corrupt their fidelity '. Another member also passed a high eulogy. No one, in effect, in either house took a view opposite. Two or three speakers, like the duke of Montrose, detected soviet tendencies ; it was ' unsafe and impolitic to encourage that spirit of deliberation among armed bodies, that lead to voluntary offers being made'. Some attention was given to the interchange point. Lord Grenville observed that, as the ' Irish militia was raised by bounty, not ballot, it would have been easy to extend their services to this country by law ' and he added that ' ministers were advised to do so but rejected that wholesome advice '.

These debates of 1804 were relatively unimportant, but they became the battle ground of the government and the opposition. All the big guns—Canning, Pitt, Addington and Fox as well as other members of the government—came into action. On the 3rd reading (16 April) of the augmentation bill the government majority was driven down to 21 in a house of 235. The *Annual Register* comments that the very small majority in favour of ministers inclined the public to suppose that the administration of Mr. Addington was fast drawing to a close.[34] Windham, referring to this division, says : ' the fate of the ministry is pretty much decided ; not of course by the mere effect of that division, but by the causes that led to it '.[35] He also alludes to it as ' a trial of strength '. Both bills became law. Followed however as they were by the fall of the Addington ministry, they had not much authority behind them ; and steps were not there and then taken to put them into force. On the offers act (chap. 32) no action was ever taken ; on the augmentation act none until the next year 1805. Three times now had the Irish offers (the spirit underlying which had however received strong lip approval in the debates) been left unaccepted. The offers act was, it is true, continued in force for another short period after 1806 and by a later act ' during the present war '. But the Irish militia regiments seem to have made few further offers, and the question of their going to England remained almost entirely in abeyance until after the passing of the interchange act (1 July 1811.. In the official Militia list issued in 1804 (20 August) all the militia, English, Scotch and Irish, are in alphabetical order together ; further than this on paper the idea of interchangeability did not progress at this time.

While the use of the force was thus under agitated discussion at Westminster the units, which had not been so very long embodied, were endeavouring to get themselves organized. In September of 1803 the official view at the headquarters in Dublin was that the ' progress of several militia regiments in discipline was not such as the urgency of the service requires or as might have been expected from the length of time they have been embodied '. The general officers to whom this warning was secretly issued were urged to exercise a more direct interference but they were told to 'feel the propriety of doing so with all possible delicacy ' and to endeavour to act 'as supporting rather than superseding the authority of the commanding officer '. Monthly reports were asked for. By the early summer of 1804 few regiments were sufficiently advanced to benefit by being encamped. The new commander of the forces, lord Cathcart, got authority[36] for two camps : the larger at the Curragh during August was attended by the north Cork, Donegal, Leitrim and Monaghan militias and the smaller at Killeady hill, near Cork, by the 2nd and 5th light battalions and the Queen's county, south Mayo and Tipperary. Some 13,000 troops in all[37]—or 15,000 by one account—were at the Curragh. The adjutant of the Donegal militia welcomed camp : 'we will soon be all together again by being encamped '. They had been having an active time, it seems. 'Our men ' he comments 'have [this was at Naas] a little more to do than they had in the old quarters—not more than three or four nights in bed and scarce a day without an escort of deserters to Dublin '.[38] They had obtained eight good recruits—locally, it would seem. At the Curragh the men were encamped 'in light marching order and ready to move on short notice '. Water had to be brought by hand a distance of nearly a mile. This was the principal inconvenience. Killeady was 'plentifully supplied with wholesome water '. The conduct of the troops is much praised. A gentleman who rode through the camp at Curragh on Sunday 12 August saw the men assembled for divine service in hollow squares round their chaplains and described them as 'most laudably attentive '. After the service they formed up and fired, in honour of the Prince of Wales' birthday, 'with the most admirable precision '. He also notes that 'not an unnecessary sound was to be heard from one end to the other of the immediate encampment '. The health was better than the average in city quarters.[39] Hardwicke commented to Whitehall that 'the camp on the Curragh of Kildare has been of great use in that county. It has served to convince the lower orders of people that. . . . troops can be moved to different points in a very short time '.[40]

During this year the lord lieutenant took notice of what had become, seemingly, something of a scandal. An order issued[41] in June refers to advertisements in the public papers for the sale of appointments of surgeon and of adjutant in regiments of militia. Offers of a militia adjutancy for sale are to be noted in the *Dublin Evening Post* in June, October and December 1803 and there are many, as well as of surgeoncies, in previous years.

One officer says that he is considering two offers. In an action for defamation brought by the colonel of the Tipperary in August 1804 a witness stated that officers commanding militia regiments were in the habit of disposing of adjutancies and surgeoncies but that he had never heard that the colonel of the Tipperary made a single shilling from such appointments.[42] There are curious particulars of these transactions in a memorial of the adjutant of the Dublin city in November 1800.[43] In another regiment the surgeon (January 1797) represents to his colonel that 'surgeoncies of militia . . . . are bought and sold every day and are at the colonel's disposal' and adds 'several surgeons in Dublin were anxious to succeed me and offered something considerable for the appointment'.[44] He passed on the appointment, presumably with permission, on a bond to pay £450 but after nine months the successor had not paid, and, in his turn, seeks the colonel's permission to resign and 'dispose of the surgeoncy'. The adjutant of a regiment in (March 1798) represents that he has seven children motherless and asks leave 'to dispose of the adjutancy for their benefit'; he mentions that the bandmaster would give him £700; he held also the appointment of paymaster—such pluralism was not uncommon then—but, as this was about to be made a distinct appointment, he proposed to keep that, after selling the adjutancy. The bandmaster was much set on the adjutancy and intimated that, if the colonel did not approve outright selling, 'there are other methods.' By this he meant that he should hold both appointments but make over to the 'ex-adjutant', as consideration for the adjutancy, his pay as bandmaster.[45] There is an official ruling in 1799 that 'militia commissions are under no circumstances vendible,[46] and any private pecuniary transaction is highly irregular'; this may however refer to combatant commissions and not to the staff appointments of the militia units, though there is no evidence of traffic in the former. Anyhow in June 1804 the lord lieutenant pronounced all this traffic 'manifestly prejudicial and injurious to the militia service' and in future declarations were to be required by persons put forward for the appointments of adjutant, surgeon and assistant-surgeon, as well as certificates by the commanding officer, that no pecuniary consideration had been given or received.[47]

Hardwicke at the time thought that early effect was intended to be given to the augmentation act (3 May). On the fall of the Addington ministry, Pitt took his seat in the commons as prime minister on 18 May 1804. On 31 May, Hardwicke[48] had received no instructions and points out that the season is advanced and that the increased demand for labourers 'independently of the competition arising from the new levies' will add to the difficulties of raising the men; the Louth, he says, had already started recruiting. He was informed (June) that he 'should defer for the present the issuing of warrants to the colonels under the act' and that the few men who had been engaged in contemplation of the augmentation could be retained. Whitehall did not come back to the subject until next year (despatch of March 1805). By then the military authorities had in contemplation another call on the Irish militia for volunteers, similar to that which had been made in 1800, and some delicacy of approach was desirable; the viceroy was told that it was 'at all events desirable in the first instance to execute the act of last session for augmenting the militia before any measures are proposed with reference to its subsequent reduction to a certain extent'.[49] Hardwicke then put out his instructions (23 March) for an augmentation to 100 rank and file per company as from the 25th; the date for completing was to be 24 June 1805.

All the 38 units were called upon to augment; the big units like the Donegal, Galway, Wexford, Tipperary and Tyrone by 300; the Louth by 270; the eight company units by 240; the two Mayo units by 210; and all the rest by 180. The target was 8,550. By 6 July 2782 had been raised.[50] Before the augmentation the strength seems to have been low. Also a draft from the Irish Militia was, as already stated, in contemplation (authorized by 45, Geo. iii, chap. 38 on 11 April). The augmentation was intended to make the draft possible.[57] The act allowed 'a certain proportion of the militia of Ireland voluntarily to enlist into his majesty's forces and royal marines'; a similar act had been passed for enlisting volunteers from the English militia. Both recited the object in view as 'the vigorous prosecution of the present war'. Not exceeding two fifths of the number then actually serving might volunteer and, if four fifths of that number were willing to enlist, then no more were to be enlisted.[52] Hardwicke's sanguine expectation, expressed to Whitehall in March, was that the volunteering was likely to produce in the course of a few months 7,000 to 8,000 'as effective soldiers as any in his majesty's service'.[53] By 27 May he had got 3,812 and a War Office return[54] gives the number to mid July as 4,617. The bounty offered had been ten guineas. Hardwicke was disappointed.[55] He attributed the failure to the fact that there were no offers of ensigncies—this had apparently been left out of the act advisedly—as there had been in the 1800 volunteering (see page 150).

There is extant an interesting letter (May 1805) from the adjutant general in Dublin to the adjutant general in London. His first point is that almost all the militia colonels were in London; the government should "speak to them". Next, no ensigncies were being offered; without this bonus they would be

4,000 to 5,000 short of the numbers required. Granting ensigncies would mean the success or failure of the measure of volunteering. He adds : 'now in fact the officers of the Irish militia are many of them as fully as good a description as the general run of those who are at present candidates for commissions in the line. They are better in so far that they are acquainted with their duty and certainly we have seldom any faults to find with their manner of performing it '.[56]

The enlistment of their men into the regulars was distasteful to the English militia colonels and, early in March 1805, they protested 'against the plan proposed by Pitt for recruiting the army from the militia'. Many were rather violent. Typical are the remarks of the marquis of Bute : 'the military plan, represented to be in contemplation of the government, if carried into execution, would tend....to extinguish that best and only constitutional defence of the country by perverting it into a stagnate reservoir for feeding the standing army. The measure, besides, seems an indirect, as well as partial, tax on the several counties....[would] reduce the lieutenants, the militia officers and magistrates to mere recruiting parties for the war minister '.[57]

The feeling of the Irish colonels was the same, as became quite evident when the milking process was repeated on a more permanent basis at the end of the year. They had, as just shown, remained absent in London while the volunteering was in progress. They no doubt thought that anyhow there would be no residuum of benefit, in strength, to their units. Not only was this so but they actually lost, owing to the fact that the men volunteered in greater numbers than augmentation men had been obtained. The final figure for the augmentation of 1805 may be taken as about 3,000 ; the number that volunteered was, as stated already, 4,617 or possibly a little more ; in the aggregate therefore the units were substantially diminished in total strength ; the Roscommon augmented by 42 and 140 volunteered ; this would, apart of course from other factors, have left that regiment nearly 100 deficient. This is not a unique case.

When it was clear that the volunteers required were not going to be obtained within the time limit, Hardwicke consulted[58] the crown lawyers about an extension, with a still later date for augmentation men. What exactly the course of things was during that summer is not clear but it was apparently decided to stop both augmentation and volunteering. Instructions were issued (24 August) for putting the establishment back to the normal from 24 October ; from the same date apparently volunteering also ceased—if it had not been stopped earlier. Augmenting to provide a margin of strength for volunteering and thus to make volunteering palatable, or as palatable as possible, to the colonels—this had been tried with only moderate success. But it was not very long before another similar effort, though on somewhat different lines, was to be made. This did not find some of the colonels very responsive (see below page 193).

During the year 1805 invasion preparations continued; there are many evidences of the alarm felt in Ireland. In January there were 780 men on guard in Dublin daily, each regiment furnishing a quota. Orders were given for the yeomanry to be purged of any corps considered untrustworthy. In February the officer commanding at Limerick received an express from Dingle that six ships of the line and three frigates were off that place and would not answer the signal. Cork too had an alarm (which proved false) and the troops were reinforced by the yeomanry. In March the Martello towers near Dublin, each of which had a garrison of six to eight, were completed and in May regiments were sent from Dublin[59] to reinforce the army on the west and south coasts. The sailing of the Cadiz and Toulon fleets was causing some disaffection. In May putting the yeomanry on duty was under consideration and inspection of the force on a large scale in Phoenix park by the lord lieutenant was arranged for the beginning of June. But afterwards the 'late alarms' were found to be groundless. In July a competent observer states that Ireland was perfectly quiet; 'I do not know' he said 'that for years I have had such strong reasons for being of that opinion'[60].

The 1804 camp was held to have been very successful 'in conciliating the public towards his majesty's army[61] in general'. The security of the maritime counties and the garrisoning of the cities and the support of the civil government throughout the interior was provided for, with some addition to the number of yeomanry put on permanent duty[62]. The camp of 1805 at the Curragh was the military event of the year. The 'panorama'* of this camp, announced the previous year[63], was opened to the public in Dublin in March.[64] It appears to have presented a grand review and a sham fight. The actual camp opened spectacularly. 'On the first [August] the troops destined to occupy this camp appeared on the ground in six divisions. The order to take up their positions being given by signal, the different points allotted to the several regiments were immediately occupied; and the command to pitch tents being announced by another signal, the whole camp was formed in little more than two minutes from the instant in which the signal was made'.[65] As regards the light infantry (a large part of which was militia) the account says 'the movement of these brigades to their posts to the sound of the

*A 'panorama' was a pictorial representation on a circular surface. They were then of fairly recent introduction.

bugle, the celerity of their manoeuvres, the brilliancy of their uniforms and the gay diversity of their various standards glancing across the hills—altogether produced a delightful effect '.[65] The day was fine.

Camping was new to most of the militia. An officer who took part in the Curragh camp speaks of it ' as initiating them into the art and mystery of encamping '.

> Great was the galloping hither and thither of staff officers of every grade and denomination for nearly an hour, until at one o'clock bang went a signal gun. . . . when the columns poured into the magnificent plain, or rather downs, of the Curragh by all the roads leading to it. Bands playing, colours flying, drums beating, bugles screaming and all the pomp, pride and circumstance of military display.[67]

The writer of this account says that a regular officer told him that he had been thirty years in the army without seeing anything like it. ' The line beneath my view ' he says ' was composed to a considerable extent of the very same men who in less than three years entered upon the career of Peninsular glory. More than twenty of the regiments [this seems an overstatement] forming that line were militia, but it was the volunteers from that body that filled up the ranks of Wellington's army '.

No ' parade state ' of the troops at this camp seems to exist, but the schemes provided for twenty two infantry battalions being present, of which nine were militia ; these were the six militia light battalions (which contained a company from each of the 38 militia corps). Besides the light infantry battalions there were : the Galway, Wexford and Kerry regiments ; and there is a statement that lord Cathcart, having a great liking for the Armagh regiment, brought it from Dublin and encamped it as his own bodyguard at the Standhouse, immediately adjoining his quarters. But beyond this there are no records of any other militia having been at the Curragh encampment of 1805. It broke up early in September and at the end of October lord Cathcart left Ireland on appointment as British ambassador at St. Petersburg. His general order on leaving stated as regards the militia : ' the regiments of militia have continued to improve in proportion to their means, and those persons of high rank, fortune and distinction who have the most frequently sacrificed other concerns and their own convenience for the purpose of giving regular attendance at quarters to the duties of the commissions they have accepted, have reason to be proud of the good effect produced by their example and presence. Had the opportunity of real service occurred, the militia should have had early proofs of the confidence and esteem of the commander of the forces '.[68]

Castlereagh had in November 1805 procured cabinet authority for a new policy—that of making 15 men per company available *annually* for the line from the Irish militia. He thought[69] that this could be effected under the existing legislation, but eventually (12 July 1806, 46, Geo. iii, chap. 124) an act was passed to cover the new principle i.e. that of a permanent ' annual tribute '. This required careful negotiation with the colonels. Cabinet authority was given in mid-November[70] for the chief secretary to begin talking them over. The letter he issued (21 November) proceeded on the lines of offering a deal : the lord lieutenant on his side would order an augmentation, with the usual proportion of field officers and noncommissioned officers, to 100 men per company —the establishment had only recently been put back to the 1795 standard—and the lord lieutenant ' trusted ' that when a colonel had accomplished this augmentation (before 1 May 1806 was the date suggested) he would, ' with a view of completing his majesty's regiments of the line, find no difficulty at that period in discharging from the regiment thus placed on a high establishment such volunteers as may choose to enter the line, not exceeding 15 per company '. Then there was reference to filling up at the 'usual bounty ' the vacancies thus created and to the ' peculiar facility of procuring men for the militia service in Ireland. There was added the statement that his excellency was ' persuaded that your lordship will readily agree to afford annually a similar aid, the amount of which has been studiously limited within bounds not likely to affect either the strength or the efficiency of your regiment '.[71]

The chief secretary reported in January[72] that he had despatched 24 letters (out of 38) ordering the augmentation to 100 men per company ; the other 14 colonels, on receiving the letter of 21 November, either disapproved or failed to answer. Of those who expressed definite disapproval lord Leitrim, the colonel of the Donegal, states that he had always ' looked upon the volunteering which has already taken place on two different occasions [i.e. in 1800 and 1805] as highly injurious to the discipline of the militia, as most grating to the feelings of the officers and as destructive of that *esprit de corps* and attachment on the part of the soldiers to their officers which is essential to the character of the militia service '. Now ' what has hitherto been resorted to only upon particular emergencies was to be a permanent system and the militia was to be converted into a mere recruiting [agency] for the line '; this, he thought, ' must inevitably disgust every officer of responsibility in the service '; if the volunteering was persevered in, ' it will in a very short time be as difficult to raise men for the militia as it is at the present for the line '.[73]

There was no attempt to force augmentation upon the unwilling. In the regiments in which it was accepted it took effect from 25 December 1805. It had solid advantages. It meant an addition to the field officers.* Castlereagh urges the importance of this in view of field officers being frequently absent attending parliament. It meant also additional noncommissioned officers, with consequent promotion for the men ; and, this time profiting by the recent experience, the authorities offered commissions, one for every 45 enlisted for general service. Accepting augmentation meant a new status, with a new obligation. In the act of 1807 for increasing the militia (passed 13 August) this new status appears : the units are there classified into (*a*) those augmented under the statute of 1804 and (*b*) those not so augmented. Those which accepted augmentation (and implicitly with it the duty to encourage volunteering) were apt to count to themselves for righteousness their compliance. Lord Westmeath in 1809[74] asked whether he was likely to get two additional companies, pointing out that it was evidently ' the interest of government to increase those regiments which were always ready to assist the recruiting of the line, amongst which I beg leave to mention the Westmeath as among the most prominent '. In May 1806 lord Granard, who then wanted the Longford militia stationed within a day's journey of Castle Forbes, was told[75] that his unit must take the ' routine of service ' and that it was also necessary ' to advert to those that had augmented '. The 10 company units were augmented to 1123 all ranks (980 privates) ; the eight company units to 901 (760 privates) ; and the rest in proportion. The first augmentations announced (November 1806) amounted to eighteen ; there was a second batch of four and, after that, others came in by ones and twos. In the big co-ordinating act of the year 1809 (see page 238) the units which had up to then accepted augmentation are named ; thirty one had and seven had not ; by May 1811 only five had not. The lord lieutenant still retained the power to augment those which so far had not been augmented. There are no statements available of the progress of augmentation, in terms of additional men enlisted.

As already stated, the act giving authority for the ' annual tribute ' was not passed until 21 July 1806 ; it provided for an annual ten days period (repeatable, if necessary) during which men might declare their intention ; the first period was to be from 24 July 1806. The results obtained in 1806 and what happened in the units on these annual occasions will be described in the next chapter.

Pitt died 23 January 1806 ; Trafalgar had been won on the previous 21 October. The period 1803 to 1805 has a certain coherence and unity, opening with the renewal of the war and

*An officer writes that ' in consequence of the augmentation he received the welcome tidings of his appointment to a majority '.

ended by the removal of serious menace from the French navy. During this period, of anxiety in Ireland as in England, the Irish militia had not stood aloof from the renewed war ; soon after the second embodiment, it offered its services as units and it had not been found possible to use them ; and, after that, its individual members had come forward for incorporation in English units, at sacrifice, in the eyes of many of its leading spirits, of what was in their view (as also in that of English militia colonels) essential to the purity of application of militia principles : the prior and overriding duty of a militia to be guarding its own national soil. In any case a long way had been traversed since the raising of the force in the year 1793. But the times had themselves changed ; and it was not so unreasonable that the militia should be expected to change in some step with the times. 'Interchange', though it had important political backing, was not as yet able to prevail, as a policy. Of the remainder of the story of the Irish militia a great part is the further development of the policies for its employment initiated during the period from 1803 to 1805.

XIII

The Militia in 1806

By the year 1806 the militia, having been now nearly three years embodied, was settling down to the routine which it was to follow for the further period, of some ten years, during which it was to remain actively under arms. If, prior to Trafalgar, there had still lingered the possibility of a 'sudden call' to the coast, that had now, though the signal stations remained manned, in effect passed. The internal state of Ireland was not however normal; and no suggestion of dispensing entirely with the force seems to have arisen. More widely, for Europe the war was definitely not yet over, even if Trafalgar had been won. The year 1806 was one of much heartsearching. Many pamphlets appeared; but, though the value and continued maintenance of the militia as a whole, British and Irish, was actively canvassed, it was greater 'disposability'* rather than abolition on which discussion turned. The points against were, naturally, brought out—progress of thought and of experience has established the validity of many—but, whatever there was in them for that age and time, it did not go anywhere near procuring a death sentence at the bar of public discussion. The force had by then some thirteen years of embodied existence but this did not make it, in that form, one of the old institutions of the country, with the usual resulting immunity. The balance of argument and of opinion must therefore be considered to have been that the force in both countries—some oneness of approaching these matters was arising—did serve some valuable public end. To review generally some features of the internal economy seems therefore, as the force is going to continue embodied a good while yet, not out of place.

A writer [1], describing the duties falling in Ireland to the troops in and about the year 1798, says:

> there was no body of police corresponding to the Royal Irish constabulary; outside the towns all the police duties had to be performed by the troops; mail coaches had to be escorted, the coastguard work had to be done, bailiffs had to be protected—in short all the work ordinarily delegated to the civil authorities was the every day business of troops'.

He goes on to say that 'one of the most arduous duties was the

*'Disposability' was the word currently used for 'availability for general service

prevention of illicit distilling '. He quotes a return for October 1794 which shows that in that month 41 distilleries were destroyed and 68 gallons of whisky, 64 barrels of malt and 2,800 gallons of pot ale were captured. Though perhaps some of the duties specified may have altered, the specification in general continued correct and, in particular, that of ' still hunting ' continued arduous in the period we have now reached. Sir Robert Peel, speaking in February 1816, said that in 1806 there had been granted 448 military parties ; in 1807—598 ; and, in the previous year 1815, there had been 1889. A house of commons return[2] shows a large number of stills seized in each of the five years ending December 1805 in the districts of Cavan and Trim. Similar seizures no doubt occurred elsewhere. There is for example a report of a serious case (February 1805) at Kittymorris in co. Antrim in which the Waterford militia were attacked ' in so violent a manner that they were at last compelled to fire '; sticks and stones were the usual weapons and missiles. There were two deaths and several were wounded. The revenue officer was subsequently indicted at the August assizes but secured a verdict of not guilty.[3] There was a very serious revenue incident in April 1797 in which several of the Armagh militia were killed and more wounded.[4] This had led to lord Carhampton procuring a decision that no more parties of soldiers should be given to assist revenue officers ; ' it had been found in its consequences destructive of all discipline '. In November 1800 the cavalry were for a time prohibited from employment on this duty. But the next year the prohibition was withdrawn as ' the working clandestinely of distilleries was growing to an alarming extent '.[5] In 1809 cavalry on many occasions went with revenue officers to seize stills.

In this irksome and unpopular duty—it has been with probability argued that desertions were largely attributable to such unsoldierly employments—the militia had to take a full share. In 1795, in a debate in the Irish house of commons[6], it was mentioned as a ' material defect ' in the Volunteers that they ' could not be made assistant to the custom house officer ' and, in this very year 1806, the commander of the forces, when consulted by Hardwicke about the continuation of the light infantry battalion organization, gave as one reason for continuing it ' the collection of the revenue '.[7] The fundamental act of 1793 said nothing about this as a duty which was to fall to the militia to be created but the ' General Regulations for the Army of Ireland ' (1794) say quite explicitly that ' his majesty's revenue would greatly suffer if proper attention is not paid, by the commanding officers of regiments and quarters detached, to the requisitions made to them by customs house officers for the aid of troops '; and that any officer refusing to employ his men in this way was to be ' immediately tried by a general court martial for disobedience of orders '.

These detachments were granted under ' writs of assistance ' which ran in the name of the king, over the signature of the chief baron of the court of exchequer; they recited that the officers of the revenue, in the due execution of their duty, ' have been frequently obstructed and violently assaulted and wounded, to the hazard and sometimes to the loss of their lives '. This duty, for the suppression of a traffic which was for their fellow-countrymen on a wide scale a means of livelihood, was not popular with the native troops and it had, in 1794, been generally inefficacious ' as in the majority of cases the still, head and worm, have not been seized, but only a part....the vessels in many cases have not been destroyed nor the pot-ale spilled '.[8] Special payments—an elaborate scale—were therefore approved for the troops employed; there was also special remuneration for the revenue officers in charge of what were in effect small military preventive or punitive expeditions. The figures quoted show how frequent these were (and how little progress was made in suppressing the traffic) and no true picture of the daily round of the officers and men of the Irish militia is possible unless this ' distressing and oppressive duty ' is realized as a continuous possibility. The quartering of detachments was affected by the exigencies of this service; there is, for example, official reference to a certain quarter as being ' well calculated in point of situation for a detachment of troops for the purpose of preventing frauds on the revenue '. This duty probably did not fall to the English militia, but the Highlands also affected illicit distilling; a parliamentary commission in 1816 on illicit distillation in Scotland refers to this ' pernicious and general practice ' and to it as a ' system of disobedience to the laws ' and to the ' violation of so many sacred engagements and depravity of morals which are inseparable from this state of active fraud '.[9]

In the interior economy of the units a new condition which came—and to stay—in this year 1806 was the ' annual volunteering ' (46 Geo. iii. chap. 124 21 July 1806). There had been in the year 1805 the ' draft ' for the line which has already (chapter XII) been mentioned. For this volunteering the line regiments allotted to receive volunteers were those then serving in Ireland and authority was given for officers and non-commissioned officers to be sent from these to the headquarters of such militia regiments as were thought most likely to provide them with recruits. What happened at the first volunteering of all in 1800 has been described in chapter X. Things were probably the same or a little worse in 1805. The Donegal colonel's sentiments have already been quoted and Castlereagh states that in 1806—after much attention had been called to the resulting disorder and indiscipline—no less than 42 parties went to Belfast from different parts of England to contend for 150 men from the Londonderry militia.[10] This was indeed a wooing of the electors on old time lines. Even as regards next year (1807) an officer can write as follows :

> with the autumn drew on the period of our annual annoyance, the volunteering, a period during which discipline was sadly in abeyance....Some weeks before the day of volunteering officers and sergeants began to drop into Naas [the writer's regiment was quartered there] each doing his bit to win the militiamen to his own corps....The volunteering was kept open for 14 days [sic] unless the quota turned out sooner, which was rarely, I may say never, the case. The consequence was that 8/10ths of those who turned out at first were in a state of beastly intoxication during the greater part of the fortnight and had generally spent every farthing of their bounty before it ended. In this they were ably assisted not only by their former comrades but by shoals of those same characters who attend the paying off of a ship's crew in our ports. At length the nuisance was at an end and the regiment returned to its ordinary habits, purged of sundry wild hands.[11]

As has been seen, even highly placed staff officers often intervened, though not by canvass in person, to get recruits for their old regiments. Lord Harrington, the then commander of the forces in Ireland, in 1810, caused a letter to be sent to certain militia colonels repeating a request which he had formerly made ' for influence in the volunteering about to take place, by endeavouring to prevail upon a few more men to extend their services to that old and distinguished corps [i.e. the 29th regiment], still serving in Portugal '.[12] Sir Arthur Wellesley himself, when chief secretary, acted similarly.[13] All this was comparatively harmless, though tiresome perhaps for the units. But the over zealous *direct* canvass, with its obvious evils, had got to be dealt with. It is surprising that this was not done at once. In July 1806 there was an order that militiamen were not to be ' tampered with in the view of inducing them to enter into particular corps of the line '[14] and at length, after the autumn volunteering of 1807 and with effect from 1 October, parties from line regiments were by administrative order strictly prohibited from interfering.[15] The next year the prohibition was made statutory ; officers and men of the line were not ' to come within ten miles of militia regiments while volunteering '.

The other way of protecting the regiments against the disorders arising from the recruiting assaults was *segregation*—not that this term is applied to it in the documents of the period. In January Charles Long, reporting to Castlereagh the reactions of the colonels to the projected ' annual tribute ', says : ' some of these make a great point of having the power to set aside a certain number who should not be permitted to volunteer'. Provision had in fact been made for this, both in regard to the English and the Irish militias, by identical legislation of the previous year. Commanding officers could select up to half the privates serving and a like proportion of sergeants and corporals, and enlistments were only to be made out of the sergeants, corporals and privates remaining. Orders provided that those set aside should be sent to outstations and that 'the whole of the proportion allowed to volunteer shall be brought to the headquarters of the regiments'. This seems sufficiently drastic but, even after it, there are complaints of men being taken whom the commanding officers wanted to retain. The regiments of militia were helped over this upsetting of their internal economy in another way, i.e. by allowing the different units to volunteer only to a limited number of line regiments, so that there should thus be no excuse for their being open to the general solicitation described by Castlereagh.

Another step taken to reduce the disorder attending the volunteering was the substitution of six separate periods of three days' each (between 24 August and 14 February) for the continuous (possible) twenty days provided for by the act of 1806. This was introduced by the 1808 act. But still the militia colonels and their officers naturally disliked volunteering, on account of the conditions it caused when it was in progress, and for the conditions in which it left the units as regards strength. A militia officer has written :

> 'few things are more annoying to a militia officer who has taken pains with his regiment than its 'minished' appearance after a volunteering. We became accustomed to it however in due time and it led to patronage and promotion. A certain number of the junior officers obtained commissions in the line and deserving privates slipped into the shoes of those noncommissioned officers who had left us'.[16]

Another consolation was a reduction in the number of military punishments : 'for this' he says 'we were much indebted to the volunteering system which sent all our scamps to the line'.

When the matter of volunteering had been mooted with the colonels several of them asked : could not their light companies be returned to them? They no doubt realised that this would mean breaking up the light battalions on which, in a military sense, so much store had been set. They stated that detaching light companies had been discontinued in England. Some of them seem to have expressed a preference for their entire battalions 'to be trained to the light infantry discipline'.[17] The feelings of the officers who were detached from their parent unit seem to have been mixed. On the one hand life with the infantry brigade was at least stimulating, especially under general Scott (see chapter X); and the officers had the distinction of belonging to a corps d'élite. But, as the light companies were usually at considerable distances from the parent units, there was difficulty in keeping up the appearance of the companies as regards uniformity of height. An officer complains that the 'springing up among the young fellows gave the outline, on parade, of a segment of a circle', the men on the flanks being 6ft. high while the centre diminished to 4ft. 5 or 8in. As already noted, there were the two masters to please; the officer already quoted received the clothing for his company from his unit but the regular commanding officer of the light infantry battalion to which his company belonged did not like the mode in which the lace was put on the men's jackets and had it altered; soon after this the company rejoined its unit and 'there was the devil to pay at the alteration' and he was ordered to alter it back again at his own expense.[18]

Lord Hardwicke consulted his military adviser on the effect on the real military strength of the country of breaking up the light infantry concentration. He was informed that the light infantry practice was more suited to Ireland where 'a line of infantry.... cannot move in connected front for the space of a pistol shot, and where every field is a post'; the grenadiers and the light infantry were 'estimable as the picket men of the army, full of that spirit and ardour which belongs to a consciousness of superior powers', but it was added that taking them away from the regiment reduced 'efficiency and self-opinion'. This was not very conclusive and Hardwicke referred the matter to London. The reply does not seem to be available but an order was issued disbanding the light infantry battalions from 24 July; thanks were expressed for the services given and it was intimated to the regiments that the companies were to be kept in a state of readiness to be brought together again.[19] This never happened. The case against centralization had force; the colonels reasonably urged their new liability to feed the line and they could quote the precedent of 1800 when the light infantry companies were brought back by Cornwallis for the volunteering of that year. Moreover the contra-invasion responsibility was not what it had been[20] and, if there was anything in keeping step with England in things military, it surely applied both ways.

An affray which happened during the repatriation marches of the light infantry companies caused considerable sensation. It throws light on the clannishness which was at all periods very characteristic of the Irish militia units. In Ireland at that time there was the king's German legion, about 9,000 strong.[21] Some 900 of these were lying at Tullamore. The light infantry companies of the Londonderry, Monaghan, Sligo and Limerick (county), were passing through Tullamore when an incident arose. It possibly originated in a Hanoverian soldier attempting to take by force from a small drummer boy of the Monaghan company a switch 'on which the boy seemed to affix much value'. The boy apparently complained to a militiaman, using offensive language about the German. Then some more militiamen came up and fell violently on the German. With the arrival on the scene of more of the German soldiers there was a general mêlée. But the Germans were more numerous and the militiamen had consequently to fall back, but not belore they had attempted to rescue one of their comrades who was being conveyed to the guardhouse. Then more Germans came on the scene. The retreating militiamen began to fire. The whole affair took place after 8 p.m. but the townspeople did not become involved. The march of other light companies through Tullamore was, next morning, stopped. But, before this had been done, the Wexford light company had come in and halted for the night. Still 'nothing unpleasant occurred between the privates and the officers of both corps passed the evening together, those of the Wexford having been invited by the Germans to their mess'. In this encounter the militia had nine wounded of whom one died, from a bayonet stab. The German legion had several wounded; twelve by ball, three by bayonet and seven by cudgel; one of these died. The conduct of the Germans in the town is stated to have been good and no racial antipathy was anticipated from the deplorable affair.[22]

This was more a sudden emotional storm that anything else. The conclusion cannot be drawn from it that the units were lawless. The strains upon them were now less and more attention was probably being paid to internal order. The printed standing orders of several units still exist, compiled in some cases from the most approved standing orders of regular infantry regiments. The following (county of Limerick militia standing order) illustrates[23] the high conception of the officer status which was held up:

> Every gentleman who comes forward to bear a commission in the militia must undoubtedly be influenced by the most laudable motives; he withdraws his attention for a time from his usual pursuits and avocations to qualify himself for a very important trust; and his fellow citizens, placing a firm reliance upon the exertion of his best endeavours in the public service, are enabled to pursue their usual employments in security.

From noncommissioned officers also a high standard was expected; the following is from standing orders of date much earlier than the last extract:

> The noncommissioned officers are to be vigilant, active, lively and trustworthy; they are commanded to enforce these orders [i.e. the standing orders] and thereby to establish regularity and uniformity. They are to treat the men with mildness and good humour when they behave well and punish the idle and negligent impartially; when upon duty they are to treat

their men with rigour if their behaviour require it, to insist upon every form being most punctually adhered to, to enforce every part of the practised discipline, confine or report every man that is negligent that he may be brought to a due punishment, and thereby convince the men that they know their duty and will make them do theirs.

Something should be said about duelling. The royal instructions to lord Fitzwilliam (December, 1794) on his appointment as viceroy, repeated in the case of subsequent viceregal appointments, spoke of the 'frequent duels and quarrels between the officers of our army' and enjoinment number 12 directed the viceroy to attend to this matter.[24] Many duels are reported in the newspapers; probably many occurred which never got reported. The duel did not certainly die at the end of the 18th century. But the English traveller John Carr (known colloquially in Ireland as 'jaunting Carr') who made a tour through the south and west parts of Ireland in 1805 and published his impressions[25]—he was a lawyer—says:

I found that duelling had very much subsided and that it was far from raising those who engaged in it in the opinion of their brother officers. From one regiment, the officers of which I knew, an Irish officer was dismissed for quarrelling and challenging, and a resolution was entered into that any gentleman of that regiment who accepted a challenge from such expelled officer should be sent to Coventry by the whole mess. The result of many enquiries upon the subject was that military duels in Ireland are rare.

In the case of the men, as we have seen, the volunteering system operated to provide, though this was not its avowed object, an outlet for the 'scamps' and 'wild hands'. But the punishments awarded continued severe. Southey stated in the next year that 'the martial laws of England are the most barbarous which this day exist in Europe, offenders sometimes being sentenced to 1,000 lashes, a surgeon standing by to feel his pulse during execution and determine how long it could be continued without killing'. In the year that Southey wrote, in the books of one militia regiment, are found the following sentences:—for desertion—900, 800, and 600 lashes; for drunkenness—800, 500 and 200; and for riotous conduct 600, 500 and 200.[26] A militia officer describes a military punishment as 'an unpleasant sight' but he adds that 'he is clearly of opinion that it is necessary to discipline the ranks of the army' which included 'so many rascals who can be kept in order by corporal punishment only—who have no sense of shame so as to fear disgrace'.[27]

To the drum major it fell to execute these decrees. The 'heads of a militia bill' (see chapter I), as drawn up as far back as 1776,[28] provided that 'it may be enacted that whenever any person serving in the militia is sentenced to be whipped . . . . such whipping shall be inflicted by the drummers of the battalion'.

In 1793 a militiaman who had been awarded 250 lashes dared his officers to whip him, saying there was ' no law for it '[29]. But that he was wrong ' was ably illustrated upon his own parchment by half a dozen drummers '. In 1799 there is an application by the drum major of the Fermanagh[30] on behalf of himself and some drummers of the regiment for remuneration for executing 31 men at Wicklow ; one guinea a head is claimed. The drummers were often men of colour[31] but whether these were allowed to administer the lashes is not stated.

By 1807 at all events the whole matter was systematized. The standing orders of the Westmeath[32] say that ' the execution of regimental punishment is peculiarly in his [i.e. the drum major's] department ' and' he is to take special care that the drummers are properly instructed in this....he is to provide proper cat-o'-nine-tails for which he is to be allowed 6d. by each man who is punished ; and he is to be particularly careful that two men are not punished with the same cat-o'-nine-tails '. The surgeon, or assistant surgeon, was required to be present at all punishments. The drum major had to count the strokes. In one case he omitted to do so though reminded by the sergeant major ; whereupon the latter struck him with a rattan. But the drum major had more humane duties also : he was in charge of all regimental letters ; he kept the colonel's postage account ; and, in one case at least, his wife had the honour of doing the colonel's washing. But still his main duty (see chapter IV) was the band ; the standing orders quoted instruct him to ' march the drummers to some field near the town and practice them [not, of course, on the human parchment] for two hours at least, as often as the weather will permit '. Down to August 1809 the drum major had, in an official sense, only a regimental existence ; after that year a man was allowed as drum major, additional to the authorized number of drummers, but paid, from public funds at all events, only as a drummer ; next year the drum major received the pay and allowances of a sergeant of militia. In the light infantry brigade before its dissolution the head of the music was apparently the ' bugle major ' and he was allowed to charge half a guinea for teaching a boy to play on the bugle.[33]

Of the amusements and sports of either the officers or the men there is little information available. A periodical, the ' *British Military Library or Journal* '[34] speaks of ' athletic exercises among the soldiers....the knotty etc.' We hear occasionally of hurley matches between two militia units. Boxing matches also took place. Brigadier general Scott (October 1801) expressed disapprobation ' at a riotous quarrel which took place ....among some of the soldiers ' and forbad ' in a most positive manner all boxing matches '. But they no doubt went on. The 'gentlemen of the Galway regiment' are spoken of as given to cockfighting. But a newspaper reference to 'the wearisome listlessness of unemployed time in country quarters', though it is in terms only as regards officers, is probably equally relevant as regards the men. The correct picture however for the reader to have before him is not a segregated quasi-monastic barrack life. The atmosphere must have been much more of a family character than that. The militia milieu was one in which wives and children teemed. In previous chapters the remarks of the commanding officer of the Kerry have been quoted and also the numbers of the women and children taken by the Wexford and the King's county to the Channel islands. In July 1809 the Armagh stationed at Clonnel had with the unit 228 women and 313 children. The women went also to camp; the Donegal at the Curragh in 1804 had nine tents allotted for their use.[35] The traveller Carr, already quoted, remarks that, when the English militia regiments were in Ireland during the rebellion 'the numbers of married men amongst the Irish regiments was astonishingly greater than those of the same description in the English regiments, to the no small and frequently jocose surprise of the Irish soldier'.[36] Officers also seem to have had their wives with them though by no means to the same extent as the men.

The presence in the units of these large numbers of children was a serious matter. It was serious when the unit was on the move, in the field (as in 1798), or on change of quarters; it was almost more serious when the unit was stationary at a quarter; these stationary periods, as we know, were not long. A newspaper of this period says:

> 'every military man who has been engaged in a regimental duty and is acquainted with its interior economy well knows to what low vices the children of soldiers bred and reared in barracks are early addicted and that from the promiscuous intercourse of a barrack life they receive and imbibe the most licentious habits'.[37]

Charitable ladies had in some cases given funds for the education of the children of militiamen. In 1807 the officers of the Cavan militia made a serious effort to deal with the matter.[38] By subscription amongst themselves (field officers 12/- a month; captains and paymasters 9/-; lieutenants, surgeons and adjutant 4/6; and ensigns 3/-) they created a continuing fund to provide for not only educating but also clothing forty boys, who might be either roman catholic or protestant. They were taught to read and write and the common rules of arithmetic and instructed in the principles of the Christian religion and duties of morality. In 1812 there is an official statement that 'many if not all of the militia regimental schools' used 'a compilation from those parts of the old and new testaments in which roman catholics and protestants would unite '.[39] The fund in the Cavan regiment provided each boy with a leather cap, a jacket and two pairs of cloth trousers annually ; it was left to the parents to supply shoes and shirts. This example was probably followed by many units. The Tipperary are stated to have been the first to establish a regimental school. In 1810 the Limerick (county) standing orders[40] state that ' in order to open the door promotion, and give every soldier in the Limerick militia an opportunity of pushing forward in the world ' the colonel ' has thought proper to establish a school ', which was under the sergeant major. Ultimately, though not until 1812, it was decided to add a sergeant schoolmaster to the establishment.[41] It had however become imperative for the authorities to recognize the problem of the children of the regiment as the militia amending act of the previous year (52 Geo. iii. chap. 29) had provided that not exceeding one quarter of those to be raised in each year for the militia of any county should consist of boys, of the age of 14 and upwards. Apart from this a strong current of desire for education was running in Ireland at this time ; ' hedge schools packed with voluntary and eager scholars ' are mentioned as characteristic of the early 19th century in Ireland.[42]

That the officers of the militia gave up not only much of their money but also of their time to the care and welfare of their men there is sufficient evidence. At the Giffard-Sankey court martial (see page 149) captain Giffard testified that ' before the soldier's pay was raised (1797), in long and laborious marches, I always regularly subsisted their wives and children at the rate of soldiers pay, at my own expense ' and the account of a colonel's disbursements shows the item ' paid for things for the regiment on the march '. For the soldier these changes of quarters, which were frequent, must have meant much expense which, without help from the officers, they with difficulty met. During the events in the west in 1798, a captain was courtmartialled for failing to march when ordered to do so ; part of his defence was that he had 26 soldiers' wives on his hands whom he had to ' billet about the place ' before he could get off.[43] The early standing orders of one of the militia units (September 1793) have the following :

> ' The officers will teach their men the attitudes of soldiers and how to address their officers, speak kindly to them off duty, endeavour to improve them in their discipline and correct such errors as creep into and prejudice the same, attend to their food and clothing, consult their ease as much as is consistent with the service, do them the strictest justice and then punish offenders without favour '.[44]

Those officers who acted in this spirit—and there is no reason for thinking that the majority did not do so— must have had some means of keeping their days relatively free from ' the wearisome listlessness of unemployed time', quite apart from the morning and evening parades, the special field days and exercises, and the half-yearly inspections which involved much keying up. A militia officer writes, referring to about this period :

> Ireland was at this time a land of general officers. I believe there was scarcely a considerable town without one. Changes were frequent among them and, as each newcomer deemed it expedient to inspect the troops under his charge, our inspections were of frequent occurrence.[45]

These military events led to much social gaiety. The inspecting officers often dined, after it was all over, with the officers and sometimes barrels of ale were provided for the men to regale themselves simultaneously.

> Then came, writes the officer just quoted 'our half yearly inspection, a great event.... which never failed of drawing an assemblage of all within ten miles around. I think there could not be less than 15 or 16 carriages on our exercise field and sundry parties resulted from the meeting'.

For these inspections the outlying companies were, at this period, brought into the headquarters, which meant four or five days of reunion and 'wet nights'. In the earlier and more troubled days Dublin castle did not think it prudent to assemble 'all the detachments from the militia at the several headquarters even for the purpose of a review' and commanding officers were told that they must do the best they could 'to make their corps appear to advantage'.[46] There is also an order that reviews were to interfere as little as possible with the assizes. These took place in the spring and autumn and were times of great gaiety. On these as on other social occasions the militia bands were in request. For instance, at the celebrations in Londonderry in December 1805 of the shutting of the gates of the city, the Waterford militia band took a part and, at the annual party given in Wexford to celebrate the birthday of the grand old man, George Ogle (see p. 2) the Tyrone band 'contributed not a little in detaining the joyous party to a late hour next morning'.[47] We hear too of a militia band playing on a barge at Seapoint, co. Dublin, regatta and, in 1809, the Tyrone band, in full uniform, accompanied the lord lieutenant on the Grand canal ; they were on the deck of 'a small and elegant passage boat' which attended the lord lieutenant's boat.

Presentations of colours were always great occasions. In August 1806 authority was given for militia units which had gone 12 years 'without receiving a supply of drums or colours or an allowance in lieu' to apply for an allowance for the supply of new colours. The interest taken in the colours does not seem quite so keen as it had been in 1793-4. But there is recorded one ceremony, in the Armagh regiment, which is interesting and worth quoting :

> A very grand and solemn scene took place at Ennis on 25 November (1805), it being the day appointed to replace the old colours of the Armagh militia. The regiment was drawn up in funeral procession before major Cope's lodgings (commanding at Ennis at present). The ancient banners were given out, with which they proceeded, the band playing solemn dirges, to the exercise ground. Here they formed a hollow square, in the centre of which the colours were burned and the ashes interred over which the regiment fired three rounds. This ceremony concluded, the regiment again formed a hollow square and were presented with the new standards. After a beautiful and glowing address delivered by the major, the consecration of the new colours was then performed by the acting chaplain....together with an appropriate and very excellent discourse. In the same evening a splendid ball and supper was given by the officers of the regiment to which the principal families of the surrounding country were invited.[48]

The colonels were full of concern about the appearance of their units on parade. This was, with more serious considerations, at the back of their antagonism to volunteering. So far as information is available, the units still had, after the close of the year 1806 and after the first ' annual tribute ', a substantial stiffening of men with ten years service; nearly half had from 3 to 4 years (i.e. had been in the unit from the re-embodiment); while the remainder were new hands. The quota for the first ' annual tribute ' (taken in September and October) was 3,285. By 14 October 2968 had been obtained and the final figure recorded in the War Office was 2,990. Most of the units which gave volunteers at all—29 gave, though less than that number had by then been augmented—gave the quota.[49] The maximum quota was, obviously, 150 (i.e. 15×10 for the 10 company units). Of the quality of these recruits to the line we can only judge indirectly. Clearly, from the efforts made to get them the line units liked to have them. The traveller Carr has some relevant observations. ' British adjutants ' he says ' allow that an Irish recruit is sooner made a soldier of than an English one ' and, though admitting that Irish *recruits* were in general of short stature owing to the poverty of their food, he adds that ' most of the Irish militia regiments that I saw exhibited very fine looking men, frequently exceeding the ordinary stature ' and, having spent some days with the Londonderry militia at Killarney, he says they were ' a complete refutation of the assertion that the Irish soldiers are shorter than the English '.[50]

Of recruiting for the militia in this year 1806 we have a vivid picture.[51] The writer speaks of ' increased activitity in completing our numbers and for proceeding, if necessary to a ballot in the county '. This officer who had a numerous party to help him attended at the towns on the market day to receive and pass the recruits furnished by each parish; they were all, he says

> on the *qui vive* in the recruiting way. It was really the church militant, for the parochial clergy took the lead in their respective parisbes.... Many parishes however contracted with Surgeon....[a civil surgeon] for supplying their quotas and it was in good hands. He was very sharp and knew the way to come round a young hand while his medical knowledge prevented many an old one from coming round him. Nothing was more common in those days than for fellows who knew right well they would not pass offering themselves to young officers and receiving a shilling or two as recruiting money. But the surgeon was not to be had in this way. He knew himself how to examine a candidate for the bounty before disturbing a farthing.

In June 1806 the militia regiments were asked to send in a return of carpenters they might have 'who are willing to be employed on government works and paid agreeable to his majesty's regulations'.[52] This is perhaps an illustration of that tranquillity which, during the greater part of that year, Ireland is reported to have enjoyed 'under the mild and conciliatory government of the duke of Bedford'.[53]

XIV

The Ballot revived

In the year 1807 there was in the militia some considerable trouble which lasted on, becoming more acute, into the next year. It never got into the newspapers, although for more than a year it was an embarrassment to the lord lieutenant and caused recourse not less than four times to the advice of the law officers. It arose out of the obsession the men got that their discharges would shortly become due, now that five years were about to be completed since they were enrolled in the year 1803. In that year, on the re-embodiment, all the militiamen—those then re-enlisting no less than those then newly enlisting—entered upon a fresh engagement. Irregularities in the attestations having led to the wholesale release in the year 1802, it might have been expected, perhaps, that, even though the re-embodiment proceedings were hurried, casualness over enlistment would be generally avoided in 1803. But this was not so. It was not however solely technically irregular attestations of 1803 but also the interpretation of those which had been quite regular, over which trouble arose in the years 1807 and 1808.

In 1803 the governors of counties Down, Carlow, Louth and Waterford had thought it advisable, and had been permitted, to raise the militia for those counties 'under the old laws' (see chapter XI); in all the rest enrolment had been, or should have been, under the oath contained in section 5 of 43. Geo. iii, chap. 2. This was:

> I will faithfully serve during the term of five years for which I am enrolled, *or for such further time as the militia shall remain embodied, if within the space of five years his majesty shall order and direct the militia to be drawn out and embodied, unless I shall be sooner discharged.*

Whatever may be the interpretation of the italicized words, they are not so much surplusage and to be left out of account. But this contention was in effect set up. It was however militiamen who considered that they had come in on a limited four years contract who first began to agitate their claim to discharge—to be discharged, that is, in the spring of 1807.

In March the Carlow militia, then 'lying in the county of Kerry', and the Louth which was at Naas—two not contiguous quarters—both made a move. The petition of the latter is said to be ' in the name of the balloted men and substitutes ' or ' what is called the four years' men '. They say that they made objection at the time of attestation but that the Speaker [i.e. Mr. Foster who was colonel of the Louth] made certain statements to them and that there were threats of prison ; ' and the honourable Speaker told us substitutes who refused to take the oath with the words ' during the war ' that we were not liable to serve one month longer than four years without a fresh bounty, because by the county we were raised and no volunteers but militiamen '.[1] They asked that as four years was then fully expired they might be discharged. The Carlow likewise put in a petition, as well as a memorial direct to the duke of York. They also claimed that they had been told, by their major, that they were not bound to serve more than four years. They thought that they were entitled to their discharge ' especially as they were balloted and forced from their respective homes and families, and abandoned their aged parents '. Their statement went on : ' some are anxious to return and others for further engagement. For that reason the regiment is very much divided in opinion, and grieved at a regimental order which was issued against a soldier insisting on discharge or otherwise, this they refer to your mental observation, expecting an immediate answer from your honour, if not, 'tis to be dreaded there will be some altercation, or further confusion, and that instantaneously, as may be said, by us unanimously in the regiment '.[2]

Not much seems to have happened on these petitions beyond some enquiry into the really irrelevant (as the law officers, in effect, subsequently advised) question of the extent to which the two regiments had in fact been balloted in 1803. But in July the officer commanding the Londonderry reports to Castlereagh that his men think that they are eligible for discharge next year (i.e. 1808) and that ' no rhetoric can convince them to the contrary ' and, most serious of all, ' so long as they have this idea not a man of those who enlisted in 1803 will volunteer into any regiment whatever '. He had about 250 who took this line and most regiments, he said, had about as many. Another colonel reported that similar ideas pervaded the whole militia. The authorities seem to have been alarmed lest a rot should set in and, with the 1807 volunteering due to begin on 1 October, on a large scale that year (see below), there was the possibility of seriously disappointing Whitehall's expectation of man power. The number who might fade away if this rot was not stopped was stated as being from 8,000 to 10,000—a number, in the words of the lord lieutenant, ' infinitely too large to be spared at this moment '.[3] The question was moreover of larger scope since the same oath (i.e. that in 43 Geo. iii, chap. 2) had been administered to the men raised under the augmentations of 1805 and 1806.

In August a circular[4] was issued to all the units. No general reading of this to the regiments was enjoined. The line taken rather was to minimize; if this misconception prevailed in any regiment or battalion there was to be investigation, followed, if necessary, by explanation in 'the most clear and circumstantial manner' of the precise terms upon which they had been enrolled and upon which (as was, with a hint of firmness, emphasized) they were to be retained. The opinion which had been furnished by the law officers was quoted at length. Briefly this was that no man, since the re-embodying in 1803 could have been legally enrolled—and the cases submitted were all of legal and regular attestations—in such a manner as to entitle him to discharge 'at the expiration of any number of years from his attestation, provided that at such time the war continues or the militia is embodied'. The men could be legally retained and the law on the subject with respect to all classes of militiamen 'was so clear as to admit of no doubt'. This opinion covered both the men who were balloted and the men who were enrolled, though in the details of the two cases there were, it was admitted, differences.

One commanding officer, lord Clancarty,[5] thought that the circular created doubts where there had been none; this was the case, not in his own Galway regiment, but in the Kerry; the government, it was argued, would never have consulted the law officers unless they had themselves had considerable misgivings. Castlereagh[6] anyhow was anxious that an interval should, if possible, elapse after the explanation, in order to make the volunteering go more smoothly. In actual fact this does not seem to have been prejudiced. But the official action did not remove the discontent. In December 1807 Wellesley, back again from Copenhagen at his Dublin post, says he has daily reports that the men raised in 1803 expect their discharge next year.[7] He himself apparently had some qualms about the government position: he expected a breeze and he did not want discontented soldiers. Lord Clancarty also thought 'the case is a much stronger one in favour of the claim than I had originally supposed it'.[8] So the law officers were once again (Jan. 1808) formally consulted. Otherwise than confidentially, no new announcement of their views (which remained unchanged) seems to have been made. In the Londonderry, where there was still trouble, a regimental order (22 January) was read every day for a week at morning parade.[9] The discontent sulked on. On 15 March, 15 men came on parade without arms. This was 'mutiny' and the lord lieutenant was seriously alarmed. The government in London were all for firmness, basing themselves on the legal opinions furnished, but they advised a very strict examination of the attestations some of which, it had appeared, were informal.[10] Wellesley was ready to come over at once and advised that yeomanry should be called out if other militia units showed a disposition to follow those who made the claim.[11] The lord lietenant's contribution was to order the colonels, usually expected to play the role of '*dei ex machina*' in militia crises, to join their regiments at once.[12] But there was, it seemed, no cause for a tragic attitude. The Londonderry men, on explanations being given them, were satisfied and expressed contrition. Their case was that the magistrates who had sworn them in had told them that the words 'such further time' in the oath were of no significance. On 19 March the lord lieutenant felt himself able to report to London that 'the thing is over and we shall have no riot on the subject of discharge'.[13]

But the wood had in fact not yet been left; and on 24 April the law officers were again consulted. The Cavan were at this time at Athlone. Sometime at the end of March a notice was taken down from the markethouse door which was as follows:—

G.R.

By order of government sent to Mr. Richard Handcock [sovereign of Athlone] for to publish in Athlone that the militia regiments of Ireland will be discharged at the expiration of their five years or else take the fresh bounty which will go in each county of the kingdom, as it is considered that the men who will serve their five years if not let go that they will desert and cause a rebellion in the kingdom of Ireland.[14]

A letter of a Cavan private of this time is also preserved:

there is great work about the men getting off, the first of their times is on the 25th of this month and they are determined to throw up their arms and will go to the guardhouse let the consequences be what it will. There is other regiments that some men has their time in and they are all in the guardhouse waiting for the issue which will be known on the 25th.[15]

The militiamen's letters appear to have been censored to see what they were thinking. A substantial packet of extracts from these exists; they are from a good many different regiments and show a widespread desire for discharge; awareness of their respective dates of attestation; and aversion from volunteering. But some see clearly that 'nothing is doing' in the way of discharge. Two of the Dublin city were overheard, whilst returning from a field day, to say that, as they were not to be discharged, they might as well volunteer—which they did a few days later. In the Tyrone some of the men subscribed to procure counsel's advice as to their right to discharge at the end of five year's service; the opinion they got supported their claim. A king's messenger going south who was attended by escorts of militia put in a report on the attitude he found among the men.[16] No wonder the lord lieutenant wished for further advice.

What happened then is not quite clear. Wellesley was not entirely happy with the legal advice which was probably then, as certainly later, against accepting informality of attestation as justifying grant of discharge. He writes, presumably referring to the latest opinion of the law officers, on 9 May :

> as soon as [a soldier] asks for his discharge on the ground of the irregularity on the face of it and that this irregularity appears, the man must be discharged. The attorney general's opinion is very good law, I dare say, for common purposes but it won't do for soldiers. In all transactions with them you must have justice as well as law on your side.[17]

The volunteering had been going well in spite of the discharge agitations and this no doubt predisposed Dublin castle towards taking things calmly. But this attitude could hardly be maintained in face of a further outbreak which occurred in July. This was serious and the trouble was at the door. It was considered an ' aggravating circumstance ' that the units affected, the north and south Down, were in camp, contiguous, the former in Phoenix Park and the latter at Chapelizod. A south Down private refused to do duty and was apparently courtmartialled. In the north Down as many as twelve men ' persisted in refusing duty ' and were confined. The lord lieutenant held that ' an example must be made before the militia will understand this business ', and the sooner the better '. The men, he said, who were brought forward, ' must be convicted and sentenced. The sentence should be put into execution before a large body of troops '[18] On 28 July, they were tried at Dublin on the charge of ' refusing to do their duty as soldiers ' and all except one were sentenced ' to receive 800 lashes each, in the usual manner '. But the court at the same time recommended a further reference to the law officers. A consultation between these and the chancellor and the deputy advocate general followed. The men tried had been substitutes and not volunteers but had had administered to them, as had others who were balloted men, the volunteer oath. But, this notwithstanding, all the legal authorities maintained the view (and, as we may feel, correctly) that ' no militiaman of any class, notwithstanding the irregularity of administering a wrong oath, is at present entitled to his discharge, or can be while the war continues and the militia remains embodied '. This opinion, with reasoned amplifications, was delivered in writing on 5 August The lord lieutenant and the commander of the forces then decided, ' taking various considerations into account to attribute the conduct of the prisoners to error rather than intention ', and they remitted the punishment. The ' opinion ' was promulgated by general order to the army by the commander of the forces and, simultaneously, to the colonels of militia from Dublin castle.

The general order was to be read at the head of every regiment in Ireland and was to be entered in the orderly books.[19]

This was of course done, but the matter was not so easily liquidated. Sir Edward Littlehales comments at the end of August on the 'very novel and embarrassing light in which the question remained'. This apparently refers to what had come out regarding the attestations in the Meath militia. There a considerable number of men were found to have been enlisted (in the words of the law officers) 'according to a form not to be found in any of the militia laws and altogether unwarranted'.[20] This difficulty was referred to London whence came approval that men so situated might be discharged. But to let so many soldiers go did not appeal to the lord lieutenant, although he expressed strong views about what had happened at the attestation of these Meath men : 'they entered under a misapprehension into the service for five years only, and they have consequently been inveigled and trepanned by the magistrates before whom they were attested'.[21]

It was decided to bring into action the colonel, lord Headfort, and let him effect a settlement on some terms which did not include discharge. He was instructed to repair to his regiment from London. But he had a 'severe Rhumatic attack' and could not go. Instead he sent an order which stated that 'as some remuneration may be due for the mistake' there was to be paid 'to each man in the predicament' two guineas which was to be charged to him. The reported results were considered satisfactory; ninety men reattested on receiving the gratuity; twenty had volunteered to the line; and twenty cases remained unadjusted.[22] Next year, as will be seen, Wellesley introduced a new form of oath, explaining that the old one had caused some trouble. But this trouble was not ended even by that change. In the year 1812 the law officers, again appealed to, again reiterated their view that no militiaman enrolled since the year 1803 could be at that day legally entitled to his discharge; and an explanatory memorandum for the benefit of private soldiers was issued in November. At that time there was also misunderstanding about terms and duration of service in the English and Scotch militias. Next year (May 1813) there was again trouble in the north Down, the men claiming that the officers by whom they were attested had told them their service was to be limited to five years.[23] Again an order, which gave a detailed legal refutation of the claim, was issued and ordered to be read at the head of each militia regiment.

But notwithstanding this apparently rather general preoccupation about discharge, the volunteering (which began as from 1 October 1807)[24] both started with a swing and turned out in the end satisfactorily for the regular army. This year Castlereagh, now since the fall of the Talents[25] ministry secretary at war, in May and July put before the cabinet proposals for largely increasing disposable strength. These included getting 5,000 from the militia in Ireland, which was to be increased by that same number. This was to be in addition to the 'draft of 15 men per company which the augmented militia regiments [of Ireland] are now liable to furnish'. His proposals went through and obtained legislative approval in acts which were passed on 13 August. Apparently the 'annual tribute' act was about to be put into force in Ireland in 1807 anyhow. This would have produced approximately 3,000 men for the line and the letters about this were, it seems, on the point of being issued from Dublin castle[26] when the new policy arrived from across the channel. The act (of 13 August) did not state a gross number, nor specific totals for individual units, as the goal to be reached; it gave a formula as governing the extent of the effort to be made, i.e. that the number to be taken was 'not to exceed such number of men then serving as will reduce the regiment below 3/5ths of the establishment'. In figures this meant that some 8,600 men had to be produced from the Irish militia. This number which included the 'annual tribute', constituted a much larger task than had been set the colonels since the first volunteering in the year 1800. Simultaneously the English and Scottish militias were set the task of furnishing respectively 16,327 and 4,160 volunteers.[27]

Contemporary accounts speak of the ardour with which the volunteering began;[28] the act permitted units in which 5/6ths of the 2/5ths turned out as volunteers within 30 days to stop at that. Several units quickly reached their permitted quota. The Kildare in three days had got its number.[29] The Westmeath, always keen to help by furnishing the demanded volunteers, had its quota in less than 15 days. The Antrim at the first parade for volunteering gave the entire number required.[30] By the end of October 5,506 men had been transferred. For the success achieved the colonels must have the main credit. On this occasion they had been left with the management of this ticklish operation. The circular sent out (26 September)[31] specifically states that it 'has been the anxious endeavour of ministers so to frame the law in all its parts as to protect the discipline of the militia and to consult the feelings of that service....' The circular ended by emphasizing 'the pressing exigencies of the public service' and referred to 'the expectation of the legislature'. Lord Sligo, in his correspondence with Dublin castle, speaks of 'a most critical moment when our all is at stake', and of his resolve to discharge what fell to him 'with that zeal and alacrity that is generally felt by those who possess great comforts and wish to preserve them by every possible exertion '.[32] But the militia colonels, English or Irish, did not uniformly take this enlightened view. At Westminster there had been much hostility to the bill. Volunteering from the militia was in fact a political issue between the late ministry (the 'Talents') and the ministry in office. A critic of the attitude taken up by the colonels attributes their dissentience to personal vanity and goes on :

> It is the vice of the militia system that the commanding officers look upon their regiments rather as personal property than as a public trust and consider every effort to render the militia force more useful to the state as an attempt to deprive them of so much of that property.[33]

By mid February the number of those who had volunteered had reached 7,335.[34] The pressure had been kept up by further admonition and an additional guinea of bounty was offered in April. At the same time, an appeal of rather a cringing nature was made to the colonels of those units, eleven in number, which had 'with much honour to themselves' furnished 5/6ths of their full quota. They were told that it was only by their 'personal and special indulgence that any additional number of men can become entitled to volunteer' and they were reminded of 'the great advantages that would result to the public service, at this important juncture, should you deem it not inconsistent with the due exercise of the discretion which has been entrusted to you by the legislature '[35] to permit men to transfer to the full extent of the full quota authorized to enlist. Lord Leitrim, who had reacted so sharply on a former occasion to the cooing of Dublin castle, spoke out strongly : he found the appeal 'totally inconsistent with the terms of volunteering held out last summer' and stigmatized it as a breach of faith towards the militia. 'I cannot' he said 'give my consent to any further volunteering from the Donegal regiment if it is left to my discretion '.[36] Other 'gentlemen of the militia' appear in Wellesley's correspondence as going even further than lord Leitrim. Not very many more men seem to have accrued from these appeals. The final aggregate reached was 8,353 of which the marines had 235. This left a deficiency of only 203. Although under the act the volunteering could have been continued until August it seems to have been shut down in June.[37]

The successful results had been obtained notwithstanding that volunteers were involved in the disastrous wrecks which took place in November off Dublin. Justice Day writes to lord Chichester (formerly the chief secretary, Pelham) of 'about 300 highmettled volunteers from our militia crammed into the holds of two transports and, within a stone's throw of the shore, consigned to irredeemable destruction'. He adds that 'this disaster will damp the volunteering spirit of our militia '.[38] The volunteers were on board the two shipwrecked vessels, the Rochdale and the Prince of Wales, and were from the south Mayo and the south Cork ; and it seems that there were, as usual, numerous women and children with them. The storm and the shipwreck scenes which it produced were terrible and in the morning, after the wild and horrible night, the shore, we are told, was ' covered with their bodies '. Very few escaped destruction. An inquest followed at which amongst others a surviving volunteer from the south Mayo gave evidence. It is expressly mentioned that he gave evidence through the medium of an Irish interpreter.[39] Volunteering, evidently, for many of the Irish country lads must have meant a ' heavy change ' and it is small wonder that a militia colonel should be found urging that it be carried out with the units away from their counties and ' far from the solicitations of parents and friends '.[40] But all honour was paid to those who perished in this tragedy. The commander of the forces in Ireland caused stones to their memory, which remain to this day, to be erected in the churchyards of Old Merrion and Carrickbrennan in which the recovered bodies were buried.[41]

Simultaneously with the volunteering and with the discontents described, strenuous efforts were being made to get up the strength of the militia. Between 1793 and 1802 balloting had been infrequent in Ireland. Much research would be needed to arrive at any certainty as to what, if any, casual resorts to it, apart from what happened in 1795 (see chap. V), there had been in this period. At all events it had not disturbed the public peace. Its reputation in this sense, derived rightly or wrongly from the early days, was in part the reason why the authorities kept clear of it in 1803. The preamble of the act of that year (43 Geo. iii. chap. 2) had, as stated in chapter 10, recited that ' the mode of raising men by ballot had not been generally adopted in Ireland '. This was true but the statement by Fortescue that its enforcement almost always meant ' desperate riots ' has been shewn to be, at the least, inexact. In some counties (e.g. Down and Louth) the governors remained constant to what they conceived to be the true militia faith and in these and in a few others balloting was, as already stated, operated in 1803. For the augmentations of the years 1805 and 1806 the men had been raised as volunteers. But for the Additional Force act (43 Geo. iii. chap. 85) the men were to be got by ballot under the militia laws. Hardwicke brought together the governors of counties and recommended to them that in those counties ' where it should be thought inadvisable to resort to an actual ballot ' they should proceed by parochial volunteers, rather than recruiting.[42] This was probably the course taken but there is a representation, in a letter from the bishop of

Meath to Pelham, of the 'folly of leaving an alternative of raising this force by recruiting rather than by ballot....The Irish members' he says 'all expressed a dread that ballot would produce an insurrection....The fact has turned out that wherever the mode of balloting was adopted the men have been raised without the least disturbance. Unfortunately there have not been more than three or four counties where this has happened'. He then speaks of Meath as one of the counties where 'the timid course' was adopted.[43]

There is no statement of the reasons why the authorities, for the augmentation of 1807-8, decided to revert to the ballot. It may however be judged that, having been forced by the military and political situation abroad to pursue a vigorous expansion policy, they adopted the method of the ballot—the reality, if the threat proved not enough—as the course most certain to give what they wanted. 'No mode of recruiting' wrote an unofficial adviser from co. Waterford 'will do—no, nothing but a ballot or compulsion of some sort'.[44] In the spring Castlereagh had been stressing that the militia were about 6,000 below establishment; both he and the lord lieutenant wanted this made good so that the 'annual tribute' might be furnished without difficulty. The troubles about discharge had shewn the existence of a considerable desire to get out; and, if this was so, it was a fair inference that men not already in the militia might not generally be anxious to come in. The troubles of those inside would almost certainly be known to potential recruits outside.

After the act had been passed (47 Geo. iii. sec. 2, chap. 56, 13 August 1807) and before any steps were taken to put it into force, the lord lieutenant consulted[45] the governors as to the best mode of carrying of it into effect. A majority favoured a course other than the ballot; either parochial assessment or enrolment by commanding officers or a combination of the two. The lord lieutenant's first inclination, when he saw the incomplete unanimity of the replies, was, as he expressed it, to proclaim—he used that now ill-omened word—each county separately, according to its stated preference. This however was thought open to objection and he decided to adhere to uniformity. The counties had never previously been formally allowed local option in matters of recruiting, although, under stress of circumstances in 1793, they had to a large extent followed their own ideas; and recently, as regards augmenting or not, they had been allowed to make choice. He was apparently nervous about ordering balloting pure and simple and wanted to do from the beginning what was, in effect, afterwards done, i.e. to give the counties choice between balloting and parochial assessment. But the law officers held that parochial assessment could only be lawfully allowed after balloting had first been proclaimed. The lord lieutenant therefore, by proclamation, 'ordered, directed and appointed that the men necessary to be raised shall be procured in all and every of the several counties by ballot in the manner directed by the act'. But the proclamation was somewhat apologetic; it recited that 'after due enquiry made and deliberation held' it appeared that this would be 'the most certain and effectual mode of carrying the act into execution'.

The preamble sets out the necessity of augmenting the regular forces; that a proportion of the militia was being permitted to transfer; and that therefore that force should be increased in limited proportion. Within six months from the date of passing there was to be raised 'a number of private militiamen equal to half the quota [i.e. standard establishment] of 35 Geo. ii. chap. 8, i.e. the Irish act of 1795', The number finally accepted as to be raised was 9,905. They were to be obtained by ballot or as volunteers and, if in the latter way, then they were to be enrolled by the colonels as arranged for the augmentation of 1805 (i.e. under the act of 1804, 44 Geo. iii. 33). If a ballot should be directed, general meetings were to be held in the normal way. Then came the provisions about the parochial procedure, the object of which method is stated to be to facilitate raising the necessary number with all convenient speed. A vestry meeting, with three days notice, summoned by the churchwardens could assess such sum to be levied on the parish as the meeting might decide. The aggregate sum received (which would be the multiplication of the quota by the average price of substitutes as fixed by general meeting) was to be applied 'for providing a sufficient number of persons to serve as substitutes or volunteers for the parish'. The churchwardens were at liberty to produce volunteers* before a deputy governor at any time before the day appointed for balloting; other people could produce volunteers or come forward themselves in that capacity.

The feeling in the country obviously could not be tested otherwise than it had been—somewhat unthoroughly, as was apparently thought in Cork where there was complaint that the governors had, in favouring ballot, conveyed to the lord lieutenant a view 'directly contrary to the sense of the most populous and respectable parish in the city'.[46] But of what was felt later, when what was in contemplation had become public, there is some evidence. Lord Sligo, always ready with counsel, supplemented the report of his consultative meeting with his deputies with these remarks:

*The terms 'volunteer' and 'substitute' are not synonymous; the former were men found before the ballot; the latter men found after. The price for the latter tended to be higher. Principals are men drawn to serve and electing to serve in person.

> The rumour of such a measure [ballot] being in contemplation had caused a universal ferment in the country and we were assured that the people of one very extensive district were preparing to fly to the mountains, leaving their harvest unreaped.[47]

He was against balloting which was ' not suited to these parts ; it would produce riot and do no good ; we are now all peace, prosperity and happiness '.[48] Another report (2 August) was that the peasants were ' sulky and generally exclaiming against the new bill, calling it an act of cruelty at this season '.[49] Castlereagh urged (21 August) pressing on the proceedings ' so as to find the substitutes in that happy state of idleness and intoxication which usually succeeds harvest '.[50] The official view in October was that ' the lower orders were better organized and more disaffected than they actually were in 1798 '.[51] In the reports of the debate at Westminster on 19 February 1808—the only general review of the 1807-8 balloting—there is little evidence of what the general feeling was before the act was put into force. Discussion turned mainly on the details of what was done and not on the fact that it was done at all ; on the latter the view taken apparently was that ' the ballot was odious to the people of Ireland '. But, however this may be—and, if true, it was probably at least equally true of England and Scotland—it is to be noted that there was no social upheaval, no popular explosions and not even any popular opposition.

What then was the course matters took in the counties? The proclamation was accompanied, on the same day, by a long circular to the colonels. The residual effect of this looking-two-ways document must have amounted to a hint that balloting was not in fact expected to be operated very generally, even though it was put forward by the proclamation as ' the most eligible mode of carrying the act into execution *in all cases* '. By recognizing ' resorting altogether to actual ballot....as liable to objection in some counties ' and by countenancing the idea of ' superseding as much as possible the necessity of actual balloting ', the lord lieutenant must have meant to convey that he did not expect much resort to balloting ; and the impression thus conveyed must have been strengthened when, only a week later, the precepts putting the parochial assessment into operation were issued. They authorized the *inhabitants and churchwardens* to levy the assessment. Ministers of religion are not officially brought into this but in practice they often took the lead. The first circular made it quite clear that, ' if, contrary to expectation, any county did not, by the means it adopted, procure the whole number required ' the deficiency must be made good ' by strictly resorting to the ballot '. It also stressed that, whatever exertions individuals might make, the county remained responsible for the required force being produced. The correspondence of Wellesley shows that for many of the counties the holding of a ballot was never expected to be a possibility.[52] *Faulkner's Journal* (which, however, probably did not represent general opinion) commented as follows :—

> 'We perfectly coincide in their opinion who prefer the ballot ; because it is the most ancient and constitutional mode ; because it has been already proved and found effectual ; because it is infinitely the most expeditious.... We have only to add that the highest confidence may be placed in the exertions of the governors and deputy governors ; they are men of the first character for loyalty, probity and public spirit; most of them have already gone through the labour of forming the present militia when it was a new and difficult measure in Ireland, and resisted by an opposition which has since fallen into contempt '.[53]

Fortunately, a member of parliament (acting, as he claimed, 'in conformity with the principles of the Irish union ') moved (19 February 1808) for papers[54] and so we know what happened in the various counties. There was a large amount of balloting but, if anything, parochial assessment was more frequently adopted. Cork (north) is perhaps not a typical county area for this purpose, but in this region over 80 parishes balloted while in over 100 the assessment method was followed. In neither Galway nor Kildare were there any ballots. In co. Sligo all the parishes balloted except four ; in co. Monaghan all balloted except two, out of twenty two ; and in co. Down all except five. In appendix IX is a summary of what was done in the areas of each militia unit.[55]

That the county authorities did not, directly they were free not to ballot, at once adopt the other method seems to follow from the re-emergence of the insurance offices ; this would not have happened unless the ballot had actually menaced. Insurance (against being drawn for the militia) seems to have been in abeyance since the year 1793. Though it was at the moment causing abuses recognized as serious in England,[56] in Ireland it was far from being discountenanced. 'We are pleased ' says *Faulkner's Journal* 'to see several insurance offices being opened, where for a very trifling premium it is engaged to find substitutes for those who may be drawn for the militia. These premiums are so very low as to obviate every even the smallest hardship of the ballot ; and the offices should therefore be encouraged as tending much to promote the good of the service '.[57] There were one or two of these in Dublin where the premium was 16/3. Insurance was active in the north. A firm at Lisburn[58] offers to insure for 10/6 any man against the risk of being drawn for either the Antrim or the Down. For the former the governors had (7 September), taken the decision to have a ballot. Insurance offices at once opened; one offered 'at the reduced price of 7/7' insurance until the number of men required by law should be completed, and engaged to find for this figure proper substitutes for those who might be drawn. Another man of the name of Kirk (who was an auctioneer and seems to have doubled the business of insuring with the duties of sub-division clerk) first of all asked a premium of 10/6 and professed himself ready, if no drawing should take place, to return the money, retaining only one tenpenny piece for his trouble and stamps'. About a week later his offer is to insure (for presumably the same sum of money) 'against the risque of the ballot not only for the present occasion but all future drawings for the space of four years; the period of service [sic]; or until the militia laws now in force shall be altered'. Before Kirk is next heard of the sovereign of Belfast had given notice of a vestry for the parish of Belfast to applot a sum sufficient to raise the quota prescribed; he makes this public 'to prevent any person from insuring against a ballot which in all probability will not now take place'. Kirk is scornful in his next advertisement of the 7/7 premium, as also of another offer which was apparently to protect men, for a premium of 11/4½ from the service for 'half a lifetime'. Of the offer that men liable to be drawn would receive protection through the parish fund he was equally contemptuous. These offers, he seems to have claimed, gave only limited protection and left the insuree liable to be assessed, or alternatively to have to insure himself, at least eight times within four years. 'So eligible [this was his new offer] are Kirk's new terms and so convinced is he of the risque he subjects himself to thereby (from his loss by a similar speculation in 1803*), that he will insure any man against the first ballot for the small sum of five tenpenny pieces'. An office was also opened at Londonderry which insured against service in the regiment of that county for the sum of 7/7 'in the present ballot or until the quota shall be completed for the county'. There is also official evidence that in county Monaghan there was widespread resort to the insurers: this note occurs; 'men raised by an insurance company and no assessment of any kind on the parish'.

In some parishes the amount obtained by the cess was supplemented by public subscription among the well-to-do and those not themselves liable to be drawn. This occurred, for instance, in county Louth, in the parish of Carlingford.[59] In these cases the burden of providing the men came out like this: first incidence of burden on fund subscribed; then, if that was deficient, a parochial cess was invoked to provide the sum deficient; if these

*This was probably in connection with ballot for the Additional Force.

methods (though the funds got together were *in amount* adequate) in fact failed to procure the quota—money will not do everything—then the compulsion of the ballot had to be invoked and the funds would be used either to give a douceur to men actually drawn or to buy substitutes, possibly from an insuring concern. Thus we have the following: 'a ballot took place generally throughout the county, the parishes not having been able to procure substitutes or volunteers within the prescribed period from the money, assessed by vestries, declared as the average bounty to be paid'. In some cases the cess seems to have been cancelled and the money returned or placed to the rate account of the parish.

The cess was in some cases baronial[60] but usually parochial. In the parish of Taney co. Dublin the assessment was at the rate of 7d. per acre.[61] The parish of Donaghmore co. Down (7 October 1807) passed the following resolutions: that 6½d. per acre be levied of the landholders in the parish; that 1s. 8d. per head be levied off all cottars in the parish likely to be balloted for; that 2s. 6d. per head be levied off all male servants and artificers liable to be balloted for.[62] Several of the parishes of Dublin[63] seem to have decided to proceed 'by assessing themselves with a certain sum of money to raise substitutes' and the parish of St. Andrew's decided on 'a parochial tax of 6d. [to be added] to the 1/- minister's money paid by each housekeeper'.[64] Of course there were difficulties; there is mention of the possibility of distraint on goods to get in the money, in some instances. Another grievance ventilated at Westminster was that absentee landlords had managed to get exemption from payment and also that taxing the tenant rather than the landlord was improper. Wellesley made the general answer to these as well as to other points of complaint that 'the mode pursued had met with the general approbation, as no representations had been made to him to the contrary'. It seems established that everything passed off without anything more than normal dissatisfaction and without any particular sense of hardship arising.

It may be useful to give a more detailed sketch of the course of the proceedings in a particular county. There is information available in regard to county Antrim; and what happened there is probably typical, or at all events illustrative, of what happened in other counties. The full details are given in appendix X. From these it might be concluded that not much, if any, effort was made to get men to volunteer and so to avoid the use of the ballot. But this was not so. This county like others was slow in getting started. By January for 30 regiments out of the 38 only 2,161[65], of the aggregate of 9,905, had been reported as raised. In some cases the preliminary steps were delayed; in others carrying into effect of agreed action tarried. The act had fixed a period—six months from the date of passing—for the quotas to be obtained; and, after that, there was a fine of £30 per man deficient. As this time (13 February 1808) drew near reminders of the penalties being incurred became fairly frequent and the parochial authorities, ministers as well as churchwardens, were not unnaturally nervous. Advertisements for recruits appear. This was especially the case in co. Antrim. One of these is on 'see the empire lines'; it is addressed to 'those high-spirited young men of character and reputation who wish to travel through their native country and have all their expenses paid'; to married men 'a certain maintenance' for wife and family in their absence is promised. It is hoped that 'all such dashing young fellows will prefer the militia of their own county to that of any other'. They are promised they shall receive their bounty in gold. In view of the troubles referred to earlier in this chapter about promises made on attestation, the following is to be specially noted: 'four years is the short period recruits will have to remain with the regiment, when they can once more return to their families'.[66] With similar misdirection, a Dublin advertisement asks for 500 men 'for only five years service' and adds (this of course is harmless) 'not to leave old Ireland'.[67] The churchwardens of Carrickfergus are also found[68] advertising for their parochial quota and offering a handsome bounty. We may judge of the part the clergy had to take in these troublesome matters from the following address of thanks passed at an Easter vestry:

> We should think ourselves deficient in our duty if we did not express our gratitude for the disinterested and generous exertions you made in reconciling the various interests of so great a number of people, which, however small, are not therefore contended for with less violence, and at your own risk securing the parish from the penalty they must have incurred by delaying to carry into effect the militia act. Your providing the recruits and sending them to the regiment while the different parties were contending about the means of raising them has our most grateful thanks.[69]

The following figures will show the aggregate numbers obtained at different dates:—16 February 1808 (six months from the passing of the act) 5504; 15th March—6736; 12 April—7667; 26 April—8770; 31 May—8974; and, by December, to which time the augmentation was kept going, the aggregate was 9,169, or a deficiency of 736.[70] Between January and early February an increase of approximately 3000 took place. In December pressure had been applied by Dublin castle; it was notified that, if by 10 January 2/3rds of the quotas were not forthcoming, the ballot was to be put forward to 22 January but on that date the ballot was positively to take place. Throughout, regimental recruiting parties were in most of the counties and, for this occasion, the policy of keeping units away from their counties was modified, in the interests of the levy. Officers who were also deputy governors were, with other influential people, got into their counties. There is the hint of possible disturbance of public order in the provision for the yeomanry to be on permanent duty at the time at which the ballot would take place.[71] But no need for this seems to have arisen. By the end of March, as the number reached was still only about 7,250, Wellesley sugge ted issue of a circular to governors informing them that judges of assize would have their attention called to the fining clauses in the act[72] but whether this was done is not on record.

In the official returns[73] the aggregates obtained by this levy are described as obtained ' since the commencement of the ballot ' or as ' added by the ballot '. These figures are of course no index to the number of balloted men (principles or substitutes) in the 38 militia units. For the balloting period May 1809—December 1810 (dealt with in the next chapter) statistics exist[74] of the recruits obtained *a*) as principles (*b*) as substitutes (*c*) as volunteers or beat of drum men. These show substantially more than 1/9th of the whole number of men then obtained as being principals or (mainly) substitutes. The proportion (not available) for the ballot period 1807-8 was probably less. But the actual numbers of the directly ballot-derived recruits for this latter period, if available, would be no measure of the real operative effect of the ballot. At the end of chapter XIII a militia officer was quoted as, in effect, referring to the threat of the ballot and, when Wellesley said in the debate on 19 February 1808, that it ' would have been impossible to have raised the number of men required.... without having recourse to the ballot ', he was probably referring to the indirect, rather than to the direct, compulsion it exerted. That the prescribed pre-ballot procedure up to and including the hearing at sub-divisional meetings of objections was in several counties gone through is clear. But, under the various stimuli applied, the prevalent inertia seems, at a very late moment, to have been made to yield. What, after it was all over, the ballot period of 1807-1808 established was the technique of the ' ballot threat ' and this was to be further developed in the ballot period 1809-10, as will be seen in the next chapter.

Through different forms and in different ways there had been a great drive for men in which the burden of supply—this time in fact as well as in theory—had been upon the counties rather than, through direct recruiting with money derived from county funds, upon the colonels. The duty of providing the men had never in theory been incident on the latter and, for a big augmentation such as that of 1807-8, their effort could not have sufficed. But it was at this time definitely realised that, when the colonels were not responsible, there was much wastage between the recruiting points and the units; the colonels, when they had not to provide the men were inclined to say: 'what does it matter? the county can provide another man'.[75]

XV

The Years 1808—1811

THE militia was now, to the extent of about a third, a new force. By the spring of the year 1808 a number approaching 9,000 had been added and about 8,400 had left. Dublin castle felt that the large addition and the very considerable outflux made it desirable, if not necessary, to assemble the troops ' with a view particularly to the discipline of the young militia soldiers and to the state of the temper of the militia and the general discipline and efficiency of the whole army '.[1] The militia was still, as always, widely scattered and the units themselves, no less than formerly, were dispersed. The Kilmainham papers[2] in March have reference to the prevalence of ophthalmia in several regiments in Ireland ; to the ' strong grounds for suspecting that in many instances the disease has been designedly brought on and the cure of it resisted '; and to punishment for ' those who shall be detected in applying irritating substances to the eyes, in order to produce the disease '. Soldiers of the 28th foot who had been accused of producing ophthalmia by anointing their eyes with ' a pernicious composition ' were apparently sent to the East Indies, by way of punishment.[3] One motive assigned for this self-mutilation was desire to get a high rate of pension. This would not apply to the militia. A newspaper however notes, in June, that ' the ophthalmia has made its appearance in one of our finest and best disciplined regiments of militia, the south Corks '. This is recorded without any suggestion of dishonourable practice.[4] In the previous December a transport had arrived[5] apparently at Cork, the troops on which were suffering from ophthalmia—in a natural way. So far only as ophthalmia was induced is it some evidence of war weariness and of desire to get out of military service.

There had last been camps in the year 1805. This year again the main camp was at the Curragh where the Donegal, Kerry, Londonderry, Cork (south), Louth, Tipperary and Leitrim were assembled[6] ; and there were six infantry regiments of the line, with a proportion of other arms. On this occasion there was no spectacular arrival-episode but there was, beside hard work and early turning in for the night, much gaiety : camp balls every Thursday at the Stadhouse, and, at the same rendezvous, ' a public ordinary every Sunday at three o'clock for ladies and gentlemen'; this was calculated to 'relieve the tedium which want of the society of [their fair countrywomen] must give, even in a camp'. A great event was the visit to the camp of sir Arthur Wellesley. He was now again being transferred from the ministerial to the military scene and was on his way to join the armament which was to sail from Cork for 'the bloody battlefields of Spain'. He 'passed the line' on the 4 July and, so great was the enthusiasm that 'had it been permitted....not a doubt is entertained that the whole army on the Curragh would have willingly accompanied the gallant general to lend their assistance to the heroic patriots of Spain'.[7] At least three Irish militia units (Galway, Londonderry and Cork north)[8] volunteered their services, as also did some English and Scotch militia units and some Irish yeomanry. These offers brought polite acknowledgment from Dublin but no more. Ireland had however the privilege, in 1809[9], of supplying large quantities of horse shoes and of oats for the army in Spain, as well as 'their beloved and gallant countryman', sir Arthur Wellesley. The other two encampments were at Fermoy and in the Phoenix Park. The former did not attract any particular attention; it was attended by about 8,000 troops in which were included the Kilkenny and the Wexford. But the newspapers are full of the Phoenix park camp. It was situated 'a small distance from Castleknock gate'. The throng which moved along the road to it on a fine Sunday in June is said to have been immense.[10] The militia regiments attending it were the Wicklow and the Down (south).

The militia by the ballot operations of 1807-8 had not much more than made up the great outflux to the line and the ordinary 'annual tribute' of 1808 was yet to come. This would send down the strength—which had never got up to the establishment. A sidelight on what was thought in the ranks about volunteering is afforded by the letters of two privates.[11] Patrick Lynch of the Meath writes to his father and mother in July: 'as for the volunteering, you need not to trouble yourself to send any word more about it, for it is a thing that will not take place in our regiment this year, and if it was tomorrow I would never think of going'. Another private, in the Westmeath, had permission to go to the county to find a substitute—this was a common way of getting out—and he went to Dublin and 'paid a guinea to Counsellor Ball for advice and thought to get out on another plan but he informed me that I could not. My mind is very unhappy while I remain here but I trust it will not be long'. Some evidence of the feeling in the ranks during the latter part of 1808 is afforded also by the desertion figures. In the months of May and June these were particularly heavy and between April and December the militia lost from this cause 672 men.[12]

But Patrick Lynch was wrong and his antipathy to volunteering was not apparently general amongst the private militiamen. The new volunteering was proclaimed to begin as from 25 August and to last a period of three days. So successful[13] was it that in that month 2,736 men[14] were transferred to the line. An improved bounty (three extra guineas) was authorized for those accepting unlimited service but a reduced bounty for 7 years service. It was expressly laid down that the men 'were to have free and unbiassed choice and not be pressed (except by inducement of higher bounty) to unlimited service'.[15] If three days did not suffice to get the men required then there were to be additional three day periods in each of the next five months. Then there might be a ten days period in March; the provision for an original ten days period, in the act of 1806, had been found by the colonels altogether too upsetting to discipline. For this year's volunteering recruiting parties were, as already stated, kept at arm's length; the business was to be conducted 'exclusively by the commanding officers of the different militia regiments'.

By March 1809 when the 1808 volunteering was closed the militia had given 3,378 (deficiency of 117) men to the line[16] and, as explained, there had been heavy desertions. Nevertheless the rank and file strength was on 1 February 1809 at a higher figure (24,768) than it had been during the whole of the preceding two years. The course of recruiting is not clear. To meet the continuing drain the colonels must of course keep on labouring at procuring men. But, although the number of the recruits joined in each month is available, it is impossible to see how, in face of the large transfers to the line, the strength was maintained as it was. It will be here convenient to note that the volunteering of 1809 began almost as soon as that of the year 1808 was finished. The act had been passed on 13 March and the circular was issued 24 April; and the transfers were to begin from 1 May, over a thirty days period in which the colonels were 'to ascertain and deliver over the number of men who may be willing to enter into the line previous to any, volunteering, as heretofore practised, is permitted to take place' (sic). Parties of the line were not to interfere 'except with your [i.e. the colonel's] full sanction and on your special application'.[17] The number to be given was such as would leave serving 3/5ths of the establishment in each regiment, whether augmented or not. The basis of the calculation was to be the establishment as it was on 13 March and the number is stated as 6,708.[18] In the end—the volunteering was several times extended—no more than 4,879[19] of whom 4,644 were for unlimited service, were obtained.

By the end of May 1809 about 2,300 had transferred and during June to September the strength of the force was below 21,000.

Castlereagh evolved an army programme—for both countries. It proposed to 'complete the militia'. Twelve months were allowed for this. In England it was purposed, if possible, to dispense with the ballot[20] and to throw the expense of raising the men not upon the counties but upon the public. Castlereagh was sanguine that the ballot there would be unnecessary. The Irish Act (49 Geo. iii. chap. 56. 3 June 1809) contemplated that the men should be got by enrolling and receiving volunteers under 44 Geo. iii. chap. 33, but the lord lieutenant might require them to be raised by ballot if this should appear necessary 'for the more speedily completing of the said militia'. The quota was to be 2/5th of the respective establishments of the several units; this meant an aggregate of 10,536. A general warrant under the act, which was to operate over 12 months from 3 June, brought it into force as from 20 July 1809. The circular then issued did not display much confidence in volunteers being forthcoming; the governors were informed straightaway that if 'the greater proportion of the quota' was not produced by 24 October, then the ballot would 'most probably be resorted to'.[21] The number of volunteers obtained by 10 November was only 2,232. Ten days earlier (31 October), when the intake would have been somewhat less, the counties 'which had not yet produced 1/3rd of the prescribed complement and in which the ballot had not been resorted to' were told that, unless 1/3rd were raised by 1 December, 'measures will then be adopted for proclaiming the county and for bringing the ballot into full operation'[22]; and 'the additional expense which must result to the county for fines [£30 per man deficient] from a failure in the completion of the levy' is also pointed out. The lord lieutenant was not satisfied; the number raised he found inconsiderable and he refers to the aid the governors might derive from 'the exertions and the co-operation of the detachments from the county regiments which are at present specially employed in the enrolment of volunteers' in the counties.

Before the 'completion' efforts were over there had been proclaimed ballots for all the units except Cork (north and south), Fermanagh, King's county, Leitrim, Longford, Meath and Sligo. The first counties proclaimed (26 August 1809) were Down and Mayo. As regards the latter it would be interesting if lord Sligo's views were available; previously he had expressed himself very adverse to any ballot. Never, never, never. Both these counties had resigned themselves to having to ballot before the 31 October circular. In the case of co. Down its authorities, as we know, had always been for ballot, on principle—though lord Downshire was dead some time. But nevertheless by 15 February co. Down (north) had not recruited any out of its quota of 240. We know a little of what was going on in co. Down because one of the few ballot books which can now be in existence is of a co. Down parish. For a transcript of this[23] thanks are due to the late Mr. Tenison Groves. The parish, that of Inch in the barony of Lecale, is in the south of the county. Drawings took place on 27 November and 11 December 1809; on 1st, 11th and 27 January 1810; and on 24 February and 27 June of the same year. There are some 380 names in the list which are divided under place groups and headed 'John Gray's return' 'Thomas Wilson's return' etc. etc. The whole list is signed at the end by the clerk for the subdivisional meeting of the barony and purports to be of all resident males of 16 to 45 years. Almost all seem to be persons of industrial and not of professional standing; there are e.g. servants, labourers, carpenters, weavers, yeomen, farmers, publicans, hatter, tailor, blacksmith, schoolmaster, flaxdresser, tinker and broguemaker; and there are two yeomanry officers, the captain and the lieutenant of the Inch Yeomen. Against the names are various notes showing the fate of the particular individual: 'drawn' (with date); 'indentures produced and sworn to—master sworn'; 'drawn and undersize'; 'drawn—certificate from . . . . discharged'; 'drawn—unfit' 'drawn—deserted'; 'drawn in 1808—substitute'. These few notes will give some firsthand idea of the ballot at work in a parish.

A ballot was proclaimed for co. Antrim on 9 January 1810 and some interesting figures for this county are available. The general meeting had to take place within 10 days after the lord lieutenant's proclamation. The lists were completed in February. In the whole county there were on the lists, after the appeals were heard and when those who made legal objections had been heard or been struck out, 24,425 names; the number required was 228. In the half barony of upper Belfast the number, after exemptions, was 4,132 and 39 were required; for the town of Belfast the number, after exemptions, was 2,772 and the number required was 25.[24] In co. Waterford, 3,199 persons were liable to serve out of a total population of 40,000.

On these Antrim figures it is no surprise that, on this occasion again, the insurance offices should be found at work. An announcement appeared immediately after the proclamation saying that offices would be opened 'in the different towns in this county' and that agents would 'deliver certificates of exemption and of obligation to provide substitutes for such men as may be drawn to serve'. The announcement went on: 'as the number to be raised is considerable and the expense of procuring substitutes well known to be unusually high, the advantages now offered to the public of insurance on so low terms as 13/4 must be obvious, the expense of exemption bearing no proportion to the risk of standing the ballot'.[25] The following is a copy of the formula of insurance issued to persons insuring : ‘ in consideration of the sum of 13/4 we hereby engage to keep Mr.....of....exempt from serving in the county of Antrim militia (by providing a substitute) should he be drawn at the ensuing ballot, to take place pursuant to the proclamation of the lord lieutenant and council of Ireland bearing date the 9 January 1810 ’.[26] Presumably the authorities accepted these certificates as transferring the liability for a man being forthcoming from the individual actually drawn to the insurance agent. Raising by volunteers and by balloting were permitted by the act to go on simultaneously. The parishioners of Dundonald in north Down advertise for three substitutes to serve in the north Down militia for *four years* [the limitation to an exact four years is again to be noted] ; twenty pounds were to be given to each of the three men by the parish and eight guineas by the government ;[27] this latter was the sum allowed by the act.

The financial strain of providing the ‘ completion ’ of the militia had increased since the ballot period 1807-8. Under the 1807 act (47 Geo. iii. session 2. chap. 56) a bounty not exceeding four guineas was allowed ; now it had had to be doubled. The period after which fines became leviable was increased from 6 months to 12. Another important provision left the counties ‘ free from any charge whatsoever ’ in respect of men enrolled, within the 12 months, either as volunteers or as balloted men ; whereas under the 1807 act, for the men raised by volunteering (and a *fortiori* for those raised by ballot), the counties had to pay, i.e. reimburse the cash advanced by the Treasury. The 1807 act directed general meetings to fix the average price to be paid for a substitute (or volunteer) and this price varied in amount from county to county ; and what one county paid had a very marked effect on what the next door county had to pay. The 1809 act on the other hand reproduced the old stipulation that the officially recognized amount should not be exceeded. There is record of a major being officially reprimanded for exceeding (though the extra sum came from his own pocket) ; but large additional amounts were given.

The financial liability of the counties in reference to providing volunteers to fill vacancies caused (*a*) by original augmentation and (*b*) by death, desertion, or lawful discharge in augmentation units needs to be stated, as over the period 1804-13 it appears—and this is not surprising—to have caused friction. The 1804 act (44 Geo. iii. chap. 33) made no distinction ; the county did not pay, either directly or indirectly, in either case. But in 1807, though for vacancies arising from augmentation the county still stood free from expense, nevertheless for *any* vacancies arising by death, desertion, or lawful discharge and filled by volunteers the county, if its unit was augmented, had to pay a sum which was

7/10ths of the money advanced by the Treasury. Under this arrangement no question could arise as to whether the man who had died etc. had been an augmentation or original establishment man—a point probably as a rule incapable of determination; see Chap. XVI—and there was also some safeguard for the public against improper charges. This 7/10th arrangement passed in 1809 into the co-ordination act and was then completed by the provision that the casual vacancies in augmented units *should* be filled by volunteers and not by balloting. In 1813 (53 Geo. iii. chap. 48) the position was logically set out, for the removal of doubts; the exposition may be completed by stating that in non-augmented units the county paid the whole bounty in respect of the filling of *all* vacancies.

The ballot proclamations 1809-10 were spread over the period from 26 August (Down and Mayo) to 8 May on which date both the city and county of Limerick were proclaimed; in 1807 the lord lieutenant had himself favoured, but had been unable to carry, the individual treatment of the counties. Mostly the proclamations, which usually state that they are made on the representations of the governors that ballot was necessary, were of one or two at a time, but on 22 December no less than fifteen were dealt with in one proclamation. In the number was Galway. Lord Clancarty, an indefatigable correspondent of Dublin castle, on this occasion again furnished his views. On receipt of the original circular he complained of the ‘ apathy of the gentry of this county in all public concerns ’; he goes on : ‘ I have no idea of being able to obtain a single man from the ballot except in the subdivision where I may be myself personally attending ’. He thinks however that they will get the men, though not by 24 October.[28] The men raised between 3 June, the date of the act, and the date (20 July 1809) of the general warrant were, it seems, not to be credited to the counties towards their quotas under the act; this, Lord Clancarty argues, increases the liability to the fine of £30 per man deficient and, giving rein to fancy, he suggests that ‘ by delaying issue of warrant till the day previous to the termination of the time prescribed, the county could be rendered incapable of complying and for Galway the fines could rise to £12,000 ’; he had sent in his certificate of deficiencies to the county treasurer.[29]

There is a newspaper account of the ballot in Galway city; it was to raise 19 men, the quota of the parish of St. Nicholas. It was held at the Thorsel; ‘ the usual order and decorum was observed, as on similar occasions, in a town remarkable for its strict obedience to the laws ’. Previously to the ballot taking place, the deputy governors presiding ‘ informed such industrious young men as might be drawn and who might not have the means of procuring a substitute and could produce good characters that a subscription would be entered into for the purpose of procuring men to fill their places '.[30] This was agreed to by a crowded court. Here we see how things were made to go smoothly. The only trace of disorder at these ballots of 1809-10 which has come to light is an attack on a constable in co. Kerry who was active in his duty. But this is a minor matter and it is possible to say with confidence that, so far as there was balloting in Ireland in 1810, it excited no opposition. This was not the case in Scotland where there were troubles and ' general hatred of the militia '.[31]

The total number to be raised was originally taken as being 10,536 but the crown lawyers subsequently decided that the quotas for Antrim, Carlow, Clare and Cork city ' should be calculated on the augmented establishments of those regiments '.[32] The aggregate quota was accordingly raised to 10,872. The 2/5th quota meant in terms of numbers the collection of 400 men for the bigger units like Galway, Londonderry, Tipperary, Tyrone and Wexford. Of these Londonderry produced in the end 173 only ; Wexford, Tyrone and Galway produced respectively 265 ; 237 ; and 345. Tipperary on the other hand was one of the few counties which exceeded its quota. Figures available in regard to this augmenting operation enable us to see the course of the levy in each county. Tipperary was one of the counties proclaimed in the group of fifteen on 22 December and gradually went ahead until it reached 428, but Tyrone, proclaimed on the same day, continued with no more than 28 recruits right into February and, as shewn, did not at the end come within measurable distance of its quota figure. The quota for an eight company unit was 320 (i.e. 2/5th of 800 or of 8 companies of 100 men each) ; this number was slightly exceeded by Cork south and by 33 by Meath. The only other counties to exceed their quotas were Clare and Mayo north ; two others, Fermanagh and Longford (non-augmented counties) proffered their exact quota of 168.[33]

No final figure for the total raised has come to light but on 17 May—which was some twenty days only before the closing day, 3 June—the aggregate reached is given as 8,288. It is not quite clear why, with the support the ballot was calculated to give, the desired total was not more nearly approached, unless it was that the authorities in many cases did not, when it came to the point, see their way to face the possible results of actual resort to the ballot. In regard to this ballot period the house of commons does not appear to have shewn any interest ; no information was called for and little or none is available. The men demanded by the authorities were undoubtedly there ; it seems almost as undoubted a fact that they were becoming, for whatever reasons, more difficult to get. The stimulus of the ballot proclamations, which had been applied on the advice of the governors, had been without demonstrable effect in most of the counties. Figures are available which shew 94 principals and 1044 substitutes as obtained by the Irish militia in December of 1809 and during 1810. Substitutes were derived from the following counties :—Antrim—214 ; Down (north)—199 ; Down (south)—53 ; Louth—129 ; Roscommon—219 ; Westmeath—94 ; and Wexford—206. Carlow, Galway and Kerry between them account for another 110. Of the principals almost all—not very numerous—are from Carlow, Down, Galway and Louth. It is strange that Londonderry, which only produced 173 out of its quota of 400, did not by the ballot get more than five principals and five substitutes.[34]

This failure to get substantial contingents out of the operation of the militia laws seems to have been the result of general causes amongst which no doubt was a growing lukewarmness on the part of the local gentry from which stratum the deputy governors were taken. There is a complaint to Dublin castle in July 1810 of the difficulty of recruiting the militia generally and a representation that ‘ the deputy governors are entitled to any assistance that can fairly be given them ; in this county we labour under peculiar difficulties and have no assistance from the Westmeath regiment ’.[35] The writer mentions the ‘ unnecessary expense and trouble ’ put upon the balloted men and the complacent attitude of the regiments about desertion ; ‘ steps should be taken to show the county that they have justice ’ i.e. over this matter of desertion . The officer who had raised the original Donegal regiment, represents his difficulty in operating the ballot in his neighbourhood ‘ from the absence of some deputy governors and the indisposition of others ’;[36] he had to attend himself at several different places. Absenteeism had in fact, since the opening years of the century, rendered the machinery of local government almost unworkable.[37] Producing ‘ disposable force ’ for foreign service was not an object inherently likely to call out local effort. The centre of political interest and of the pleasurable play of intrigue had departed to London. As regards invasion, Ireland was now in a cold stage, as the measures taken at the end of 1809 show. The lord lieutenant paid off the gunboat establishment which had been adopted ‘ when invasion was expected ’; he says that ‘ in the present reduced state of the enemy’s navy, no such apprehension [i.e. of invasion] can reasonably be entertained ’. The Sea Fencibles were at this time mustered (and paid) in Ireland four days only each month ; in England only one day : practice in this matter was assimilated. The yeomanry too had their days of exercise, for the winter to begin with, reduced from four to two.[38]

A militia commanding officer, who may be the same officer[39] who in 1807 proposed to Wellesley a scheme for making up from the militia nine battalions for service in Europe, in January 1809 airs interesting views about the force. He professes his object to be to render it more useful. Volunteering, or 'reduction' as he calls it, has been resisted 'not so much from military pride as from political motives'; those who have done this have, from the balloting act, found themselves in possession of regiments 'considerable above the establishment originally attached to them'; on the other hand those who have given their quotas are scarcely, if at all, above their proper number. Reduction by voluntary transfers in all the units which are above the fundamental establishment [i.e. that with which they started after the re-embodiment] would produce equality among the counties; would counter the efforts of political opponents and, lastly, provide 'a sufficient force to replenish ten regiments'; if this is not done he cannot see on what grounds 'extension of the militia service throughout the United Kingdom or rather their commutation into fencibles is, or ought to be, resisted'. The only reason, he suggests, could be that the colonels 'being men of influence, dislike emigration from their domestic comforts'; but as 'they now almost assimilate themselves to general officers and obtain with facility a dispensing power of being present [with their regiments], to them it can be of no consequence whether their regiment is at Athlone or at Canterbury'. Opulent individuals might possibly be driven out from a service 'in which they can no longer find tranquillity and repose'. Such men would be better out of the force; 'a more active service would rather improve than mortify officers' and 'men of property would be more induced to remain than they are with the prospect of doing nothing'. He thinks that 'some stimulus is absolutely requisite to vivify the force. At times it breaks forth from the languor which marks its existence; but even then, though beautiful in appearance and splendid in decoration, it soon falls again into that listlessness which resembles sleep and that murmuring idleness which generates decay'.[40]

This might almost be a picture of any force condemned by circumstances to a merely garrison life. As a picture of the Irish militia at about the period of the two ballots its value, as it is presented anonymously, cannot be rightly estimated. But its correctness seems inherently probable. The force was now one which was old in arms. It was, among other things, weighed down, as was its English counterpart, with an immense mass of legislative provisions which seriously taxed those locally responsible for its administration.[41] As far back as the year 1796 Pelham had obtained a first reading for a bill 'for amending and consolidating into one the different acts relating to the militia'.[42]

But it went no further. How much more necessary was consolidation as the years went on and elaborate acts followed one another, session after session ! In 1802 the English militia law was consolidated (42 Geo. iii. chap. 90) and all the legislation back to the act of 1796 (26 Geo. iii. chap. 107), which was the act on which the main Irish act of 1793 had been modelled, was repealed. This was a very long act, as was the *separate* act for Scotland passed on the same day (26 June). In that same month the house of commons at Westminster, warming to its new Irish work, set up a committee to consider the Irish parliament's militia acts made in the 33rd, 34th, 35th, 36th, 37th, 38th, 39th and 40th years of the king ; the journals record that they were read ! From this committee came a bill (probably drafted in Dublin) which was presented in December and, after consideration in committee, printed as amended ; it is consequently available for consultation.[43] It is very long and was to a large extent, it would seem, drafted from the English act (i.e. chap. 90). Indeed the preamble specifically recites that ' it is expedient that the militia of Ireland should be placed on the same establishment and, so far as local circumstances will permit, be made subject to the same laws and regulations as the militia of England '. The preamble also makes the point that ' it would greatly tend to the better execution of [the militia laws] if the whole of the provisions were comprised in one act of parliament '. That this ' bill for establishing a general system for the militia [i.e. the Irish militia]....similar to that adopted for the English militia by Mr. Yorke's act ' was actually referred to ' the gentlemen of Ireland....so that they might have full opportunity of considering it in all its parts before it was proceeded on ', as was clearly intended by the lord lieutenant, does not appear. It became urgent that the ' speedy enrolment ' bill (see page 00) should have priority of attention and, when this had been passed (17 December 1802), the practical task of raising the new militia absorbed the colonels. The consideration of the bill was deferred twice and it was afterwards ' not proceeded in '. Assimilation of the Irish to the English militia law probably encountered opposition. That was to go too fast. Besides in the process the two forces might stand to lose some of their separate individualities.

Consolidation of the different acts remained in abeyance until in 1805 Castlereagh (probably) had the matter taken up afresh. But there is no mention of any parliamentary action in that year nor indeed until sir Arthur Wellesley's chief secretaryship. In August 1808 consultations of the colonels of militia, ' whose sentiments the lord lieutenant desired to collect ', took place. They each received a printed ' abstract ' which ran to 152 clauses and 60 folio pages of type. Their notice was directed to ' the necessity of simplifying the existing acts....and of rendering their provisions better adapted to the actual situation and circumstances of this country .,[44] It would have been interesting to have the ' sentiments ' on the draft bill of even one of the colonels but any reports sent in no longer exist nor any summary of them. This draft was probably, with some changes possibly, the bill subsequently introduced ; it was probably (perhaps almost certainly) the same as, or largely based upon, the draft bill referred to in the Castlereagh despatches ; but this latter draft is unfortunately no longer in existence. The bill (and act) of 1809 and the bill as referred to by Castlereagh—he gives an outline—seem to have represented a fresh tackling of the co-ordination problem and did not simply follow the draft of 1802.

The parliamentary proceedings on this massive piece of legislation went on intermittently from 6 February until 19 June (royal assent). It was already in committee in February and, after amendment, was ordered for further consideration ; this was several times deferred ; when it came up in May for actual consideration it was recommitted and reported with further amendments. Then it appeared that still further amendments were considered necessary and it was again recommitted. After again many deferments of consideration, further amendments were made and it was passed. All this was in the commons, but in the lords, where considerable interest was taken in militia matters, it went through easily. That the bill was so frequently put back seems to show that members, or a section of them, were either reluctant to let it go or too lazy to face the laborious task of examining it. It was printed twice before the final engrossment. The hesitation may have been due to disinclination to endorse what was possibly put forward as being in the main a parliamentary draftsman's matter and to suspicions that, under this pretext, some new departures were being smuggled through. No doubt in the end assurances were officially given that it did not alter things very much. To many the militia law was the keystone of the constitution.

Of all this deliberation nothing (beyond the record of one point raised) remains, except a somewhat perfunctory account of Wellesley's second reading speech.[45] This probably survives because it was Wellesley who made it. Codification is always a dull subject and the Irish newspapers took no interest and procured themselves no reports. Wellesley specified as his object ' to reduce all [the several acts] into one and to amend and class under proper heads the different provisions they contain '. He said that ' the provisions in the act of 1793 which were found at the time efficient for the raising and training the then first levied militia in that country were afterwards found inadequate when the militia had been once embodied ' and that ' in the acts since passed there have been incorporated many provisions which are, in various instances, inconsistent and contradictory '. He mentioned only four specific points :—(i) clearing up the question of the oath ; (ii) securing power for the governors to *compel* the alteration of the ballot lists whenever the lord lieutenant should call for this ; (iii) enabling him to substitute the mode of parish assessment for the ballot ; (iv) authorizing the governors to raise men for the militia by volunteering. The Castlereagh memorandum had made the point made by Wellesley about the non-permanent outlook of the act of 1793 and said that ' the clauses of [his draft] are expressed in general terms with a view to answer for all future times and occasions '.[46]

The memorandum gives an outline of the arrangement of the bill then contemplated and specifies seventeen points as ' the principal, if not the only, changes which have been made, exclusive of arrangement, consolidation and verbal emendation '. The majority of these are of relatively minor importance ; three are points subsequently brought forward by Wellesley (i to iii). Enactments for authorizing parochial assessments and for raising men by volunteering were not new but were apparently regarded as not yet part of the general law. Castlereagh does not think it necessary to mention volunteering which had, in fact, been going on from the very earliest days. Both Wellesley and Castlereagh mention the question of the oath on which the latter's statement is : ' the clause in the militiaman's oath, respecting the obligation to Ireland, has been omitted, as also the ambiguity of expression as to the militia being called out within five years and, in the clause of the act limiting the militiaman's service to Ireland, an exception is put in for the case of their volunteering individually to go to England '. The oath, as it stands in the co-ordination act, binds balloted men, substitutes, and volunteers, only to service in ' the militia of Ireland ' and not to service in the militia ' in Ireland ', as oaths prescribed in previous acts had done. As pointed out (see chapter XIV) the alterations made in the oath did not, in fact, dispose of the difficulties.

There was not in this bill any mention, however generally worded, of bringing the Irish militia and the English under a uniform law, as there had been in the preamble of the 1802 draft. This was not practical either at that time or later. The nearest approach ever made to it—and not a near approach—was made in 1811 by the interchange act (see chapter XVI) and some subsequent legislation. To assess precisely in what respects the English and Irish militias differed in law and in their practice would be very laborious indeed and, until some one has made a detailed study of the former for the period of the Napoleonic wars, almost impossible. Wellesley incidentally noted one difference : many of the expenses which fell on the parishes in England (e.g. expense of raising recruits who volunteered into the army) were in Ireland defrayed by the Treasury. Fortescue suggests a difference: that whereas, according to the view he seems to favour, the ballot was always a source of trouble and disorder in Ireland, this was not so or not equally so in England or Scotland. But this view is hardly borne out by the facts. Reference has been made to the troubles of an acute character in Scotland in 1797 and to the troubles at certain times in England. The index to *County Lieutenancies* will illustrate this. The absence of any marked trouble in Ireland at any time since the original raising and the exaggeration of what took place then and on the augmentation in 1795 have also been noted. That there was in Ireland an indisposition, fairly general though by no means universal, to make use of the ballot is not in doubt. But this indisposition was not limited to Ireland. What was in effect a general and, as may be claimed, normal healthy reaction to interference with personal liberty can hardly be represented with accuracy, or indeed without imputation on Britain, as a manifestation peculiar to Ireland. When the Irish code of militia law was sorted out and re-enacted in the year 1809—then was the opportunity, had this been desired, to drop the ballot altogether from the statute book as regards Ireland, if Ireland was really so different in its attitude to it. But this was not considered nor even mooted. The ballot was re-enacted in the co-ordinating act.

At the end of the year 1810 Ireland was a good deal disturbed and there were many affrays, in dealing with which the militia were called upon to participate. Miscellaneous demands for military detachments continued. A new category of these was for meeting opposed tithe valuations.[47] This was discussed at Dublin castle in December. The chief secretary in January 1811 reports to the lord lieutenant an attempt to disarm the Wexford militia at Clogheen.[48] In April the colonels were confidentially consulted by the Castle about the reported circulation of two pamphlets deemed inflammatory: 'the Painter cut; a vision' and 'Supposed speech of Bonaparte'. But most of the colonels —some took no notice of the communication—could discover no trace of the pamphlets; one took the occasion to represent that 'danger may be apprehended from the detached state of the regiment and the length of time it has been in its present quarter'. There were also at this time allegations that in a northern county the militia were being tampered with and that hopes had been expressed that 'the schemes in contemplation might be accomplished before the expected interchange of the British and Irish militias'.[49] This was the coming event a shadow of which was apparently discernible even to those not possessing official information.

XVI

The Years 1811—16; interchangeability; the service of the Irish Militia in England; second disembodiment; reembodiment and final disembodiment.

In the year 1811 interchangeability at last became realized fact. As appears in chapter XIII Hardwicke had supported it strongly. Cornwallis, on the other hand, in spite of the close connection which many (Castlereagh included) saw between interchangeability and the Union, does not seem to have been interested. Wellesley favoured the policy but in July 1807 he writes that he had not been able 'to prevail upon ministers to adopt the plan of a reciprocal interchange of the militia of the two countries' though, he says, 'I went far towards it'.[1] About the same time the secretary of state, lord Hawkesbury, was discussing with the duke of York bringing over to England the next winter part of the militia.[2] But this was unilateral and interchangeability was bilateral. It had much unofficial support. The traveller Carr (1806) writes: 'I hardly know a measure which would be more gratifying to the Irish than [interchange of militia]; it formed a frequent subject of conversation with the officers of several Irish militia regiments who declared it as their opinion that the intercourse would have a strong tendency to attach the Irish to this [i.e. England] country and to civilize Ireland by a conformation of habits. I conversed with several intelligent private soldiers and found among them a strong desire of association with the English in this manner'.[3] Those who supported interchangeability wanted not only the benefits of the Irish militia going to England but also the corresponding benefit of the English militia coming to Ireland. On the theory that Ireland needed the services of a force the size of the Irish militia obviously they could not part with some thousands of troops without their being replaced. In 1813, when the second contingent was being arranged for, the lord lieutenant was simultaneously calling for reinforcements; but in 1811, when the first lot went to England, there does not seem to have been any qualm about letting them go.

If opinion in Ireland was as favourable as it always was to letting the Irish militia go to England, the question arises : why did nothing happen before the year 1811 ? This has been discussed in chapter 00. Did the opposition of the king and that of the English militia colonels continue to be an obstacle ? If so, how was this obstacle finally removed in 1811 ? What the catholic leaders in Ireland had been concerned about in the year 1804 was the absence of facilities in England for the catholic militiamen to pursue the catholic worship—or rather the possibility, as they feared, that attendance at protestant worship might be imposed. As has been seen, this point of view received powerful support in that year from liberal opinion in the house of commons. Occasionally there had been difficulties about alleged compulsion put upon the catholic militia in Ireland to attend the parade protestant service on the Sunday. But these had not been of the magnitude of a grievance. Why then should it be expected that the Irish militiaman should be any worse treated in this respect in England ? The answer is—and it has force —that what was on the whole avoided in Ireland, in a catholic environment, would not so certainly be avoided in England, in a protestant environment.

It might perhaps have been expected that the co-ordination bill of 1809 would have been made the occasion for obtaining guarantees on this matter. But that act does not envisage the Irish militia going, otherwise than individually, to England ; it went through, as pointed out in the last chapter, easily in the end ; this was, as already suggested, probably on some assurance that it contained no new principles. But on the interchange bill, which was before the house of commons during May and June 1811, the catholic question was raised on every possible stage. The ministerial assurance that the desired guarantee would be provided by an order of the military authorities, as in Ireland, was not accepted and the insertion of a special clause to provide a *statutory* guarantee was, in various forms, urged. A clause was offered stating that ‘ the Irish catholic militiaman when transferred to England should be entitled to the same civil, military and religious exemptions as were enjoyed by him in Ireland ’. But this was not acceptable ; it assumed that the Irish catholic in Ireland was in fact content under his restrictions. On the report stage a thoroughgoing clause was moved against the government but it was negatived without a division and the bill passed.

No doubt the reason for the firm stand made by ministers is to be found in the general attitude they held to catholic emancipation. They did not explain their attitude ; they simply stonewalled, reiterating that the statutory provision asked for was unnecessary. The whole of this parliamentary stage-battle may be regarded as a tactical incident in the general fight for catholic emancipation. On the other aspects of the bill there was less contention. Lord Palmerston thought it 'the most important that had been made since the Union, and could not but think the Union incomplete till it was adopted;' uniting all classes of both countries was, he thought, the most weighty argument for the bill. The minister introducing it, stressed the necessity for united efforts at home which could never, he said, be fully attained while 'our militias are confined to one country'. Portugal did not, he conceded, at the moment cause concern but how much better if it had been possible to send as reinforcements 'those valuable troops [i.e. the regulars] in Ireland'. He admitted however that the moral and political effects were infinitely greater than the military; 'new connections and friendships would be formed, not confined to one class or degree but extending generally through both nations'. He feared however 'the opposition of a certain class of gentlemen connected with the militia service'.[4] This was duly forthcoming and was strongly expressed on familiar lines; the bill 'went to affect the first principles of subordination'; it would put the officers at the mercy of the men, as the former would have to follow the decision of the latter; half might volunteer and half not—which would have the effect of producing two services; it might deprive the militia of the talents of the ablest of its officers, as 'it was a different thing to an English county gentleman to go over to Ireland and to an Irish county gentleman to come over here with his regiment'; and other similar (and largely English) arguments. Lord Holland, at the end of the house of lords debate (18 June), summed up the position fairly, saying that he 'was of opinion that the bill as it stood really went to consolidate the efforts of the empire and therefore, though it considerably trenched upon the old principles of the militia acts, yet the former advantages so much outweighed any inconveniences from the latter that the bill should have his support'.

The royal assent to the act was given on 1 July. The object of it is recited to be promotion of the better defence and security of the United Kingdom by extending the services of 'the present regular militia of Great Britain and the militia of Ireland to all parts of the United Kingdom'. For such service all persons commissioned, raised and enrolled, whether by ballot or otherwise, were, after 1 July, to be under liability. The force to be raised for extended service was to be called 'the militia of the United Kingdom'. The limit of service in Great Britain or Ireland was to be two years and no more than 1/4th part of the English militia were at any one time to be employed in Ireland nor than 1/3rd part of the Irish in Great Britain; but during invasion or rebellion the limits of duration of tour of service and of proportion expatriated were not to stand. Units that had served overseas (either way) were, for a period, not to be liable again, except in case of invasion or rebellion. The service oversea of the existing personnel was to be voluntary ; those who so volunteered (sergeants, corporals and drummers included) were to take a new oath to 'serve in any part of the United Kingdom of Great Britain or Ireland' during the period for which they had been enrolled to serve.

The bill had been first mentioned in parliament on 14 May. News of this seems soon to have gone round Ireland. Quick off the mark, Westmeath on parade 'in consequence of intimation of the bill for interchange of militia' volunteered 'to extend their services in such a manner as may be most consistent with the good of his majesty's service';[5] and there was an outbreak or wave of offers of service in England such as in earlier days. A list forwarded to London (25 May) by the lord lieutenant contains 23 units (929 sergeants, 415 drummers and 16,218 men). These offers obviously were not delayed, even in predominantly catholic units, until catholic worship facilities had been statutorily guaranteed and were made some time before the bill was finally passed into law. They must have preceded the important Aggregate meeting of the catholics of Ireland which was assembled in Dublin on 28 May to discuss the bill.[6] The speeches made at this meeting, though insistent on the need for a statutory guarantee, were not unbalanced ; one speaker made specifically the point that they were not bent upon 'annoying ministry', while another urged that, however strongly they felt about the probable results to catholics of the measure, they should not 'refuse their aid to ensure the salvation of an empire ; they were embarked upon a common cause'. Daniel O'Connell spoke at length, in opposition, urging amongst other points that the bill was a conspiracy 'to take away our native army from us' and that it was 'not a transfer but an annihilation' of the Irish militia.

By the end of July no less than 34 (19,146 privates) units out of the whole 38 had volunteered.[7] The alarmist prediction made on 27 May by Wellesley Pole that 'if the bill should be passed without [unequivocal provision for attendance at catholic worship] catholic privates may refuse to embark'[8] was wide of the mark. In the Clare regiment, for one, the prospect of service in England is stated to have acted as a stimulus to recruiting. The lord lieutenant's recommendation was that units should be removed according to the priority of date at which they made a tender of their services. The total number of men that might be sent (1/3 of the number voted by parliament on the establishment for the current year) was 14 units or 10,332 of all ranks. But this was a maximum. In practice the number of men sent was much less, as the units, simultaneously with getting in readiness to go, were being reduced through ordinary volunteering; this implies that there were men who preferred (induced probably by higher bounty) to transfer to a regular unit rather than to go to England as members of their own militia unit. It was subsequently found that, as the numbers of some of the 14 units were so reduced an additional unit could be got within the allowed total and so the Meath militia were proposed for inclusion and sent*.[9] In the first 15 units which volunteered none of the Ulster county units appear. The men (and the officers also) were allowed to be accompanied by their wives and families without restriction. The embarkation (1811) and disembarkation (1813) returns show the extent to which advantage was taken of this privilege. Thus the Louth on their return disembarked (with officers and non-commissioned officers) 1,317 strong; in this number there were 260 women and 311 children, with 606 privates. Two more illustrations: the Roscommon in April 1813 were 911 strong, in which number were 164 women and 175 children; and the Clare, disembarking, out of a total party of 625 had 106 women and 123 children.[10]

The passage afforded some new and unpleasant experiences. The wife of a sergeant of the Cork north (which claimed the honour of being the first regiment embarked (Cove, 19 August)[11] 'had the misfortune to fall overboard and would unquestionably have been drowned, had not colonel Crawford.... instantly plunged into the sea, though in boots and regimentals, and by his exertions kept the poor woman's head above water until a boat was got ready'. In this same regiment, on its arrival at Portsmouth, there was an alarm of fire, as a consequence of which some men leaped overboard and were lost. The transports conveying the Louth, Clare and Mayo, after having been unable to leave Dublin bay for some time owing to contrary winds, struck the storm and were driven into Milford with great loss of top gear. To add to this trouble contagious fever appeared and those of the troops who were not already affected were transferred to the lazaretto there. The Leitrim were 23 days in reaching Deal and the King's county a similar time in getting to Plymouth dock. The voyages are referred to by a contemporary newspaper as a 'first nautical exploit which no doubt must have appeared pregnant with great and alarming peril'. No doubt; and especially to

*The Meath establishment of rank and file was 760, of whom 182 were deficient. Of the remaining 578, 482 embarked and the remaining 96 were accounted for as follows: left on recruiting 16; sick absent 38; not volunteered 28; in charge of sick at Cork 4; absent with leave 10. They took 118 women and 126 children.

Mayo men after the unit's alarming experiences in Dublin bay in 1807.

To a large extent the Irish militia units replaced in England British militia units in stations where the latter had been quartered. The north Cork, Dublin city and Limerick county were on duty in the dockyards at Portsmouth and guarding French prisoners there. The units seem to have received warm welcomes in England. There was much hospitality for both officers and men from local institutions (the Plymouth Commercial Coffee News room is mentioned); from local notabilities; and from English militia and other regiments. The Sussex militia when visited at Portsmouth by their colonel, the duke of Norfolk, gave an 'elegant entertainment' to the Tipperary. An officer of this regiment who participated wrote home that 'the duke of Norfolk entertained us as much by his vivacity as his wine, in the best style of lively hospitality—the men get the best beef and mutton for 6d. a pound and one pound of bread each day for 1½d.; potatoes and turnips are also cheap and plenty'. The Roscommon who had a short but rough passage to Bristol were a great success at Plymouth. The *Plymouth Chronicle* wrote:

> The Roscommon regiment of militia which have been for some weeks in this garrison has already distinguished itself by its good conduct and steady discipline. The men attend divine service at the chapel (roman catholic) at Stonehouse where their silence and devotion may shame many of their protestant brethren. The ignorant part of the people in this country consider their Irish fellow subjects as being eccentric in themselves, and as savage in their dispositions as the people of New Zealand. Almost every old woman had a tale relative to them and trembled for her virtue. How surprised must these wretched ignoramuses appear when they find that there is not a regiment in this garrison that behaves better in every respect than the Irish, peaceable and well disciplined as they are. We conceive it our duty to bear public testimony to this, in order to silence all cavillers and to convince those who deny them an equal participation of privileges in civil and religious offices that they should blush for their intolerance.[12]

The *Hampshire Telegraph* says (September) of the Limerick county: 'they are a fine body of men and discovered so much of the steady and well disciplined soldier as to excite the praises of those who saw them on parade'.[13] Lord Westmeath was himself with his regiment at Dover where, writes an officer, 'we were sumptuously entertained at dinner by the mayor and corporation who, to numerous good things, were profuse in adding their sincere approbation of our conduct since our arrival among them'.[14] The Sligo seem to have been stationed at Windsor; this being so, it is satisfactory to find recorded that they were 'an excellent disciplined regiment and for propriety of conduct cannot be surpassed'.[15] The Tipperary, almost exclusively catholic, were over 1,000 strong. Their own records supply some graphic particulars : a reception of the duke of Clarence (when, at Chatham, he dined at the mess) by the men of the flank companies of whose unusual stature their officers were very proud ; the conferring by the duke of the title ‘ Duke of Clarence’s Munster regiment of militia ’; then an incident which led to the regiment being moved to Dover where, as is specifically stated, one of the vaulted chambers in the castle was fitted up for roman catholic worship. The incident illustrates again how the personnel of the Irish militia units clannishly held together.

The town authorities had imprisoned an officer of the grenadier company who was a favourite of the soldiers and so the latter, while the officers were at mess, broke open the gaol and carried the officer back on their shoulders. This happened seven months after their arrival in England. But provocation did not come only from the Irish militiaman. The Leitrim were quartered in Bristol in 1812. A sergeant of the regiment was accosted one day by an individual who asked him how he liked the country. He then ‘ began to abuse the sergeant by damning him and everyone from his country. A second man came up and with a carving knife cut the sinews of the sergeant’s right leg, so that the poor fellow was not able to be moved from the public house to which he was immediately conveyed ’. The account adds : ‘ the conduct of the whole regiment since they have been among us has been truly exemplary ’.[16] At a review of the Limerick county on Portsea common in December the duke of Clarence addressed the regiment ‘ with his hat off ’ (presumably a compliment) and observed that ‘ the project of interchanging the militia of the two countries had originated with himself who had recommended it strongly to the Prince Regent ’![17]

The units were frequently moved in England : the following is a list of the quarters of the Clare : Ipswich, Woodbridge, Harwich, Horsham, Brighton, Chichester, Haslar, Gosport. The comparative absence of recorded ‘ incidents ’, though there were some, goes to show that the spirit of fraternization which, as we have seen, greeted the Irish militia on their arrival in England, continued and that things proceeded normally and without any unusual friction. On their return journey the Westmeath took 11 days over the voyage from Spithead to Cove ; the orders issued[18] on this voyage happen to be available and they contain, amongst other things, the following :—

> The men’s rum to be mixed with about three waters that one half may be given to them by the quartermaster at 12 o’clock and the other half reserved for them until 6 p.m.

and this :—

The dinner drum to be beat at two o'clock each day. Every officer's servant is held responsible for the tying up of his master's dogs to prevent them from dirtying the deck and annoying the company.

The service of the two militias alongside one another in Ireland and also in England brought into the open two differences of treatment which, as long as the forces were not juxtaposed, caused no difficulty. In Ireland the English colonels found that, while they received allowance for the clothing of their effective numbers only, the Irish colonels received it (and had received it since the first formation in 1793) on the establishment numbers. An illustration given showed that the colonel of a certain unit ' should his corps continue in its present state for the entire year ' stood to receive, though this seems to have been an extreme case, an emolument of over £1,110 ' independent of his pay and other allowances '. The duke of York however opposed any alteration of the position of the Irish colonels.[19] They had apparently always done well financially while at home ; in November 1797 a commanding officer tells his colonel who had been complaining about the financial burden of the regiment : ' I am sure the regiment ought not to be an expense ; on the contrary it should be worth a thousand a year '. The other difference came to light through the complaint made by the Irish militia officers in England when they found themselves called on to pay the property tax ' from which they considered themselves exempted under the comprehensive terms of the interchange act '. They got no satisfaction ; they were told that they had compensating advantages.

A contemporary statement[20] is that the underlying purpose of the interchange was to have at hand in Ireland a militia ' not influenced by the local interests or prejudices of that country .... to assist in the suppression of the disturbances which may arise from the disappointed hopes of the majority of the people respecting their civil or religious privileges. The policy of the measure ', so the statement proceeds, ' will not be questioned, provided that of subjecting them to such disappointments be established '. Twenty-five English militia units were sent to Ireland. These considerably more than replaced the Irish militia units that left. Ireland was in fact, though this is not anywhere stressed, left with a predominantly English garrison. In the autumn (1811) an attack on Ireland was again regarded as probable—to come from the Boulogne flotilla. The defence position was again reviewed and the commander of the forces recommended that such detachments (except those for revenue purposes) as were out (probably numerous as always) should be called in and yeomanry substituted. There were 1,304 aiding the police and 588 on revenue duty. But, in spite of the military advice that dispersion would ' render [the troops] liable to be cut up in detail on the landing of an enemy ' the lord lieutenant was against the proposal to call in detachments.[22]

The chief secretary (who in January 1810 had written to Whitehall ' we are weak in our garrison and weaker in our generals ')[22] continued to be alarmed and to fear invasion ; the army was even less efficient than when he had raised the question in July 1810, though he admitted that the interchange of the militias had relieved some of his apprehensions. Some still remained ; ' we all ' he said ' suppose [invasion] will take place whenever the enemy may evade our fleets '; he expected a force to land and advance to Dublin and ' he has not the smallest doubt that this calamity must infallibly happen under our present military arrangements '. These alarms were apparently shared in London : ' every despatch we receive almost shows the cabinet are aware of the intention of the enemy to invade Ireland '. This was at the end of November 1811.[23] In February next year the enemy's fleet was thought to have been descried off Kinsale and in the south of Ireland the troops and the yeomanry were in readiness to act on the shortest notice. The Kinsale rumour turned out to be false, but, in March, the French fleet was observed to put to sea from Lorient.[24] In May there was expectation of them off Broadhaven ; and in August a fleet was seen off Blacksod harbour but was probably only the West Indian fleet.[25] By September Peel had succeeded Wellesley Pole and he then reported to London that the country was ' very tranquil '.[26]

Certain measures had been taken in 1811 besides the interchange. There had been in May another act modifying in detail but continuing the recruiting of the ' annual tribute'. By the time its operation ended 2,795[27] volunteers had been obtained but the lord lieutenant, in October, bewails that ' volunteering for the militia becomes more difficult '.[28] In July five of the units still not ' augmented ' had accepted augmentation and had thus become contributories to the ' annual tribute '; these included the Donegal, about the augmentation of which the views of lord Leitrim have been quoted. An alteration had been made to enable the colonels to get more patronage in the shape of the bonus commissions for their young officers : they were now to be allowed to keep an account current with the government and to bring forward, from one volunteering to another, any surplus volunteers in respect of whom they had had no credit towards bonus commissions. Thus the Cork city which, between October 1807 and March 1811, had furnished 515 volunteers had received only 8 commissions ; on the basis of one commission for each 50 volunteers, that unit was left with a surplus of 115 in respect of whom no commissions had accrued to them.[29]

There were in Ireland in 1812 about an equal number of Irish and English militia units. There is no particular information available as to how these two militias got on together there. They were no doubt for the most part in different garrisons and contact between them was possibly purposely kept limited. An unfortunate occurrence arose in the case of the Nottingham and Dublin city militias which were together in Dublin in 1811. This was apparently 'the consequence of a mistaken sensibility upon military pre-eminence which is always to be found in associated bodies of men, whether armed or unarmed'.[30] Anyhow they were satisfactorily and dramatically adjusted at a public reconciliation on St. Stephen's green during which the band of each regiment played the national tune of the other.[31]

In this year cropped up again the old trouble of the claims to discharge. This time it was in the Fermanagh [32]where balloted men were asserting their right to be discharged. This is not surprising if the statements made to entice men into this unit were as misleading as those which have been quoted in the case of the Antrim (chap. XV). The question was once more reviewed and the law officers again expressed the opinion that 'no militia private soldier of any class who has been enrolled since 1803 can at this day be legally entitled to his discharge'. An explanatory memorandum for the benefit of private soldiers was issued. There was, it appears, at this time trouble also in the English and Scottish militias about their terms of service.[33] The Irish act of 1809 (the co-ordinating act) had introduced for *balloted* men a *fixed* 5 years but this did not apply, as certain men of the north Down the next year with downed arms claimed, to men balloted under any previous act.

Perplexity about how to get men for the militia (and as volunteers for the line) seems to have been growing. An order issued in May 1812 as to prompt payments being made for aid in suppressing stills suggests that 'militiamen may possibly have been prevented from extending their service [i.e. transferring to the line] by their claims not having been settled'.[34] In August the authorities urged that an improper number of officers and men was employed in the militia on recruiting service. The lack of men was no doubt the cause of the enactment (April) that not exceeding 1/4th of those to be raised for the militia of any county should be boys; they were to be of the age of 14 and upwards; to be raised by beat of drum; and drum-beating was to be—this was specifically ruled—in the unit's own county only. The volunteering of 1812 had been good but in December Peel was seriously considering the position of the militia. In October the 23 units in Ireland had an establishment of 16,435 but on this there was a deficiency of 3,885; the 15 units in England were similarly weak.

The increased bounty paid to recruits since 1811 had not had the success anticipated. Completion of the establishments or reduction of them more nearly to the strength were the alternatives put before Whitehall; to promote the former, the course taken in 1807 (i.e. the ballot with the permitted alternative of parochial assessment) was the suggestion.[35]

In January 1813 the lord lieutenant,[36] dealing with the ballot, makes a point not perhaps hitherto brought clearly out, i.e. that this method is limited to completion of the several corps to the establishment at which they were originally fixed: for the augmented part of each company (i.e. the 71st to the 100th man in each company) ' there is ' he says ' no claim on the county for any man to be raised by ballot '. A regiment, for example, with an original establishment of 560 and an augmented establishment of 800 and an actual strength of (say) 573 must be exempted from the operation of the ballot. This limits the usefulness of the ballot. He goes on to refer to the ' few instances in which the ballot has been resorted to in Ireland and the difficulties which might be found in carrying it into effect in many parts of the country, in consequence of the defective state of the civil arrangements necessary for that purpose '. Dublin castle seemed to lack adequate information on the results of balloting; a return in December from the Commissioners of military accounts[37] showed that ' men have been raised by ballot in one instance only, leaving it doubtful in many others '. They suggested reference to the governors and deputy governors of counties; this was subsequently made[38], with somewhat unsatisfactory results, in May 1813. The lord lieutenant's final recommendation was that the colonels should be ordered to enrol volunteers; that they should be reminded of the liability to fine for every man deficient; and that they should be given four months for getting their quotas. These proposals were approved without delay and on 26 February 1813 the orders for giving them effect were issued.[39]

The result does not seem to be available. Almost certainly things went poorly because at the end of July all the colonels were warned that reduction of establishment would follow the non-completion of the augmented establishments.[40] Prior to that, on 21 May, there had been a new act (53 Geo. iii. chap. 48) the precise policy underlying which is not quite evident. It makes important provisions for the removal of doubts ' enter tained as to . . . . by whom and in what proportions bounty [on raising volunteers for the militiaj ought to be paid '; it also altered the provisions about the liability for fines for men deficient. By the end of May the figures for the number of balloted men actually serving had been collected from the county authorities;[41] they gave a total of 1,738 but 13 counties had made no return—

probably because their records were so defective that they could not do so; some of those sending returns reported 'no information'. Of the numbers returned there were in co. Antrim 488; in co. Down 938; and in co. Sligo 210; of the other counties which gave information Galway had 60.

The lord lieutenant again reviewed the situation in October 1813.[42] He does not give the results of the efforts made since the beginning of the year but the presumption is that there had been little success, as he now poses the question whether he is to reduce the corps found deficient on present establishment, at the end of four months. He again goes over the arguments for and against the ballot and his conclusion is that it would not be productive. 'Exclusive' he says 'of the prevalent objection to the bringing that measure into operation here, it is necessary under the provisions of the existing militia laws that in all augmented regiments a complete apportionment of the men should have been made, so that it can be ascertained by authentic documents which of the men were of the augmentation and which of the original establishment; also which of the latter belonged to each parish etc. If this proceeding had been adopted, the ballot may be resorted to, so far as to complete the deficiency of each parish, etc. to its quota in the original establishment, but no further, and in such case the deficiencies in the augmentation must be supplied by volunteering; it is however apprehended that the apportionment has not been made effectually in any instance; where it has not, the ballot cannot be used and the numbers in such case can only be filled by enrolling volunteers'. As regards the latter course, he says that 'the late efforts to complete the militia of this country', even supplemented by the liability to fines 'to which the counties are subject whose quotas shall continue deficient', show that it will be unproductive. But Whitehall did not accept his recommendation and he was informed in November 1813 that 'any measures for the reduction of the Irish regiments of militia to their original establishments should for the present be suspended'.[43] In that month the country was disturbed. Reduction had, it seems, in fact been proposed to some units and there had been protest.[44]

In the summer of 1813 the 1811 contingent of Irish militia returned to Ireland and the fresh contingent of 16 units sailed. This time the Ulster counties were well represented by the Antrim, Down (north and south), Fermanagh, Londonderry and Monaghan. The selection was made by priority of offer, as before. As also in 1811 there was a liberal permitted complement of wives and families; the north Down, it appears, took (in addition to a low strength of 362 privates) 125 women and 164 children.[45] The men were granted before embarking two days leave[46]—

exclusive of the time taken for going to and from their homes at the rate of 15 miles a day. In August the duke of Richmond had been asking for a few regiments of British militia; his successor, lord Whitworth, in November writes to the secretary of state that he knows not ' how we are to spare our militia. Indeed we have now but scarcely sufficient to preserve any tolerable degree of order in the country '.[47] But there was no question apparently of bringing the Irish militia back.

In 1813 the fear of invasion had passed and the Longford, in the midlands, found the innkeepers unaccommodating and the welcome for troops not what it had been.[48] ' Tip us a smile, sweet landlady ' said a Sligo militiaman to his hostess at the inn ' and charge the novelty in the bill tomorrow '. The England to which the Irish militia had now gone was one of industrial unrest. That an Irish military force which by its critics was declared inherently unsuitable for dealing with domestic disturbance at home should find itself the guardian of law and order in England was anomalous, though, on the theory of the said critics, unassailable. In this position more than one regiment found itself. The Louth on 6 May are reported as on their way to Warrington (Lancs.), a district disturbed by Luddite activities. They had been at Huntingdon on April 30 and ' they travel in carts, with the utmost expedition '. In similar predicament, with Castlebar and the Cornwallis strictures no longer presumably remembered against them, were the Kilkenny. According to a regimental record,[49] after a few weeks in Dublin spent in ' breaking bounds and hearts ', they felt ' the manners of the contemplative merchant of Liverpool ' a great contrast. They moved from there to Nottingham, then an industrial storm centre; and ' their activity in suppressing the insurrection of the Luddites ' (according to this account) led to their being moved away; their stay was certainly not long. It happens that a report exists formally made at the time to London by the magistrates[50] and this gives a different version. It commends the officers and the colonel for their unwearied exertions to promote the peace and tranquillity of the town; admits that great provocation had been given by the townspeople to the Kilkenny men and that ' there exists a considerable disposition on the part of many of the inhabitants to use expressions to and in the hearing of the soldiers which have a manifest tendency to influence their passions and to excite them to violent conduct '. But there had been disturbance on three successive days between the private soldiers of the regiment and the townspeople which left the magistrates no option but to ask for the removal of the regiment. Later they were at Harwich when they were ordered to Gosport to take part in the great Portsmouth review. On this trek they surprised their officers by making a long before-breakfast march, without anyone falling out—they were keen to come up with a great prize fight. At the review the duke of York took special notice of the regiment and its band; this had a magnificent uniform and the regimental account quoted says that the colonel, lord Ormonde, spent £1,500 a year on his band.

Marshal Blücher, who was at the review, tried, the account states, to get 400 Kilkenny militiamen for Flanders, but only 370 came forward and the plan was dropped; had they gone 'they would' the account suggests 'have become heroes of Waterloo as they deserved to have been of Castlebar'. That this Flanders visit should have been a possibility at all resulted from the act of the previous year (54 Geo. iii. chap. 1 24 November 1813). A circular letter issued under this from Whitehall alike to British and to Irish militia units invited officers and men to extend their service as wholes to any part of Europe or to transfer in blocks to the line.[51] But this measure for 'the vigorous prosecution of the war' had very little success. The officer commanding the Monaghan militia (who were at Plymouth dock) said that no men of his corps were likely to extend 'notwithstanding every exertion has been made by the whole corps of officers'; and he adds; 'the Irish regiments of militia have been for nine months in each year during these last seven years called upon and every possible means made use of to induce them to extend their service; these men therefore who now compose this regiment have long since made up their minds on that subject'.[52] In most cases refusal was due to what they considered inadequate provision for their wives. One unit however, the Cavan, made an offer which was in these terms: 'to serve as a militia regiment in any part of Europe upon any service and upon any terms that the Prince Regent shall think proper, for the period of one year from the date of being sent out of the United Kingdom'.[53] But the oath prescribed by the act required the men to serve 'during the remainder of the war, and until the expiration of six months after the termination thereof'. No provisional battalion was formed under this act from the Irish militia but an English militia brigade of just under 2800 men actually went to Bordeaux.

The ordinary annual transferring went on during 1813 but was less successful than it had been in the previous years. Those colonels who had not completed their quota in the previous year were 'empowered' (which certainly meant 'expected') to make good the deficiency of 15 a company. Yet another expedient was authorized (54 Geo. iii. chap. 10 [6 December 1813]); the restrictions and conditions of the interchange act were suspended and power was thus given to employ in England and correspondingly in Ireland a larger number of militia units from the other country. This gave the means of meeting the Irish government's cry for more troops. Sidmouth had promised (9 December) that 3,000 British militia would be embarked for Ireland with all possible despatch.[54] The lord lieutenant reported a ' rooted and rancorous hatred of government ' as existing. Peel pressed for more troops from England. Sidmouth stressed the difficulty of finding them but on 19 January he said 5,556 more English militia were to go to Ireland. The conversion of the yeomanry into local militia was considered in January by the lord lieutenant, but lukewarmly : ' they can scarcely be deemed an efficient force. The numbers though large on paper are small in point of fact ; the expense enormous '.[55]

But in truth by this time the heart had gone out of the fighting and it was getting impossible to have appeals taken seriously. There were obvious signs of Napoleon's end being at hand. During that winter (1813-4) ' le drame de l'empire touchait au dénouement ' (Maurois). In April he fell. In that same month recruiting for the Irish militia was suspended and the recruiting parties were called in, though it appears that in the early part of the year the linen trade was bad and recruits inclined to come in freely.[56] Early in June steps preparatory to disembodiment were taken ; and in July the discharges of those whose service expired on disembodiment of their corps was effected. This constituted the greater part of the force, for, of the total of some 19,300 then in the militia, some 12,300 were due for discharge ; of the remainder the discharge was due to come in later years and these could be brought back if there should be a fresh embodiment before expiry of service. There was a definite decision not to discharge, as was done at the peace of 1802, the men who had not completed their period of service ; to these their liability to be called upon again was fully explained.[57]

The adjutant-general in Dublin was stressing at the end of July the importance of ' giving back to the general population, at this period when labour is required [i.e. for harvest work] as many hands as possible ' and he adds ' it would have been well if we could have done this sooner and to a greater extent '.[58] Many of the units were of course in England; some of these were held up in Bristol for many weeks owing to want of transport and did not leave until August. About half were not disembodied until October or November ; most of the others went in August.

Nine however were kept embodied ; these were the Armagh, Donegal, Roscommon, Wexford, Tyrone, Cork (north), Londonderry, Mayo (north), and the Tipperary. This selection may have been made on the basis of selecting the strongest ; five of those retained were 10 company regiments. But in England at all events retention of particular units was largely fortuitous : it was explained that several had been disembodied before the government 'saw the propriety, from peculiar circumstances, of forbearing from any further reduction.'[59] In January there had been 23 English militia units in Ireland and 18 were still there in December. Peace—so Peel urged—would not help much to remove the causes of internal trouble and he felt that the disbanded militiamen 'who have been good soldiers may be worse civilians when they get among their friends'.[60] In the English militia in Ireland there was considerable dissatisfaction 'on the subject of the period of their servitude' and about 150 men of the north York laid down their arms declaring that they would do no more duty.[61] The general question of retaining militia still embodied was agitated vigorously in both houses of parliament and the legality challenged. This was met by the law officers pointing out that as the law was silent as to when the militia, being already embodied, could be *disembodied*, the discretion rested with the executive. What it amounted to, claimed those who were objecting, was that 'the militia was not to be disembodied whilst the American war or the congress at Vienna should continue'. But Sidmouth would not go beyond the general formula that 'the foreign and domestic calls for military service rendered it necessary that the militia should continue embodied'. Lord Donoughmore said that, whatever the view about continuing the militia was in England, 'in Ireland it was far from being a burthen: it was looked up to as being a service of advantage and emolument, and afforded a considerable patronage to the government'. The counties to which the embodied units belonged were reimbursed from public funds the payments they might have to make for the maintenance of wives and families.

The writer of an official memorandum[62] (June 1814), made, with a view to another ballot which he thought should be held to complete the militia as soon as possible, two proposals: first that men enlisted for a county not their own should be transferred to their own county regiment to complete therein their service; second, that the governors and deputy governors should allot the men who remained undischarged to particular parishes. As regards the former, there had always been much slackness, notwithstanding attempts to stop the practice, followed quite unblushingly by some colonels, of recruiting outside their own counties. This we hear of the Wexford, on their march to Dublin to embark in September 1813, picking up in co. Fermanagh some 200 men. Men thus obtained, just as much as men obtained within the county, should, as already pointed out, have been allocated to a particular parish. The statutes insist on this repeatedly. If men were not allocated, what was the value of the county and parish lists as a basis of calculating liabilities? For instance, if a man were discharged unfit for service or on any other permissible ground, how and by what parish was he to be replaced if in fact he had never been assigned to a particular parish? It seems most probable that the parish lists were never at any time in workable order; they were much criticized in the debate on 19 February 1808.

That the lists should be unsatisfactory is not surprising, as the constables charged under the acts with the duty of originating and maintaining them were probably in most cases rather illiterate men and the work of keeping them up adequately probably called for some administrative competence. It also called for a constant and efficient touch between the regimental and county authorities which, even if cordial relations existed, was in all probability seldom achieved. There are cases where the treasurers of counties clearly find themselves unable on the facts before them to resolve questions of incidence of charge as between the stock purse of the unit and the county funds.[63] The fact that units were hardly ever, except on eve of disembodiment, in their own county must in itself have led to muddle. Another point was that individual men might be assigned to the original (or 1795 establishment) or they might be augmentation men. To the two categories different conditions applied, to some extent. Clearly they should have been kept rigidly separate in the records of the county as well as in those of the units. It is difficult, on the information available, to resist the conclusion that the whole matter of allocation was enveloped in confusion in many, if not in most, counties. The records of monies 'presented' and raised by the counties for the militia show different figures as given at different times for the same presentment (assize). Also the treasurers are unable sometimes to understand, and often even to find, their predecessors' records on the subject. A very complicated business over which is written 'mole ruit sua'; and it is not incorrect to take the view that the militia balloting system, which can hardly be classed as a success, failed as a system (and not only in Ireland but in England also) as much because of administrative unworkability as through unacceptability on general grounds. The moment the county unit moved out of its county and ceased to be, as theory at all events required, a county organization functioning on a county basis *within* the county and in touch with the county administrative machinery (exiguous at best), breakdown of the recruiting arrangements was already in sight. Adequate centralized control was obviously necessary. For this accurate and complete centralized statistical information was indispensable; but, although the statutes habitually order returns to be made to the government, it seems fairly clear that what was received was not adequate to provide a coherent basis for administrative decisions, as has been seen earlier in this chapter.

The men and the officers (except those of the retained units) accordingly returned to their homes. It is not possible to quote any contemporary firsthand account of their feelings on the occasion. The financial settlement with them did not presuppose possibility of a fresh embodiment at an early date. At the disembodiment in 1802 there had been earnest attempts to deal with the unemployment aspects of the demobilization; in 1816 there was considerable similar solicitude; but at this disembodiment in 1814 the main concern found expressed is that the process should, in the interests of the social economy, be as gradual as possible. But Peel in July 1814 was considering 'the employment of the better description of militia soldiers as special constables....under the permanent police act'. The theory as regards the officers was that they had the property which had been their 'qualification' for their commissions to fall back upon. But doubts are by some writers[64] stated as to how far qualifications had in fact been enforced. Anyhow there are at this time many memorials from captains asking, in virtue of the long service which many of them seem to have had, for some provision and representing that the property which was their 'qualification' for their commissions had, owing to general causes, gone; and further that they were no longer entitled to the statutory disembodiment allowance provided for lieutenants (2/6 a day) and for ensigns (2/- a day) under the annual pay and clothing acts (see e.g. 54 Geo. iii. chap. 177. 30 July 1814). There is no record of the discharged militiamen causing disorder. 'The measure of disembodying the Irish militia' says the lord lieutenant on 27 August 'has been attended with no difficulty'.[65]

The probability is that there were celebrations not different from those which had taken place in 1802 and from those which were to take place after the final closing down. The *Ennis Chronicle* published a panegyric of the Clare militia and an old officer testified to their good conduct in 1798.[66] No doubt other regiments received also a similar meed of county applause. Generals supervised the disembodiment proceedings. Scandals came to light in a few of the units: monies due to soldiers for 6 to 10 years and improper use made of the family money; and the report on one disembodiment says: 'one child of 10 years old is kept as a drummer [a paid rank]; he is said to be a good fifer'. There is a record that the general presiding at the Monaghan disembodiment, amongst other more serious complaints, reported that the commanding officer had permitted 'a disorderly chairing of officers'. The officer, in explanation, said he was in the orderly room when a number of the men 'burst in and were about to carry me out when I seized a bayonet and with the assistance of the clerks I got them out, locked the door and was proceeding with the business when some officers came to the door and repeatedly requested I would submit ' i.e. to be chaired. And ' chaired ' he was.[67] Chairing also occurred, was in fact very general, at the final disembodiment (see page 262).

There is little to be said about the Irish militia during the period known as the Hundred Days. The retained units, which had been in November 1814 very much under strength (the company establishment was 100), had by May 1815 run down still further ; and by 25 June, on an aggregate establishment of 9,100, 3,647 were wanting. But Napoleon was to return from Elba and the troubles were to begin again. In April the cabinet advised the Prince Regent to withdraw 1,200 cavalry and 4,000 infantry from Ireland ; this left there about 2,000 of the former and 12,500 of the latter.[68] The lords justices (then acting in the absence of the lord lieutenant in England) did not like these withdrawals. On 23 June Peel writes to Dublin : ' for the purpose of reinforcing the duke of Wellington it is intended to send out of the United Kingdom every regular soldier. We must therefore immediately take means for supplying as well as we can the immense loss we are about to sustain. Inclosed is the act (55 Geo. iii. chap. 77. 14 June 1815) authorizing you to order the Irish militia to be embodied. I think we ought to embody every regiment that is not so weak and inefficient as to be of no service '.[69] Before this, in May, Wellington had complained, in the letter from Brussels in which he said that he had an ' infamous army ', that the government ' had not called out the militia either in England or Ireland '.[70]

There had been a *general* warrant on 4 May for completing *certain* regiments to their respective ordinary establishments specified in the act 49 Geo. iii. chap. 120, and the retained units were instructed[71] to enrol volunteers to fill up the vacancies in their establishments. But on the other hand during the months from March onwards there were, under specific instructions issued in April, large discharges, both from the embodied and also from the disembodied units, of volunteers and substitutes who had completed 5 years service ; but they might extend their services with a bounty of 6 guineas and on taking the oath under the interchange act.[72] General re-embodiment, for counties with militia not embodied, was ordered by proclamation of 26 June. This stated that it was ' expedient....in the present situation of the country, there being the prospect of an immediate war with France, to authorize the drawing out and embodying the militia '.[73] It took effect for all units on 17 July.[74] Discharges of the volunteers and substitutes of 5 years service continued after the embodiment but on the other hand the counties were busy recruiting. In Kilkenny there was a meeting of governors and preparations for a ballot—which was not however held.[75] The *Ennis Chronicle* gives a vivid picture: 'the enthusiasm with which the veterans of the corps crowded to the standard....is scarcely to be credited, while the eagerness of recruits swelled the muster of the corps....and the numbers who follow them continue to fill our streets beyond anything occasioned by the bustle of our late assizes'.[76] In co. Monaghan a large number of those who had been discharged joined again.[77] The Mayo north records[78] show considerable numbers, probably also discharged men, as reattested. By 25 July that regiment shows 119 recruits; the Tipperary 105; and the Cork north 79; all these were retained units. But discharges still take place and on a return (25 August) very heavy desertions are shewn; these are probably men who did not turn up as they should have done. There are still heavy discharges in several units (Londonderry 147). But, notwithstanding discharges and desertions, the net strength was increasing. On 1 September it was 14,925; it had increased 1,172 since the last return; there were still 5,025 wanting to complete; of the units Clare and Kerry were actually up to establishment.[79] The strength continued to increase under active recruiting until January 1816. At this time there were 23 English militia units in Ireland. In June 1815 the yeomanry had been called upon again, so as 'to relieve in some degree the regular military force in Ireland and to render it, as far as circumstances will permit, disposable for general purposes'.[80] Earlier in the year the lord lieutenant thanks the cabinet for having taken on themselves a large measure of responsibility 'for withdrawing so large a part of the regular force [from Ireland]' but he realized that 'the peace of Ireland must be fought for and maintained in France....and be firmly established by the destruction of Bonaparte and of the revolutionary government'.[81]

The time from the second re-embodiment, i.e. during the autumn and winter of 1815, offers nothing of note. The units of the Irish militia were not, even in this St. Martins summer, for the most part allowed to remain in their own counties. Some offered to extend their services to Great Britain. The old routine, now so well established and doubtless become bone of their bone, went on again. The momentum of the machine, though it had during the disembodied period run down, was not spent. Recruits were no doubt easily absorbed. As always, calls for protection of excise officers and magistrates were numerous. The battle of Waterloo had taken place before the militia was in arms again. A captain of the Longford was, indeed, at that battle 'in order to satisfy my curiosity relative to the campaign there' and he accompanied the duke of Wellington's army to Paris; he hurried home to Longford when he heard that the Irish militia was called out.[82] It is perhaps a little surprising that they were kept out so long. But duty as an army of occupation still kept (in October 1815) over 50,000 troops[83] on the continent and the state of Ireland was considered to require retention of the militia. In September the lower Shannon district was so disturbed that a force very considerably larger than Cornwallis took to the west in 1798 had been ordered there.[84] In December, Ireland was reinforced substantially. In January 1816 there was the idea of sending there as reinforcements troops from France and on the 19th of that month the lord lieutenant, mentioning that the militia then consisted of about 17,000 men, speaks of being under the necessity of keeping it out, in whole or in part, 'until we have accomplished the salutary work we now have in hand, that of reducing this country to a state of tranquillity and of obedience to the law'. But in February the state of the country was considered to be improved and the commander of the forces proposed gradual reduction of the militia.[85]

The Prince Regent's warrants (issued February and March)* ordering dis-embodiment recited his desire 'to take the first opportunity of releasing his majesty's subjects from the burthen and expense occasioned by the war;' they were, on their return to 'their respective parishes and places of abode', to remain subject to the same orders and directions as they were by law subject to before they were drawn out and embodied. By the end of March the number of units was down from 38 to 20. A month later, though five English militia units still remained in Ireland, all the Irish, finally now, had been let go. The long odyssey round Ireland—many individuals had served since the original raising of the force—was over and the now engrained military life was at an end.

On the final day the Longford 'paraded at half past six in the morning....and no man was permitted to quit the barrack yard until the whole were paid their balances, their fourteen days bounty and all other just claims'.[87] From the Kilkenny we have a more hilarious side of this most momentous parting. 'The men had provided two chairs neatly ornamented, in which they placed the officers successively and chaired them through the principal streets, the drums and fifes playing favourite national tunes and the men cheering, during the greater part of the afternoon'. In the Tyrone the colonel, the earl of Caledon, issued an order the night before the disembodiment thanking everybody and earnestly requesting the soldiers 'to show their discipline to his orders by separating without noise or tumult....and to return to their respective homes with as little delay as possible'.[88] And this is what apparently took place, not only in the Tyrone but generally.

*By 20 March orders had been issued 'for disembodying the entire of the Irish militia'.[86]

The lord lieutenant gives the number of privates to be let go as about 16,000. He was alive to the difficulties they would 'probably experience in procuring support for themselves and their families and the evil which may result from their indiscriminate intermixture amongst the lower orders of the people who, in certain districts, particularly, are prone to licentious habits and insubordination to the laws'. A large proportion had, it appears, been enrolled during the last year and these had some years to serve; if they were induced 'to continue in a profession to which they had for some time been habituated' and to go into the line, then the counties would have to be compensated for the charge of filling their places. He had no other suggestion to make as regards the disembodied men but he realized that, if they were to be got into the line, legislation would be necessary and this, he saw, might be inexpedient.[89] 'Is it not possible' writes an officer of the military staff in Dublin to a brother officer in London 'to do something on your side of the water in favour of the poor fellows lately turned adrift from the militia in this country by permitting them to enlist into the army?' Later this same officer, who was one of those employed to carry out disembodiment proceedings, writes to Peel: 'I made some observations in dismissing the militia. I was instructed to caution them against enlisting into the line and the common reply was 'colonel, what can we do?'[90] No doubt many of them, notwithstanding that they were apparently under oath not to enlist into the regulars, did this. Sidmouth seems to have perceived psychological inappropriateness in beginning volunteering for the line again. Anyway nothing seems to have been done to meet the social problem caused by the disembodiment of the considerable number of men involved.

The request of the captains for an allowance (which in 1814 had been negatived) was in February 1816 again put forward. A memorial, sent to London by the lord lieutenant, stated that:

> when the militia force was first called out, it was arranged upon different principles....The captains were appointed from a class of men whose fortunes rendered them independent of military pay and who, upon the militia extending their service, retired from the profession; for persons of this description the legislature did not deem it necessary to make any provision. In the progress of the war, other claims to promotion were put forward and acknowledged; length of service, attention to military duties and general good conduct became at length the real grounds of preferment, so that at the present hour the captains of militia are generally men promoted from subaltern situations and whose chief provision for themselves and their families is derived from their profession.[91]

They anticipated from disembodiment melancholy results for themselves; they would not be able to get into any other profession. There is a moving letter from a captain to his late colonel : ' compelled by the wants of my wife and my little children to adopt the only thing which is open to me at present, namely the precarious and dependent situation of a public auctioneer '. Previously to ' appearing to the public in that capacity through the medium of the newspapers ' he feels it 'a duty imperative on him ' to resign his commission as captain.[92] Nothing seems to have been done to meet the hardship of the captains nor for the paymasters who put in printed petitions in Januery 1815 and again in May 1816. The latter represented the ' vary great increase of trouble and responsibility which has accrued to them during the last 10 years from the frequent volunteering and transfer of men from militia to line and from recruiting toreplace such volunteers '.[93]

This was the end, for about forty years, of the Irish militia as an embodied force. They then went into Sleepy Hollow. 'The permanent staff ' says a regimental record ' from disembodiment grew gradually less and less, vacancies not being filled up, until at length in the beginning of 1855 it consisted of but a few old cripples whose one duty was to receive their pay monthly '.

In July 1816 Peel reported to London that since he had been connected with Ireland he never recollected it less disturbed.

XVII

Women and Children

The Irish militia, as circumstances fell, remained continuously—more continuously than ever anticipated—on 'actual service'. Had they, according to a peace time militia routine, alternated between annual periods of 28 days as soldiers and the rest of the year as civilians, it would not have been necessary to take account of the existence of wives, who are anyhow not usually in the military picture. There was not then, nor for a long time, in Ireland, for the wives and families of those Irishmen who became *permanently* soldiers (i.e. for those serving as regulars) any 'poor-rate law, nor any other sort of allowance subsisting for these objects'. England 'a country far less famed for their charity, clemency or urbanity religiously provide for the wives and off-spring of the well-deserving soldiers, from the moment those worthy objects are deprived of the means of support by the absence of their husbands'. The wives and children, the widows and orphans, of the regular soldier, in England, received 'the benefit of the poor-rate law, in value from 2 to 3 shillings a week for each woman and at the rate of 1/6 a week for each child'. The fate of the wives of Irish soldiers is referred to by sir Jeremiah Fitz-patrick, M.D. Inspector of Health for the Land forces, as being 'itinerant beggary' and the negative policy followed as producing 'sea ports....crowded with the begging widows of Irish soldiers and sailors'. We hear also of the heartrending scenes when a regiment embarked for foreign service and of the endeavour of the 'wives, children and helpless infants....to return to their once homes, for now they have none (although on their native soil) there to become common beggars'. Wellington put the matter abruptly: wives, from the moment of their husband's enlisting, went 'not "upon the parish" but upon the dunghill, to starve'.

Such miseries would be known to many of those who were potential Irish militiamen and would be not without influence on militiamen actually serving when there arose question of their serving out of Ireland. About the preference which the Irish militiaman came to enjoy over the regular soldier in Ireland there were two views. Those who asked for the latter an act of justice (which would also aid recruiting and lessen desertion) put it this way:

In Ireland the family of the militiamen remaining in his native county in great measure, in a comparatively pampered state and risking little or no danger, has some provision made for it ; but none for the disconsolate family of him who to conquer for the empire is sent to meet toil danger and death.

This statement, as will be seen, puts somewhat too high the covenanted advantages available to the militiaman for his family. But there were apparently those who thought—this is the second view—that he had some natural right or claim to better treatment :

I could be no friend [so this position is stated in 1797] to the appearance and figure of an Irish militia if I would have held out equal advantages to the wives, widows and orphans of common marching soldiers.

The Irish militiaman was, during the period of his ' actual service ' down to 1816, neither an in-and-out nor, technically, a permanent soldier. Even if he became, as he so soon did, continuously a soldier, there were thought to remain reasons for a preferential treatment of his wife and family different from that accorded to the wife and family of the man *voluntarily* enlisted to be a *professional* soldier. The act of 1793 had contemplated a force ' chosen by lot '. This constituted, in theory at all events, a difference and there resulted the creation, as regards treatment of wife and family, of a new category. Also, apart from any theoretical case for eligibility derived from the circumstance of ballot-compulsion, practical recruiting considerations, both in 1793 after the passage of the bill as well as continuously throughout constituted a case for some family-concession for the militiaman ; and this even though his service became, in fact, of quasi-permanent character and his military pay and emoluments, consequently, as continuous and not less in amount than those of the permanent soldier—who had no money allowance to provide for his wife and family but could, in England though not in Ireland, ' have them on their parish for bread '.[1]

The act of 1793 contained no provision for allowances to wives, under any circumstances ; this was probably one of the points, commented upon by Castlereagh and others, wherein the act showed marks of having been drafted ' not for all time ' but for an immediate purpose. In 1793 no one foresaw developments. At no time, and certainly not then, was there any marked policy of ' married men not eligible ' nor even of ' unmarried men preferred '. But the question of the position of entrants into the force who were married quickly proved a difficulty ; and there were not wanting those who were ready to work up a grievance. The debates are unfortunately inadequately recorded and the lament recently expressed that little is known ' about the physical conditions under which our [i.e. in Ireland] forefathers lived is justified '.[2] But in the house of lords, and not in the commons, a voice was raised about the absence of provision for the family of militiamen and it was urged that it would be 'impossible for their people to exist, especially in the manufacturing north'.[3] The press also made the point[4] that the only solid objection to the bill was absence of provision for the wives and children of balloted men. Nothing however was put in and parliament separated. What happened on the resumption has been stated in chapter III and some evidence was given of the need for relief—which is however obvious.

In the first families bill, of 1793, the words governing eligibility are 'called out to actual service' and 'ordered to march'. The next act, that of 1795, is slightly more precise: to be entitled to the family allowance a man must be on active service, or, as it is also put, have 'marched out of the county'. This remained the basic condition. But as most of the militia units were during most of their service between 1793 and 1816 out of their counties and on active service the case of the man who was eligible but had not marched out would have been rare.

Another distinction between one militia family and another would be: whether they followed the regiment or did not. For a wife who was drawing the allowance to join the regiment was not in order. The 1793 act says specifically that the allowance is given 'provided she [the wife] does not join the regiment'. The point does not seem to be mentioned again until the 1799 act laid it down specifically that if they did join they were 'for ever after precluded from receiving any allowance under the act'; under this act, as will be seen, the allowances were much less restricted. Of the number of those who followed the regiment some indications are available.

Particulars of the number of women and children who embarked with the units sent to England in 1811 and in 1813 have been given and of the women and children taken by the Wexford and King's county to the Channel Islands in 1799 (chap. 00). These were cross-sea journeys but there is also evidence that in their peregrinations within Ireland* the units were accompanied by large numbers of wives and children. These figures, so far as they go, indicate that the majority of the married militiamen took their wives and children about with them and it would consequently seem that travelling with the militia round Ireland, there might have been, at almost any time in the period 1793-1816, an army of women and children almost as numerous as the militiamen themselves. The largeness of these figures is evidence that those who did not follow the regiment were relatively

*The Armagh militia in July 1809, at Clonmel and Cahir and two other detachment stations had 228 women and 313 children.[5]

few. The proportion of these would be reflected in the sums presented at the spring and summer assizes for 'family money'.

Returns of this expenditure were made to the Irish house of commons in 1799 and to the house of commons in 1803.[6] The earlier years are covered by both returns. The former show sums as having been presented, as we should expect, for militia families at the assizes of most of the counties in the years 1795-8; those of 1804 on the other hand show only a minority of the counties making a presentment and, consequently, some not showing money as presented when the earlier returns had shewn this. After 1795, as will be seen, increased numbers became entitled; in 1797 and 1799 the generous policy was reversed. In so far as figures when given by both returns for any year or assize do not always agree their accuracy is open to some question. The expenditure shewn discloses marked differences: whereas in some cases relatively large sums are reported, in others the expenditure was trifling; Cavan is an instance of the latter and Galway and Tyrone of the former. The same county will at one time be spending heavily and at another lightly on this head. Kilkenny in the two assizes of the year 1800 voted £478 but in the previous and subsequent years £30 and £26 respectively. In some cases it is explained that this was due to decrease in the number of men who were married though, after the act of 1795, the numbers participating might have been expected to be more. The cost per year of a full family's allowance is roughly £10. On this basis the Kerry, which is an extreme case, had in 1795, 1796 and 1797 respectively 130, 184 and 306 eligible families. These would be all non-followers. In connection with these allowances, there are allegations of fraud to which the figures, so far as it is now possible to interpret them, seem to give some support.

The family of a militiaman who was not eligible for any allowance from the county would in most cases 'follow the regiment'. The colonels might try to exercise some control over the numbers following. The remarks of a colonel which suggest wish to do this have been quoted, but how far they could absolutely control the number is not clear; the remarks rather suggest that restriction could be exercised only by personal influence and that, if that was not effectual, there was no option for the colonel but to acquiesce in the regiment taking about a very large number. Some considerable time after the force had been embodied, the consent of the colonel to marriage had to be obtained and this created what was in effect a 'married establishment'. Any limitation of the categories which could receive the statutory relief obviously tended to put up the number of those who followed. Private charity so far as it was applied to those not following, would operate to increase the number of these.

The relief provided by the act of 1793 was not available for substitutes; this, though logical, created grievance; the *Freeman's Journal* comments[7] thus:

> The surety of being absent from [their families] but a few months [this is *not* how it worked out] prevents the militiaman's removing his wife and children from their usual place of residence or seeking for them the kind of livelihood usual to the wives and children attached to marching regiments. In this case distress must inevitably follow in many instances to the families of the substituted whose service being voluntary and not compulsory allows him no aid from legal provision. The militia of Dublin in particular is almost completely filled by substitutes, the greater part of whom are manufacturers and heads of little families and who must necessarily be embarrassed by their absence. We understand that the governors, impressed by the representations of these poor fellows, have come to the resolution of instituting a subscription in order to form a relief fund....To this expedient every humane citizen must wish success.

In September 1794 the *Dublin Evening Post* says:

> We have heard of an act of last session to provide for the families of militiamen in certain circumstances. What a bubble must that act be if it be still necessary to recur to the humanity of individuals to rescue the despairing wife and the helpless child of the soldier of his country from famine.

As stated in chapter III the original act does not appear to have extinguished hardship. That subscriptions, of which we hear a good deal, were necessary in order to supplement supports this view. Under the act, on a unit being ordered to march the commandant was to give notice to the parishes and they were, with 8 days, to hold a vestry; if it then appeared that 'any militiaman chosen by lot or any corporal drummer or fifer....shall have left his family less able by means of his absence to support itself',* then a weekly allowance might be ordered for such family. For a wife (whether with or without children) this was 2/- and, for each child born in wedlock under the age of 10 years, 1/-. There was as yet no aggregate maximum. The money was to be raised by a cess or parish rate to be imposed at a vestry and was to be issued weekly by the 'rector, vicar, curate or churchwarden'. Vestry books under the years 1793 and 1794 record the proceedings in connection with this matter; the following is from the parish of Dundalk (9 October 1793):

> The question being proposed whether a cess should be laid on the parish for the support of the wives and children of the men elected into the militia by ballot, and now serving in their corps, the same was rejected by all present except one voice. Resolved that no cess shall be laid on the parish at present for the wives and children of the militia.[8]

Here the claim was, to begin with at all events, not accepted. In the parish of St. Peter, Drogheda, money was raised by a

*This remained the formula of eligibility throughout. The acts provide machinery for testing claims to be 'less able' and safeguards against abuse.

penny rate to provide for six wives and ten children. In 1794 the parish of Enniskillen co. Fermanagh decided that a cess was not to be levied for making provision for wives and children left behind by persons balloted into the Fermanagh militia.[9] In the case of Drogheda the number of those relieved was small; and in the cases of Dundalk and Enniskillen, it may well be that the number was also small and that, in consequence, the parish took the view that the case could be met by private charity.

In 1795 a new act was passed. Though not very long, it was three days in committee. On report some of the amendments made were again amended; and finally on the third reading it was 'amended at the table' and a rider was added. It was then little more than a fortnight since it had been read the second time and committed. It would therefore seem that the early passing of it was regarded as a matter of some urgency, though all the three militia bills of that year were driven through early in the session. There were several differences from the 1793 act:—

i. A maximum allowance of 4/- for wives and children together was introduced.
ii. Outside this maximum, 2/- a week for a mother or father and 1/- for sister or brother when they had been 'entirely or chiefly supported by the militiaman's industry' might be given. (for balloted men only).
iii. The allowances were to be paid by the treasurer of the *county* out of money raised by public cess within the *county*.

But the important and expensive feature of the new act was that it extended eligibility for family allowance to 'privates serving in the militia of this kingdom'; the title was a bill for the 'more *effectual* support of the militiamen's families. It met with some opposition. Both the Speaker and Mr. Stewart supported the inclusion of substitutes as beneficiaries; with them came the large body of what are called in the act of 1797 the 'enlisted families'. It was urged that the extension of benefit would give rise to grievance on the part of the regulars but the commander of the forces did not accept this. Another peer urged—and this probably accounts for the generous extensions of benefits—that it would 'encourage men to enter the militia to which an augmentation was to be made'. Under the general act of 1797 and, more specifically, under the act passed in 1799 to amend the act of 1795, eligibility for the family allowance was again, as in the beginning, restricted to balloted men. In the act of 1795 the only preferential treatment left to the balloted men was eligibility for the new allowance then instituted for fathers, mothers, sisters and brothers.

Though the wide scope of this new act must have tended to restrict the numbers of women following, it was apparently considered too expensive—in the next session two amending bills were brought forward. The first, by a private member, was rejected almost at sight. Then Pelham introduced a bill to amend and explain the 1795 act. This got to the stage of being 'agreed to with amendments' but later there was a decision that 'consideration be deferred to a very distant day'.[10]

The 1797 act, which was a general one, made provision for the families of men then being re-enlisted, and gave them the same allowance as they had been getting before reenlistment; but after the date of the act, apart from the families of the re-enlisted men, the allowances were to be restricted to families of men actually chosen by lot—as already stated. The 1799 act was wholly one to amend that of 1795. Since the passsing of that act, it pointed out, the pay of all sergeants, corporals, drummers* and privates had been considerably increased and this made it unnecessary 'to extend the allowances to the families of militiamen who shall or may after the passing of this act be enlisted to serve in any militia of this kingdom'. Families of men chosen by lot before or after the act were, it seems, left in enjoyment of all they had before this act was passed.

In 1799 returns of militia expenditure were, as stated, called for by the Irish legislature. Whereas the county of Sligo gives a certificate that no money had been paid on account of the militia families during the five years since the act of 1795, Tyrone reports 295 families as recipients and the city of Limerick 130 families. A member of the house of commons, presumably grounding his criticisms upon the returns sent in, obtained an order[11] that the treasurers of the counties Clare, Fermanagh, Galway, Kerry, Mayo, Sligo, Limerick, Waterford and Wexford should attend at the bar of the house; those particular counties showed the biggest expenditure under the families-concession and it was disproportionate in many instances to the numbers of men in the regiment. On this, a member mentioned that the colonel of the Sligo regiment 'had given such bounties to his men as precluded the necessity of their families claiming at all under the bill'.[12] The orders for the attendance of the treasurers were in most cases discharged. There had possibly been some scandals and there may have been, on general grounds, a move for economy; and the reversion to restriction of the privilege of the allowance was probably the result of what was disclosed in the returns.

When the Wexford and King's county were sent to the Channel islands in 1799 no special arrangements appear to have been made. The number of wives and children allowed to go was not restricted, and a great many went. Some must have remained behind in Ireland and these, so far as they were wives of

*Men in these ranks were eligible for the allowance though they had not come in by ballot.

non-balloted men, were presumably provided for either by the officers—they seem to have often put their hands in their pockets—or by county charity of some sort. But when in the year 1801 Cornwallis was promoting the general volunteering movement he sought to make special provision[13] (see chapter X, page 163) for the wives and children of 'those soldiers.... who have so zealously volunteered their services to any part of the United Kingdom'. Any private, as well as noncommissioned officer (and not only those who had been chosen by lot), who left his family 'less able' (the usual formula) was to have the allowances; two justices of the peace could extend them to fathers and mothers, and to brothers and sisters under 10 years of age, provided that they had been entirely or chiefly supported by the militiaman's industry and were part of his family resident with him at the time of his being enlisted to serve in the militia'. It is not clear how these allowances, so far as they were not covered by the act of 1799, could legally have been paid*, but, as the militia did not go then to the United Kingdom, the matter rested there.

At the 'speedy enrolment' of 1803 a new formula appears (43 Geo. iii. chap. 142). In addition to the noncommissioned officers, any man serving or enrolled as a 'balloted man or substitute, hired man, or volunteer respectively', provided he came within the 'less able formula, was to be entitled, from the time of marching out, to allowances. The sum for the wife was however reduced to 1/- and nothing was allowed to fathers etc. The balloted man again kept a preference in two respects: he could have the child's allowance for three of his children whereas others could have it for one only; and he did not, as did the non-balloted man marrying after embodiment, require to have the commanding officer's consent before marrying. Apparently a grievance arose[14] that those chosen by ballot were badly treated under the 1803 arrangements and in 1804 the 2/- allowance was restored for the wives of those who had been chosen by lot before 1 November 1803 and who were then 'actually serving in their own proper person'; the right to draw allowance for wives and children up to 4/- weekly and a conditional (not absolute) right to the allowance for fathers etc. were also restored to them.

The next act, that of 1809, confirms to the wives of balloted men the allowance of 2/- weekly—it had been continued by acts of 1806 and 1807—and similarly of 1/- to the wives of non-balloted men; these allowances were payable whether there were any children or not; if there were children, an allowance might be drawn for two irrespectively of whether the father had been

*The circular to the governors requested them to convene the magistrates of the county and ask them 'to take every step necessary for carrying the said regulations into effect'.

balloted or not and, if there was no wife living, it might be drawn for a maximum of four children. There was an overriding provision that the families of non-balloted men (i.e. of substitutes or volunteers) who had married after the date of being called out into actual service were not to get allowances unless they had been married with the consent of the colonel.

The act of 1811 repealed that of 1809. It provided many safeguards against irregularities ; there was to be a formal declaration signed by the applicant with a certificate by the commanding officer ; these had to be countersigned by the adjutant. A justice of the peace had independently to enquire into the circumstances of the family and to endorse the declaration and certificate ; he was also to review the grants every three months, making fresh enquiry into the circumstances. The consent of the colonel was made a condition of eligibility in the cases of balloted men. The non-balloted men enrolled after the act were to be ineligible, but any of these who were drawing allowances at the time of the passing of the act could retain them if they had not been married in actual service and after the act of 1803.

All this legislation so often altered emphasizes what is said in chapter XVI about the burden of work arising for the county and the regiment from the militia administrative duties they had to perform. The treasurers and justices of the peace had the definite duty of protecting, or trying to protect, the county purse. In the units the adjutants had the duty of keeping a register alphabetically and by companies of all family tickets issued.[15] By no means all the men in any regiment or battalion would be natives of that county and so between the county and the regiment no doubt there arose many difficult questions. The counties were not, it seems, always prompt with payment. There is a memorial from the married men of the Clare regiment that their wives and families had remained (April 1798) without the 'allowances granted by parliament' since the previous May.[16] In 1810 the Kilmainham papers[17] contain several requests made to headquarters in Dublin for payment of their money. Many no doubt lived far away from the source of payment and, with the changes as regards eligibility, they may often have been confused as to where they were in the matter.

The lot and way of life of the militia wives who did not follow the regiment was not of course different from those of other women in Ireland thrown on general charity or on their own resources ; and there is nothing more to be said about them than has been said. As regards public help the distinction between those who followed and those who did not was rigidly maintained. A standing order[18] says :—

The wives of the noncommissioned officers and privates (who have or may hereafter obtain certificates which entitle them to receive the family allowance) that return to the regiment will be deprived of such certificates and will also be deprived the liberty of coming into barracks and associating with their husbands.

The women who, with their children, passed their lives with the regiment are much more distinct, as a social category, and consequently more interesting. This being so, it is a pity that more information is not available about them. For knowledge of their mode of life, as of other sections of the 'people' at the end of the xviiith century, we have to search far, and find little. Contemporary generalisations are scanty; for generalisations to be made now the materials in existence are also limited. This part of the militia community deserved, and on occasion received, the attention of the Army Medical Board of Ireland. What they have recorded does not afford a very pleasing picture. In some general remarks (February 1800) on women and children with units, made primarily with reference to two English militia units which were in Dublin from July 1798 to December 1799, they have the following criticisms:

Our official experience enables us to state with some confidence that a multitude of women and children attached to any corps produce many formidable inconveniences. They are generally the medium through which contagious diseases are first introduced amongst the soldiery and they invariably preserve the sources of infection, until by repeated irruptious it has exhausted its virulent effects; the filth and unventilated state of a barrack room in which the wives and children of soldiers are lodged can only be conceived by those who have frequently visited such apartments before cleansing day.... The Irish militia have so great a proportion [of women] as absolutely to render barrack cleanliness and ventilation nearly impracticable.[19]

The same body in December 1801 report as follows:—

It will form part of such a plan [i.e. a new army system] to restrain within moderate bounds the number of women and children that shall be permanently attached to our army; independent of the mischief resulting from contagious diseases which have very commonly been introduced amongst the troops through this medium, the most serious inconveniences have heretofore always been felt in disposing of the wives and children of soldiers when their regiments were ordered on foreign service.[20]

What might be expected sometimes to strike the eye in barracks may be gathered from the following standing order:—

No dogs, fowls, baggage or lumber of any kind, belonging either to officers [sic] or men should be kept in or admitted into any of the men's rooms.[21]

The life of the families was thus, according to modern standards, often of the greatest squalor.

The question then arises: why did the women and children follow the regiment in such large numbers? The answer is twofold; partly it was economic. They were frequently left without homes when their men went off and with no status except that of spongers upon charity or mere mendicants. On the other hand there was with the units for some of them a more or less recognized status, though this could hardly have been so for (e.g.) as many as 285 women—the number the King's county took to Jersey in 1799 (see page 147). The Irish militia unit provided, in this no doubt like other marching regiments, all its ' services ' from within. In the sphere of the domestic needs of the militiamen, as was pointed out in one of the debates on the families bill, there was, specifically, need for women. A military periodical of 1812[22] says : ' There is no doubt that a certain number of respectable wives of soldiers are very necessary in a regiment '. We find these in militia records spoken of as the ' barrack women '; as ' boiling the victuals ' and as employed as ' mess women or cook '. In one case it is laid down that for this latter work the wives of privates were to have the preference and any wives of sergeants or corporals so employed were to be ' discharged '. This seems to imply that payment was made for the performance of the cooking duty the receipt of which by the wives was of less importance to the non-commissioned officers with their higher pay. The following extract from a set of standing orders[23] makes the position clear :—

> A woman shall be allowed to each mess, to cook, keep the mess utensils clean, and to wash the linen ; who shall be allowed the same rate of provisions as a man, and fourpence from each, weekly, for his washing.

But there must have been many women amongst the large number following any particular unit who did not earn money for duties performed and these would have been wholly dependent on what their husbands could provide for them out of small pay. An order of 1799 which prohibited women from marching with the troops ' to meet the enemy ' laid down that each woman was to receive, in addition to sixpence a week lodging money [presumably for whole family, i.e. wife and children, of any], fourpence a day ; of this twopence was to be charged against the husband. This points to twopence a day as the proportion of a soldier's pay which was regarded as available for the maintenance of his family under barrack conditions.

How were all these women and children lodged ? Even when the whole unit was together—which, as the reader will know, was not common—it must have been difficult to provide bare roof covering. The quotation given from the Army Medical Board earlier in this chapter shows that even in Dublin the lodging arrangements were promiscuous and of low standard. In the provincial towns and villages conditions were possibly better but, possibly also, worse still. Then there was the case of the detached company and the detachment of even smaller dimensions. It is also not uncommon to hear of the noncommissioned officers being billeted at such distances that they had to walk three or four miles to their parades. The women, or a portion of them, on occasion, went to camp; a Donegal militia record[24] speaks of nine tents assigned 'for the use of the women'. On some of the major occasions, such as e.g. the Bantry march, they were left behind, but this was not always so. The contra-invasion orders issued in the years after 1798 (see page 148) seem to have required that the women and children should not march with the units (i.e. 'to meet the enemy') but in 1798 there were certainly considerable numbers of women with Cornwallis in the west; an order of the end of August says they are to be left with the sick and the heavy baggage at Athlone: but a certain number followed Lake's column even in its four days forced march.

On the ordinary, and so frequent, changes of station the women and children must have undergone considerable hardship. In chapter XIII the statement of captain Giffard and an extract from a commanding officer's disbursements have been quoted (page 206). The latter probably refers to some special expenditure which was necessitated by the movement of a large retinue of women and children. The actual moving must have been complicated by their presence. These marches usually started very early in the morning and sometimes, when the change of quarter was to some distant place, covered several successive days. The total number of cars allowed for a regiment of 8 companies[25] in 1808 was nearly 100 but this number, even if obtainable, did not include provision for the conveyance of the women and children: it is stated to be for the conveyance of baggage and camp equipment. No doubt the women and children traipsed along with 'lifts' of longer or shorter duration; probably the women, as distinct from the children, had to cover long distances actually on their feet; and, though we may pity them, *they* may have thought it child's play, or may not. There is a Sligo militia record that, when they went to England in 1811, they were permitted to take with them their wives and children without restriction and that provisions on the transports, as well as conveyance, were free. The authorities were thus not unmindful of the wives. In 1811 some of those who had gone to England with the units wished to return; in a strange country they may have found things harder for them than in Ireland; and the Irish government[26] ordered a transport to take back those who wished to return and allowed them 10/- each on landing to carry them to their homes. In February 1814 the north Mayo, on their way to Plymouth, marched through London; if their march strength included a large host of their women and children there must have been many spectators in the streets.

Historians of military formations seem seldom to make any reference to soldiers' wives. But this book is the history of a social institution as well as of a military formation and not many probably would espouse the view that it is only the marchings and counter-marchings that matter. Élie Halvéy[27] regrets that Fortescue's history ' too often degenerates into a history of campaigns '. To get a complete picture it is necessary not to regard a military unit as something taken clean out of the civil population. Though perhaps the ' home front ' is something of a modern discovery it has always existed and had influence on the course of events. Even regular formations do not live and fight in entire segregation from the home and family. Certainly a force like the Irish militia did not even nearly approach a condition of monastic isolation. It was still, however much exiled geographically from its counties, within Ireland and remained still almost umbilically attached to the parent ' people ' which gave it birth. The Irish militiaman was mostly married and many childrened and it is impossible not to take account of these ' military encumbrances ' (if the phrase is at any time appropriate). That is the justification for introducing this sketch of what there was behind the parade ground.

XVIII

What then was this force ?

In a recent study of the question of public order[1] in England it is stated that a ' knowledge of the use and organization of the militia, in this period [i.e. early xviiith century], is fundamental to a correct understanding of the problem of order ' and that, in the deficiency of this knowledge ' several problems connected with [the problem of order] cannot as yet be clearly answered Long before the period of this book (i.e. in the xviith century) ' the keeping of public order became more and more the prime task of the militia ' and, it is noted, ' the number of instances in which military help was called for immediately on the outbreak of disorder ' was large. For the prevention of minor breaches the officer responsible was the constable—an office filled ' by a combination of election and rotation and wholly unpaid '. But when things went beyond minor breaches, the magistrates had no effective instrument at hand upon which they could rely. It is therefore not surprising to hear of ' the importance which . . . . was attached to the militia by contemporary statesmen '.

The army, both officers and men, regarded employment in suppressing riots with disgust, and the tendency was for them to be less and less used for this purpose. By the last decade of the xviiith century the militia, which had in the main taken over the repressive duties, came to be considered of less value and reliability for the work owing to ' their closer contact with the populace '. But the dislike of repressive duty ' was not shared by the yeomanry, and for this reason authority came to regard them as a substitute which it could use without restraint or misgivings '. They had been created in 1794. They were ' almost exclusively the product of the land and the landowning classes. They could be quickly summoned to any centre of disturbance in the provinces and their response to the call of the landlord and parson magistrate of the period was both eager and enthusiastic '.[2] Lord Fitzwilliam, on his arrival in Ireland, was very anxious, as we have seen, to have such a force. He no doubt brought with him experience of the role of such a body of men in the maintenance of public order. For this was a serious question in the xviiith century, not only in Ireland, conventionally perhaps regarded as the land of Donnybrook, but equally in England. Benjamin Franklin, in 1769, has some comments which are relevant to this :

Do you Englishmen then pretend to censure the colonies for riots ? I have seen within a year riots in this country [England] about corn ; riots about elections ; riots about workhouses ; riots of colliers ; riots of weavers ; riots of coalheavers ; riots of sawyers ; riots of sailors ; riots of Wilkites ; riots of government chairmen ; riots of smugglers, in which customs house officers and excisemen have been murdered, the king's armed vessels and troops fired at etc.....Here indeed one would think riots part of the mode of government[3].

Then again there were the turnpike riots ' most extensive between 1735 and 1750 ' and spoken of as ' among the most widespread and turbulent manifestations of popular discontent in the xviiith century '.[4] Does one hear some Irishman saying : ' do you English then pretend to censure Ireland for riots ?'

This was the English background and course of development. By the time (1793) when an Irish militia was created, or recreated, the Volunteers were no longer, according to Grattan and others, the active (though amateur) guardians of public order that they had been—or rather they held, and acted upon, their own views of what was contrary to it. The duty of maintaining this, when matters went, as they often did, beyond minor disturbances, was therefore at that time neither being carried out, nor, as the Volunteers were anyhow a self-constituted body, was it regularly and officially provided for at all. Whatever therefore the parish constables could not cope with—and they could cope with little—passed naturally within the sphere of the militia and it is correct to say that, in the post-union period at all events, apart from acting as ' a school where professional soldiers [subalterns and privates] were trained for service in the line '[5] its functions had become, very largely, solely that of police. Not that, from the beginning, there had not been abundance of police work. Some remarks relevant to this have been quoted earlier. When the English militia came to Ireland in 1798 they were amused that an escort of soldiers seemed to be needed in Ireland merely for taking a pickpocket to a county goal. An English member of parliament who made a critical tour round Ireland in 1813 has the following remarks :—

' In England the execution of the law is committed to the hands of the people ; here, the authority of the police is vested in the military ; for, so impotent is the civil power that the warrants of the magistrates are executed by the soldiers '.[6]

He refers also to the desirability of the government ' devising means of rescuing the law (except in extreme cases) from military execution ' and, in another place, to ' the increasing presence of a military force. Scarcely a village is entered without a detachment being obtruded on the traveller' and of forces being 'spread over the face of a nation, for the purpose of executing the laws, or of protecting or enforcing the payment of revenues'.

Repelling invasion is obviously a purely military duty and invasion, for Ireland in 1796 and 1798, had been a reality; and it seemed more or less, though gradually less, near being so on later occasions. Of this the training and preparation had to take account for a long time after those years. The organization and equipment of the force were of course at all times on military lines. On the other hand it is to be noted that it was rarely *used* in the regiment or battalion formation. Did they ever form up for action in a thin red line? The answer is that they were almost always used in detachments (garrisonally, or in actual exercise of force) or as individuals. Even for the parades and reviews, so dear and essential to the xviiith century military mind, there were many difficulties in getting them together as whole regiments or battalions; militia officers are often found lamenting the infrequency of the 'entire' of the regiment being together. The service in England no doubt involved concentration of the units and in 1813 sending them to the continent as *wholes* was statutorily adopted (see page 235). But the active duties performed by the Irish militia (and also probably by the English and Scotch) were preponderatingly in the civil sphere. This 'comparative military insignificance' of the militia is probably the reason for its neglect by historians of the army.

When it came however to active contra-insurrection duty, the military and police functions were both exhibited. This was super-police work and a little more; and of the force as engaged in it 'the more police, the less military they' is perhaps a correct description. The success that they had in this work (admitted contemporaneously; in post-Union reflection after the turmoils and by competent modern historians such as Lecky) seems to have amounted to this: that, so far as they had been 'regularized' (i.e. veneered over more or less thickly with xviiith century military *discipline*), they were able to deregularize themselves. They in fact, quickly and as if, some might say, to the manner born, went through the same sort of adaption process as the British regular army in the later stages of the Boer war. In passing, it may be remarked that that war and the Irish rebellion were both much more than wars; they were tragedies in the lives of two peoples of which the human interest far surpassed the military interest. This adaptation seems to be what the British army had only partially been able to achieve in the American war.[7] That war had not been a case of putting down all the disorder 'with four regiments', as general Gage confidently advised[8]. It is described as a war in which the Americans converted themselves 'from an army into individuals; all our superiority of discipline and knowledge of arms was immediately lost and the battle came to be determined by man to man'.[9]

Ireland, in the insurrection part of 1798, was left almost entirely to the non-regular forces at its disposal. It seems possible that with a bigger regular force the actual result of the fighting would have been no better and might have been worse. Camden saw[10] that cavalry 'cannot charge a line armed with pikes'. The technique and possibilities of pike warfare had been carefully thought out by the United Irishmen. A paper[11] found in the writing box of lord Edward Fitzgerald says:

however well exercised standing armies are supposed to be, by frequent reviews and sham battles, they are never prepared for broken roads or enclosed fields, in a country like ours covered with innumerable and continued intersections of ditches and hedges, everyone of which are an advantage to an irregular body and may with advantage be disputed against an army as so many fortifications and entrenchments....The apparent strength of the army should not intimidate, as closing in on it makes its powder and ball useless, all its superiority is in fighting at a distance, all its skill ceased and all its action must be suspended when it once is within reach of the pike.

What is anticipated in these quotations seems to have happened. A Dublin castle official writes (30 May 1798):

We have sometimes done wrong in charging the pike-men with our cavalry....In the first attack on Rathangar....we lost 20 men killed and wounded of the 7th Dragoons....You need not mention this disaster. We did not make any bulletin of it.[12]

Those in command of the anti-insurrection forces do not seem to have occupied the time which they had for preparation in thinking out what *they* were going to have to face, notwithstanding what should have been the lesson of the American war. Bishop Percy, who was in touch with government opinion, remarks (30 July 1798):

It is very certain that some of them [i.e. the generals] have not shone in their conflicts with poor undisciplined rebels.[13]

So far as there is a generally held view and formed historical judgment of the Irish militia in an active military capacity and as a national institution, it would seem largely to rest on what they did, did not, or are now thought to have done, in 1798. For the formation of this judgment the authority who had most influence is Cornwallis. It is on him, for example, that Lecky relies and Lecky is the principal historian writing impartially about Ireland in the xviiith century. The prepossessions, political and military, with which Cornwallis may be considered to have assumed office in Ireland have, to some extent, been already suggested (chapter IX). But one aspect of his earlier experiences which is relevant has not been mentioned. He had in the American war found himself, an exponent of European tactics, confronted with practitioners of irregular warfare. To this he had with difficulty accommodated himself; it was probably psychologically impossible for him to do so. He had, it seems likely, come away from America with a profound distaste for irregular gadfly warfare and with at least an 'imperfect sympathy' for its exponents. A contemporary criticism is that, as a result of the American war, he posessed 'in a peculiar degree' the qualities of 'a peculiar caution and tardiness', and it is said that 'in his operations against the rebels in Ireland and to repel a ridiculous invasion, he conducted himself with as much deliberation, and with as slow a detail, as if Bonaparte had invaded this kingdom in person at the head of 100,000 men'.[14]

This was the man who, never having been in Ireland since his subaltern days, found himself, with all his admittedly great qualities of character, in front of the problems left by Camden. Lecky admits that 'his judgment of [the state of feeling and society that he found] in some respects was not altogether just. Arriving at a time when the rebellion had received its death blow, he certainly underrated the efficiency of the yeomanry and the militia who, in spite of their great want of discipline, had virtually saved the country, and had shewn in these last weeks qualities of courage, vigilance and energy which Camden and Castlereagh abundantly recognized'.[15] No one passed more severe strictures on the Irish militia than did Cornwallis.[16] The word 'licentious' is in this connection employed by him. It seems to connote to some extent at all events 'atrocities' and 'methods of barbarism'. Relevant to this is a remark of the duke of Leinster in 1796: 'with regard to the militia, I entertain the same opinion that I do of all the troops in the world, viz. that their conduct will depend upon the discipline established by the generals and commanding officers'.[17] So far as 'licentiousness' indicates that they were, in the dictionary interpretation of 'licentious', 'unrestrained by strict rules of correctness', this might have been so. But for those finding themselves up against irregular and guerilla warfare 'discipline' may easily be in the nature of a fetish. Anyhow it is perhaps fair to enquire: were other armies, and regular ones at that, much different? Of the French army of that period it was stated in 1804 that they were of all armies the most licentious; provided that orders were obeyed in the field, French generals never concerned themselves about what went on in quarters; and Wellesley, writing in June 1809 to Castlereagh from Spain about the serious state of discipline of his army, says: 'we are an excellent army on parade, an excellent one to fight; we are bad in quarters, when campaigning'.[18] The charge of licentiousness against the Irish militia should, it seems, naturally be estimated by the standards set by the regular forces of the time.

Had the Irish militia been in fact and practice raised by direct county effort, it might have retained more completely, instead of progressively losing, the character of a non-professional army. Élie Halévy, speaking of the English militia, says : 'we can hardly call a militia of paid substitutes in any true sense a militia. A force of this kind, so far as the common soldiers were concerned, was a professional army '.[19] If this is true of a militia of 'substitutes ', it is equally, if not more, true of a militia of volunteers or enlisted men. The Irish militia was in 1803 recreated, almost entirely, by the enrolment of volunteers directly by the colonels. In 1807-8 and again in 1809-10 there was reversion to the ballot, but the force cannot in the main be considered to have been much other than a professional army—of limited functions however. If as a result of circumstances the men in the ranks lost the non-professional character, the officer rank also, as the war became prolonged, underwent similar transformation. In 1798 Wilberforce[20] can speak of 'the circumstance which rendered our militia [i.e. the English] so dear to us, as a constitutional force ' and then mentions that it was 'officered by country gentlemen, men of property, of family, of domestic connections, of personal influence '. In 1805 a member of parliament expressed the view that 'the constitutional principle of the militia rested almost entirely on its being officered by men of property ; and he therefore highly disapproved of giving commissions in the militia to unqualified [i.e. without a property qualification]) persons.... He thought half-pay officers ought to get commissions in the line '.[21] The fact is that, with the coming of the industrial revolution, 'the traditional grades of rural society were blurred, indeed destroyed '.[22]

The course of social development was not exactly the same in Ireland; the following from the *Freeman's Journal*[23] in 1814 is probably correct :

> It is well known that, with the exception of the colonels only, the commissioned officers of the militia regiments are no longer men of rank and fortune. The change of quarters [i.e. the constant changing], the fatigues of regular duty, and the necessity of quitting home, made it necessary for them to quit ; but their situations have unquestionably been filled of late more usefully to the country, for they have been taken by young men who have made the service a profession. But these young men have no fortunes now to which they can retire.

The paper then goes on to refer to representations which have been made to the various lord lieutenants on this. It seems probable, in view of this social change, that, in the later stages at any rate, the property qualifications for officers cannot have been insisted upon but nevertheless they continued to be a requirement under the statute (see 49 Geo. iii. chap. 120) which was never modified. But, in spite of this growing professionalization, few, if any, officers of the militia—it is almost safe to say—were ever, except perhaps in very few cases, non-regimentally employed in the higher direction. It has often been argued that the ethos of the auxiliary forces has not been really understood amongst those who fill the staff appointments of the army. In the case of the Irish militia the higher direction and control whether at the highest or at the immediate contact level, was, besides being in the hands of regular officers, also in the hands of non-Irish officers. Abercromby writes to general Knox in Ireland in November 1797:[24] ' Ireland is to me a new country, you have got new principles and a species of military force with which I am unacquainted '; and later, and pathetically,[25] ' the affairs of this kingdom are of so complicated a nature and so much beyond my sphere that I cannot venture to form any opinion on them '. No doubt the ' imperfect sympathy ' between commander and commanded was greatest in the case of Abercromby. Between battalions and regiments with a purely Irish personnel and the purely English (or Scotch) higher command, the high social and political position which the colonels possessed was a factor calculated to cause difficulty. As already stated, they did not always suffer generals gladly; they were prone to behave challengingly to lord lieutenants; some were what Cornwallis calls ' opposition colonels '.[26] He has harsh things to say about the colonels.[27] He was only too aware that he had to persuade and not simply order, even though he had the double power of lord lieutenant and commander of the forces. He naturally did not like this inhibition nor a military force so constituted that he was in fact so much inhibited. Camden had written[28] on ' how much temper and caution is to be used in the management of a militia army ' and Cornwallis himself recognized[29] that ' the same sense of subordination and an equal zeal and energy cannot be expected from the officers in general of troops of this description as may naturally be looked for amongst those who have chosen the army as their profession '.

But he was perhaps not always ready to make the necessary allowances for what were, in his eyes, even after his experiences of irregular warfare in America, their military defects. The truest word on this matter is perhaps that of a civilian observer who remarks,[30] with reference to the Irish militia in England, that : ' they are commanded by their own county officers who understand their nature and can better manage them than Englishmen can possibly do. Irish nature requires a vigorous but a flowing rein. English system, which is well adapted to English nature, only makes it [i.e. Irish nature] restive and violent and, while it provokes its mettle, does not increase its speed'. Throughout, the Irish militia was a lump of Irish life being pressed into an English mould. This has to be remembered but scarcely ever is. Psychologically it meant something. Regular generals naturally liked troops that were regular. But the Irish militia, though conscientiously aspiring all the time to conform to regular standards, were congenitally irregular. It was as exponents of irregular warfare that they were *à priori* likely to shine, and did shine. The most successful contact between the force and an English general seems to have been that between general Scott and the light infantry of which, by his understanding and insight, he made what all accounts represent as a fine military body. Possibly the general who found the least use for the militia was general Knox who, during his command in the north in the difficult year 1797, would have liked to sack the lot (see page 109).

The question naturally arises: how far was the Irish militia a militia? This of course raises the prior question: what is a militia? It was called a 'constitutional force' by which is meant that, in conception at all events, it was the citizen army of an anti-militarist nation. The English, and the Irish, were both anti-militarist. The continuing 'keen discontent, widespread complaints, even the beginnings of revolt'[31] which followed Pitt's militia act of 1757 are indication of something deeper seated than a mere innate xviiith century propensity to riot, especially over something new like turnpikes etc. Even as late as 1796 there was a riot at Bakewell in co. Derby about the militia balloting.[32] These were anti-militarist demonstrations. The militia, 'an army composed of propertied men with a personal stake in the preservation of public liberty and enlisted only for a very short period' was 'the army of the nation in opposition to the standing army, the army of the king'. The appointment of the officers by the lord lieutenants—in this fencibles differed from militia (see page 92)—continued throughout. But, as regards Ireland, all this theory has not perhaps the same relevance; and, more and more, amenability to, and actual selection of the men by, ballot came to be stated and currently regarded as the essential feature of militia.[33] In the debate of 1803, raising the force by bounty was described by Windham (who was 'unfriendly to the [militia] system adopted in England, still more to that adopted in Scotland, but to that of Ireland unfriendly in the highest degree')[34] as a 'total subversion of the whole constitutional principle of the militia'. Some of those who asserted this were in fact not on any grounds in favour of a militia force. But this would not be true of Castlereagh who admitted that 'balloting was undoubtedly the constitutional mode of providing the militia'.[35] There were of course other features which characterized a militia viz. the purposes for which it could be used, the geographical limits (' indisposability ') within which it could operate and the duration of the service of those serving in it.* According to Windham, it was then (1803) ' neither a militia nor a regular army but partaking of all the ill qualities without embracing any of the virtues of either '; and it is the case that, with the progress of the war under the pressing need for troops, the features peculiar to militia tended to get dropped. But they did not entirely disappear and, as one of these, disembodiment duly supervened on the three successive terminations of the war in 1802, 1814 and 1816.

There was at the beginning suggestion that a militia was not suitable to Ireland. As the ' very organization of the militia [i.e. landed proprietors leading their tenants and all that] presupposed an agricultural nation '[36], it might have been thought that it was *peculiarly* suitable to Ireland, not only in 1793 but throughout the period, in all of which the Industrial Revolution had scarcely touched that country. The Speaker Mr. Foster thought that it was suitable and did not budge from that opinion. Lord Downshire always resisted any change which implied the contrary. The act of 1795, with its recognition of recruiting from a regimental stock-purse, produced from him the comment : ' I find by the late act that my militia is to become part of a standing army and that I am to raise men to complete my regiment by beat of drum—a thing I do not like nor know well how to set about '[37]. A correspondent of Pelham, writing in 1798, says frankly : ' the militia system is not fit for Ireland—for a thousand reasons which must strike you but principally on account of the badness of its officers who are appointed by the colonels solely for the purpose of making an electioneering interest '; and he continues : ' I cannot help lamenting that you did not follow up your plan of making fencible regiments of them '.[38] Nothing is known of this plan but others had the idea and it was talked of from time to time. In 1797, though there was some popular dislike of fencibles, there was some support for conversion to fencibles. There seems however no reason for supposing that, with fencibles instead of militia, a different and better corps of officers would have been available. There are the same official complaints of absence from duty of the fencible officers in Ireland as there are in the case of militia officers, though the justification was less as the fencible officers had not county duties to attend to nor wives and children in peril, as those of militia officers often were, through

*In the American war the states had continual difficulties owing to the insistence of the men of the militias on returning to their homes at the end of their period of service.

civil disturbance. Some of the fencible units in Ireland, like other troops, got a reputation for 'licentiousness'. The opinion of the adjutant-general in Ireland in 1805, on the class of the officers sent to the line from the Irish militia has been quoted (page 189) and it is favourable. What was wrong with the officers of these two forces was not peculiar to them; it is said by Halévy that 'the average English officer possessed no more knowledge than that which he had managed to pick up at a preparatory school between the ages of ten and fifteen'; they were all alike too little professionally minded. 'The English officer was a man of fashion, who regarded war as a sport, not a science'.[39]

Though the disuse of the ballot removed the recruiting of the militia to a large extent out of county hands, the position of the force was very far from becoming as entirely non-county and non-regionally connected as would have been a fencible force; the main features of such a force are enumerated on page 92. Through the county provenance of the officers and also of the men (however limited balloting and however extensive recruiting outside county limits), the units still had a specifically county basis. The counties, if they produced actual men as a result of ballot, had no expense but, if they did not, a financial obligation arose. The presentments for militia recruiting purposes came twice a year before the county at the assizes and were of course subject of discussion (see e.g. page 104 for one of the few records of such discussion). It is perhaps not realized how much money in the aggregate the counties must have produced, for the wives and families, and also especially for recruiting. The former was the equivalent of a poor law obligation but, as shewn in the preceding chapter, it was a charge which did not arise, in Ireland, in respect of others than the dependants of militiamen. Of the charges incurred by the counties for recruiting the militia it is possible to give some illustration. In 1795 co. Clare paid £1,220 for the augmentation of the militia; co. Donegal £1,110; the county of Dublin, between May and November £1,112; co. Limerick £1,920; co. Louth, in March to December, £449; and Westmeath £527. In some cases the sums are smaller than these and in others there is no payment. Again in 1797 the re-enlistment (see page 105) caused the counties great expense: co. Antrim £1,137; co. Londonderry £539; and Tipperary £1,140. Over the period from 1797 to 1802 we find co. Tipperary bearing the following charges:—1797 (summer) £1,465; 1798 (spring) £1,049; (summer £1,455; 1799 (summer) £805; 1800 (spring) £630; 1801 (spring) £495; 1802 (spring) £800.[40]

Sometimes the militia could not get the money properly due from the county. The military authorities in such case, if appealed to, referred the regiments to their county authorities for redress, but, when the Wexford were in Guernsey, they made a representation through the general there and the Home Office to the lord lieutenant that 'since the formation in 1793' [they had] never received any assistance from the county: 'marching guineas' (£515 5s. 0d.) for 453 were due. On the authority of the lord lieutenant these were paid, many months later.[41]

The militia was obviously an issue in local or county politics, but it was never in any sense a *political* or even politically-minded force in the way that its predecessor, the Volunteers, had been. The same could not perhaps with equal correctness be said of the yeomanry; the circumstances in which it originated would account for some difference and the definitely class line that it seems to have taken in 1798 is evidence of different impulse. The militia never had the unity of momentum that the Volunteers had. Though a territorially raised force, it was by policy not quartered territorially (as shewn above) and, being kept on the move more or less perpetually, and often, to the extent found possible, segregated from the general population, it was probably outside any definitely political local movements. Lord Blayney[42] speaking in 1797 said that 'the militia are all politicians [and] consequently bad soldiers'. But it is not likely that the number who were really politically conscious was ever, even at the time lord Blayney made his remark and still less at any other time, very large. When the rebellion came in 1798 they seem, with little exception, simply to have done, or attempted to do, their soldierly duty. There was no question of their being pronouncedly *for*, if not of their being specifically *against*, the insurrectionary movement; they were simply for their employers—which most persons regard as the correct attitude for soldiers. A commanding officer said as early as 1793: 'if they are ever tried the difficulty will be to restrain them'.[43] On the one hand they showed, as would have been expected of Irishmen, on many occasions *élan* and even perhaps *trop de zêle*; but on the other it seems the fact that, when the acutely difficult trial came, they remained subordinate to their officers who were able—and this must be recorded to their credit—to hold the men steady; and there was never any question (unless, as their critics have held, at Castlebar) of the instrument, admittedly not of the highest tempered steel, bending or breaking in the hand—as the United Irishmen on the one hand hoped and as their English commanders and their political superiors on the other dreaded.

In this book the militia of Ireland has been treated mainly from an Irish point of view and as a national force, (p 147) without much impact, direct at all events, on the great drama being enacted in Europe during the period. A hundred years earlier Jacobite emigration from Ireland had given to foreign armies great commanders; and it is estimated[44] that between 1691 and 1791 no less than 480,000 Irishmen took service under the French flag. Such military effort as Ireland put into the European fighting of the Napoleonic wars was through participation in the military undertakings of the British armies. Some figures showing the extent of this in the case of Abercromby's force in Egypt have been given (chapter X). In an article on *Irish levies in the great French war*[45] Dr. Chart says that 'for the first time for several generations Irish soldiers were seen in large numbers fighting in the British ranks. From 1793 to 1815 probably at least 150,000 Irish recruits passed through the army. How well they fought let Badajoz, Barrosa, Wellington attest.' From returns extant in 1917 'he found that between September 1806 and January 1813, 88,409 recruits were sent to the Line, most of whom eventually found their way to the Peninsula'. He mentions that 'in 1808 the 85th Connaught Rangers received no fewer than 511 men from this source (Irish militia) alone; in 1809, 278, and in 1810, 299'.

Of the Irish militia as a source of recruits for the Regular Army during the Revolutionary and Napoleonic wars[46] Oman states: 'Nothing, for example, was more usual than to find such things as 100 of the King's County militia joining the 31st or Huntingdonshire Regiment. When the 77th or East Middlesex regiment returned from India in 1808, it was completed, before going out to the Peninsula, from the 1st West York, north and south Mayo, Northampton, and south Lincoln militia.....The '1st or Loyal Lincoln was filled up in 1808, before sailing for Portugal, from the Dublin, King's County, south Devon, and Montgomery militia. Instances might be multiplied *ad nauseam*. It was quite exceptional for any English corps to contain a preponderance of men from its own nominal district, and nearly all of them had from a fifth to a fourth of Irish.

It is impossible to exaggerate the advantage to the Peninsular Army of the system, the invention of Castlereagh when War Minister, which enabled it to draw in such a heavy proportion on the militia for recruits. The men thus obtained had all had at least twelve months' drill and discipline, in a corps which had been under arms for many years:....'

So says Oman. I cannot claim to have seen the nominal rolls nor to have read all the military memoirs of the period, but my impression, for what it is worth, is that his estimate is if anything on the conservative side. To give an example, sergeant William Lawrence of the 40th or 2nd Somerset Regiment says[47] of this period that not merely the 27th or Inniskilling Regiment but his own battalion were mostly Irish, and a number of the rank and file who appear in his anecdotes bear Irish names or are stated to have been Irishmen. There were after all inducements to volunteer into the Line. Bounties were high and home service in wartime unattractive. Militia colonels were less un-co-operative than they had been in the earlier days. 'The militia would be drawn up in line, and the officers of the regiments requiring volunteers would give a glowing description of their several corps, describing the victories they had gained, and the honours they had acquired, and conclude by offering the bounty. If these inducements were not effectual in getting men, coercive methods were adopted: the militia colonel would put on heavy and long drills and field exercises that were so tedious and oppressive that many men would embrace the alternative, and volunteer for the regulars'.[48]

HIBERNIA OFFICINA MILITUM.

Bibliography

(Detailed references are given, chapter by chapter, in support of statements under Notes and References. The following is an analysis of the sources available but is not exhaustive).

A. ORIGINAL SOURCES

MANUSCRIPT MATERIAL—IRELAND.

1. *Dublin Castle.*
Fane papers.
State of the country papers, 1790-1795.
Calendar of official papers, 1790-1831.
Rebellion papers.

2. *National Library of Ireland.*
Kilmainham papers. Correspondence and papers of the Commander of the Forces in Ireland from 1780 to 1894; transferred from the Royal Hospital, Kilmainham. These are quoted as Kil. papers.

Richmond papers	(MS. No. 58-75)
Melville papers	(MS. No. 54-55b)
Buckingham correspondence	(MS. No. J, 39-40)
Lake papers	(MS. No. 56)
Papers of Lt. Col. Brown	(MS. No. 131)
Records of Westmeath militia	(MS. 177 and 178).

3. *Public Record Office of Ireland.*
Notes made at the Four Courts by Dr. D. A. Chart and Mr. Philip Crosslé before 1916.

4. *Public Record Office of Northern Ireland, Belfast.*
Miscellaneous correspondence; and Downshire letters on loan from the Marquis of Downshire.

5. *County Museum Library, Armagh.*
Letter book of Armagh Light Co. as part of the Light Brigade.

6. *Journal of lt. colonel William Blacker* (1777-1855).
Now in possession of Mr. T. G. F. Paterson, curator of the County Museum, Armagh.

7. *Donegal militia papers.*
Left by Lord Clements (afterwards Earl of Leitrim) who was colonel of this unit.

MANUSCRIPT MATERIAL—ENGLAND.

8. *British Museum.*
Pelham, Hardwicke, Percy, Windham, Auckland, Liverpool, Vansittart and Peel papers. Of these the Pelham and the Hardwicke papers must be considered major sources.

9. *Public Record Office, London.*
Chatham and Abbot papers.
H.O./100 series. This, consisting of the official correspondence between Dublin and London, is, over the whole period 1793-1816, one of the major sources.
W.O./68 and other series, various. These constitute a very extensive collection and comprise correspondence books ; regimental records of general and other orders ; records of service ; marching orders ; enrolment books, etc., etc. In them may occasionally be found other records such as *e.g.* colonels' accounts with regimental agents ; attestation forms etc. There is also practically a complete series of muster and pay rolls for every unit of the Irish militia for the whole period 1793-1816. This is the only continuous run of contemporary records of the Irish militia. There is no collection available of the general orders issued by the commander of the Forces. The Army Medical Board issued periodical reports ; these were in M.S. and when available, provide valuable information, statistical and general ; but there is no continuousset of them. In proportion to its extent I have not found these W.O./- papers as useful as the Kilmainham papers.

10. *Letters of Lord Castlereagh to his wife.*
These cover mainly the time of his active service with the Londonderry militia. In possession of Lord Lothian.

11. *War Office, London—Library.*
Special and miscellaneous returns. These mainly manuscript papers are concerned with the period from 1799-1816 and are the principal body of statistical information available (scanty for the earlier period), other than what is available in the H.O./100 series.

12. *Papers in possession of Marquis Camden*, Bayham Abbey.
The extant correspondence of the lord lieutenant is mainly to be found in the Pelham papers (see No. 8) and in the H.O. 100/- series at the P.R.O. London. But in the collection at Bayham some letters not otherwise available were found to be included.

B. PRINTED MATERIAL

1. *Records of Parliament.*
Statutes at large passed in the Parliament held in Ireland, Dublin 1765.
Statutes at large.
Lords Journals, Ireland.
Commons Journals, Ireland.
Lords Journals.
Commons Journals.
A summary of the legislation is contained in appendix XII. These important records do not appear to have been consulted in anything that has

appeared about the Irish militia in print, except in Fortescue's *County Lieutenancies* which however begins from 1803.

2. *The Dublin Gazette.*
3. *Publications of the Historical manuscripts commission of Great Britain.* Dropmore MSS., Charlemont MSS., Lothian MS. Carlisle MSS., Rutland MSS.
4. *Collections of contemporary correspondence* (other than 3).

Correspondence of Marquis Cornwallis. Ed. Charles Ross, 3 vols. London 1859.

Correspondence etc. of Viscount Castlereagh, 2nd marquis of Londonderry. 12 vols. London 1848-53.

Wellington. Civil correspondence and memoranda, Ireland, London, 1860.

Wellington Despatches. 12 vols. London 1834-1838.

Colchester, lord (Charles Abbot). Diary and correspondence of, 3 vol. 1861.

Auckland, lord. Journals and correspondence of. 4 vols. 1860-2.

Beresford, right hon. John. Correspondence illustrative of the last thirty years of the Irish Parliament. London. 2 vols. 1854.

George iii. Letters of. Ed. Bonany Dobree. London, 1935.

Drennan, William. The Drennan letters (1776-1819). Ed. Chart, 1931. Belfast.

Plunket, lord. Life, letters and speeches, by Hon. D. Plunkett. 2 vols. London, 1867.

5. *Contemporary historians ; publicists ; and travellers.*

The Annual Register.

Mullalla, James. A view of Irish affairs....to the close of the parliamentary session of 1795. Dublin, 1795, 2 vols.

Barrington, Sir Jonah :

Historic Memoirs of Ireland. 2 vols. London, 1833.

Personal sketches of his own times. 3 vols. London, 1827-32.

Rise and fall of the Irish nation. 3rd vol. 1832. Paris, 1833.

Plowden, Francis :

Historical Review of the State of Ireland. 3 vols. London, 1803.

History of Ireland from its union with Great Britain to Oct. 1810. 2 vols. Dublin, 1811.

Dupin, Charles. View of the history and actual state of the military force of Great Britain. 1822. 2 vols. London.

Gamble, John. A view of society and manners in the north of Ireland. in 1812-1813. London.

Wakefield, Edward. An account of Ireland, statistical and political. 2 vols. London, 1812.

Smyth, George Lewis. Ireland : historical and statistical. 3 vols. 1844-49.

Curwen, J. C., M.P. Observations....on the state of Ireland principally directed to its agriculture and rural population. 2 vols. London, 1812.

Carr, John. The stranger in Ireland, or a tour in the S. and W. parts of that country in the year 1803. London, 1806.

Hoare, Sir. R. Colt. Journal of a tour in Ireland. A.D. 1806. London, 1807.

6. *Newspapers ; Dublin and provincial.*

These constitute an indispensable source, for parliamentary reports on Irish matters as well as for valuable information on general matters ; for illustrative ' faits divers '; and for purely Irish aspects of events not likely to be given in English newspapers. Under Notes and References will be found a list of the newspapers most frequently quoted from in thisbook ; others are mentioned where referred to in the Notes and References.

7. *Newspaper cutting books.*

British Museum. Fragments cut from newspapers concerning Ireland.
Cambridge University Library—three.
National Library of Ireland—cuttings from *Kilkenny Moderator* (1859).
Articles cut from *Irish Times*, 1898.

8. *Contemporary Magazines* (other than military) e.g.

The Sentimental and Masonic magazine.
Walker's Hibernian magazine.
Antholol gia Hiberdica.
Dublin magazine.

9. *Contemporary military magazines.*

British Military Library or Journal. 2 vols. 1801.
Ansell's Monthly Military Companion. 2 vols. 1801-2. Dublin.
Royal Military Chronicle or British Officers' Monthly Register and Mentor. 13 vols. Dublin, 1811-1817.

10. *Militia Standing Orders.*

Armagh Militia (manuscript). (See appendix V of this book).
21st, or Royal County Limerick militia. Athlone, 1810.
Standing orders to be observed by the 6th or Westmeath Reg. of militia. Dublin, July 1807.
Standing orders of the Clare militia. Ipswich, n.d.
North Down Standing Orders. Drogheda, 1801.
(These four are in the national Library of Ireland).
Standing Orders : Leitrim Regiment. Waterford, 1809.
Standing Orders, D. Company, Cork South militia. Dublin, 1808.
(These two are in Armagh County Museum Library).
Roscommon militia Standing Orders. Limerick, 1801.

11. *Contemporary Pamphlets.*

Consideration on the heads of a militia bill. Dublin, 1776. (L. F. Irwin).
Address to the commons of Ireland on the militia bill brought in March 25, 1778 (L. F. Irwin).
An essay on the use and necessity of establishing a militia in Ireland and some hints towards a plan for that purpose. By a country gentleman. Dublin, 1767.
Considerations on the present state of the military establishment of this Kingdom. Dublin, 1768.
*These are pre-*1793 *pamphlets.*
On the defence of Ireland. Dublin, 1795.
Conduct of the Admiralty in the late expedition of the enemy to the coast of Ireland. London, 1797.
Strictures on the present state of public credit and public security. Francis Burroughs. Dublin 1797.

General Observations on the state of affairs in Ireland and its defence against an invasion. By a country gentleman. Dublin 1797.

Impartial Relation of the military operations which took place in Ireland, in consequence of the landing of a body of French troops under General Humbert in August, 1798. Dublin, printed for J. Milliken. 1799.

Observations on a Pamphlet lately published by an officer entitled "Impartial Relation of the military operations etc. etc....." Dublin, printed for T. Stewart, military stationer. 1799.

An impartial narrative of the most important engagements which took place between his majesty's forces and the rebels during the Irish rebellion. Dublin, 1799. (There were four editions of this and the title is not in all exactly the same). Published by J. Jones.

An account of the late insurrection in Ireland. 4th edition. London, [c. 1799]

A concise account of the material events and atrocities which occurred in the late rebellion, with the causes which produced them. Dublin, 1799.

Proceedings of a general court martial held in Dublin barracks on captain J. Giffard of the Dublin militia. Dublin; printed....for J. Milliken, 1800.

An Irish catholic's advice to his brethren; Denys Scully. 1st edition Dublin 1803.

Five letters to the men of Ulster by a Derry bleacher. 1804 (? Belfast).

12. *Vestry Records.*

An ancient Irish parish—Donaghmore, co. Down. Cowan, 1914.

Vestry records, parish of Aghalow Caledon, co. Tyrone. 1691-1807. Marshall.

Minutes of the Vestry for the parish of Dundalk. In Tempest's Annual, 1936.

(*These records, when available, may be useful for particulars of ballot proceedings, votes of money for women and children, etc; those mentioned are of course only a sample*).

C. SECONDARY AUTHORITIES

1. *Militia regimental histories.*

A Short History of the Royal Longford militia 1793-1893. H. A. Richey, B.L. Dublin, 1894.

An Outline of the history of the county Wicklow Regiment of militia, together with a succession list of the officers of the regiment. E. E. B. Evans. 1855, n.p.

Historical record of the 2nd (now 80th) Royal Tyrone Fusilier regiment of militia from the embodiment in 1793 to the present time. Quartermaster John Cove. Omagh, 1872.

Records of the Monaghan militia. Quartermaster William Watson, 1871. Published in *The Northern Standard*. Monaghan. March-April, 1928.

There were similar compilations for the Waterford militia, 1885; for the Tipperary Clonmel, 1890; and for the S. Cork, 1906.

These regimental histories are, with the exception of that for the Longford militia, almost entirely uncritical and written without any general knowledge of the Irish militia as a whole. There are no doubt some others which I have not seen. After the Crimean war there seems to have been a revival of interest in the Irish militia units and some attempt was made to write up the regimental stories but it was then too late and the accounts written up, apparently at the instance of the War Office, are not well done. I have looked at some of these, at the Public Record Office.

2. *Archaeological journals.*

Louth.

Ulster Journal of Archaeology.

Cork Historical and Archaeological journal.

Waterford.

(These sometimes contain comtemporary material).

Army Historical Research Journal. 1909.

3. *Histories of counties, cities and towns.*

History of co. Longford. James P. Farrell. Dublin, 1891.

History of Sligo, county and town. W. G. Wood-Martin. Dublin, 1882-92.

Limerick ; its history and antiquities. M. Lenihan. Dublin, 1866.

History of the county and city of Limerick. P. Fitzgerald and J. J. McGregor. Dublin, 1827.

(*These sometimes contain contemporary material*).

4. *Other books* (*mainly modern*) *consulted.*

(The following have a London imprint unless otherwise stated).

Gough, viscount, the life of and campaigns of. R. S. Rait. 2 vols. Westminster, 1903.

O'Brien, George. The economic history of Ireland in the eighteenth century. 1918.

The Economic history of Ireland from the Union to the Famine, 1921.

Castlereagh, the political history of : Sir J. A. R. Marriott (1936).

Peel, Sir Robert. C. S. Parker. 3 vols., 1891.

Chart, D. A. The Irish levies during the great French war. English Historical Review, vol. 32, 1917.

A new and enlarged military dictionary. Charles James. 3rd ed. 2 vols. 1806.

Lennox, lady Sarah. Life and letters of 1745-1826. 2 vols. 1901.

Bantry Bay. Ireland in the days of Napoleon and Wolfe Tone. P. Brendan Bradley. 1931.

Curran, J. P., life of. W. H. Curran. 2 vols. 1819.

Grattan, Henry. Memoirs of the life and times of. 5 vols. 1839-46.

Beloff, Max. Public order and popular disturbances, 1660-1714. 1938.

Reith, Charles. The Police Idea ; its history and evolution in England in the xviiith century and after. 1938.

Fortescue, hon. John. A history of the British Army. 13 vols. 1899-1930.

The county lieutenancies and the Army. 1803-1814.

Rogers, Patrick. The Irish volunteers and catholic emancipation. 1778-93. (1934).

Jacob, Rosamund. The rise of the United Irishmen. 1791-4. 1937.

An Old Highland Fencible Corps. (The Reay Fencibles). I. H. Mackay-Scobie. Edinburgh and London. 1914.

The House of Downshire. Its history 1600-1868. H. McCall. (no place). 1881.

Sir Ralph Abercromby, 1793-1801; A memoir. Lord Dunfermline. Edinburgh, 1861.

With the "Thirty Second" in the Penninsula and other campaigns. Harry Ross-Lewin. Edited by John Wardell. Dublin, 1904.

Notes and References

H.O. and W.O. references are to Home Office and War Office papers in the Public Record Office, London.

By the words Down papers ; Bayham papers ; Clements papers ; Blacker papers ; Kil. papers ; Chart Notes ; and Crosslé notes are quoted the sets of papers specified in the Bibliography (p. 291).

B.M.Add.MSS stands for British Museum, Additional MSS ; D.C. for Dublin Castle ; and W.O. Special Returns for a MS volume of War Office Special and Miscellaneous returns (p. 292).

Various Irish newspapers are referred to by the following abbreviations :—

F. J. Freeman's Journal	*D.E.P.* Dublin Evening Post
Hib. Jour. Hibernian Journal	*N.S.* Northern Star
B.N.L. Belfast News Letter	*Mor. Post* Morning Post
Faulk. Faulkner's Journal	*Saund.* Saunder's Journal.

The Cornwallis Correspondence is quoted as *Corn. Corres* ; the Castlereagh Despatches as *Castle. Desp.* ; the Auckland correspondence (published) as *Auck. Corr.* ; the Auckland papers (B.M.Add.MSS) as Auck. papers ; The Ulster Journal of Archaeology as *U.J.A.* ; the Parliamentary Register as *Parl. Reg.* ; the Journals of the House of Commons (U.K. or G.B.) as *Commons jn.* ; the Journals of the House of Commons of Ireland as *Commons jn. Ire* ; the Dictionary of National Biography as *D.N.B.* ; the Historical Manuscripts Commission as *H.M.C.* ; and the Sentimental and Masonic magazine as *Sent. and Mas. Mag.*

Chapter I.

1. There is no critical, or indeed any, study of the history of the principle and practice of militia in the period 1660 to 1793.
2. In 1760 in order to deal with Thourot some militia elements in Ulster turned out.
3. B.M.Add.MSS 33,118. Pelham papers.
4. Copies in Oireachtas and Bodleian libraries.
5. H.M.C. Charlemont i, 279 ; to Charlemont.
6. Pamphlet. *Consideration on the heads of a militia bill.* Addressed to Mr. Ogle. Dublin 1776.
7. *Parl. Reg.* 1785 iv. 234 (and 291 for Ogle's speech in that debate).
8. *Commons jn. Ire.* xviii. 402. **9.** *Parl. Reg.* iv. 285.
10. H.M.C. Lothian ; to earl of Buckingham.
11. H.M.C. Carlisle ; letters of 8 and 16.9.1781.
12. H.M.C. Dropmore vol. i ; to Grenville, 10 May.
14. See no. 3.
14. Patrick Rogers. *The Irish volunteers and Catholic emancipation* 1778-1793. Belfast, 1934, p. 45.
15. H.M.C. Rutland, vol. iii for quotations in this and next paras. generally.
16. *Parl. Reg.* iv ; 229 and foll.
17. H.M.C. Rutland. iii. 182. **18.** *Parl. Reg.* iv. 266.
19. H.M.C. Dropmore, i, p. 249.

20. H.M.C. Charlemont, ii. 19 to Dr. Haliday. **21.** Crosslé notes.
22. Rogers *op. cit.*, p. 197. **23.** H.M.C. Dropmore i, 583.
24. Down papers.
25. DC ; Fane correspondence. 18.11.1792.
26. *DC ; Fane correspondence.* 18.11.1792 to Dundas.
27. *DC ; Fane correspondence* ; letter to attorney general. **28.** See no. 24.
29. *Fane correspondence* ; letter to Dundas of 11.12.1792. **30.** See no. 21.
31. *Fane correspondence* ; letter to Pitt 4.12.1792. **32.** See no. 24.
33. *Dublin Gazette*, 24.12.1792. **34.** See no. 26.
35. Fane correspondence.

Chapter II.

1. Down papers. **2.** F.J. 14.1.1794. **3.** F.J. 28.4.1794.
4. B.N.L. 21.1.1793. **5.** *Parl. Reg.* xiii, 145.
6. *Parl. Reg.* xiii, 391. **7.** See no. 1 ; letter of 15.2.1795.
8. *Sent. and Mas. mag.* April 1794.
9. B.M. ; newspaper cutting book (see Bibliography) ; source not stated.
10. *Commons jn. Ire.* 19.3.1793. **11.** *Hib. Jour.* 25.3.1793.
12. *D.E.P.* 26.3.1793 gives the division list. **13.** See no. 11.
14. See no. 10. **15.** *B.N.L.* 8.3.1793.
16. See chap. i, note 4. **17.** *Parl. Reg.* xiii, 389.
18. *Parl. Reg.* xiii, 387. **19.** H.O. 100/48.
20. *Castle. desp.* viii. 40. **21.** *Parl. Reg.* xiii, 565.
22. Giffard-Sankey court martial ; proceedings printed as pamphlet. Copy in H.O. 100/102.
23. Down papers ; letter dated 9.9.1793. **24.** Clements papers.
25. B.M.Add.MSS. 33, 119. **26.** *Parl. Reg.* xv, 84.
27. *Parl. Reg.* xiii, 145. **28.** See chap. 1, note 6.
29. Quoted by R. S. Rait in *Life of viscount Gough* 1903 i, 7.
30. Down. papers ; letter dated 17.4.1793.
31. *D.E.P.* Jan. 1793.
32. H. Joy. *Historical collections relative to the town of Belfast*, 1837.
33. H.O. 100/43.
34. Rosamund Jacob. *The Rise of the United Irishmen.* 1937, p. 166.
35. Rogers, *op. cit.* p. 311-2.

Chapter III.

Newspaper references are to issues of 1793 unless otherwise indicated.

1. Newspaper cutting book ; Bradshaw collection. Camb. Univ. Library.
2. W.O. 68/221. **3.** *F.J.* 23/. and 27/4. **4.** *N.S.* 1/6. **5.** H.O. 100/40.
6. *F.J.* 18/5. **7.** *Sent. and Mas. mag.* v, 190. **8.** *F.J.* 25/5.
9. *F.J.* 28/5. **10.** *D.E.P.* 30/5. **11.** See no. 1. **12.** *Hib. Jour.* 27/5.
13. *D.E.P.* 25/5. **14.** 29/5. See also *Cork Gazette* 18/5.
15. *Faulk.* 1/6. **16.** *Sent. and Mas. mag.* June 1793. **17.** See no. 1.
18. Charlemont letters. R.I. Academy. **19.** *F.J.* 4/7.
20. *Ennis Chronicle* ; 29/7. **21.** See no. 4. **22.** 9/7.
23. B.M. newscutting book. **24.** *Sent. and Mas. mag.* July 1793.
25. *F.J.* 13/7. **26.** See no. 23. **27.** H.O. 100/39. **28.** See no. 23.
29. *D.E.P.* 31.12. **30.** H.O. 100/40. **31.** See no. 23.
32. *A View of Irish Affairs*, 1795, pp. 199 and 261. **33.** 28/5.
34. H.O. 100/40. **35.** H.O. 100/39.

36. Jacob. *op. cit*, 170. **37.** See no. 35.
38. Cf the Turnpike riots 1735-50 and the riots on introduction of the New Style.
39. *William Pitt*; Basil Williams 1913, i. 405.
40. *Correspondence of duke of Bedford* 1842, ii, 267-70.
41. *Victoria County History*, Surrey, i, 427 and the *Gentleman's Magazine*, xvii, 43.
42. *Annual Register* 1761. **43.** H.O. 50/29.
44. *Annual Register* 1797. Reports of these Scotch riots appeared in the Irish papers. (D.E.P. and Faulk.)
45. Fortescue. *The County Lieutenancies and the Army*, 1909, p. 22.
46. *Faulk*, 25/5. **47.** *D.E.P.* 8/6. **48.** *D.E.P.* 21/5.
49. *N.S.* 8/5. But this is not confirmed by *Gazette* announcements.
50. References in this paragraph to H.O. 100/40 and/41.
51. *Parl. Reg.* xiii, 417.
52. *With the Thirty Second*, as edited by Prof. Wardell. 1904, p. 2; (originally published 1834 as *The Life of a Soldier*).
53. *Faulk*, 29.9.1793. **54.** *F.J.* 7/11.
55. D.C. papers; carton 620/18A. **56**. *Faulk.* 21/5.
57. *Walkers magazine*, June. **58.** *F.J.* 24/10. **59.** See no. 23.
60. *F.J.* 4/7. **61.** *F.J.* 12/9. **62.** *F.J.* 30/8.
63. Quotations in this para from W.O. 68/221. **64.** Clements papers.
65. Fortescue *op. cit.* pp. 42-45. **66.** *New Cork Evening Post*, 9/5.
67. *Ennis Chronicle*. **68.** *New Cork Evening Post*, 6/5. **69.** *Faulk.* 8/6.
70. Down. papers. **71.** Crosslé notes. **72.** *Hib. Jour.* 3/6.
73. *F.J.* 22/8. **74.** References in this para. to *F.J.* (dates in June).
75. *D.E.P.* 1/6. **76.** *Hib. Jour.* 20/10. **77.** *Hib. Jour.* 28/11.
78. *F.J.* 5/12. **79.** *F.J.* 28/11. **80.** *F.J.* 31.12.1793 and 5.1.1794.
81. *D.E.P.* 10.12.1793 and 5.1.1794. **82.** *Cork Gazette* 29/5.
83. *Cork Gazette* 23/6. **84.** *New Cork Evening Post* 16/12.
85. See no. 23. **86.** *N.S.* June 8/12. **87.** *Parl. Reg.* xiii, 443.
88. *Faulk.* 19/7, *F.J.* 10/8, also *D.E.P.* 3/9 and 12.9.1794.
89. *D.E.P.* 14/9. **90.** *F.J.* 18/8. **92.** *D.E.P.* 9/11. **92.** *Faulk.* 9/7.
93. *D.E.P.* 3/10 and 9/11.

Chapter IV.

1. *Parl. Reg.* 1793, xiii, 386. **2.** *Parl. Reg.*, xiii, 399.
3. B.M.Add.MSS. 33, 119 (Pelham).
4. Bayham papers, Leinster to Camden; 6.3.1797. **5.** H.O. 100/47.
6. *Lords' jn.* Ire. 1.3.1794.
7. H.O. 100/50. **8.** H.O. ./49. **9.** H.O. ./47. **10.** H.O. ./53.
11. Quoted in *U.J.A.* xii, Oct. 1906.
12. *Faulk.* 10.8.93. **13.** *Faulk.* 20.8.93.
14. *F.J.* 30.5.93. **15.** *F.J.* 20.4.93. **16.** Blacker papers.
17. Clements papers. **18.** D.C. circular; 23.6.1804.
19. *Hib. Journ.* 31.5.1793. **20.** B.M.Add.MSS, 33, 118.
21. B.M.Add.MSS. 33, 119. **22.** B.M.Add.MSS. 33, 119.
23. B.M.Add.MSS. 33, 113. **24.** See note 55, chap. III.
25. B.M.Add.MSS. 33, 118. **26.** *New Cork Evening Post*, 28.10.1793.
27. D.C. Fane papers. **28.** *D.E.P.*; 26.9.1793. **29.** *F.J.* 2.12.1793.
30. *Hib. Jour.* 14.8.1793. **31.** *D.E.P.* 27.12.1794.
32. *Historical review of the state of Ireland*, ii, part I, 435.

33. *D.E.P.* ; 5.9.1793. **34.** *F.J.* 3.8.1793. **35.** *D.E.P.* 3.12.93.
36. *D.E.P.* 9.7.93. **37.** *D.E.P.* 26.9.93. **38.** *F.J.* 25/5.
39. *Sligo Morning Herald*, 24.5.1793. **40.** H.O. 100/40.
41. *F.J.* 17.9.1793. **42.** *Ennis Chronicle.* **43.** H.O. 100/41.
44. B.M.Add.MSS. 33, 119.
45. Regimental order book, Armagh militia. **46.** Down. papers.
47. See no. 48.
48. e.g. in *Walker's Hibernian magazine.* Sept. 1794.
49. Letters to his wife. **50.** *F.J.* 23.7.1793. **51.** *D.E.P.* 3.10.1793.
52. *F.J.* 10.4.1794. **53.** *Faulk.* **54.** Clements papers.
55. Down papers. **56.** *Ibid.* **57.** *Desp.* viii, 91.
58. General order, 30.4.1801.
59. *D.E.P.* 26.4.1796. **60.** Chart notes. **61.** *Hib. Jour.* 20.8.1794.
62. B.M.Add.MSS. 33, 129. **63.** *F.J.* 4.6.1793.
64. War Office. Special returns. 1799-1816.
65. Down papers. **66.** *Sent. and Mas. mag.*, June 1794.
67. *D.E.P.* 5.11.1793. **68.** *Walker's mag.* Oct. 1793.
69. Charles Lever. *Jack Hinton the Guardsman.*
70. Down papers and Clements papers. **71.** Down papers.
72. *F.J.* 8.8.1793. **73.** Kil. papers, section iii. vol. 78.
74. General order. **75.** General order, 11.6.1795. **76.** W.O. 68/221.
77. Blacker papers. **78.** *Faulk.* 4.6.93.
79. D.C. circular letter, 19.9.1793. **80.** *Sent. and Mas. mag.* Aug. 1794.
81. *F.J.* 19.12.1793. **82.** *D.E.P.* 16.8.1794. **83.** See no. 69.
84. N.S., July 31—3 Aug. **85.** *Parl. Reg.* vol. xv.

Chapter V.

Note.—All references to dates are to dates in 1795 where not otherwise indicated.

1. H.O. 100/56. **2.** *Commons jn. Ire.* xvii (Feb. 1797). *Commons jn.* vol. 58 (1803), 295.
3. *D.E.P.* 27/2. **4.** F.J. 28/2. **5.** *Commons jn. Ire.* vol. xviii.
6. See no. 16. **7.** *D.E.P.* 21/5. **8.** See no. 5.
9. *View of Irish Affairs*, ii. 261. **10.** *B.N.L.* 3/4. **11.** *D.E.P.* 26/3.
12. Kil. papers, sec. 111, vol. 229. **13.** Down. papers. **14.** *F.J.* 5/2.
15. D.C. State of the country papers. **16.** D.C. State of the country papers, 11/4.
17. For Five Mile House affair see *F.J.* 14/4 ; *Faulk.* 6/4 ; and D.C. State of the Country papers.
18. *Sent. and Mas. mag.* April. **19.** State of the Country papers.
20. *Faulk.* 6/4. **21.** *New Cork Evening Post.* **22.** H.O. 100/54.
23. D.C. papers. **24.** *Drennan Letters*, ed. D. A. Chart, 1931, letter 585.
25. B.M.Add.MSS. 33, 105. **26.** *D.E.P.* 17/11. **27.** B.M.Add.MSS. 33, 113.
28. *On the Defence of Ireland.* Dublin 1795. **29.** H.O. 100/54.
30. H.O. 100/54. **31.** *Sent. and Mas. mag.*, June. **32.** *F.J.* 23/6.
33. See no. 31. **34.** See no. 32. **35.** *F.J.* 20/6. **36.** *Morn. Post*, 4/7.
37. *Morn. Post*, 20/7. **38.** *F.J.* 30/6. **39.** *F.J.* 40.
40. John Ferrar, *A View of Dublin*, 1796, 127. **41.** *F.J.* 4/7.
2. *D.E.P.* 6/8. **43.** *F.J.* 23/7. **44.** *Morn. Post*, 5/12.
45. *Hib. Jour.* 14/8. **46.** *Morn. Post.* 23/5. *F.J.* 21/5, *Hib. Jour.* 22/5
47. *Faulk.* 3/1. **48.** *F.J.* 25/7.

49. *The King of the Beggars.* Sean O' Faolain, 1938, 261.
50. B.M.Add.MSS. 33, 101. **51.** D.C. State of the Country papers.
52. B.M.Add.MSS. 33, 129. **53.** See no. 50. **54.** *Mor. Post*, 1/10.
55. *D.E.P.* 5/11. **56.** *D.E.P.* 8/12. **57.** See no. 50.
58. *British Military Journal*, 1801, i, 286-7. **59.** *Hib. Jour.* 24/8.
60. D.C. papers. **61.** *F.J.* 26/11. **62.** B.M.Add.MSS. 33, 119.
63. *Faulk.* 24/9. **64.** *D.E.P.* 16/7. **65.** *D.E.P.* 4/4.

Chapter VI.

1. B.M.Add.MSS. 33, 101, Pelham. **2.** *Ibid.*
3. B.M. Add.MSS. 33, 129. **4.** H.O. 100/60.
5. B.M.Add.MSS. 33, 102. **6.** B.M.Add.MSS. 33, 113.
7. D.C. papers ; letter 25/12/1792. **8.** H.O. 100/61.
9. Down. papers, 7/8. **10.** H.O. 100/54. **11.** Crosslé papers.
12. B.M.Add.MSS., 33, 104. **13.** Blacker papers.
14. Castlereagh ; letters to his wife.
15. B.M.Add.MSS. 35, 774, Hardwicke ; despatch 22.9.1804.
16. See no. 4. **17.** H.O. 100/68. **18.** Down papers.
19. B.M.Add.MSS. 33, 102, Pelham. **20.** B.M.Add.MSS. 33, 113, Pelham.
21. Based mainly on Clements papers. **22.** H.O. 100/62.
23. H.O. 100/62. **24.** See no. 19. **25.** H.O. 100/56. **26.** H.O. ./62.
27. Down letters, 15/2/1795.
28. See no. 19 ; Camden to Pelham 30.8.1796. **29.** H.O. 100/47.
30. *Faulk.* 8/10. **31.** *D.E.P.* 10/9. **32.** Down. letters. **33.** See no. 8. Camden 22/9.
34. *Faulk.* **35.** *Life and letters* ; 1901, ii. 125. **36.** See no. 19.
37. *Hib. Jour.* 2/9. **38.** *Hib. Jour.* 17/8. **39.** See no. 19.
40. H.O. 100/61. **41.** *Ibid.* 10/9. **42.** See no. 19. **43.** See no. 40.
44. *Hib. Jour.* 25/11 ; *Saund.* 24/11. **45.** *F.J.* 20/8 and 24/11.
46. *Hib. Jour.* 24/10. **47.** *Saund.* 24/11.
48. B.M.Add.MSS. 33, 103 ; 9.1.1797. **49.** H.O. 100/61.
50. B.M.Add.MSS. 33, 118. **51.** B.M.Add.MSS. 33, 102 ; *D.E.P.* 29/12.
52. *D.E.P.* 27/12. **53.** See no. 19. **54.** *D.E.P.* 27/12.
55. See no. 14. **56.** See no. 19.
57. George Bennett, *History of Bandon.* 1869, 490. **58.** *Faulk.* 27/12.
59. *Hib. Jour.* 26/12. **60.** Kil. papers. **61.** Down. papers.
62. Blacker papers. **63.** Down. letters.
64. Quoted in *Short History of the Royal Longford Militia*, H. A. Richey, p. 88.
65. *Memoirs of Grattan*, 1839-46, vol. iv, 265. **66.** Down papers.
67. B.M.Add.MSS. 33, 103 ; to Pelham 2.1.1797.
68. B.M.Add.MSS. 33, 119. **69.** *Faulk.* 10.1.97. **70.** *Faulk.* 5.1.97.
71. *Faulk*, 10.1.97. **72.** B.M.Add.MSS. 33, 103.
73. *D.E.P.* 31/12 ; *Faulk*, 5.1.97. **74.** B.M.Add.MSS. 33, 130.
75. B.M.Add.MSS. 33, 129 ; 26/12. **76.** *F.J.* 29/12. **77.** *Faulk*, 17.1.1797
78. *D.E.P.* 29/12 ; *F.J.* 27/12.
79. Pamphlet ; *Conduct of the Admiralty in the late expedition of the enemy to the coast of Ireland.* Lond. 1797.
80. See no. 19.
81. Pamphlet : *An Irish catholic's advice to his brethren* ; Denys Scully ; 1st edition. Dublin, 1803.
82. *Faulk*, 21.1.1797.

Chapter VII.

Note.—All references to date are to dates in 1797 where not otherwise indicated.

1. B.M.Add.MSS. 33, 103, Pelham. **2.** BM.Add.MSS. 33, 103, Pelham.
3. *Commons jn. Ire*, vol. xvii, pt. 1. **4.** *Parl. Reg.*, vol. xvi, 7.3.96.
5. See no. 3. **6.** See no. 3. **7.** Down. papers. **8.** See no. 7.
9. *D.E.P.* 3/2. **10.** See no. 7.
11. Down papers ; Camden to Downshire, 4/2. **12.** *Faulk*, 6/7.
13. *Hib. Jour.* 28/4.
14. *Commons' jn. Ire*, xviii, 1799. **15.** H.O. 100/67 to Portland 30/1.
16. See no. 3. **17.** W.O. 35/13.
18. Kil. papers, sect. ii. vol. 363.
19. Kil. papers, sect. iii. vol. 78. **20.** Act of 1797. **21.** See no. 3.
22. Down. papers ; to lord Downshire 14/1.
23. *F.J.* 7/2 ; BM.Add.MSS. 33, 103 ; Cooke to Pelham 28/1.
24. *Walker's Hib. mag.* Feb. 1797. **25.** *Corn. Cor.* iii. 14.3.1799.
26. *Hib. Jour.* 13/2. **27.** B.M.Add.MSS. 33, 103.
28. See *The Man Wellesley* by Muriel Wellesley 1937, p. 259, and Wellington despatches ix, 575-6.
29. See no. 27. **30.** H.O. 50/30 18.2.1799.
31. H.O. 100/67 ; 30.1.1797 and H.O. 100/94 1.11.1800, both to Portland.
32. BM.Add.MSS. 33, 113. **33.** B.M.Add.MSS. 33, 105.
34. See no. 32. **35.** *Ibid.* **36.** Down papers 31/1.
37. B.M.Add.MSS. 33, 103 ; Carhampton to Pelham 5/2. **38.** Down papers.
39. B.M.Add.MSS. 33, 103 ; Knox to Pelham 19/4 ; Lake to Pelham 1/4.
40. B.M.Add.MSS. 33, 105 ; Knox to Pelham 25/9.
41. B.M.Add.MSS 33, 104 ; Dalrymple to Pelham 25/6.
42. B.M.Add.MSS. 33, 103. **43.** BM.Add.MSS 33, 104 ; Dalrymple to Pelham, 25/4.
44. *Secret Report*, Irish House of Commons. Dublin 1798, 301. App. XXX.
45. *Ibid*, p. 286.
46. See no. 42. **47.** B.M.Add.MSS. 33, 104 25/4. **48.** *Faulk.* 13/5.
49. With scrapbook of newspaper cuttings ; Bradshaw collection, Camb. Univ. Library.
50. The *Courier* (London) 8/6. **51.** *Faulk.* 9/5.
52. See correspondence pubd. in *D.E.P.* 18/4.
53. Kil. papers ; section iii, vol. 238. **54.** B.M.Add.MSS. 33, 104.
55. See no. 50 ; detailed account of the affair.
56. B.M.Add.MSS. 33, 103 ; further letter 1/5 in B.M.Add.MSS. 33, 104.
57. See *D.E.P.* 23/5 for words objected to.
58. H.M.C. Dropmore iii, 3/11. **59.** H.M.C. Dropmore iii. 2/11.
60. B.M.Add.MSS. 33, 105 ; letter to Pelham 3/10. **61.** See no. 62.
62. D.N.B. article ; Luttrell, Henry Lawes.
63. *Hist. Brit. Army*, Fortescue, iv. part I, p. 572.
64. This view was stated emphatically to Camden by the duke of Leinster, 18.8.1796. Bayham papers.
65. H.M.C. Dropmore iv. 266. See also bishop Percy's view in BM.Add.MSS. 32, 335 fol. 71, quoted in chap. XVIII.
66. B.M.Add.MSS. 33, 106 ; fol. 282.
67. See Fortescue's remarks on the behaviour of the regular cavalry at Castlebar. *Hist. Brit. Army*, iv, part 1, p. 593.

68. Quoted in *The Floating Republic* (Mainwaring and Dobree) 1935, p. 100.
69. *Corn. corr.* ii, 335, 30.3.98. **70.** *Corn. corr.* ii, 415.
71. J. Holland Rose, *William Pitt and the Great War*, 1911, p. 354.
72. *Auck. corr.* 1861-2, iii, 397. Lord Clare ; March 1798.
73. Nat. Lib. Ire. Melville papers. Abercromby wrote, 18.2.1798 : " the affairs of this kingdom are of so complicated a nature, and so much beyond my sphere that I cannot venture to form any opinion on them.".

Chapter VIII.

1. Quoted in Fortescue ; *British Army* iv. part i, p. 575. See B.M.Add MSS. 33, 105.
2. Kil. papers. **3.** Down. papers, 12/4.
4. *Auck. corr.* iii, 19/3 ; Cooke to Auckland.
5. *Auck. corr.* iii, 19/3 ; Cooke to Auckland, p. 442.
6. B.M.Add.MSS. 34, 454, Auck. papers. **7.** *Saund.* 2/2.
8. *Faulk*, 1/5. **9.** Figures given in return amongst D.C. papers.
10. *Commons jn. Ire*, vol. xviii, 1799, appendix ccvii. *Commons jn.* vol. 59, 474-495.
11. Armagh mil. regimental records.
12. Nat. Lib. Ire. Lake corres. MS. 56.
13. B.M.Add.MSS. 35,924. **14.** Down papers ; see receipt dated 14/3.
15. J. Holland Rose, *op. cit.*
16. *Commons jn. Ire*, vol. xviii. **17.** B.M.Add.MSS. 34, 454.
18. *Secret Report.* Dublin 1798, app. xxx. p. 320.
19. *Ibid*, p. 311.
20. *The Press* 9.11.97. **21.** *Historic memoirs of Ireland* 1835, p. 267.
22. B.M.Add.MSS. 32, 335. Percy papers, 30/7 .
23. *Ibid.* **24.** *D.E.P.* 5/6. **25.** *Saund.* 28/5.
26. *Saund.* 8/6. **27.** *Faulk.* 12/6. **28.** *Hib. Jour.* 8/6.
29. John Carr. *The Stranger in Ireland.* Lond. 1806, p .409.
30. *U.J.A.* iv, 228-31. **31.** *D.E.P.* 2/6. **32.** Down papers 27/6.
33. *Secret Report*, p. 8. **34.** Plunket ; *Life letters and speeches* (1867) i, 70.
35. *A concise account of the material events and atrocities which occurred in the late rebellion*, Dublin 1799, p. 57.
36. Printed in *Impartial Relation of the military operations* etc. Dublin 1799.
37. See Down papers, letter of 13/9 ; also Auck. papers ; BM.Add.MSS 34, 454. Beresford to Auck. 15/9.
38. Regimental record. **39.** *Corn. corres.* ii, 408.
40. B.M.Add.MSS. 33, 106. Pelham. **41.** H.M.C. Charlemont ii, p. 304.
42. H.M.C. Dropmore iv. 264. **43.** Down. papers.
44. *Auck. corr.* iii. 435. **45.** BM.Add.MSS. 33, 105.
46. B.M.Add.MSS. 34, 454. Auck. papers.
47. *Sermons* by rev. W. B. Kirwan 2nd edit. Lond. 1816.
48. Quoted in Rosebery's Pitt, 1891, p. 210.
49. Nat. Lib. Ire. Lake corres. M.S. 56. **50.** See no. 45.
51. See no. 45. **52.** See no. 45.
53. *Castle. Desp.* i, 219. For reliance of United Irish on disaffection in I.M. see *Secret Report*, p. 311.
54. See no. 45. **55.** See no. 45 ; date probably early in June.
56. *D.E.P.* 5/6.

Chapter IX.

1. Donegal mil. regimental records. P.R.O.
2. *Auck. corr.* iv, 40.
3. See his reference to a " wrongheaded absurd colonel of militia " and his comment that " the brotherhood are numerous "; *Corr.* ii, 334.
4. *Corr.* ii, 416. **5.** *Castle. Desp.* i, 219.
6. W.O. 1/612, to Dundas 1.7.1799.
7. Richey. *op. cit.* The author expressly says (p. vi) " the regimental records, both voluminous and in excellent preservation, form the basis of this work " ; this para is based on this book.
8. *Ibid*, p. 25.
9. Quoted in Richey, p. 35. See also criticism of giving an opportunity for general action in B.M.Add.MSS. 34, 454 fol. 469, Auckland papers.
10 *Corn. corr.* ii. 414.
11. See articles in *Kilkenny Moderator*, 1859 (scrapbook in Nat. Lib. Ire.).
12. See no. 16.
13. *Life and military services of viscount Lake*, 1908, H. W. Pearse, p. 122.
14. Richey, *op. cit.* p. 33. On the conduct of this unit further information in Kil. papers, sec. vi, vol. 430.
15. Barrington. *Historic memoirs of Ireland.* 1835, ii, 279.
16. Richey, p. 33. **17.** H.O. 50/29.
18. Quoted by Richey p. 33. **19.** *Ibid.* **20.** *Faulk*, 28.3.1799.
21. *Castle. Desp.*, 1, 378 and ii. 112.
22. Lord Granard quoted by Richey, p. 33.
23. From review *Times Lit. Sup.* 1.8.1936 of *An outline of Brit. mil. history* by Cole and Priestley.
24. See *Studies in Irish History* ; Litton Falkiner, 1902, p. 284.
25. Richey, p. 30.
26. *Observations on a pamphlet lately published by an officer*, etc. Dublin 1799.
27. *Historic memoirs of Ireland*, ii, 279.
28. *Letters of George iii*, Dobree, 1935, p. 239.
29. The composition of the force is given in the *Impartial Relation.*
30. See no. 11.
31. W. H. Maxwell, *History of the Irish Rebellion in* 1799, 1845, p. 241.
32. Remark attributed to Humbert.
33. *Op. cit.* i, 179, speech, 15.1.1800. See also similar view expressed by Mr. Frederick Falkiner in debate 22.1.1799. (Report printed for James Moore, Dublin, 1799).
34. Vereker was called the " Irish Leonidas " see *F.J.* 27.8.1799.
35. *Corn. corr.* ii, 390. **36.** Given in *Impartial Relation.*
37. Particulars from *An old Highland fencible corps.* History of Reays, 1914. I. H. Mackay Scobie.
38. For effect of Castlebar on Cornwallis see letter quoted in *Nineteenth Century*, July 1916 (article by R. H. Murray). But Lecky attributes this letter to lord Auckland.
39. See *Impartial Relation.*
40. *Faulk*, 15/9..
40. In the History of the Reays, p. 223, it is stated that the 3rd light battalion and the Armagh militia were first brought up because they headed their brigades that day.
42. B.M.Add.MSS. Auck. papers, 34, 454, fol. 485. **43.** Blacker papers.
44. See no. 23.

45. Nat. Lib. Ire. Melville papers, Captain Taylor to col. Brownrigg, 14.9.1798
46. *Castle. Desp.* i, 345.
47. H.M.C. Charlemont MSS. Report 13, app. viii.
48. Down papers 10/9. **49.** *Ibid,* 12/9. **50.** *op. cit.* i, 179.
51. B.M.Add.MSS. 35, 919. Hardwicke fol. 88.
52. Regimental record, W.O. 68/23. **53.** See no. 51. **54.** Down papers.
55. B.M.Add.MSS. 33, 119, report 1.3.1800. **56.** Down papers.
57. Down papers. **58.** Kil. papers.

Chapter X.

1. B.M.Add.MSS. 33, 105, Pelham. **2.** *Ibid.*
3. *Auck. corr.* iv. 17. **4.** See no. 1. **5.** H.O. 100/84. **6.** H.O. 100/83.
7. *Corn. corr.* iii, 79. **8.** *Ibid,* p. 76. **9.** *Ibid,* p. 79.
10. H.O. 100/84, and W.O. 35/14. **11.** B.M.Add.MSS 33,103, Pelham.
12. *Corn. corr.* iii, 111. **13.** *Ibid,* p. 113. **14.** H.O. 100/74.
15. 6.4.99. adj. gen. circular. **16.** Kil. papers, sect. iii, vol. 411.
17. Kil. papers sect. xv., vol. 195, p. 151. **18.** H.O. 100/94, 1.11.1800.
19. Kil. papers, sect. xv., vol. 195, p. 196.
20. B.M.Add.MSS. 35, 924, Hardwicke. **21.** H.O. 100/83.
22. H.O. 100/102. **23.** Circulars D.C. 9 Nov. and 12 Nov. 1799.
24. *Corn. corr.* iii, 79. **25.** *Castle. Desp.*, ii, 405.
26. *Corn. corr.* iii, 130. *Castle. Desp* ii, 402.
27. *Commons jn. Ire,* xix, pt. i. **28.** *Corn. corr.*, iii, 165.
29. *D.E.P.* 23.1.1800. **30.** H.O. 100/93.
31. Report in *F.J.* 21.1.1800. **32.** H.O. 100/90.
33. *Corn. corr.* iii, 178. **34.** *Ibid* p. 202.
35. B.M.Add.MSS. 37, 891, fol. 206-7. **36.** H.O. 100/90.
37. *Ibid*, and B.M.Add.MSS. 37,891.
38. *The 85th King's Light Infantry.* Ed. C. R. B. Barrett, 1913.
39. *Records of 54th Regt.* 1881. **40.** Vane, *Durham Light Infantry,* 1914.
41. B.M.Add.MSS. 35, 774, Hardwicke.
42. Lord Dunfermline. *Sir Ralph Abercromby,* a memoir, 1861, p. 254.
43. Varley. *The Veteran,* i, 103. London 1838, for statement about Netley army and *F.J.* 21.5.1801, for newspaper report.
44. *Cambridge Modern History,* ix, 683.
45. War Office. Special Returns.
46. Reported at length in *Faulk,* 19.2.99, and also in *F.J.* same date.
47. *D.E.P.* 24.5.1800. **48.** Adjt. gen. order 6.9.00.
49. *Faulk,* 6.9.00.
50. Report on light inf. brigade by Brig. Gen. Scott dated 10.6.01 in H.O. 100/103.
51. Blacker papers. **52.** D.C. papers, mil. 1803, carton 522.
53. Kil. papers, section ii, vol. 411, p. 237. **54.** Clements papers.
55. D.C. papers.
56. For this incident see *Castle. Desp.*, iii, 231 and foll.
57. *Proceedings of a general court martial* held in Dublin barracks on captain J. Giffard of the Dublin militia, Dublin, 1800.
58. Reports in *F.J.* 7/3 and *Faulk* 27/1.
59. B.M.Add.MSS. 35, 775. Letter to Charles Yorke, 17.9.1803.
60. *Hist. Brit. Army,* iv, part ii, p. 886. **61.** *Castle. Desp.* iii, 419.
62. *Commons jn.*, vol. 59, 725.
63. H.O. 100/104. **64.** Reports in *D.E.P.* 24 and 28, Feb., 1801.

65. *Faulk*, 31/3 and 2.5.1801. **66.** See no. 33. **67.** W.O. 35/15.
68. See no. 45. **69.** B.M.Add.MSS. 33, 119.
70. *Ibid*, 33,114. **71.** H.O. 100/103, 30.7.1801.
72. H.O. 100/104, 18.9.01. **73.** B.M.Add.MSS. 33, 114, 14.8.01.
74. H.O. 100/102. **75.** Clements papers. **76.** Regimental records.

Chapter XI.

1. B.M.Add.MSS. 35, 773, Hardwicke. **2.** B.M.Add.MSS. 35, 711, fol 193. See also *ibid* 33, 119 Pelham.
3. *Diary and correspondence of lord Colchester*, 1861, i. 299. **4.** See no. 2.
5. See no. 1. **6.** B.M.Add.MSS. 33, 119.
7. B.M.Add.MSS. 33, 114, Pelham. **8.** Clements papers.
9. B.M.Add.MSS. 35, 771, Hardwicke to Pelham 28.1.1802.
10. See no. 1., 24.4.1802.
11. P. Fitzgerald and J. J. McGregor, *History of county and city of Limerick*, Dublin, 1827.
12. Blacker papers. **13.** See no. 8.
14. Commons debate, 16.8.1803 : report in *Faulk*, 22/3.
15. See references to the law officers of the crown from military department in B.M.Add.MSS. 35, 925, fol. 181.
16. See no. 1. **17.** W.O. 17/1127. **18.** B.M.Add.MSS. 35, 924.
19. Clements papers, letter 13.5.1802. **20.** See no. 1. **21.** See no. 18. 5.5.1802.
22. Clements papers ; report 29.5.1802. **23.** See no. 1. **24.** See no. 1.
25. See no. 18, fol. 270. **26.** See no. 18, fol. 270, 5.5.1802.
27. See no. 15. **28.** H.O. 100/109.
29. B.M.Add.MSS. 35, 772 ; to Wickham 5/6.
30. Specific statements to this effect in Clements papers, e.g. " they went off very peaceably and no disorder occurred ".
31. W.O. 68/222. **32.** *Castle. desp.* iv, 23.3.33., and 14.11.02. Wickham to Castlereagh.
34. Circular from Wickham to colonels 24.11.02 ; copy in Clements papers.
35. B.M.Add.MSS. 35, 771. **36.** B.M.Add.MSS. 35, 925, fol. 181.
37. See. no. 34.
38. D.C. circular to colonels ; 28/11. Copy in Clements papers.
39. *Ibid.* **40.** See no. 35. Hardwicke to Pelham 14/11.
41. *Faulk* : 19.5.03. *F.J.* 15/3 and 26.3.03. **42.** B.M.Add.MSS. 35, 773.
43. Blacker papers. **44.** Regimental records. **45.** *F.J.* 5.4.03.
46. *F.J.* 5.4.03, 26/3. **47.** W.O. 35/15.
48. *Commons jn.* 59, 474-95. **49.** *Dublin Gazette*, 17-19 March, 1803.
50. W.O. 17/1128. **51.** H.O. 100/111.
52. B.M.Add.MSS. 35, 777. **53.** *Ibid.*
54. B.M.Add.MSS. 33, 114.
55. *Commons jn.* vol. 59. see also H.O. 100/139, despatch dated 10.8.1807.
56. *Waterford Archaeological society journal*, vol. 17. A Carrick man's diary 1787-1809.
57. W.O. 68/386. **58.** H.O. 100/111.
59. *Faulk*, 22.3.1803. *D.E.P.* same date.
60. B.M.Add.MSS. 35, 925 ; reports of Army medical board 1.7., 1/8 and 1.10.1803.
61. B.M.Add.MSS. 35, 775. **62.** *Commons jn.* vol. 59.

Chapter XII.

1. H.O. 100/111. **2.** Blacker papers. **3.** *Faulk*, 13.7.1803.
4. D.N.B. s. v. Fox, Henry Edward.
5. B.M.Add.MSS. Hardwicke 35, 925. Army medical board report; 1.10.1803.
6. H.O. 100/112. **7.** B.M.Add.MSS. 35, 775, fol. 17.
8. Kil. papers, sect. xv., vol. 79. **9.** *Faulk*, 10.12.1803.
10. H.O. 100/112. **11.** B.M.Add.MSS. 35,775, fol. 8, 15 and 62.
12. B.M.Add.MSS. 35, 775, fol. 8, 15 and 62.
13. B.M.Add.MSS. 35, 775,
14. B.M.Add.MSS. 35, 775, 28.9.1803.
15. Clements papers.
16. B.M.Add.MSS. 35,775; letter to Charles Yorke; 17.9.1803.
17. H.O. 100/111 and ./119. **18.** B.M.Add.MSS. 35, 774.
19. *Ibid.* **20.** Louth offer; B.M.Add.MSS. 35, 774; 5.4.1804.
21. *Commons jn.* vol. 59, 680.
22. John Cove. *Historical record, Tyrone militia*; Omagh 1872, p. 62.
23. B.M.Add.MSS. 35, 772, fol. 17. **24.** *Ibid.*
25. H.O. 100/122. **26.** H.O. 100/120 and 122, 24.3.1804.
27. B.M.Add.MSS. 35, 774; despatch 12.3.1804.
28. H.O. 100/122, 8.3.1804. **29.** B.M.Add.MSS. 35,774, letter 12.3.1804.
30. *Annual Register* 1804, p. 71 note.
31. *Faulk*; which gives long accounts of the parliamentary debates of April 1804.
32. *Annual Register* 1804. **33.** *Hansard.* **34.** as 32, p. 73.
35. *Dublin magazine*; Jan. 1813. **36.** H.O. 100/121.
37. *Faulk*, 26.7.1804. **38.** Clements papers, letter July 1804.
39. *Faulk*, 14/8/1804. **40.** B.M.Add.MSS. 35,778.
41. Clements papers. D.C. circular 23.6.1804. **42.** *Faulk*, 18.8.1804.
43. H.O. 100/92. **44.** Down. papers; for all these details.
45. Down. papers, letter 9.5.98. **46.** Kil. papers, sect. iii. vol. 77.
47. Clements papers. **48.** H.O. 100/120 and B.M.Add.MSS. 35,775.
49. H.O. 100/120 and B.M.Add.MSS. 35, 775.
50. B.M.Add.MSS. 35, 774 Hardwicke, despatch 8.7.1805.
51. *Castle. desp.*, viii; 6.11.1805.
52. H.O. 100/126; instructions issued 2.5.1805.
53. B.M.Add.MSS. 35, 775 and H.O. 100/125; despatch 23.3.1805.
54. W.O. Special returns. **55.** B.M.Add.MSS. 35, 775, despatch 29.5.1805.
56. H.O. 100/31; 16.5.1805.
57. Nat. Lib., Dub. *Buckingham papers* MS. no. 00; report of meeting of deputy lieutenants and militia officers at Thatched House, London.
58. B.M.Add.MSS. 35, 775.
59. Details in this para. from *Faulk*; Jan. to May.
60. Vansittart correspondence; B.M.Add.MSS. 31,230.
61. H.O. 100/126; Hardwicke 15.7.1805. **62.** B.M.Add.MSS. 35,774.
63. *Faulk*; 20/12/1804. **64.** *Faulk*; 19.3.1805.
65. *Faulk*; 3.8.1805. **66.** *Faulk*; 3.8.1805. **67.** Blacker papers.
68. *Faulk*; 12.11.1805. **69.** *Castle. desp.*; viii; 6.11.1805. **70.** *Ibid.*
71. Chief secretary to colonels 21.11.1805, copy in Clements papers.
72. See no. 69, p. 44. **73.** Clements papers.
74. D.C. papers military 1809, carton 538. **75.** Kil. papers, sect. iii. vol. 94.

Chapter XIII.

1. *Irish Times* ; 30.5.1898. **2.** *Commons jn.* vol. 61, 796.
3. Carrickfergus, 17 August. *Faulk.* 22.8.1805.
4. *Faulk* ; 18.4.1797, and B.M.Add.MSS. 33, 106, fol. 287.
5. D.C. order, 9.4.01. **6.** *Parl. Reg.* iv. 222. **7.** H.O. 100/132.
8. *General Regulations for the army*, 1794.
9. *Commons* : *Accounts and papers* 1816.
10. *Castle. desp.*, viii, 57. **11.** Blacker papers.
12. Kil. papers, sect. iii, vol. 40, fol. 470.
13. Wellington ; *Civil Corres. Ire.* 17.1.07. **14.** W.O. 68/223.
15. Kil. papers, sect. xv., vol. 321, fol. 65.
16. See no. 11. **17.** H.O. 100/132. **18.** See no. 11. **19.** See no. 14.
20. Kil. papers, sect. ii. vol. 260. **21.** Kil. papers, sect. iii, vol. 94, fol. 4.
22. Reports in *Faulk*, 31/7 and 7.8.1806.
23. *Standing orders of the 21st or Royal Limerick county militia* ; Athlone 1810. **24.** H.O. 101/2. King's letterbook, 1791-1803 ; and B.M.Add.MSS. 33, 119, fol. 214. King's instructions to lord Hardwicke.
25. Carr. *op. cit.* p. 241. **26.** W.O. 68/387, regimental record.
27. Blacker papers. **28.** See chap. i, note 6. **29.** *F.J.* 5.10.1793.
30. D.C. papers, carton 620/9. See also Kil. papers, sect. iii, vol. 69, fol. 72.
31. *Journal of Army Historical research*, ix, 250. See also W.O. Special Returns ; adj. gen. return 14.3.1815.
32. *Standing orders issued by the colonel to be observed by the 6th or Westmeath regiment of militia* ; Dublin, July 1807.
33. Order book ; Armagh light. inf. co. Nov. 1801.
34. i, 423, 1801. **35.** W.O. 68/223, regimental record.
36. Carr. *op. cit.* p. 405. **37.** *Faulk* ; 31.1.1807.
38. Edward Wakefield. *An account of Ireland* ; *statistical and political.* 2 vols. London 1812, ii, 443-6.
39. H.O. 100/166. **40.** See no. 23. **41.** W.O. 35/16, fol. 108.
42. *Green Fields* by Stephen Rynne, 1937.
43. Down. papers, letter 31.10.1798.
44. Standing orders, Armagh militia 1793. See Appendix V, of this volume, article 6.
45. Blacker papers. **46.** Kil. papers, sec. iii, vol. 229.
47. *Faulk* ; 21.10.1806. **48.** *Faulk* ; 3.12.1805. **49.** H.O. 100/134.
50. Carr, *op. cit.* p. 395. **51.** Blacker papers. **52.** W.O. 68/233.
53. *Annual Register*, 1806, p. 263.

Chapter XIV.

1. H.O. 100/139. **2.** H.O. 100 **3.** H.O. 100/144.
4. W.O. 68/223, 673. **5.** Wellington *op. cit.*, letter 4.1.1808.
6. Nat. Lib. Ire. Richmond papers, letter 21.8.1807.
7. *Ibid*, letter 19.12.1807.
8. Wellington *op. cit.*, letter 8.1.1808. **9.** H.O. 100/144.
10. Richmond papers. Wellesley letter 22.3.1808.
11. *Ibid*, letter 21.3.1808. **12.** H.O. 100/144.
13. H.O. 100/144. **14.** H.O. 100/131. **15.** H.O. 100/131.
16. Wellington *op. cit*,. p. 393. **17.** *Ibid.*, p. 413
18. H.O. 100/147. **19.** H.O. 100/145 for all this paragraph.
20. H.O. 100/148. **21.** H.O. 100/145. **22.** See no. 20.

23. Kil. papers, sec. xv., vol. 89, fol. 126. **24.** H.O. 100/140.
25. *Castle. desp.* viii, 53 and 72.
26. Wellington *op. cit.*, p. 112.
27. Fortescue, *County Lieutenancies*, p. 186. **28.** *Faulk* ; 3.10.1807.
29. Kildare and Westmeath figures from *Faulk.*
30. *Faulk* ; 22.10.1807. **31.** H.O. 100/148. **32.** H.O. 100/142.
33. *Faulk* ; 4.8.1807. **34.** H.O. 100/144. **35.** D.C. papers, carton 536.
36. Clements papers. **37.** War office Special returns, fol. 419.
38. B.M.Add.MSS. 33, 112, fol. 202. Pelham.
39. *Faulk* ; at inquest 21.11.07. **40.** H.O. 100/142.
41. *Faulk* ; 7.4.1808. **42** B.M.Add.MSS. 33, 775, July 1803, Hardwicke.
43. See no. 38. fol. 46 letter of Sept. 1803. **44.** H.O. 100/142.
45. H.O. 100/148. Report by lord. lieut. to S. of S. 10.9.1807.
46. *Southern Reporter*, 12.9.1807. **47.** H.O. 100/148.
48. H.O. 100/142, letter of 3/8/1807. **49.** H.O. 100/142.
50. See no. 6. **51.** Richmond papers ; letter of Oct. 1807.
52. Wellington *op. cit.*, 9.12.1807. **53.** 26.9.1807.
54. Report in *Faulk.* **55.** *Commons Accounts and papers*, 1808.
56. Fortescue *op. cit.* p. 192. **57.** 1.10.1807.
58. *B.N.L.* 9.10.1807. The references in the rest of this para. all to *B.N.L.* Sept. and Oct.
59. PRONI. Three letters to colonel of Louth mil.
60. e.g. in co. Clare. *F.J.* 17.10.1807.
61. Vestry book. In 1810 it was 3½d. per acre and in 1813 5d. per acre.
62. Extract from vestry book. **63.** *Faulk* ; 13.10.1807.
64. *Faulk* ; 20/10. **65.** H.O. 100/114.
66. Advert. of parish of Belfast. *B.N.L.* 5.1.1808. **67.** *F.J.* 4.11.1808.
68. See no. 66. **69.** *B.N.L.* 3.5.1808. **70.** H.O. 100/144 and 145.
71. Wellington *op. cit.* Letter of 6.1.1808.
72. *Ibid.* Letter of 6.1.180i, p. 380.
73. War office, Special returns, fol. 397.
74. *Ibid.*, printed return after fol. 621.
75. D.C. papers, letter of 8.7.1810.

Chaper XV.

1. H.O. 100/144. **2.** Kil. papers, sec. xv. vol. 321, fol. 126-7.
3. *Fr.J.* 25/9/1807. **4.** *Faulk* ; 21.6.1808. **5.** H.O. 100/144.
6. *Faulk* ; 9.7.1808 and *Leinster Journal* 14.5.1808.
7. *Faulk* ; long account 9.7.1808.
8. *Faulk* ; 16/7 and 9/8/1808 ; also H.O. 100/145. **9.** H.O. 100/151.
10. *Faulk* ; 28/6/1808. **11.** D.C. papers ; carton 536.
12. W.O. 17/- series ; monthly returns. **13.** *Faulk* ; 30.8.1808.
14. H.O. 100/146.
15. D.C. papers, circular 13/8/1808, carton 536.
16. All but 100 for unlimited service ; see War Office Special Returns and return in Wakefield, *Op. cit.* ii, 833.
17. H.O. 100/151. **18.** Fortescue ; *County Lieutenancies*, p. 223.
19. War Office Special Returns fol. 525. **20.** See 18, p. 222.
21. H.O. 100/152. **22.** *Ibid.*
23. Belfast Public Library. Biggar papers.
24. Wakefield, *op. cit.*, ii, 692-3. **25.** *B.N.L.* 16.1.1810.

25. *B.N.L.* 16.1.1810. **26.** *B.N.L.* 16.1.1810. **27.** *B.N.L.* 24.11.1809.
28. D.C. papers 16.8.1809.
29. D.C. papers, to sir E. Littlehales, 30.7.1810. **30.** *F.J.* 12.3.1810.
31. Fortescue, *op. cit.* p. 237. **32.** H.O. 100/155.
33. Figures in H.O. 100/152. **34.** War office, Special returns.
35. D.C. papers, 1810, carton 541. **36.** Clements papers 9.4.1810.
37. Elie Halévy ; *A history of the English people in* 1815 ; book ii, chap. i. Pelican edition.
38. H.O. 100/152. **39.** W.O. 1/1116. **40.** *F.J.*
41. Fortescue, *op. cit* p. 106. **42.** *Parl. Reg. Ire.*, xvi, 184, 7.3.1796.
43. *Commons Papers* ; public bills 1802-3, 27. **44.** H.O. 100/146.
45. *Wellington's speeches in parliament*, ed. Gurwood, 1854, i, 50.
46. *Castle Desp.* viii, 41. **47.** H.O. 100/159.
48. Nat. Lib. Ire., Richmond papers W. W. Pole to duke of Richmond.
49. H.O. 100/163.

Chapter XVI.

1. Nat. Lib. Ire. Richmond papers, 15.7.1807. See also Wellington; *Op. cit.* p. 115.
2. Nat. Lib. Ire. Richmond papers, letter to Richmond 18.8.07.
3. *Op. cit.* p. 523. **4.** *Parl. debates*, xx. 130, 13.5.1811.
5. H.O. 100/161, 25.5.1811. **6.** Reported at length in *F.J.* 30.5.1811.
7. H.O. 100/164. **8.** H.O. 100/163. **9.** H.O. 100/161.
10. Figures from H.O. 100/170.
11. *F.J.* (Aug.-Sep.) is the authoritity for all the facts quoted in this and the next para.
12. Quoted in *F.J.* 8.11. **13.** *Ibid* 17/9.
14. *Ibid* 26/11. **15.** *Ibid* 24/9.
16. *Annual Register*, 1812. Chronicle, p. 107. **17.** *F.J.* 3.12.1811.
18. Nat. Lib. Ire., M.S. 178. **19.** H.O. 100/169.
20. *Annual Register*, 1811, chap. vii (published 1812). **21.** H.O. 100/162.
22. H.O. 100/158.
23. Letter 22.11.1811 ; W. W. Pole to Mr. Ryder, H.O. 100/165.
24. H.O. 100/166. **25.** H.O. 100/167. **26.** H.O. 100/168.
27. War office, Special Returns. **28.** H.O. 100/162. **29.** *Ibid.*
30. *F.J.* 4.10.1811. **31.** *F.J.* 21/10/1811.
32. Kil. papers, sect. iii, vol. 159. **33.** Kil. papers, sect. xv. vol. 89.
34. *Ibid.* **35.** H.O. 100/168. **36.** H.O. 100/169.
37. D.C. Calendar of official papers, 1812, carton 548. **38.** H.O. 100/170.
39. H.O. 100/169. **40.** H.O. 100/171 and 173. **41.** H.O. 100/170.
42. H.O. 100/173. **43.** H.O. 100/174. **44.** Richey, *op. cit.* p. 64.
45. H.O. 100/170. **46.** Kil. papers, sect. xv. vol. 89, fol. 182.
47. H.O. 100/174. **48.** Richey, *op. cit.* p. 63. **49.** See note 11, chap. IX.
50. H.O. 50/461. **51.** H.O. 100/174. **52.** *Ibid.*
53. H.O. 100/175. **54.** H.O. 100/174. **55.** H.O. 100/176.
56. Blacker papers. **57.** Kil. papers, sect. xv. vol. 89, fol. 314, 328-9 and 324.
58. D.C. papers, mil. 1814, carton 556.
59. Sidmouth, *Parl. debates*, 11/1814.
60. To Sidmouth, H.O. 100/178, 18.5.1814. **61.** H.O. 100/182.
62. D.C. papers, mil. 1814, carton 556.

63. W.O. 68/223. A circular issued 23.12.1806 stated that the Treasury and the treasurers of counties "indispensably required" certain comprehensive statistics.
64. e.g. by Wakefield, *op. cit.* ii, 819. **65.** H.O. 100/180.
66. *Regimental record.* W.O. 68/23.
67. H.O. 100/182 and D.C. papers, 1814, carton 556.
68. H.O. 100/183.
69. Quoted in C. S. Parker, *Sir Robert Peel.* 1891, i, 177.
70. *Despatches*, xii, 358. **71.** H.O. 100/184. **72.** H.O. 100/184.
73. The formula of the act 55, Geo. iii, chap. 77 (15.6.1815).
74. H.O. 100/184. **75.** *Kilkenny moderator* 1859. See note 11, chap. IX.
76. 15.6.1815. **77.** Watson, *Records of the Monaghan militia*, 1871.
78. Regimental records, W.O. 68/325. **79.** H.O. 100/185.
80. H.O. 100/184. **81.** *Ibid.*
82. *History of the Longford militia.* Richey, *op. cit.* p. 68. **83.** H.O. 100/186.
84. H.O. 100/185.
85. H.O. 100/186 and ./189. **86.** H.O. 100/185 and ./189.
87. See no. 82. **88.** *op. cit.* chap. XII, note 22.
89. H.O. 100/169, letter 26.3.1816.
90. Nat. lib. Ire., Correspondence of lieut-col. Brown. M.S. 131.
91. H.O. 100/189.
92. Miscellaneous correspondence relating to Armagh militia in PRONI.
93. See no. 91.

Chapter XVII.

1. The quotations in these paragraphs are from letters at different dates from 1795 to 1798, of sir Jeremiah Fitzpatrick, M.D. H.O. 100/174. He interested himself in the question of soldiers' wives. Much of what he says is confirmed by a speech of Mr. Bagwell in house of commons ; *Faulk*, 21.6.1803.
2. *King of the Beggars.* Sean O'Faolain, 1938, p. 153. See also pp. 54-55.
3. Lord Enniskillen ; reported in *Faulk* ; March 1793.
4. *Faulk* ; 18.6.1793. **5.** W.O. 68/387 (i).
6. *Commons jn. Ire.*, xviii ; appendix ccvii, and *Commons jn.* 59, pp. 474-95.
7. 10.8.1793.
8. Quoted in *Tempest's Annual* (Dundalk) 1936.
9. References supplied by T. G. F. Paterson.
10. *Commons jn. Ire.*, xvi.
11. *Commons jn. Ire.*, xviii, 4.3.1793.
12. Report of debate of 4.4.1799 in *F.J.*
13. H.O. 100/102, fol. 207 ; printed letter to mil. colonels (forwarding regulations) and circular to governors of counties ; both dated 25.8.1801
14. See Mr. Foster as reported in *Faulk* ; 25.2.1804. See also *Faulk* ; 20/3 and 31.3.1804.
15. *Standing Orders, S. Cork mil.* D. co. 1808 (printed). See for a 'Family Ticket register book'. W.O. 68/400.
16. Kil. papers sec. iii, vol. 350, 346.
17. Kil. papers, sec. iii, vol. 124.
18. Westmeath mil. See note 32, chap. XIII.
19. B.M.Add.MSS. 33, 119 (Pelham) fol. 177.
20. *Ibid.* **21.** See no. 15.

22. *Military Panorama*, or officers' companion, October 1812.
23. See no. 15. **24.** W.O. 68/223. **25.** See no. 15.
26. *F.J.* 19.10.1811.
27. Elie Halévy A. *History of the English People in* 1815. (Pelican edition). Book iii ; bibliography of the Army, p. 231.

Chapter XVIII.

1. Max Beloff. *Public Order and Popular Disturbance.* 1938, p. 147.
2. Charles Reith. *The Police Idea* ; its history and evolution in the xviii century and after. 1938, p. 19.
3. Evarts S. Scudder. *Benjamin Franklin.* 1939, p. 186.
4. G. H. D. Cole. *Persons and Periods*, p. 103.
5. Elie Halévy. *A History of the English People.* Book i, p. 107. (Pelican edition.)
6. J. C. Curwen, M.P. *Observations on the State of Ireland* (made in 1813), principally directed to its agriculture and rural population. 2 vols. London 1818, p. 152.
7. *Cambridge Modern History*, vii, 232-3.
8. Van Doren. *Benjamin Franklin.* 1939, p. 504. See also remark of general Braddock to Franklin on p. 227.
9. *Royal Military Chronicle* ; or British Officers Monthly Register and Mentor. 1810-17, i, p 327.
10. Chatham papers. Letter to Pitt 29.5.1798.
11. *Report from Secret Committee of the House of Lords.* Dublin, 1798, p. 61.
12. Nat. Lib. Ire. Lake correspondence. M.S. 56.
13. B.M.Add.MSS. 32, 335. fol. 71, Percy. **14.** See no. 9.
15. Lecky. *History of England in xviiith century.* Library edition, viii. chap. xxx, 183.
16. See Correspondence vol. ii.
17. Bayham papers. Letter to Pelham 18.8.1796.
18. *Castle. desp.*, vii. 86-9. See also Halévy *op. cit.* pp. 116-7.
19. Halévy *op cit.* 100. **20.** *Parl. Hist.* vol. xxxiii, col. 1508.
21. *Annual Register.* 1803, p. 105. **22.** See no. 19. **23.** 14.5.1814.
24. Nat. Lib. Ire. *Lake corres.* M.S. p. 56.
25. Nat. Lib Ire., Melville papers. 18.2.1798. **26.** H.O. 100/93.
27. To Dundas H.O. 100/93.
28. 30.1.1797, after Bantry. H.O. 100/67. **29.** H.O. 100/94. 1.11.1800.
30. John Gamble. *A View of society and manners in the north of Ireland*, 1813, p. 341.
31. See no. 19.
32. Sidney and Beatrice Webb. *English Local Government. The parish and the county.* 1906, p. 426.
33. Edward Wakefield. *Ireland*, vol. ii, 821. ' The Irish militia do not merit the name, for they are not raised by ballot, but by a bounty raised by a county cess '; and *Annual Register* 1803, p. 103, ' an army of mercenaries '.
34. Report in *Faulk* ; 22.3.1803. **35.** *Ibid.*
36. See no. 19.
37. Crosslé notes. Letter to Dublin Castle, 31.7.1795.
38. B.M.Add.MSS. 33, 106. Richard Griffith, 6.9.1798.
39. Halévy *op. cit.* 117.

40. See note 6, chapter xvii. **41.** H.O./84, fol. 458.
42. In D.C., Fane correspondence. **43.** *Ibid.*
44. Sir Charles Petrie, *The Jacobite Movement*, 1949, pp. 103 and 105.
45. *English Historical Review.* October 1917.
46. Oman. *Wellington's Army*, 1809-1814. London 1912, p. 209. See also George O'Brian, *Economic History of Ireland in the Eighteenth Century.* 1918, p. 18.
47. *Autobiography.* ed. G. N. Bankes, pp. 194 and 227-8.
48. Morris. *Recollections of Military Service in* 1813, 1914 and 1915, pp. 8-9. London 1845.

Appendices

APPENDIX I.

Property Qualifications.

Deputy Governors	£200 a year or to be heir to £400 a year.
Commandant (lieut. col. or major)	£2,000 a year or to be heir to £3,000 a year.
Lieut. colonel	£1,200 a year or to be heir to £1,800.
Major	£300 a year or heir to £600.
Captain	£200 a year or heir to £400 or younger son to a person of £400 a year.
Lieutenant	£50 a year or £500 personal or son of a person of £100 a year (or £1,000 personal).
Ensign	£20 a year or £250 personal or son of a person of £50 a year (or £300 personal).

In the case of deputy governors the whole and, in the case of the commandant and lieut. colonel, a moiety of the qualification to be within the county.

APPENDIX II.

Lord Hillsborough's calculations of the numbers to be provided by each county on the basis (a) of acres and (b) of hearths in the county. (*See page* 24).

County	Acres	Hearths
Cork	1,400	1,700
Kerry	310	445
Limerick	525	640
Tipperary	850	685
Waterford	370	380
Dublin	175	550
Kilkenny	410	400
Kildare	325	220
King's county	365	330
Queen's county	340	340
Wexford	456	470
Wicklow	360	240
Carlow	170	100
Clare	625	370
Galway	1,105	525
Leitrim	295	275
Mayo	1,135	525
Roscommon	460	400
Sligo	345	330
Antrim	516	600
Armagh	200	600
Down	500	850
Louth	160	285
Meath	465	510
Monaghan	240	470
Cavan	350	400
Donegal	900	550
Fermanagh	330	250
Londonderry	360	600
Longford	190	225
Tyrone	510	710
Westmeath	355	310

32 *counties.*

APPENDIX III.

Quarters of the Militia in IRELAND from 29 *August*, 1794, *by companies.*

Antrim	Cork harbour (4), Midleton (2), Cloyne (2).
Armagh	Castlebar (2), Sligo (3), Ballina (1), Newport (2).
Cavan	Cootehill etc. (6).
Carlow	Cove fort and Spike island, Ram head and Hawbowline (5).
Clare	Ballyshannon (5), Manor Hamilton (1).
Cork city	Charleville (6), Millstreet (2).
Cork S.	Carrick-on-Shannon (2), Boyle (3), Ballinamore Cloone and Mohill (2), Elphin and Stokestown (1).
Cork N.	Mitchelstown (7), Mallow (1).
Down	Cork (12).
Dublin city	Cavan (6), Killeshandra (1), Crossdoney (1).
Dublin co.	Maryborough (6).
Drogheda	Ross (1), Enniscorthy (1), Taghmon (1).
Donegall	Athlone (8), Castlerea (2), Roscommon (1).
Fermanagh	Newry (6).
Galway	Dundalk (9), Carrickmacross (1).
Kerry	Waterford (7), New Geneva (1).
King's co.	Killarney and Ross castle (3), Tralee (2), Dingle (2), Castleisland (1).
Kilkenny	Carrickfergus (8).
Kildare	Kildare (5).
Louth	Kinsale (6).
Leitrim	Trim (4), Kells (2).
Limerick city	Cork (6).
Limerick co.	Mullingar (7), Castlepollard (1).
Longford	Carlow (4), Ballitore (1), Kilcullen bridge (1).
Londonderry	Drogheda (8), Navan (1), Balbriggan (1).
Monaghan	Galway (7), Tuam (1).
Meath	Charles fort (8).
Mayo	Parsonstown (7).
Mayo S.	Skibbereen (2), Bantry (2), Macroom (2), Dunmanway (2).
Queen's co.	Coleraine (5), Magherafelt (1).
Roscommon	Cashel (8).
Sligo	Monaghan (3), Belturbet (2), Clones (1).
Tyrone	Galway (10).
Tipperary	Youghal (10).
Westmeath	Wexford (6).
Waterford	Limerick (8).
Wicklow	Strabane (5), Omagh (1).
Wexford	Ennisfallen (10).

APPENDIX IV.

Order of precedence of the 38 *militia units, as settled at ballot* 8 *August* 1793 (*see page* 66) ; *this remained unaltered except as there stated.*

1. Monaghan
2. Tyrone
3. Mayo north
4. Kildare
5. Louth
6. Westmeath
7. Antrim
8. Armagh
9. Down
10. Leitrim
11. Galway
12. Dublin city
13. Limerick city
14. Kerry
15. Longford
16. Londonderry
17. Meath
18. Cavan
19. King's county
20. Kilkenny
21. Limerick county
22. Sligo
23. Carlow
24. Drogheda
25. Queen's county
26. Clare
27. Cork city
28. Tipperary
29. Fermanagh
30. Mayo south
31. Roscommon
32. Cork south
33. Waterford
34. Cork north
35. Dublin county
36. Donegal
37. Wicklow
38. Wexford

APPENDIX V.

Standing Orders to be strictly observed by the Armagh Militia 16 *September* 1793.

Article 1. The officers are required by their alertness, implicit obedience to all lawful commands, as well as their uniformity of dress, to set their n.c.o.s proper examples and thereby gain respect.

Artcile 2. Noncommissioned officers are the eyes and springs of a regiment. The most exact impartial and strict authority must be exercised over them by the officers, at the same time treating them with courtesy and civility that they may carry an equal command and enforce due obedience from the men.

Aricle 3. With the regiment in general the officers are ordered to carry a proper command and to enforce the respect they are entitled to from serjeants corporals drummers and private men, not suffering them either to address or pass them without paying the usual compliment.

Article 4. In addressing with a pike or forelock the serjeants are to have their arms advanced and the men to carry their arms steady on their shoulders, march up boldly, speak out and deliver their business, if without arms by bringing the right hand smart to the side of the hat and retiring behind the officer when his orders are delivered. Passing an officer with arms the serjeants to advance their pikes and men to carry their arms ; if without arms march past and bring up the right hand smart to the hat.

Article 5. The officers are strictly required not to suffer an answer to a reprimand or to a fault found on the parade or under arms. The consequences are dangerous, therefore the man who behaves so unmilitary is immediately to be confined.

Article 6. The officers will teach their men the attitudes of soldiers and how to address their officers, speak kindly to them off duty, endeavour to improve them in their discipline and correct such errors as creep into and prejudice the same, attend to their food and clothing, consult their ease as much as is consistent with the service, do them the strictest justice and then punish offenders without favour.

Article 7. Officers are desired to be perfect in the practised discipline and the standing orders and to make themselves well acquainted with the names and characters of the men of their respective companies.

Article 8. At mounting guards, upon the march, at exercise and in the barrack rooms as well as upon the parades, strict attention is required—if otherwise, censure will ensue.

Article 9. The n.c.o.s are commanded to pay the greatest respect to any officer upon every occasion particularly to young officers and if they presume to take liberties upon their inexperience a courtmartial will be held upon them for a breach of this order.

Article 10. No n.c.o. or private to pull off their hats when under arms to any person whatever.

Article 11. The n.c.o.s are to be vigilant, active, lively and trustworthy ; they are commanded to enforce these orders and thereby to establish regularity and uniformity. They are to treat the men with mildness and good humour when they behave well and punish the idle and negligent impartially ; when upon duty they are to treat their men with rigour if their behaviour require it, to insist upon every form being most punctually adhered to, to enforce every part of the practised discipline, confine or report every man that is negligent that he may be brought to a due punishment and thereby convince the men that they know their duty and will make them do theirs.

Article 12. The n.c.o.s are further ordered to make themselves perfect in all forms of duty and returns, to be strictly careful and honest in all money matters which they may transact betwixt the officers and soldiers, to attend to the markets and lay out the money as ordered, not to connive at any frauds or bargains that may be carried on underhand and come to his knowledge afterwards which is a very great crime, and above all they are commanded not to receive any premium or goods for recommending tradesmen to work for their companies.

Article 13. If any n.c.o. is known to use bad language to the men or treat them improperly, he will be reduced for the same.

Article 14. A n.c.o. of each company to be orderly for the day to make morning and evening reports to the officer of the company as well as to the serjeant major and to attend parade orders ; they will therefore always remain in the barracks or in quarters to answer any call unless the regiment is under arms.

Article 15. If any n.c.o. suffers a private to give him an answer when he is reprimanding him he will be reduced for not carrying a proper command, for altercations of that kind tend to mutiny ; therefore must be nipped in the bud.

Article 16. When off duty n.c.o.'s are ordered to treat the men civilly but not with too much intimacy. They are to explain to them the nature of the discipline and the necessity of practice. They must convince the men of the utility of the Articles of War and private regulations in keeping up harmony, good order, obedience and regularity and by an authority to punish and keep the idle and bad from offending and they should and must assist all the men lately joined in the different branches of business they are to learn and by their example prompt the old men to treat the young kindly ; they should advise the best men to associate with them to set forth to their view the consequences of behaving ill and by their good example to sway them ; they must insist upon their being punctual to their duty and alert in turning out for guard exercise or rollcalling. They are commanded to know every man's name in the company, his age, size, parish and character, to answer off at once if a question should be asked, and above all they are commanded to enforce the highest respect for their officers.

Article 17. The orderly n.c.o. of each company to be responsible that the number of men demanded by the serjeant major are in proper time warned for the duty and paraded in proper order. He is to receive all orders relative to the interior government of the company he belongs to and to report the same to his officers. Particularly he is to observe and call the rolls at tattoo beating and to report to the serjeant major who is to collect the whole and deliver them to the adjutant and subaltern for the day that the c.o. may be immediately acquainted with any extraordinaries that may have happened.

Article 18. No private to presume speaking to an officer or n.c.o. when reprimanded upon duty. If he thinks himself injured he is afterwards to make his complaint in a regular manner to the officer who commands the company to which he belongs ; if that officer refuses to redress his complaint he is then to appeal to the c.o. of the regiment.

Article 19. When an officer passes a sentry upon his post he is to stand perfectly steady and pay the compliment due to the officer's rank viz. to a general, governor, field officer, or any other doing duty in the same garrison —presented arms ; if the commanding officer of the regiment should be under the degree of a field officer, he is still entitled to the above compliment ; to all inferior officers—carried arms.

Article 20. All sentries to walk or stand upon their post (except in their box) with supported arms ; they are not to sit down on their post. When ordered to challenge to do it remarkably loud, coming always on challenging to the first position of Charge bayonet known by ported arms, they are to adhere to the orders given to them under pain of a severe punishment for neglect of duty.

Article 21. If any man presumes to speak under arms or is unsteady or introduces false motions or shows an unwillingness to his duty, he is to be sent to the drill for the first offence, to the Black hole and drill for the second and tried by a court martial for the third.

Article 22. If any man is ill used by another he is to make a regular complaint and not to pretend to do himself justice by ill using the offender, or if any private aids or assists at any quarrel among his companions he shall be deemed a principal and treated accordingly.

Article 23. Whenever any man is taken from one company to another to be made a n.c.o. or for the grenadier company that company from which he was taken has a right to choose a man from the company to which he was made a n.c.o. reserving one file only for the captain's choice and if the man taken is made a grenadier the company to choose a man from the battalion with the above reservation of the captain's choice of one file.

Article 24. Where the companies are not formed and named from the baronies belonging to the county they are to draw for the men that join except the grenadiers who are to choose their men out of the whole battalion.

Article 25. The articles of war and the standing orders of the regiment to be read once every two months by the major, adjutant, or whom the C.O. of the regiment shall appoint at the head of the battalion under arms, and at the annual meeting when not called out to actual service three times at least during the time they are assembled.

Article 26. No man will have a pass or furlough granted him by the C.O. without its being first signed on the back by the officer commanding his company.

Article 27. When the regiment is dispersed in cantonments the company's assignments of their accounts with the proceedings of all courts martial held in these quarters to be sent to the C.O. of the regiment with the monthly returns.

Article 28. A captain has an undoubted right when absent from or present with his company to appoint whomsoever of the regiment he pleases to pay his company. In case a captain does not appoint any particular person to pay his company the C.O. will appoint the subaltern commanding the company it being his duty but the person so appointed by the C.O. must account with the captain of the company for all debts and credits of casualties etc. etc. etc., must charge the captain with the repair of all arms broke at exercise and suchlike contingencies and must give the captain credit for the contingent allowance which is solely the property of the captain.

APPENDIX VI.

Numbers of rank and file to be raised as directed by : *A.* 33. *Geo. iii. c.* 22, *and B.* 35 *Geo. iii. c.* 8.

	A	B		A	B
Cork-city (8)	488	612	*Leitrim* (6)	350	460
Cork north (8)	488	612	*Mayo north* (7)	350	536
Cork south (8)	488	612	*Mayo south* (7)	350	536
Kerry (8)	488	612	*Roscommon* (8)	420	612
Limerick-city (6)	305	460	*Sligo* (6)	350	460
Limerick county (8)	420	612	*Antrim* (8)	488	612
Tipperary (10)	560	764	*Armagh* (8)	420	612
Waterford (8)	488	612	*Down* (12)	770	916
Dublin-city (8)	420	612	*Louth-county* (6)	356	460
Dublin-county (6)	280	460	*Drogheda* (3)	183	232
Kilkenny (8)	420	612	*Meath* (8)	488	612
Kildare (5)	280	384	*Monaghan* (8)	488	612
King's county (8)	420	612	*Cavan* (6)	350	460
Queen's county (6)	356	460	*Donegal* (10)	560	764
Wexford (10)	560	764	*Fermanagh* (6)	356	460
Wicklow (6)	356	460	*Londonderry* (10)	560	764
Carlow (5)	244	384	*Longford* (6)	280	460
Clare (6)	356	460	*Tyrone* (10)	560	764
Galway (10)	560	764	*Westmeath* (6)	350	460

The aggregate number to be raised under the act 33. Geo. iii, chap. 22, was 14,948 and, under the act 35, Geo. iii. chap. 8, 21,660.

Units of 8 companies or above are denominated ' regiments ' and those of less than 8 companies ' battalions '.

There were from the beginning battalions for the cities of Dublin, Cork and Limerick. The county of Cork (i.e. without the city) had two units ; Mayo also had two units. Down was for several years one regiment of 12 companies, but was individed into two battalions. Drogheda was a small 3 company unit separate from the county of Louth ; it was later incorporated with the Louth unit.

The number of companies in each regiment or battalion is shewn in brackets

The order in which the units are shewn is that in the act of 1793.

APPENDIX VII.

Sir Ralph Abercromby's order of 26 *February* 1798.

The very disgraceful frequency of court-martials, and the many complaints of irregularities in the conduct of the troops in this kingdom, having too unfortunately proved the Army to be in a state of licentiousness which must render it formidable to every one but the enemy, the Commander-in-chief thinks it necessary to demand from all generals commanding districts and brigades, as well as commanding officers of regiments, that they exert for themselves, and compel from all officers under their command, the strictest and most unremitting attention to the discipline, good order and conduct of their men, such as may restore the high and distinguished reputation which the British troops have been accustomed to enjoy in every part of the world. It becomes necessary to recur, and most pointedly to attend to the standing orders of the kingdom, which, at the same time that they direct military assistance to be given at the requisition of the civil magistrate, positively forbid the troops to act (but in case of attack) without his presence and authority, and the most clear and precise orders are to be given to the officer commanding the party for this purpose.

The utmost prudence and precaution are also to be used in granting parties to revenue officers, both with regard to the person requiring such assistance, and those employed on the duty. Whenever a guard is mounted, patrols must be frequently sent out to take up any soldier who may be found out of his quarters after his hours.

A very culpable remissness having also appeared on the part of the officers respecting the necessary inspection of barracks, quarters, messes etc. as well as attendance at roll-calls and other hours, commanding officers must enforce the attention of those under his command to these points and the general regulations for all which the strictest responsibility will be expected for themselves.

It is of the utmost importance that the discipline of the dragoon regiments should be minutely attended to, for the facilitating of which the Commander-in-chief has dispensed with the attendance of orderly dragoons on himself, and desires that they be not employed by any general or commanding officer, but on military and indispensable business.

APPENDIX VIII.

Dates and Places of principal engagements between His Majesty's forces and the insurgents during May-July 1798 ; *with particulars of the militia units engaged.*

Date	*Place*	*County*	*Militia units engaged*
24 May	*Naas*	Kildare	Armagh
	Clane	Kildare	Armagh
	Dunlavin	Wicklow	Wicklow (light co.)
	Kilcullen (1st)	Kildare	
	Prosperous	Kildare	Cork (city)
	Athy and Narraghmore	Kildare	Tyrone (light co.)
	Kilcullen (2nd)	Kildare	
	Baltinglass	Wicklow	Antrim
25 May	Ballymore-Eustace	Kildare	Tyrone (light co.)
	Hacketstown	Carlow	Antrim
	Monasterevan	Kildare	
	Carlow	Carlow	Armagh ; Cork (north) light co.)
26 May	Tara Hill	Meath	
	Leixlip	Kildare	
27 May	*Oulart*	Wexford	Cork (north)
	Ballitore	Kildare	Cork (north)
	Kilthomas	Wexford	Antrim
	Ballinrush	Wexford	Antrim
28 May	*Enniscorthy*	Wexford	Cork (north)
	Rathangan	Kildare	Cork (city)
30 May	Newtownmount-kennedy	Wicklow	Antrim
	Forth (1st)	Wexford	Meath
	Forth (2nd)	Wexford	Donegal
31 May	Curragh	Kildare	Londonderry ; Dublin (city)
1 June	*Newtonbarry*	Wexford	King's County
	Ballycanew	Wexford	Antrim ; Cork (north)
4 June	*Tubbernerneen*	Wexford	Armagh ; Antrim ; Londonderry (grenadier co.) ; Tyrone (light co.) ; Cork (north).
5 June	*New Ross*	Wexford	Dublin (county) ; Donegal ; Meath ; Clare ; 4th Light battalion.
8 June	Timahoe	Kildare	Limerick (city).
7 June	*Antrim*	Antrim	2nd light battalion ; Monaghan.

9 June	*Saintfield*	Down	Monaghan
	Arklow	Wicklow	Cavan; Armagh; Cork (north); Antrim; Londerry (grenadier co.); Tyrone (light co.).
10 June	Maynooth	Kildare	
12 June	*Ballynahinch*	Down	Monaghan
	Borris	Carlow	Donegal
13 June	Ballyellis	Wexford	
18 June	Kilbeggan	Westmeath	
	Kilcavan	Wicklow	
20 June	Ballinascarty	Cork	Westmeath
	Ovidstown	Kildare	
21 June	Ponsonby Bridge	Dublin	Cork (city)
	Goff's Bridge	Wexford	Light infantry battalions.
21 June	*Vinegar Hill*	Wexford	Sligo; Meath; Roscommon; Dublin (county); Armagh; Cavan; Antrim. 1st and 4th Light battalions; Londonderry (grenadier co.); Tyrone (light co.).
23 June	Goresbridge	Kilkenny	Wexford
	Coolbawn	Kilkenny	Waterford; Down.
	Doonane	Kilkenny	Waterford.
	Castlecomer	Kilkenny	Waterford; Wexford; Wicklow; Down.
25 June	Hacketstown	Carlow	Antrim.
26 June	*Kilconnell Hill*	Kilkenny	Wicklow; Wexford; Down
29 June	Fox's Hill	Kildare	Limerick (city)
2 July	Ballyraine Hill	Wicklow	
3 July	Carnew	Wicklow	
5 July	*Whiteheaps*	Wicklow	Louth; Leitrim
11 July	Clonard	Kildare	
12 July	Longwood Nineteen-mile-house	Meath	Limerick (city).

(*The principal engagements are in italics*).

This table has been compiled from various sources; its completeness and its complete accuracy cannot be guaranteed.

APPENDIX IX.

Balloting in Ireland in 1807-8, *extent of adoption of.*

Antrim	Ballots, except apparently in half barony of Lower Belfast.
Armagh	No ballots, except in two (out of 19) parishes.
Carlow	A ballot (pro forma) took place in each parish.
Cavan	No information.
Clare	No information.
Cork (*city*)	Ballots in three out of thirteen parishes.
Cork (*south*)	Ballots in 84 out of 91 parishes.
Cork (*north*)	Ballots in 86 out of 114 parishes.
Donegal	Militia raised throughout county by parochial assessment.
Down (*south and north*)	Ballots in all parishes (59) except five.
Dublin (*city and county*)	No ballots.
Fermanagh	No information.
Galway	Out of 110 parishes at least 31 ballotted.
Kerry	About 1/3 of the parishes ballotted.
Kildare	No information.
King's county	No ballot; all men raised by subscription.
Kilkenny	No information.
Leitrim	No ballots.
Limerick (*city and county*)	No ballots.
Londonderry	Ballots in half barony (4 parishes) of Tierkeeran; in fifteen parishes no ballot.
Longford	Ballot in five parishes (57 men) out of twentyone.
Louth	Ballot generally throughout the county.
Drogheda	Ballot (three parishes).
Mayo (*south and north*)	Ballots in 29 parishes out of 76.
Meath	Ballot in one parish only but this was not enforced.
Monaghan	Out of 22 parishes 20 ballotted.
Queen's county	No information that any parish ballotted.
Roscommon	Out of 57 parishes two were ballotted (for 8 men).
Sligo	All parishes (28) ballotted except four.
Tipperary	No information that there were any ballots.
Tyrone	Out of 27 parishes 11 ballotted.
Waterford	No ballots.
Westmeath	Ballots in all parishes
Wexford	Nothing to show that any ballot took place.
Wicklow	Divided into four districts; first district raised all its quota (35) by ballot; no ballot in two others; in the fourth, ballot in one parish for five men.

Note: the above is a summary of returns rendered to the House of Commons; the information is given in different forms and the course taken is not in all cases quite certain, especially in the case of the counties which either sent no return or sent it after the others had been printed. (House of Commons; Accounts and Papers, 1808, fol. 333).

APPENDIX X.

The Ballot in county Antrim in 1807-8.

Half Baronies	*Observations*
Upper Belfast ..	At the 1st and 2nd meetings of the governors on 7 September and 20 October 1807 the sum agreed on as the fair average price of a substitute was five guineas, but at an especial meeting on 28 December it was voted by one of a majority that £16 per man might be levied by the vestry of the parish of Belfast for each man required ; the men were drawn by ballot, and substitutes found for those who had insured or were drawn in the parish of Belfast, or who had subscribed 2/6.
Lower Belfast ..	The average price here did not exceed for substitutes five guineas per man ; vestries were held in the parishes of Carrickfergus, Carmoney, Ballymore, Inver, Island Magee and Kilroot. The average price paid for substitutes was about £20 ; the difference between that sum and five guineas was paid by voluntary subscriptions, by insurers or by the persons drawn, who had neither subscribed or insured.
Upper Antrim ..	No vestries held here ; the men furnished by ballot. Substitutes were found by insurers, only in one or two instances, in which the ballotted men were enrolled.
Lower Antrim ..	No vestries ; all drawn by ballot, and substitutes found by voluntary subscriptions and insurers.
Upper Masserene	The men were all drawn by ballot ; vestries were held for the parishes of Lisburn, Derryaghy, Glenavy, Camlen, Tullyrush and Aghagallon. £10 per man was assessed for Lisburn and five guineas for the others ; substitutes were found for all but one man, who was enrolled, and is now serving.
Lower Masserene	Drawn by ballot ; and substitutes found by parish meeting and voluntary subscriptions.
Upper Toome ..	All drawn by ballot, and substitutes found by insurers ; no vestries.
Lower Toome ..	All drawn by ballot, and substitutes found by insurers ; no vestries.
Upper Glenarm ..	Drawn by ballot ; no vestries ; substitutes proved by voluntary subscriptions.
Lower Glenarm ..	Vestries held in the parishes of Glenar, and Tukmackreven, five guineas per man asessed ; Ardclinas, the principals enlisted substitutes ; and Lede, substitutes procured by an insurer.
Upper Dunline ..	Men raised by ballot ; vestries assessed five guineas per man to assist in procuring substitutes.

Lower Dunkine ..	Men raised by ballot; vestries assessed five guineas per man to assist in procuring substitutes.
Cary	Men raised by ballot; vestries assessed five guineas per man to assist in procuring substitutes.
Kilconway ..	Drawn by ballot, no vestries held.

Note: the above is an exact copy (punctuation, which is erratic, included) of the Antrim return as presented to the House of Commons; folio 333. Accounts and Papers 1808. The other returns are summarized in appendix IX.

APPENDIX XI.

Dignities in and conected with Ireland from 1793 *to* 1816.

(*a*) *Secretaries of state, Home department.*

June 1791 ..	Henry Dundas ((viscount Melville).
July 1794 ..	Duke of Portland.
July 1801 ..	Lord Pelham (earl of Chichester).
August 1803 ..	Charles Philip Yorke.
May 1804 ..	Lord Hawkesbury (earl of Liverpool).
February 1806 ..	Earl Spencer.
March 1807 ..	Lord Hawkesbury (earl of Liverpool).
November 1809..	Richard Ryder.
June 1812 ..	Viscount Sidmouth.
January 1822 ..	Robert Peel (sir Robert Peel).

(*b*) *Viceroys.*

January 1790 ..	Earl of Westmoreland.
January 1795 ..	Earl Fitzwilliam.
March 1795 ..	Earl Camden.
June 1798 ..	Marquis Cornwallis.
May 1801 ..	Earl of Hardwicke.
March 1806 ..	Duke of Bedford.
April 1807 ..	Duke of Richmond.
August 1813 ..	Lord Whitworth.

(*c*) *Chief Secretaries.*

April 1789 ..	Robert Hobart (earl of Buckinghamshire).
January 1794 ..	Sylvester Douglas (lord Glenbervie).
January 1795 ..	Viscount Milton (earl of Dorchester).
March 1795 ..	Thomas Pelham (earl of Chichester).
March 1798 ..	Viscount Castlereagh (marquis of Londonderry).
May 1801 ..	Charles Abbot (lord Colchester).
February 1802 ..	William Wickham.
February 1804 ..	Sir Evan Nepean.
March 1805 ..	Nicholas Vansittart (lord Bexley).
September 1805..	Charles Long (lord Farnborough).
March 1806 ..	William Elliot.
April 1807 ..	Sir Arthur Wellesley (duke of Wellington).
April 1809 ..	Robert Dundas (viscount Melville).

October 1809 .. W. Wellesley Pole (lord Maryborough and earl of Mornington).
August 1812 .. Robert Peel (sir Robert Peel).

(*d*) *Commanders of the Forces.*
1793 General Robert Cunninghame (lord Rossmore).
1796 Earl of Carhampton.
1797 Lt general sir Ralph Abercromby.
1798 Marquis Cornwallis.
1801 General sir William Medows.
1803 Lt. general Henry Edward Fox.
General lord Cathcart.
1806 General earl of Harrington.
1812 General sir John Hope.
1813 General sir George Hewett.

APPENDIX XII.

Irish Militia Statutes.

A. *Pre-union.*

1. *General.*—33 Geo. iii. chap 22.—Main act—(see chap. II).
   35 Geo. iii. chap. 8. Explaining and amending [33 Geo. iii. chap. 22]. (see chap. V).
   36 Geo. iii. chap. 3. Explaining and amending the two previous acts.
   37 Geo. iii. chap. 19. Explaining and amending the laws in force relating to the militia.
   37 Geo. iii. chap. 20. Pay of militia officers.
   38 Geo. iii. chap. 62. Further explaining and amending the laws in force.
   39 Geo. iii. chap. 30. Further explaining and amending the laws in force.
   39 Geo. chap. 31. Militia voluntarily offering may be employed in Great Britain or elsewhere. (See chap. X).
   40 Geo. iii. chap. 1. Authorizing king to accept services of volunteers from militia. (See chap. X).
   40 Geo. iii. chap. 91. Authorizing continuation of service of men due for discharge before 24 June, 1801.
   40 Geo. iii. chap. 92. Amending main act.
2. *Pay and Clothing Acts.*—(see chap. II, p. 19). There was an act in each year from 1793 to 1800.
3. *Families of militia men.*—33 Geo. iii. chap. 28. 35 Geo. iii. chap. 2. *[37 Geo. iii. chap. 19]. 39 Geo. iii. chap. 49.
   *Part of this act is concerned with the women and children.

B. *Post-union.*

1. *General.*—41 Geo. iii. chap. 6. Increasing the number of field officers in militia. (See chap. X).

42 Geo. iii. chap. 109. Authorizing discharge of certain militiamen. (See chap. XI).
43 Geo. iii. chap. 2. For more speedy enrolment of militia. (See chap. XI).
43 Geo. iii. chap. 33. Repeating previous act and making fresh provisions. (See chap. XI).
44 Geo. iii. chap. 32. Authorizing acceptance of militiamen for service in Great Britain. (See chap. XII).
44 Geo. iii. chap. 33. For augmentation of militiamen in Ireland. (See chap. XI).
45 Geo. iii. chap. 38. Allowing militia voluntarily to enlist into regular forces and marines. (See chap. XII).
46 Geo. iii. chap. 31. Continues preceding act.
46 Geo. iii. chap. 124. Authorizing acceptance of volunteers from militia for line. (See chaps. XII and XIII).
47 Geo. iii. chap. 55 [session 2]. Allowing militia voluntarily to enlist in line.
47 Geo. iii. chap. 56 [session 2]. Increasing militia of Ireland. (See chap. XV).
48 Geo. iii. chap. 64. Amending [46 Geo. iii. chap. 124].
49 Geo. iii. chap. 5. Allowing militia voluntarily to enlist in line.
49 Geo. iii. chap. 56. Completing the militia of Ireland.
49 Geo. iii. chap. 120. Amends and reduces into one act the laws for militia of Ireland [149 clauses]. (See chap. XV).
51 Geo. iii. chap. 30. Amends [46 Geo. iii. chap. 124] and [48 Geo. iii. chap. 64].
57 Geo. iii. chap. 118. Permits interchange of British and Irish militias. Chap. XVI.
52 Geo. iii. chap. 29. Amends [49 Geo. iii. chap. 120] and [51 Geo. iii. chap. 118].
53 Geo. iii. chap. 48. Amending laws for raising and maintaining militia.
54 Geo. iii. chap. 1. Accepting service of militia of Great Britain and of Ireland for service in all parts of Europe. Chap. XVI.
54 Geo. iii. chap. 10. Amends interchange act [51 Geo. iii. chap. 118].
54 Geo. iii. chap. 179. Amending [49 Geo. iii. chap. 120].
54 Geo. iii. chap. 11. Pensions of sergeants of militia.
55 Geo. iii. chap. 77. Authorizes re-embodiment of British and Irish militia. (See chap. XVI).
55 Geo. iii. chap. 168. Explaining and amending the laws relating to the militia of Great Britain and Ireland.

2. *Pay and Clothing Acts.*—In the United Kingdom parliament an Irish militia pay and clothing act was passed each year from 1801 to 1815.

3. *Families of militia men.* 43 Geo. iii. chap. 142. (See chap. XVII).
44 Geo. iii. chap. 34. Amending preceding act.
49. Geo. iii. chap. 86. Altering provisions of two preceding acts. (See chap. XVII).
51. Geo. iii. chap. 78. Altering provisions of preceding act.
52. Geo. iii. chap. 28. Amending preceding act.

Index

Mentions of particular units of mil. are indexed when the unit is referred to specially, not as a rule when the reference is part of an enumeration.

Index entries such as " ceremonial duties ", " precedence ", " dispersion ", " bands " etc. are to be taken, if not otherwise specified, as references applicable generally to the whole force.

In the case of the leading *personae*, references in the text are as a rule indexed only where they have special significance.

The only abbreviations used are ' mil ' for militia, and ' co ' for county.

THE END.